studysync®

TEACHER'S EDITION

Emotional Currents

GRADE 12 | UNIT 4

studysync®

studysync.com

Send all inquiries to:
BookheadEd Learning, LLC
610 Daniel Young Drive
Sonoma, CA 95476

1 2 3 4 5 6 7 8 9 LMN 20 19 18 17 16
A
2016 G12U4

studysync®

GRADE 12 UNITS

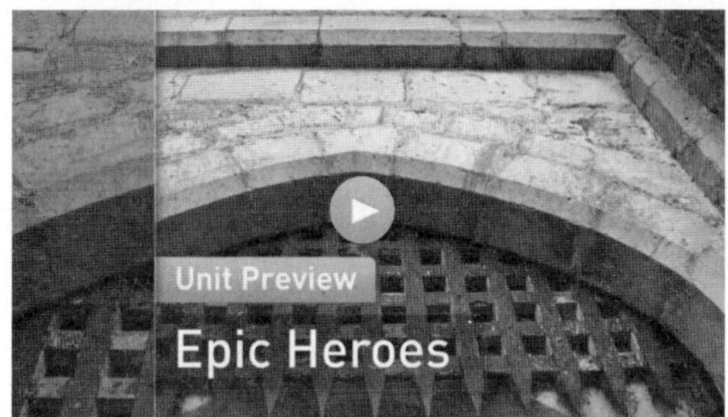

Epic Heroes

UNIT 1

Overview • Pacing Guide • Instructional Path
Extended Writing Project • Research • Full-text Study

The Human Condition

UNIT 2

Overview • Pacing Guide • Instructional Path
Extended Writing Project • Research • Full-text Study

An Exchange of Ideas

UNIT 3

Overview • Pacing Guide • Instructional Path
Extended Writing Project • Research • Full-text Study

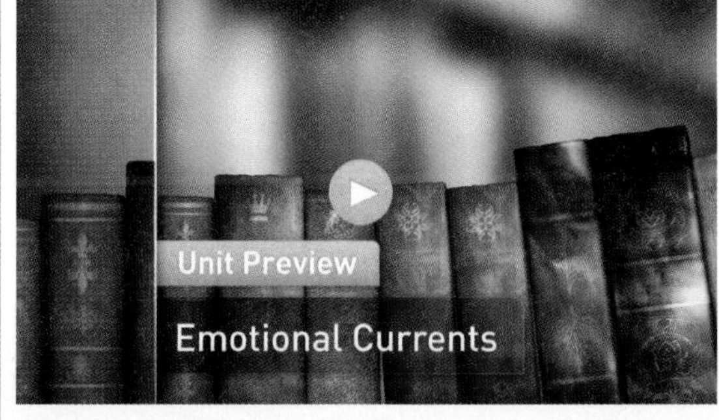

Emotional Currents

UNIT 4

Overview • Pacing Guide • Instructional Path
Extended Writing Project • Research • Full-text Study

Welcome to StudySync

StudySync's comprehensive English Language Arts program for Grades 6-12 is a hybrid print and digital ELA solution. The program leverages cutting edge technology to create an engaging, relevant student and teacher experience. StudySync's multimedia content is available 24/7 from any desktop, tablet, or mobile device. In addition, the program's print resources allow for flexible, blended implementation models that fit the needs of every classroom.

StudySync's Core ELA curriculum was built from the ground up to fully align with the Common Core State Standards for English Language Arts. StudySync provides standards-based instruction that teachers can easily customize, scaffold, and differentiate to ensure all students are ready for college, career, and civic life in the 21st century.

STUDYSYNC TEACHER'S EDITION

The StudySync Teacher's Edition is designed to help you understand, pace, plan, and deliver the StudySync Core ELA curriculum to your students. In this **Teacher's Edition** you will find:

1. A list of StudySync Materials available in both your digital teacher account and this print Teacher's Edition.
2. A guide to StudySync's Core ELA Curriculum and additional content.
3. An overview of StudySync Teacher Tools and ideas and inspirations to help you get started today.
4. Resources for each Core ELA Unit in your grade:

Unit Overviews A big picture look at the key texts and skills.

Pacing Guides A day-to-day plan for integrating all Unit content from the Instructional Path, Extended Writing Project, Research, and Full-text Study with hints for reteaching and shortcuts.

Instructional Path Detailed Lesson Plans for each First Read, Skill, Close Read, and Blast.

Extended Writing Project Detailed Lesson Plans for each Extended Writing Project.

Research A teacher's guide to delivering the Research Project.

Full-text Study A Full-text Reading Guide with key passage explications, vocabulary, discussion and close reading questions.

DESIGNED FOR TODAY'S CLASSROOMS

StudySync combines the best of print and digital resources to meet you where you are and take you where you want to be—allowing low-tech and high-tech classrooms to take full advantage of StudySync's **rigor, relevance, and flexibility.**

RIGOR AND RELEVANCE

StudySync engages students with a learning experience that reflects the ways they experience the world by providing multiple opportunities for collaboration, social interaction, and exposure to rich media and thousands of classic and contemporary texts.

In addition, StudySync challenges students and helps them meet rigorous academic expectations with:

- Access to diverse characters and points of view with an expansive digital library, searchable by grade level and Lexile®-level.
- Close reading instruction with various levels of text complexity.
- In-depth studies of canonical and contemporary texts, representing all genres including literary and informational.
- Multiple opportunities for developing foundational language and literacy skills, all while building content knowledge and helping students make meaning.
- Practice and application of analytical writing to sources, with prompts and rubrics tied to the CCSS.

FLEXIBILITY

PRINT AND DIGITAL OPTIONS

Whichever format is right for your classroom—digital, print, or a combination of both, StudySync provides a successful learning experience for all students.

In addition to this Teacher's Edition, a *Student Reading and Writing Companion* is also available to allow students to complete assignments on or off line. This consumable handbook for students gives students printed access to all readings in a Core ELA Unit's instructional path, including First Reads, text-dependent Think questions, Skills lessons, Close Reads and writing prompts. The purpose of the student print support is to provide students with close reading opportunities so they may continue through the course successfully even without daily access to digital. *Please see page xi for a full overview of all StudySync materials available in both print and digital.*

MULTIPLE IMPLEMENTATION MODELS

Whether you are using blended instruction, a flipped classroom, or a traditional format, StudySync provides the flexibility to meet your instructional needs. For example, you can:

- Use print options in conjunction with a projector to engage students in a whole-class discussion regarding a text, an assignment, or a StudySync® TV video.
- Have students work in pairs, small groups, or individually to read, annotate, and answer think questions. Students can work on a single computer or shared devices; alternatively they can annotate directly in their student workbooks.
- Schedule time in computer labs for students to bring their Reading & Writing Companions and submit writing online and complete peer reviews.

Specific examples of using StudySync for whole-group, small-group, and individual instruction are provided on page *xxx* of this guide.

TIPS TO DIFFERENTIATE

Classrooms have a mix of interests, learning styles, and skill levels. Integrating technology makes it easier for teachers to better differentiate and personalize instruction without substantially adding to their workload.

StudySync allows teachers to customize their lessons and to:

- Scaffold assignments based on students' interests and reading abilities
- Make assignments and choose texts based on Lexile®-levels
- Access an extensive library of 6–12 content, texts, and excerpts
- Target specific learning objectives, skills, and Common Core Standards
- Tailor instruction to whole-class, small group, or individual needs
- Offer access support—including audio support, closed captioning, and vocabulary support

CUSTOMIZING YOUR CURRICULUM

With StudySync, you can build the kind of program you've always wanted to teach.
You have the ability to:

- Assign a Library text with the existing prompt or write your own
- Modify assignments for differentiated learning levels
- Access Skills Lessons separately from the Units and assign as stand-alone lessons, or pair with another text of your choosing
- Customize assessments by creating your own rubrics and peer review prompts

Leverage StudySync's online platform and peer review system with **your own content** by:

- Creating your own writing assignments
- Adding your own Library items to your account, including images and videos

COLLABORATION AMONG TEACHERS

StudySync facilitates collaboration by allowing you to share teacher-created content, rubrics, modified assignments, and new library items with other educators in your subscription. Have a rubric used specifically by your district? Have an assignment that every English teacher in your department will be utilizing? These only need to be created once, helping teachers save time and focus on working together.

SUCCESS FOR ALL LEARNERS

StudySync supports students every step of the way. Students experience a seamless online experience for reading and writing, submitting assignments, and writing and receiving reviews with tools that encourage close reading and critical thinking. Students access their assignments and then can view completed work and reviews received in their own online "binder."

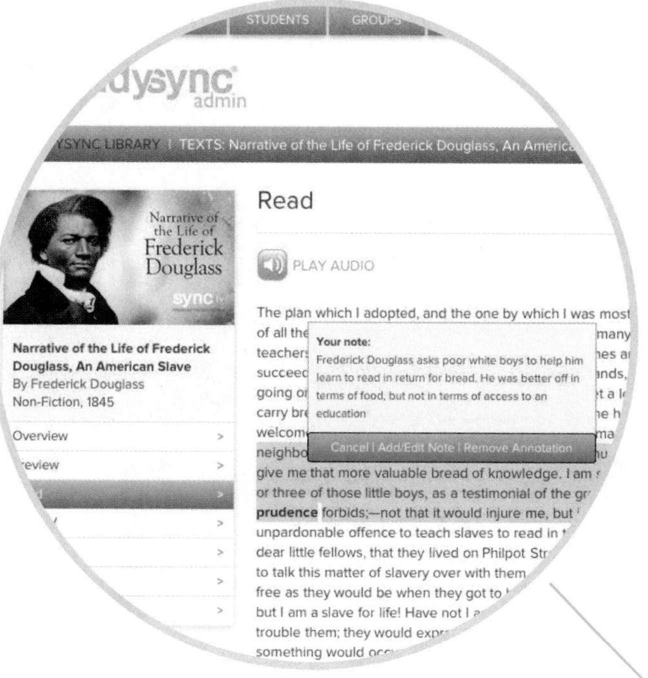

Support for All Levels of Learners

- Grade and Lexile®-leveled filters for Digital Library of texts
- Access Path for EL support
- Differentiated learning tools including customizable groups, prompts, and rubrics
- Print materials for work offline

Online Learning Tools

- Collaborative learning platform with online student binders and social learning network
- Online teacher and anonymous peer review platform
- Online test practice similar to PARCC, Smarter Balanced, and other high-stakes test formats

Audio/Visual Resources

- Audio narration of text
- Audio text highlight option
- Online annotation tool
- Closed Captioning of video resources
- Engaging StudySync® TV & SkillsTV videos

PROFESSIONAL DEVELOPMENT

StudySync's Professional Development is on target and ongoing. Our Professional Development Platform in ConnectED and the Teacher Homepage tab within StudySync provide online learning resources that support classroom implementation and instruction and connect explicitly to the standards. All audiovisual, multimedia, and technology resources include suggestions for appropriate implementation and use.

The **Professional Development course** provides an extensive overview of StudySync as well as support for implementing key instructional strategies in the English Language Arts classroom. The **Teacher Homepage** provides access to digital resources and up-to-date articles on "What's New" with StudySync features and content, plus "Ideas and Inspirations," with tips from featured StudySync users and the StudySync Curriculum team.

Review the Professional Development guides and videos within the StudySync Professional Development Implementation course in your ConnectED account and the content on your Teacher Homepage. Then turn to StudySync's Getting Started Guide to begin!

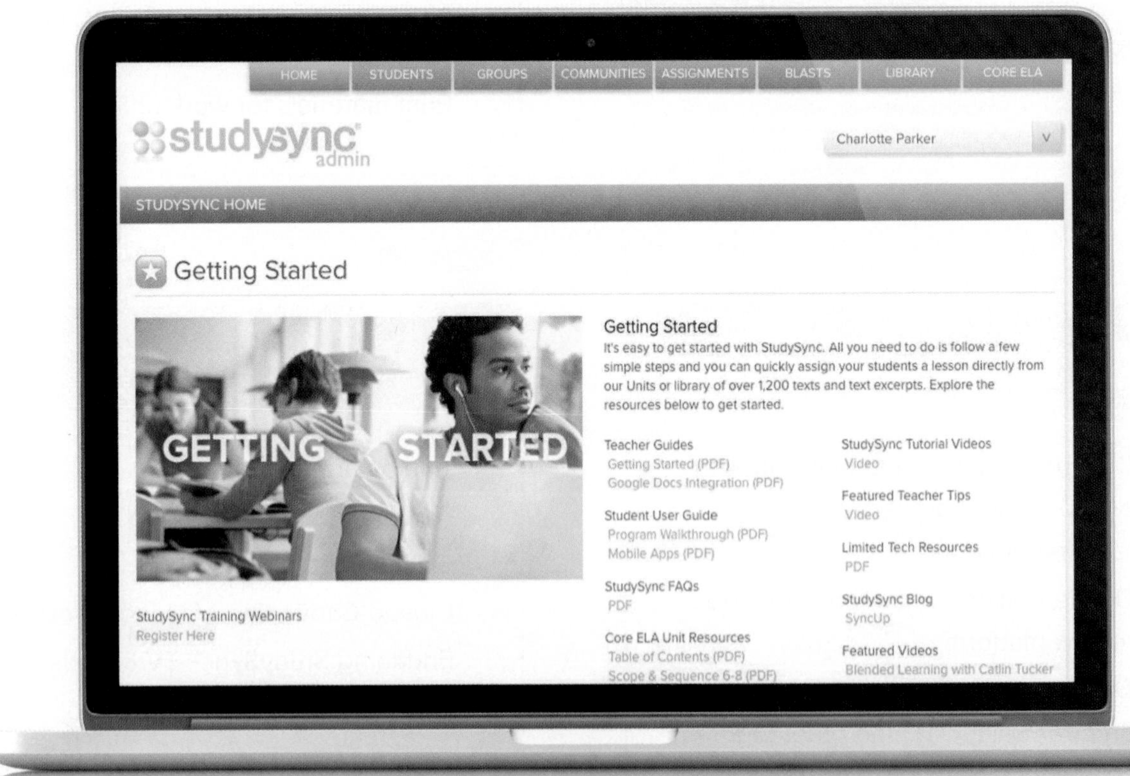

STUDYSYNC MATERIALS

	Digital Teacher Account	Print Teacher's Edition	Digital Student Account	Student Reading & Writing Companion
Scope and Sequences	●			
Grade Level Overviews	●			
Core ELA Unit Overviews	●	●		
Core ELA Unit Pacing Guides	●	●		
Complete Lesson Plans	●	●		
Core Handouts	●			
Access Handouts	●			
Text Selections and Lessons	●		●	●
Reading Skill Lessons	●		●	
Blast Lessons	●		●	
Extended Writing Project Lessons	●		●	●
Writing Skill Lessons	●		●	●
Research Project Guide	●	●		
Full-text Reading Guide	●	●		
End-of-Unit & End-of-Course Digital Assessments	●		●	
Printable Assessments	●			

Please note that excerpts and passages in the StudySync® library, workbooks, and PDFs are intended as touchstones to generate interest in an author's work. The excerpts and passages do not substitute for the reading of entire texts, and StudySync® strongly recommends that teachers and students seek out and purchase the whole literary or informational work in order to experience it as the author intended. Links to online resellers are available in our digital library. In addition, complete works may be ordered through an authorized reseller by filling out and returning to StudySync® the order form enclosed in this workbook.

CORE ELA UNITS

StudySync's Core ELA curriculum consists of 4 **Core ELA Units** per grade. Each unit covers 45 days of instruction for a total of 180 days of instruction at each grade. A complete **Scope and Sequence** outlines standards coverage for each grade, and **Grade Level Overviews** provide teachers a more in-depth look at the reading and writing instruction in each unit. **Pacing Guides** offer detailed 45-day plans for delivering each unit's content.

Each Core ELA Unit is organized around a unique theme and essential question that challenges students to examine texts through an engaging, challenging lens. Each unit contains five key components:

1. Overview
2. Instructional Path
3. Extended Writing Project
4. Research
5. Full-text Study

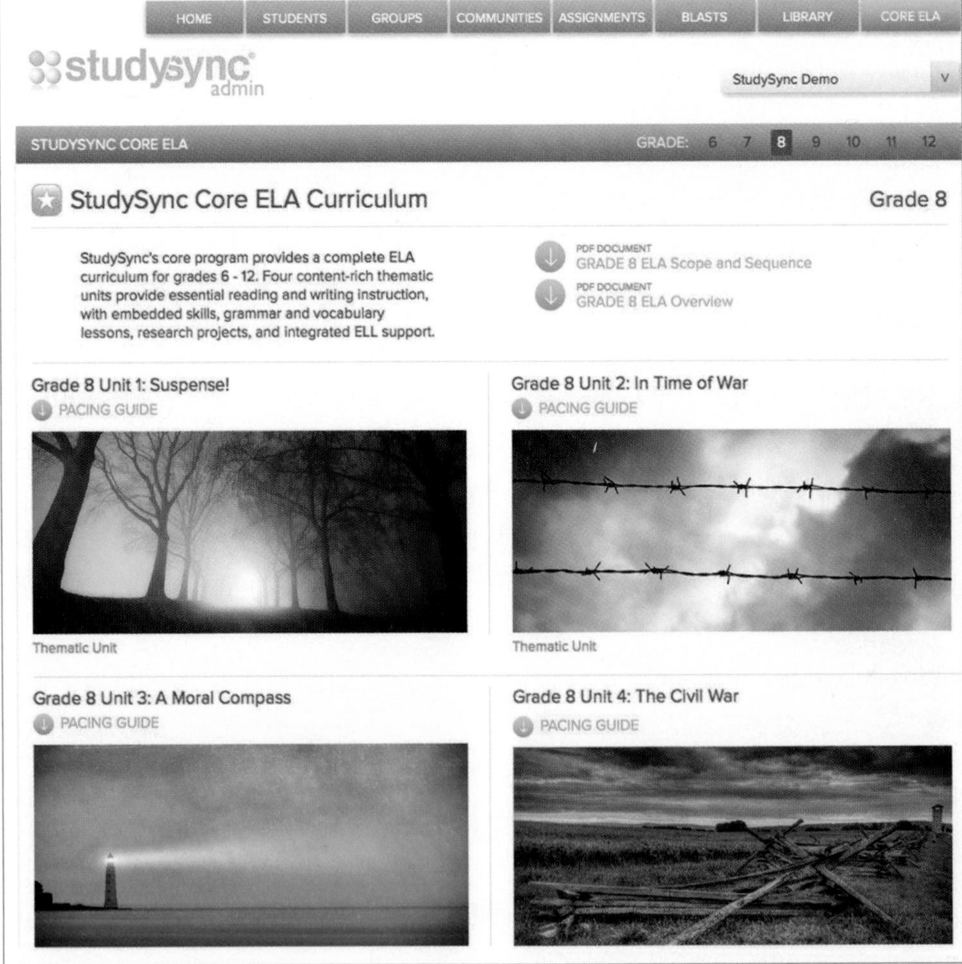

OVERVIEW

The Overview of each Core ELA Unit provides a video preview and an introduction to the unit. The Overview also contains lists of readings, key Skills, standards, and other important general information about the unit.

PACING GUIDE

Pacing Guides provide a 45-day plan with day-to-day guidance for implementing each Core ELA Unit. They outline when and how to incorporate instruction from the Instructional Path, Extended Writing Project, Research Project, and Full-text Study. An additional Pacing Guide column helps teachers draw connections between the Full-text Study and the shorter text selections in the Instructional Path.

Pacing Guides also offer ideas for substituting lessons, revisiting difficult concepts, creating multidisciplinary strands of instruction, and designing independent reading programs. These guides show teachers how to bring StudySync's wealth of resources together to create dynamic, engaging learning environments for their students.

DAY	INSTRUCTIONAL PATH	EXTENDED WRITING PROJECT	RESEARCH PROJECT	FULL-TEXT STUDY	CONNECTING FULL-TEXT STUDY TO THEMATIC UNIT INSTRUCTIONAL PATH LESSONS
23	**SKILL** Media			*Harriet Tubman: Conductor on the Underground Railroad* Chapter 5 "Flight" **COMPARE** to *Old Plantation Days*	
24	**CLOSE READ** *Harriet Tubman: Conductor on the Underground Railroad*	**EXTENDED WRITING PROJECT** Literary Analysis		*Harriet Tubman: Conductor on the Underground Railroad* Chapter 6 "The Underground Road"	
25	**FIRST READ:** *The People Could Fly: American Black Folktales*			*Harriet Tubman: Conductor on the Underground Railroad* Chapter 7 "'Shuck this Corn'"	**LINK** to *Harriet Tubman: Conductor on the Underground Railroad* – Ask students to consider the premise of the folktale and discuss why the ability to fly like a bird would be so attractive to African American slaves. In what way does Harriet Tubman help slaves to "fly"?
26	**SKILL** Compare and Contrast	**EXTENDED WRITING PROJECT** Prewrite		*Harriet Tubman: Conductor on the Underground Railroad* Chapter 8 "Mint A Becomes Harriet"	
27	**CLOSE READ** *The People Could Fly: American Black Folktales*	**SKILL** Thesis Statement		*Harriet Tubman: Conductor on the Underground Railroad* Chapter 9 "The Patchwork Quilt"	**LINK** to *Harriet Tubman: Conductor on the Underground Railroad* – How does Harriet Tubman's marriage to John Tubman keep her a "caged bird"? How is this ironic given John's status?

INSTRUCTIONAL PATH

The Instructional Path of each Core ELA Unit contains ten to twelve texts and/or text excerpts from a variety of genres and text types. Program authors, Douglas Fisher, Ph.D. and Timothy Shanahan, Ph.D., developed the instructional routines around these texts to support best practices in reading instruction.

Instruction around texts begins with a First Read lesson. First Read Lesson Plans include think alouds to help teachers model key vocabulary and comprehension skills for students before they read. Students read and annotate texts using either their digital accounts or their print Student Reading and Writing Companions, and First Read lessons conclude with a series of text-dependent Think questions that challenge students to provide textual evidence to support their understanding of the text.

At least three First Reads in every unit also include a StudySync® TV episode, one of the hallmarks of the program. Lessons with StudySync® TV contain additional metacognitive questions in which students reexamine short clips from the video to analyze how students in the model discussion construct meaning and express themselves effectively using academic vocabulary and discussion skills.

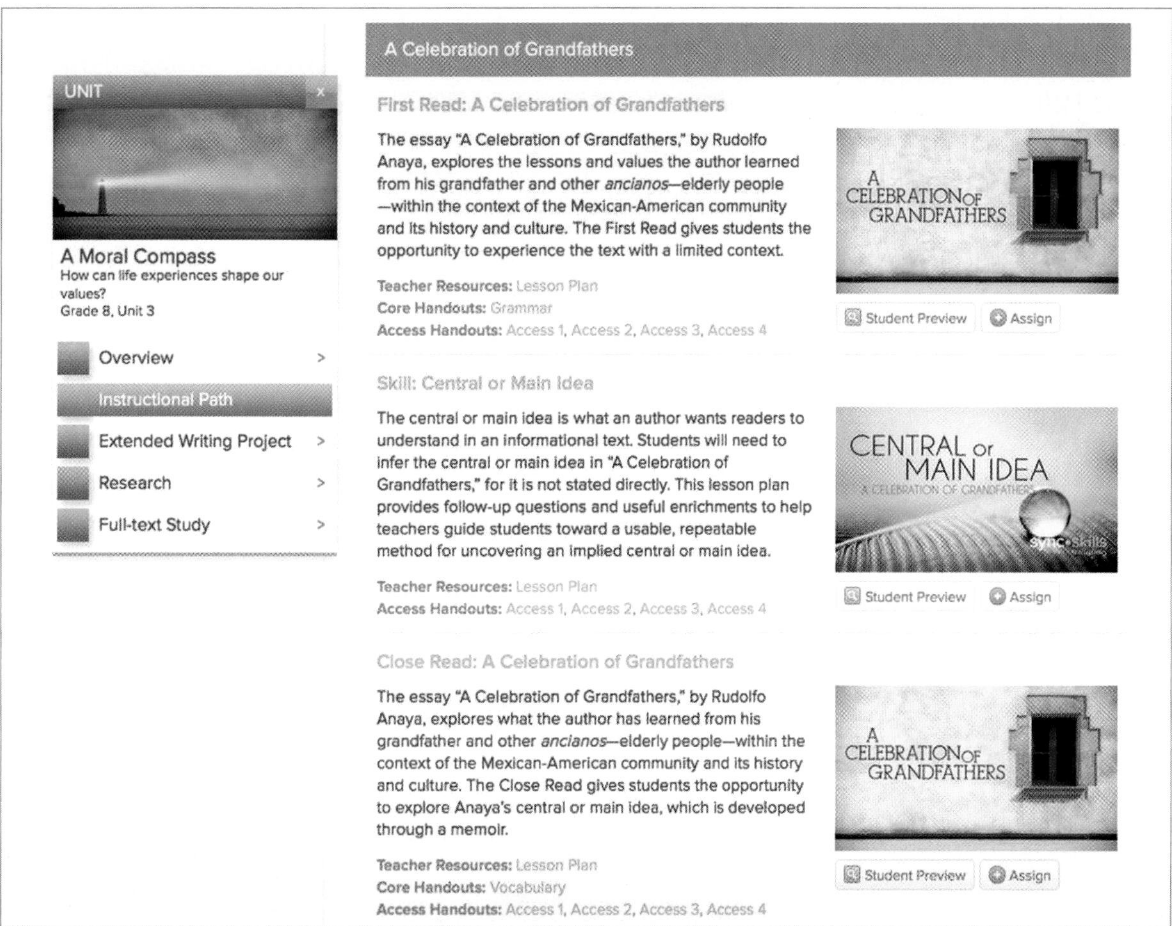

Reading Skill lessons follow First Reads, and apply the Gradual Release of Responsibility Model to deliver explicit instruction that helps students master key skills and reading strategies. Over the course of a unit, students will complete two to three of these lessons each week, offering teachers many opportunities to formatively assess student mastery and growth.

Close Read lessons culminate the instructional reading routine. Close Read lessons begin with an emphasis on vocabulary instruction as students refine or confirm their analyses of vocabulary from the First Read. Close Read lessons then challenge students to apply skills and reading strategies as they reread and annotate the text in preparation for writing their own short-constructed responses.

StudySync Blasts, the fourth lesson type found in the Instructional Path, typify the program's commitment to creating an engaging, twenty-first century context for learning. Each Blast is a short reading and writing lesson with its own research topic and driving question to which students respond in 140 characters or less.

Every assignment in the Instructional Path includes an in-depth Lesson Plan, available to teachers in their digital teacher account and this print Teacher's Edition, with both a Core Path and an Access Path of instruction. The Core Path contains the regular instructional routines that guide students toward mastery. Many lessons also contain Core Handouts—Grammar mini-lessons, Graphic Organizers, Vocabulary quizzes, or Student Writing Models.

The Access Path of each Lesson Plan contains guidance for using the Access Handouts to scaffold and differentiate instruction to insure equity and access for all students. Access Handouts provide a range of important scaffolds for English Learners and Approaching grade-level readers.

Beginner EL → Access 1 Handout
Intermediate EL → Access 2 Handout
Advanced EL → Access 3 Handout
Approaching grade-level → Access 4 Handout

EXTENDED WRITING PROJECT

Writing is an integral part of StudySync's Core ELA curriculum. The curriculum features comprehensive instruction in narrative, informative/explanatory, and argumentative writing forms, and in a wide variety of modes, including full-length essays and narratives, short constructed responses, peer reviews, Blasts, and the digital annotations of texts.

Each unit contains an Extended Writing Project (EWP) that focuses on one of the three primary writing forms and is woven into the instructional fabric of the unit. By the end of the year, each student generates a full-length narrative, informative/explanatory essay, literary analysis (in argumentative form), and an argumentative essay.

Numerous writing Skill lessons in each EWP provide instruction on skills essential to every form. EWP lessons contain Lesson Plans, Core Handouts, and Access Handouts that follow the same conventions as lessons in the Instructional Path.

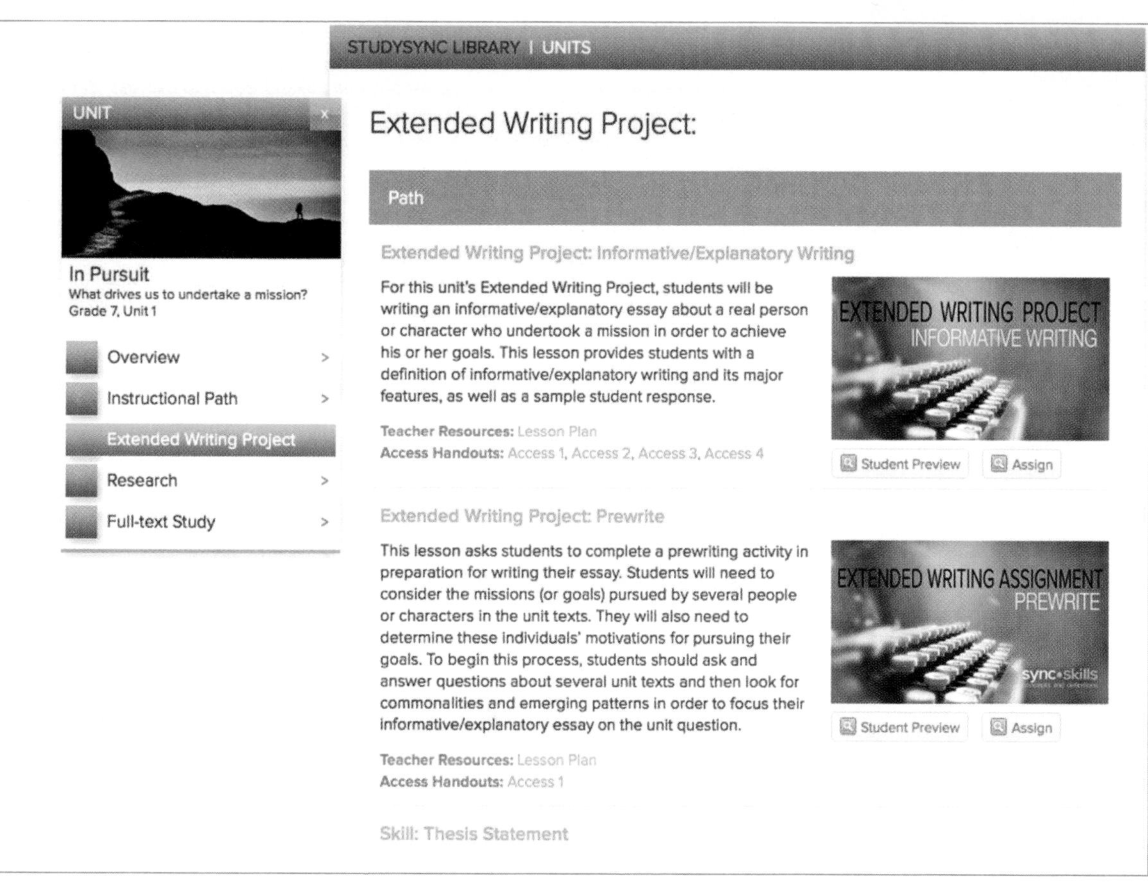

RESEARCH

In addition to the short research students complete in Blast assignments, each Core ELA Unit also contains an in-depth research project in which students explore a new angle of the unit's theme and essential question. This research project is fully integrated into the Pacing Guide, and builds on and complements the unit's key skills. Research projects deepen content knowledge, allow students to read more widely, and offer students the opportunity to present their claims and findings in a variety of formats that address key speaking and listening standards.

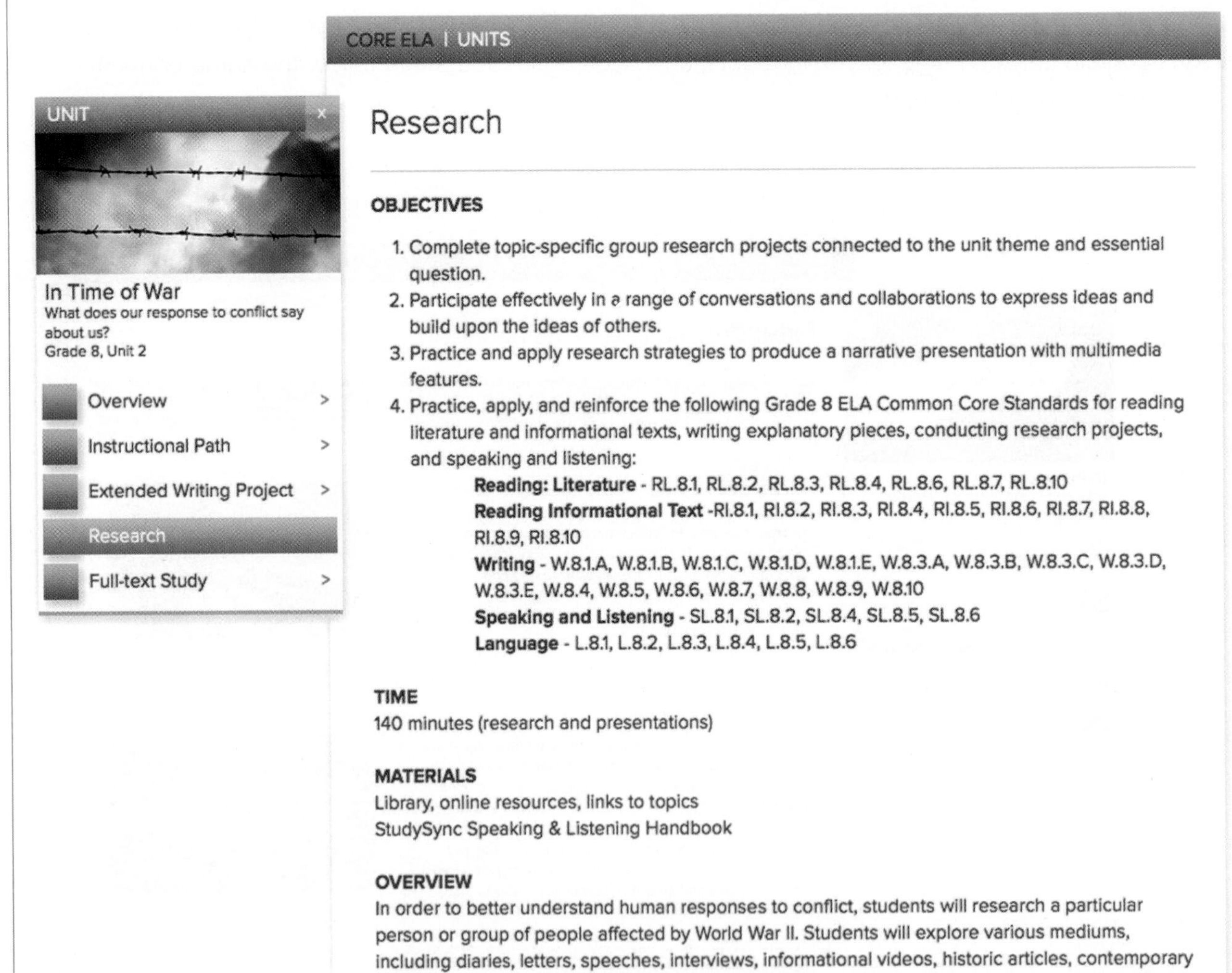

FULL-TEXT STUDY

Each Core ELA Unit contains an anchor text. An excerpt of this anchor text is included alongside other literature and informational texts in the Instructional Path. This anchor text is the recommended Full-text Study for the unit and the Pacing Guide for each unit provides teachers a recommended schedule for reading this text alongside the excerpts in the Instructional Path. The Pacing Guide also contains helpful hints to help teachers make direct connections between sections of the anchor text and lessons from the Core ELA Unit.

The Full-text Study Reading Guide supports the close reading of the complete anchor text. Reading guide lessons preview key vocabulary words and include close reading questions. Each Full-text Study Reading Guide section identifies a key passage that will help teachers guide students through an exploration of the essential ideas, events, and character development in the anchor text. This passage will also serve as the jumping off point from which students will engage in their own StudySync® TV-style group discussion.

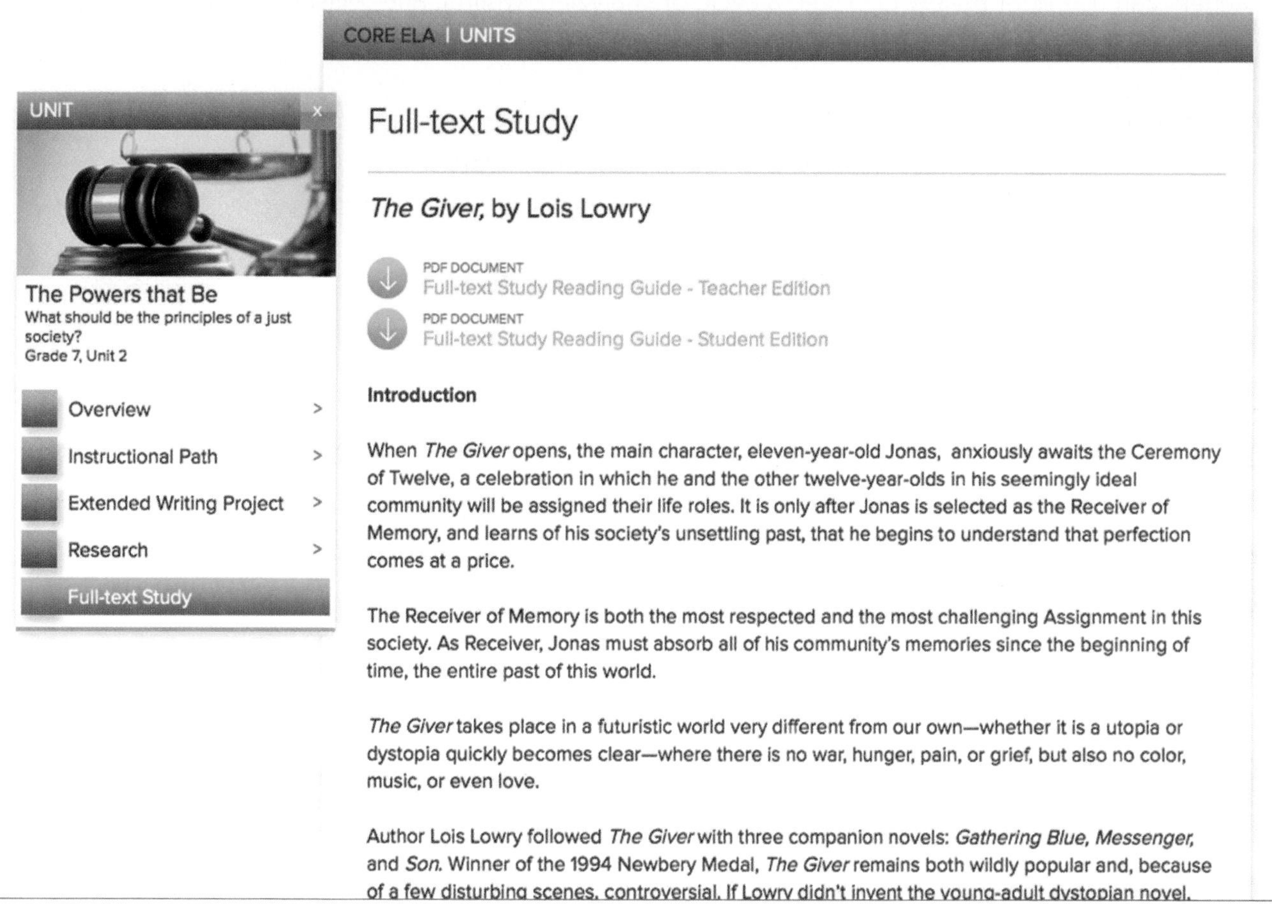

ASSESSMENT

FORMATIVE ASSESSMENT

StudySync supports all forms of assessment. Teachers provide feedback on student writing, using either the ready-made Common Core-aligned rubrics in the program or their own customized rubrics created in StudySync. Lesson plans point teachers toward minute-to-minute formative assessment opportunities. Students self-assess and peer review regularly. First Reads, Skills, Close Reads, and Extended Writing Project process steps offer medium cycle formative assessment opportunities for students and teachers to chart progress toward key learning outcomes.

ANONYMOUS PEER REVIEW

Teachers can use peer review to initiate a cycle of analyzing, writing, and revising that turns students into skilled writers and critical thinkers.

Students learn to:

- Respond frequently and meaningfully to the texts they are reading.
- Engage in multiple forms of writing, including expository, narrative, and persuasive.
- Provide timely, anonymous critiques of other students' writing.
- Thoughtfully analyze and revise their work.
- Write to an authentic audience they know will be reading their work immediately.

StudySync capitalizes on the collective intelligence in a classroom by leveraging the valuable voices of students in the learning process. The anonymous peer review feedback helps students take an active role in supporting each other in the development of their skill sets. Peer review is not anonymous for teachers. They have a window into all student work in order to mediate the process and provide appropriate direction and support.

SUMMATIVE ASSESSMENT

In addition to the formative assessment opportunities embedded throughout StudySync, each Core ELA Unit includes an end-of-unit summative assessment and each grade level includes an end-of-course assessment. These unit and end-of-course tests are located in the Online Assessment tool in the ConnectED account. They can be delivered digitally or in print. They offer robust reporting options, including tracking student proficiency with the Common Core State Standards. This assessment format provides important practice for online standardized tests for students.

ADDITIONAL CONTENT

To go along with the Core ELA curriculum, StudySync continually provides new and additional content that allows teachers to easily customize and differentiate curriculum. The Library, Blasts, Skills, Full-text and other units, and other additional resources provide teachers thousands of extra lessons to go along with the Core ELA curriculum and make StudySync a dynamic, twenty-first century content solution in their classrooms.

LIBRARY

The extensive StudySync digital library consists of more than 1,000 texts and excerpts with supporting digital tools and lesson materials for close reading and critical writing assignments.

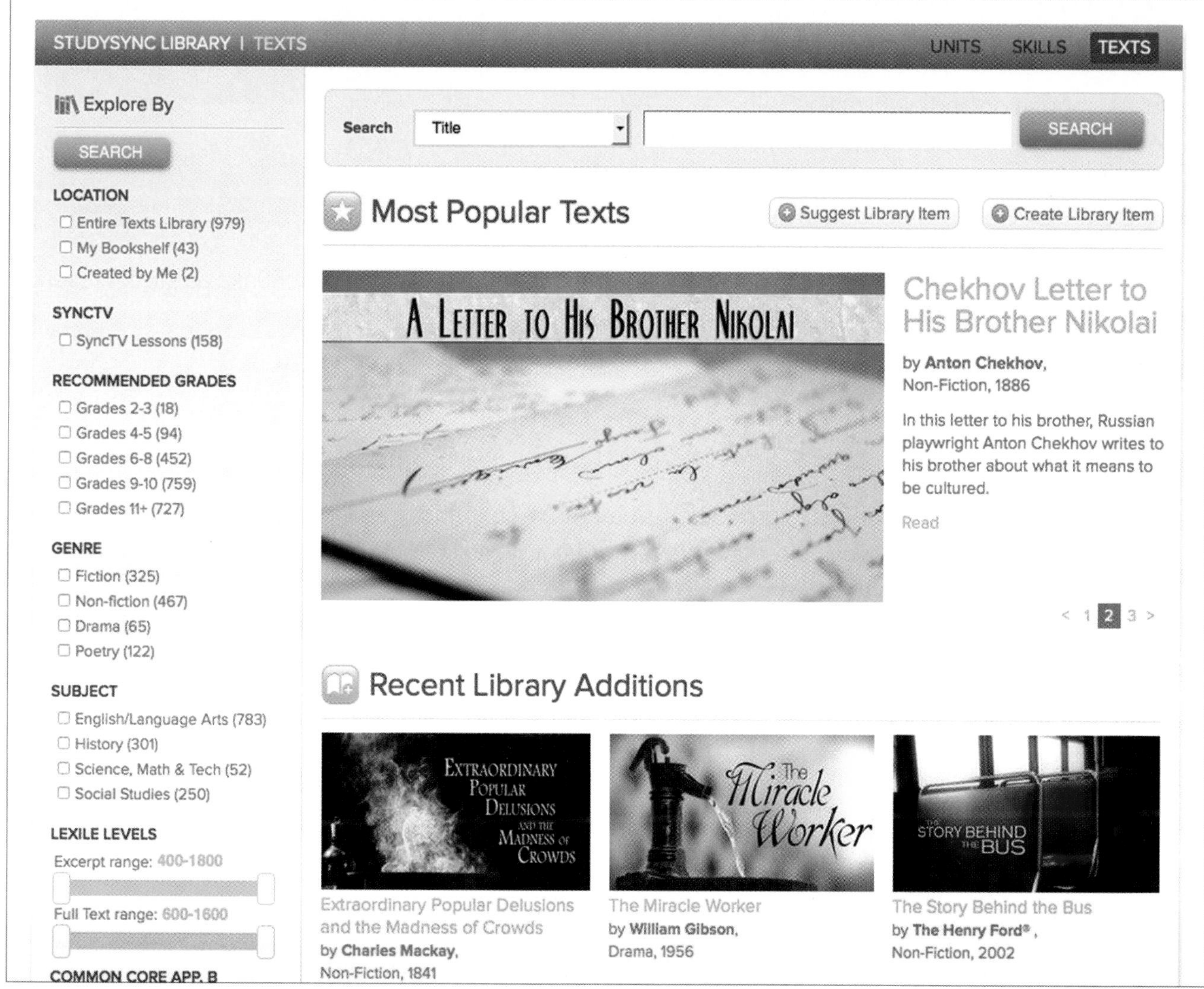

The StudySync Library is an ever-expanding resource that grows to fit the needs of all teachers. Looking for a passage of Twain's non-fiction to teach alongside *The Adventures of Huckleberry Finn*? Want to provide your students background on the political turmoil of 1960s America? Need a place to send students as a jumping off point for their own literary explorations? The StudySync Library is your answer.

To facilitate easy searching, in addition to title, author, keyword, topic, and genre searches, all texts in the Library can also be sorted by:

- Lexile®-level
- Genre
- Common Core Appendix B exemplars
- StudySync® TV Library items
- Publication date

Every Library selection includes:

- Professional audio recordings to support readers of all levels and develop speaking and listening skills
- Online annotation and highlighting
- Common Core-aligned writing prompts

Every Core ELA Library selection includes:

- An Audio Text Highlight tool that breaks texts into grammatical and syntactical chunks as students follow along with the authentic audio
- Auto-graded quizzes to formatively assess student reading comprehension
- Key vocabulary supports
- Text-dependent Think questions

As the StudySync Library continues to grow, these features will expand to selections beyond those included in the Core ELA program to provide teachers even greater flexibility and options for designing their own curriculum.

Texts with StudySync® TV lessons include additional, engaging multimedia lesson supports like:

- Movie trailer-like Previews
- StudySync® TV episodes
- Short-answer Think questions

BLASTS

In addition to the Blasts embedded in the Core ELA Units, StudySync digital teacher accounts house an ever-growing index with hundreds of Blasts that explore contemporary issues and other high-interest topics. StudySync releases new Blasts every school day, staying on top of all the latest news and providing fresh content to help teachers create engaging, relevant classrooms.

Students respond to the short informational texts and driving questions with 140-character or less Blast responses that allow them to practice clear, concise writing. The peer review platform allows students to read and respond to one another's Blasts, creating a social learning environment that teachers can easily mediate and monitor. Teachers may even elect to join the StudySync National Blast Community which enables students to read and respond to the Blasts of students from all over the United States.

Teachers can easily differentiate weekly Blasts by choosing to target any of the three Lexile® versions to students. Teachers even have the option to use the StudySync platform to create their own Blasts.

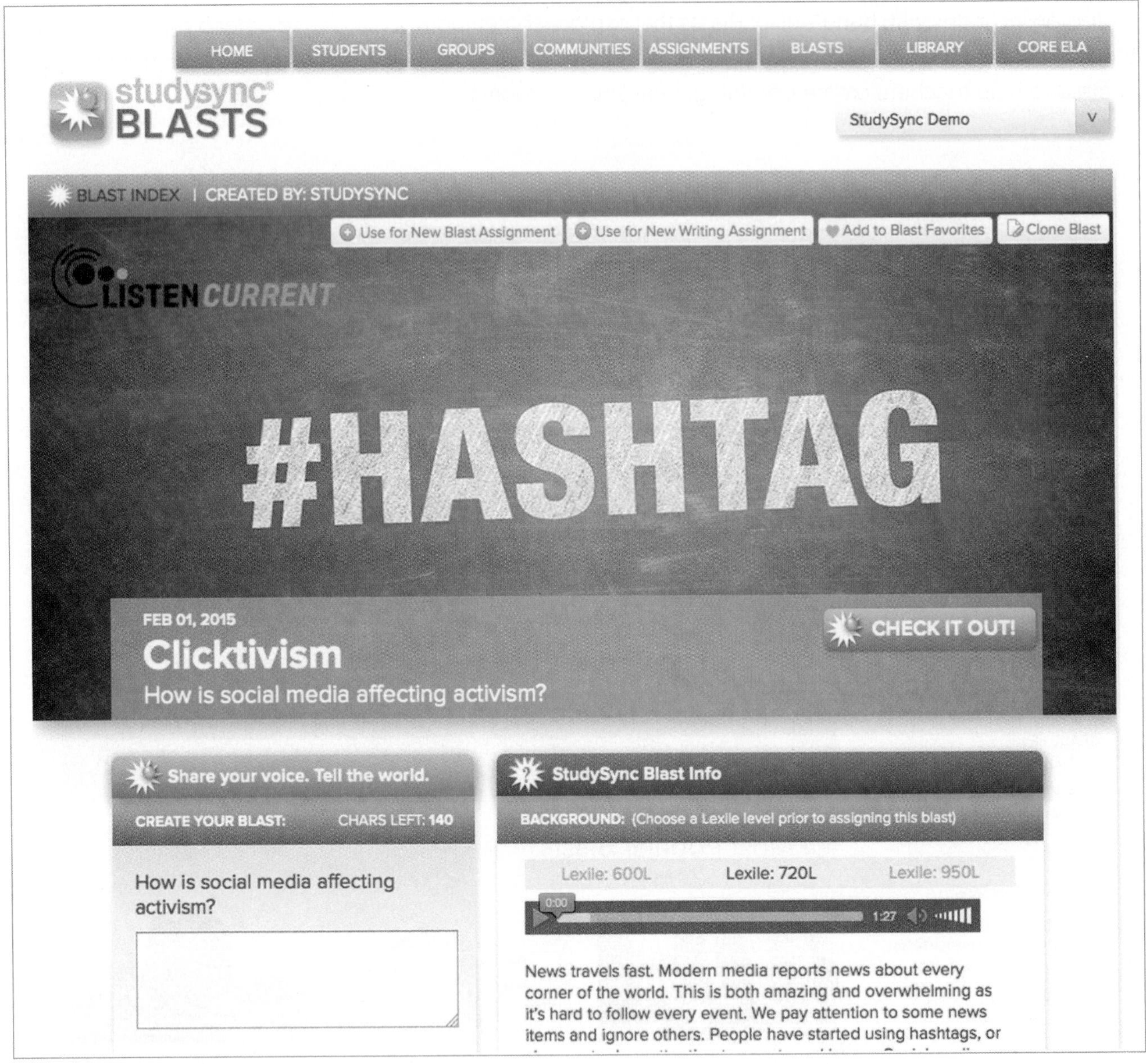

Teachers may also choose to select **Listen Current** Blasts. These weekly Blasts feature a background-building radio story to capture students' attention and help build key listening skills.

SKILLS

StudySync Skill lessons instruct students on the key reading, writing, and language skills and strategies necessary for mastery of the Common Core State Standards. The Skills index in every StudySync digital teacher account allows teachers to search for Skills lessons by grade level, topic, or keyword.

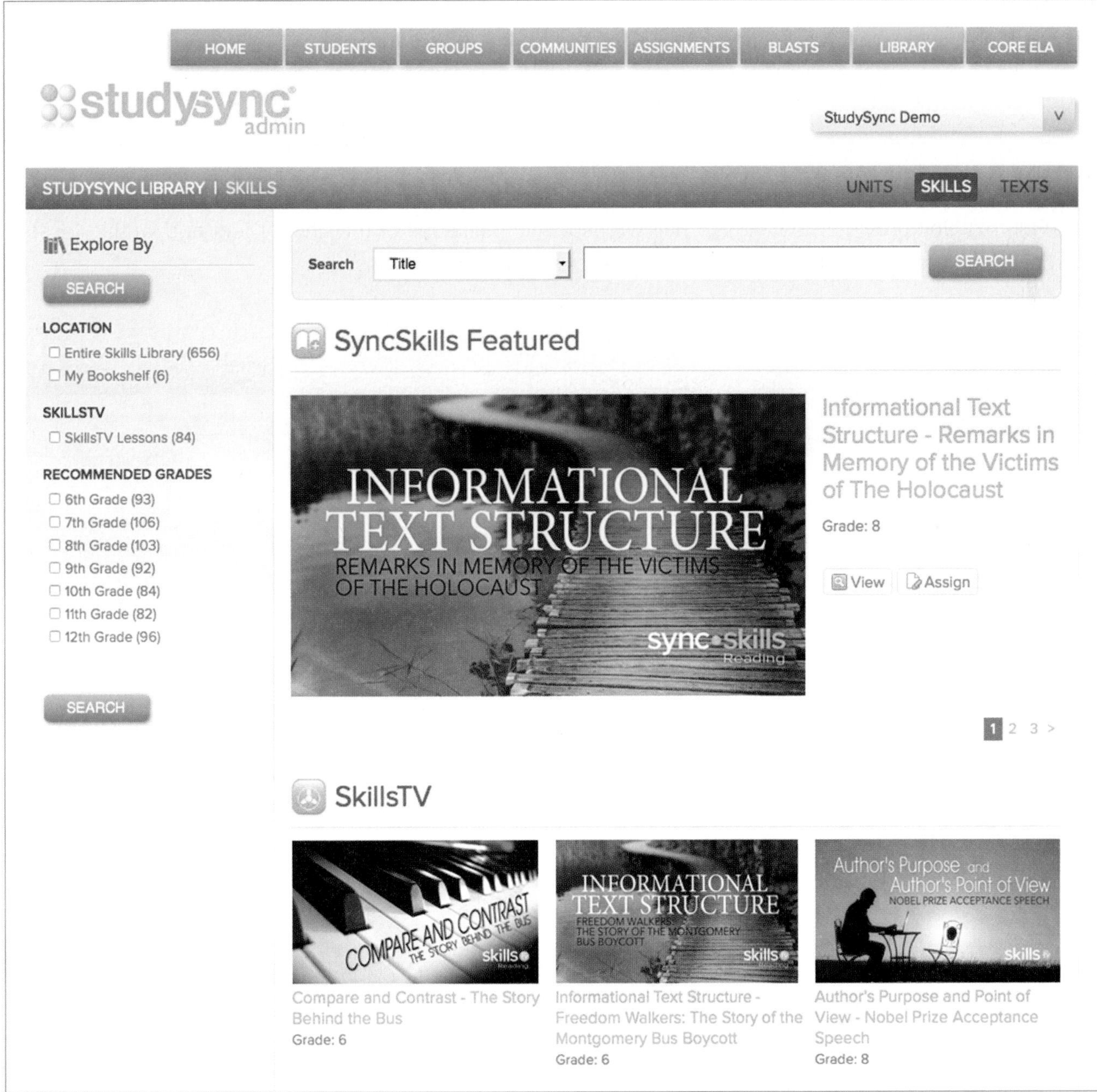

Skill lessons apply the Gradual Release of Responsibility Model. First, students learn the definition of the skill or strategy they'll be applying and watch a Concept Definition video in which students define and break down the key components of a skill or strategy. Next, teachers guide students through a "we do" portion of the lesson, facilitating discussion with follow-up questions from the lesson plan. Many Skills lessons contain SkillsTV videos in which students dramatize the application of a particular skill or strategy.

Lastly, students apply their new knowledge to short questions that ask students to both demonstrate mastery of a standard and provide textual evidence to support their understanding. Teachers receive immediate feedback on these short, formative assessments.

FULL-TEXT UNITS

Each text selected for a Full-text Study in the Core ELA Units also contains a corresponding Full-text Unit. This Full-text Unit provides readings to pair with specific passages of the anchor text and writing lessons that challenge students to compare anchor texts to additional selections.

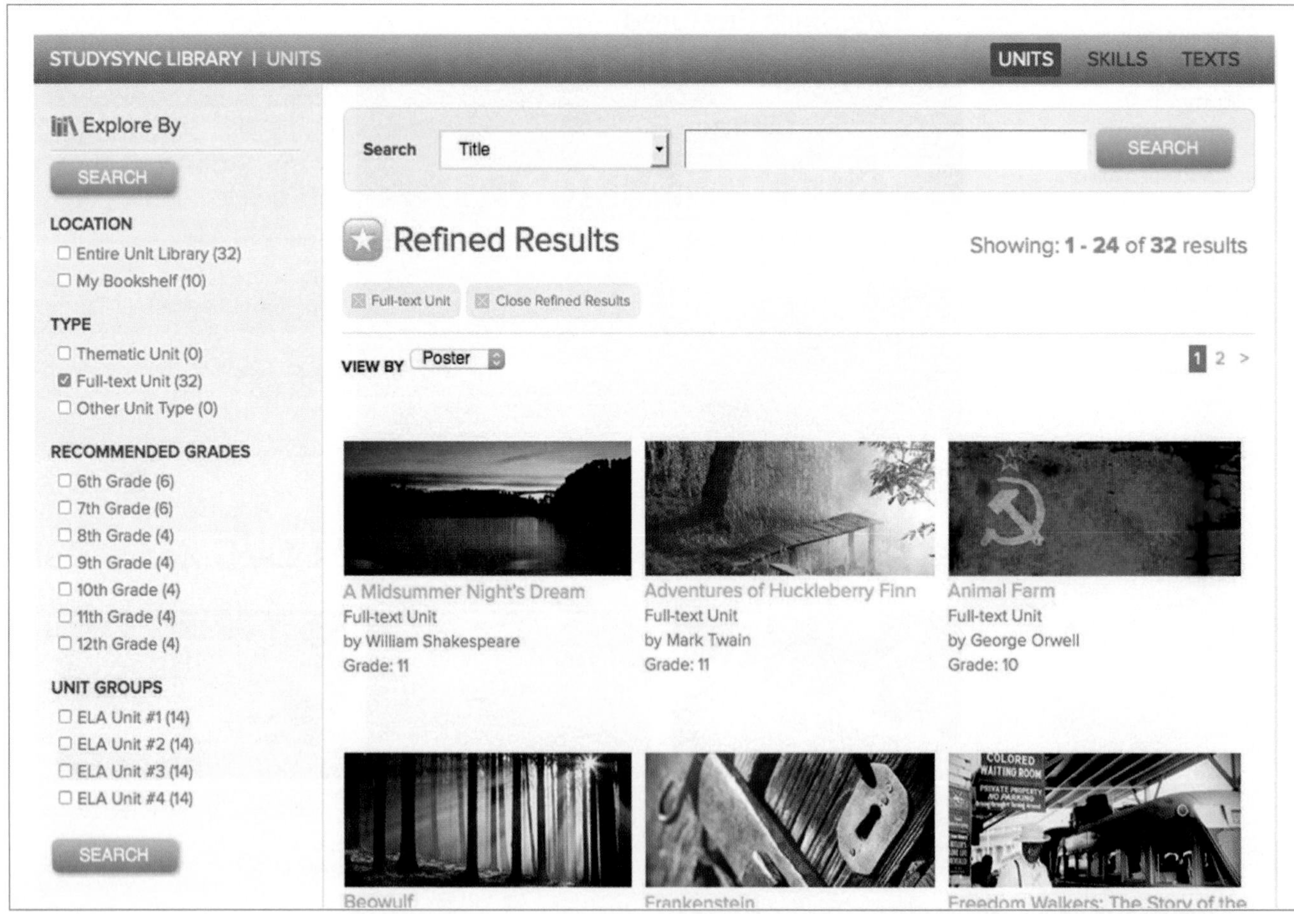

These Full-text Units are not a part of a grade level's 180 days of instruction, however teachers may wish to draw from them to incorporate materials from other disciplines or develop an alternative, novel-based approach to instruction.

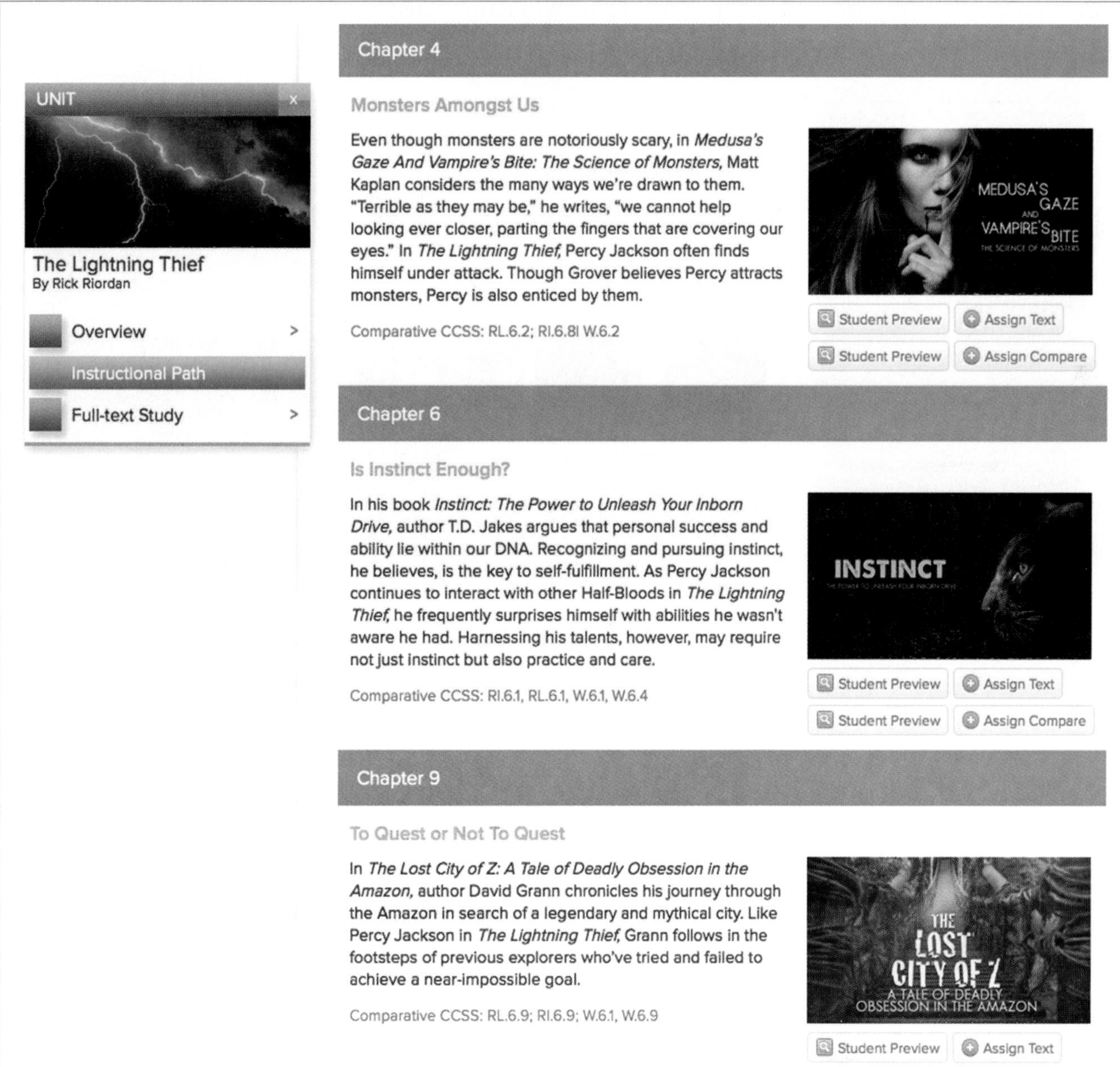

OTHER UNITS

In addition to Core ELA and Full-text Units, StudySync offers teachers a wide range of English Learner, Literature, and Composition Units from which to choose. In the ever-growing Units sections of the Library, teachers will find instructional content that allows them to further customize and differentiate curriculum to suit the unique needs of their students.

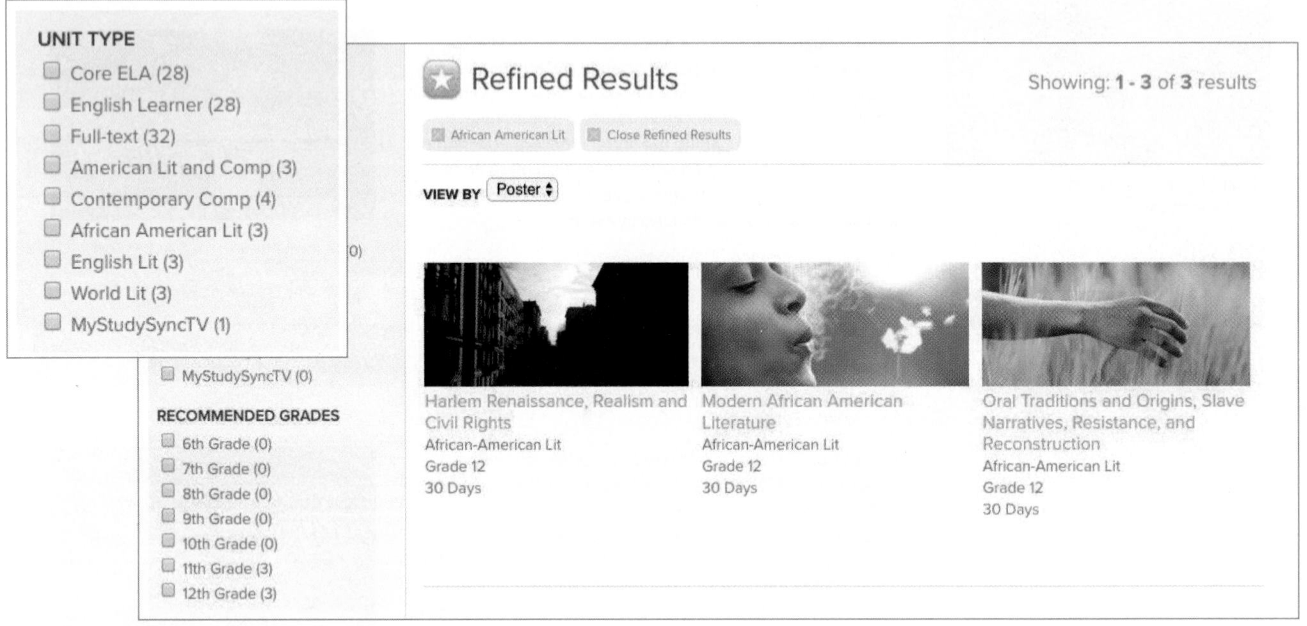

ADDITIONAL RESOURCES

- **Grade Level Assessments** documents contain printable versions of end-of-unit and end-of-course assessments for each grade.
- **Placement and Diagnostic Assessments** aid initial evaluation of student skills to decide on an appropriate instructional level for the student.
- **Foundational Skills** covers phonics, decoding, word recognition, and fluency to help build the skills that lead to students reading independently.
- **Speaking and Listening Handbook** addresses every Common Core ELA standard for speaking and listening and offers usable, repeatable methods and tools for helping students develop and master essential speaking and listening skills.
- **Grammar, Language and Composition Guide** provides additional instruction and practice that can be used for reteaching or preteaching.

- **Vocabulary Workbook** offers students additional opportunities to build and expand their vocabulary.
- **Spelling Workbook** teaches spelling patterns and concepts that apply to various word lists.
- **Standard English Learners Handbook** offers in-depth background information about different instructional routines that can be used with SELs to help them develop their Standard English and understand when it is appropriate to use it.
- **Language Transfers Handbook** provides cross linguistic transfer analysis to help teachers understand the language of students in their classroom.
- **Research-based Alignments** provides a summary of key research findings and recommendations for best practices of instruction in English Language Arts, focused on Reading, Writing, Speaking and Listening, Language, and Media and Technology. Following each section, alignment of the recommendations of the research to specific instruction within StudySync is provided.
- **The Glossary** offers basic summary of essential ELA terminology for each grade level.

Additional Resources

PDF DOCUMENT
Placement and Diagnostic Assessment

PDF DOCUMENT
Foundational Skills

PDF DOCUMENT
Speaking & Listening Handbook

PDF DOCUMENT
Grammar, Language, and Composition Guide

PDF DOCUMENT
Vocabulary Workbook

PDF DOCUMENT
Spelling Workbook

PDF DOCUMENT
Standard English Learners Handbook

PDF DOCUMENT
Language Transfers Handbook

PDF DOCUMENT
Research-base Alignments

PDF DOCUMENT
Student Glossary

PDF DOCUMENT
Teacher Glossary

DESIGN YOUR INSTRUCTION

As outlined above, StudySync provides a rich resource of materials for all ELA students and teachers. Our dynamic, ever-growing curriculum allows for teachers to customize instruction to meet their needs. Whether in a low-tech or high-tech environment, StudySync provides multiple opportunities for whole group, small group and individual instruction. Below are some specific examples of how teachers can integrate StudySync's key features into a variety of classroom contexts.

StudySync Content	Whole group	Small group or pairs	Individuals
Preview and/or Introduction	Project the multimedia Preview and view as a class. Read the Introduction as a class. Follow with a quick discussion about the images and information in the Preview and Introduction.	Have students turn and talk after watching the Preview and reading the Introduction. What images and information stood out? How did their interpretations differ?	Based on the Preview and Introduction, have students jot down predictions, questions, and/or inferences about the text.
First Read	Project a text on the screen. Model specific skills including using context clues to determine difficult vocabulary words, and using reading comprehension strategies to parse difficult passages.	Allow students to read and/or listen to the audio reading of the text in pairs or small groups, stopping to discuss thoughts and new vocabulary words as they annotate.	Students read and annotate the text, utilizing the audio or Audio Text Highlight feature as necessary. Alternatively, students can annotate in their print Companion.
StudySync® TV	Project the episode and view as a class. See the corresponding lesson plan for discussion prompts for specific sections of the episode.	Using prompts from the lesson plan, have students hold their own StudySync® TV discussions. Afterwards, briefly share with the whole class ideas that were discussed.	Ask students to jot down ideas from the StudySync® TV episode and their own discussions that might assist with their writing.
Think Questions	Think Questions may be discussed and answered as a class, using the text as support.	Think Questions may be discussed and answered in pairs or small groups before reviewing correct answers with the entire class.	Think Questions may be answered individually, using the text as support.

Skills	Project the Concept Definition video and as a group read the definition of the Skill. If there is a SkillsTV video in the Model sections of the lesson, watch and discuss as a class.	Have students work in pairs or small groups to read through the text in the Model section, stopping throughout to discuss questions and ideas. Work your way around to each group to provide feedback.	Have students individually complete the mini-assessments that conclude Skills lessons. When all students are finished, project the questions and discuss correct answers.
Close Read	Review vocabulary analysis from the First Read. Ask students to compare their context analysis of vocabulary against the actual definitions. Review key skills students will apply in the Close Read.	Close Reads can occur individually or in small groups. If assigning Close Reads for small group work, have students discuss and explain their annotations to one another as they go.	Have students reread and annotate the text in order to complete the Skills Focus questions and prepare themselves for the writing prompt that follows.
Write	Discuss the prompt as a class, making sure students understand the directions and expectations. Display the rubric for the assignment as well.	Allow students time to brainstorm ideas or discuss the prompts with their peers, referring to the text, StudySync® TV episode, and/or previous discussions.	Students individually submit responses to the assigned prompt.
Peer Review	Remind students of your expectations for the peer review process, and inform them of specific directions for this assignment.	In pairs or small groups, have students discuss what they will look for in their peers' responses, based on the directions and rubric. What will an exemplar response include? Report ideas to the whole class.	Students complete peer reviews individually, using the guidelines established.
Blasts	As a class, hold a brief discussion about the prompt. After students read the Background information, discuss the Quikpoll and Number Crunch as a class. Ask students to make predictions on how their peers will answer the QuikPoll, and how the results might differ if answered by another class, age group, etc.	Students should read the Background section in small groups and record notes in their handbooks. Have students discuss questions and ideas that came up as they read. Ask students to split up the Research Links, so that each student researches 2-3 sites and then reports the information back to their peers.	Students may read the Background information individually, as well as the information from several Research Links. After discussing the information with their peers, they should craft their 140-character response to the prompt and complete 5 or more peer reviews.

studysync®

Teacher's Edition

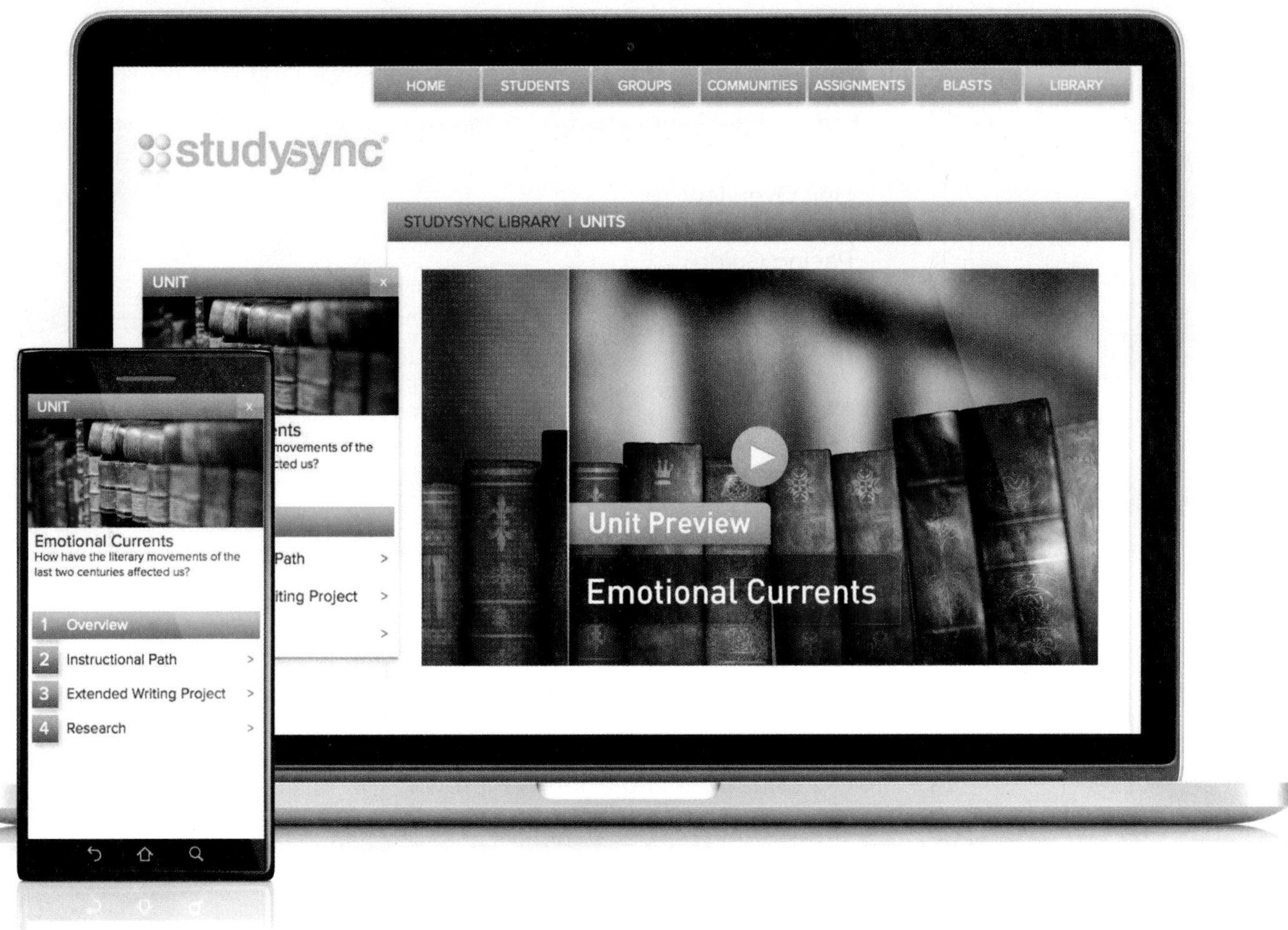

How have the literary movements of the last two centuries affected us?

Emotional Currents

Emotional Currents

OVERVIEW MATERIALS

INSTRUCTIONAL PATH

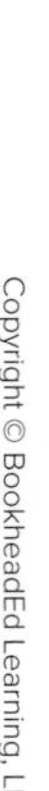

EXTENDED WRITING PROJECT

RESEARCH

FULL-TEXT STUDY

Overview Materials

Emotional Currents

OVERVIEW

UNIT TITLE

Emotional Currents

UNIT DRIVING QUESTION

How have the literary movements of the last two centuries affected us?

UNIT OVERVIEW

What is the role of literature—both classic literature and contemporary—in creating pop culture? Even people who don't read for pleasure can see the influence of books in the United States today, from hit television shows like *Game of Thrones* to top-grossing movies like *Gone Girl* to trendsetters like *The Hunger Games* or *Twilight*. These books are released and seem to be everywhere instantly. Yet classic books still permeate our culture. Edgar Allan Poe's gothic influence can be felt every Halloween; each Valentine's Day, references to finding a Mr. Darcy abound. In this Grade 12 unit, students will address this question: How have the literary movements of the last two centuries affected us?

A vast array of literature makes up this Grade 12 unit, as your students explore three literary movements from the past two centuries through several genres, including poetry, short stories, novel excerpts, speeches, and a national anthem. The unit begins with the classic romantic poem "The Rime of the Ancient Mariner," in which a sailor describes his harrowing journey to the ends of the earth and back. Other selections include excerpts from the realist novels *Pride and Prejudice, House of Mirth,* and *O Pioneers!*; an excerpt from Virginia Woolf's modernist classic *Mrs. Dalloway*; and speeches in time of war by Winston Churchill and Franklin Delano Roosevelt. Throughout this unit, students will explore how literary movements are expressed in different genres and by a variety of authors.

Blasts tie the unit's driving question to both historical and contemporary topics, such as how radio and new technology affect political speech, and the role of marriage in the United States in the twenty-first century. The Extended Writing Project guides students through a rigorous writing process in order to help them develop an informative research essay.

TEXTS

The Rime of the Ancient Mariner	Poetry
Young Goodman Brown	Short Story
The Masque of the Red Death	Short Story
Pride and Prejudice	Novel
The Glass Menagerie	Drama
Wuthering Heights	Novel
The House of Mirth	Novel
O Pioneers!	Novel
Mrs. Dalloway	Novel
The Star-Spangled Banner	Song
Be Ye Men of Valour	Speech
D-Day Prayer	Speech

FULL-TEXT STUDY

Pride and Prejudice

EXEMPLAR TEXTS

Pride and Prejudice

ASSIGNMENT TYPES

Blasts: 8
First Reads: 12
Reading Skills: 14
Close Reads: 12
Extended Writing Project Prompts: 5
Writing Skills: 7

STANDARDS FOCUS

RL.11-12.1, RL.11-12.2, RL.11-12.3, RL.11-12.4, RL.11-12.5, RL.11-12.6, RL.11-12.9, RL.11-12.10
RI.11-12.1, RI.11-12.4, RI.11-12.5, RI.11-12.6, RI.11-12.9, RI.11-12.10
W.11-12.2.A, W.11-12.2.B, W.11-12.2.C, W.11-12.2.D, W.11-12.2.E, W.11-12.2.F, W.11-12.4, W.11-12.5, W.11-12.6, W.11-12.7, W.11-12.8, W.11-12.9, W.11-12.10
SL.11-12.1, SL.11-12.2, SL.11-12.3, SL.11-12.4, SL.11-12.5, SL.11-12.6
L.11-12.1.A, L.11-12.1.B, L.11-12.2.A, L.11-12.2.B, L.11-12.3.A, L.11-12.4, L.11-12.6

KEY READING SKILLS

Tone
Setting
Irony
Compare and Contrast
Character
Media
Theme
Author's Purpose and Author's Point of View
Connotation and Denotation

KEY GRAMMAR SKILLS

First Read: The Masque of the Red Death - Syntax
First Read: Wuthering Heights - Italics
First Read: Be Ye Men of Valour - Verb Phrases
Extended Writing Project: Draft - Usage
Extended Writing Project: Revise - Hyphenation Conventions
Extended Writing Project: Edit/Proofread/Publish - Spelling

KEY WRITING SKILLS

Audience, Purpose, and Style
Research and Note-Taking
Thesis Statement
Organize Informative Writing
Supporting Details
Introductions and Conclusions
Body Paragraphs and Transitions
Sources and Citations

EXTENDED WRITING PROJECT

As students make their way through the unit, they will compile evidence, as well as a number of opinions and ideas, related to how the literary movements of the past two centuries affect us today. The Extended Writing Project for this unit helps students synthesize those ideas through a well-constructed informative/explanatory research paper on one author from the unit and the literary movement with which he or she is associated. Small, manageable tasks lead students through the prewriting, planning, drafting, revising, and editing/proofreading/publishing steps of the writing process, while skill lessons offer modeling and instruction on criteria within each step specific to the writing form.

ADDITIONAL TEXTS

These additional texts from the StudySync library are related to the unit theme and/or time period. Teachers can choose to include some of these texts in addition to the texts in this unit to create a customized course of instruction for their students.

Ode on a Grecian Urn, by John Keats (1819)
My Last Duchess, by Robert Browning (1842)
Jane Eyre, by Charlotte Bronte (1848)
A Tale of Two Cities, by Charles Dickens (1859)
Tess of the d'Ubervilles, by Thomas Hardy (1891)
Dulce et Decorum Est, by Wilfred Owen (1917)
Dubliners, by James Joyce (1914)
Do Not Go Gentle into That Good Night, by Dylan Thomas (1951)

studysync®

GRADE 12 UNIT 4: EMOTIONAL CURRENTS

PURPOSE

This pacing guide will help you utilize the wealth of resources offered in each StudySync Core ELA unit. The pacing guide weaves lessons from every segment of this Core ELA unit: the Instructional Path, Extended Writing Project, Research Project, and Full-text Study.

The pacing guide presents a suggested plan to cover all content in this unit. You may cover all of these lessons in class, or you may decide to divide the assignments between in-class work and homework. Of course, no one understands your students' needs like you do, and one of the key benefits of StudySync is the ease with which you can adapt, alter, eliminate, or reorganize lessons to best meet the needs of your students. The Shortcuts and Additional Activities section at the end of this pacing guide contains recommendations to help in that regard.

ORGANIZATION

The pacing guide divides the unit into 45 days. Instructional days often have more than a single task. For example, all of the activities on row 1 are suggested to be covered on the first instructional day. Pacing is based on an assumption of 50-minute instructional days, but since schedules vary from school to school, you may need to modify the suggested pacing to fit your unique needs.

The column labeled "Full-text Study Connections" often identifies other texts in the StudySync Library that complement the chapter in the Full-text Study students are reading on a particular day. Though these comparative texts are not considered part of the 45 days of Core ELA instruction for this unit, they are listed in the pacing guide in case you would like to include additional texts as part of this unit.

There are no activities or lessons planned for the final two days of the unit, which are dedicated to assessment.

CORE ELA UNIT

DAY	INSTRUCTIONAL PATH	EXTENDED WRITING PROJECT	RESEARCH PROJECT	FULL-TEXT STUDY	FULL-TEXT STUDY CONNECTIONS
1	**UNIT PREVIEW** **BLAST** Emotional Currents **BRITISH LITERATURE & HISTORY** The Triumph of Romanticism (1750–1837)		**SPEAKING & LISTENING HANDBOOK** Handbook "Research Using Various Media" Section **RESEARCH PROJECT PART I** Break students into small groups and assign each group a topic to research (see list of topics under Research tab) and begin research (in class and/or online).		
2	**BRITISH LITERATURE & HISTORY** The Victorian Age (1837–1901) **BRITISH LITERATURE & HISTORY** The Modern Age (1901–1950)		**RESEARCH PROJECT PART I CONT.** Students should continue to research.		
3	**FIRST READ** "The Rime of the Ancient Mariner"		**RESEARCH PROJECT PART I CONT.** Students should continue to research.		
4	**SKILL** Tone		**RESEARCH PROJECT PART II** Groups should work collaboratively (in class and/or online) on a presentation to present their information to the class.		

DAY	INSTRUCTIONAL PATH	EXTENDED WRITING PROJECT	RESEARCH PROJECT	FULL-TEXT STUDY	FULL-TEXT STUDY CONNECTIONS
5	**CLOSE READ** "The Rime of the Ancient Mariner"		**RESEARCH PROJECT PART II CONT.** Students should continue working to create their presentations.		
6	**BLAST** Modern Day Albatross		**RESEARCH PROJECT PART II CONT.** Students should continue working to create their presentations.		
7	**FIRST READ** "Young Goodman Brown"		**SPEAKING & LISTENING HANDBOOK** "Presentation Skills" **RESEARCH PROJECT PART III** Allow a couple of groups to present for the class.		
8	**SKILL** Setting		**RESEARCH PROJECT PART III CONT.** Allow a couple of groups to present for the class.		
9	**CLOSE READ** "Young Goodman Brown"		**RESEARCH PROJECT PART III CONT.** Allow a couple of groups to present for the class.		
10	**FIRST READ** "The Masque of the Red Death"				

DAY	INSTRUCTIONAL PATH	EXTENDED WRITING PROJECT	RESEARCH PROJECT	FULL-TEXT STUDY	FULL-TEXT STUDY CONNECTIONS
11	**SKILL** Irony			*Pride and Prejudice* Chapters 1–4 **COMPARE** to *Jane Austen, a Life*	**LINK** to *Pride and Prejudice* – Challenge students to find examples of irony in the first two chapters of *Pride and Prejudice*. Note, if needed, that there are many examples of verbal irony in Mr. Bennet's responses to his wife in Chapter 1 (underplaying his true reactions) and *dramatic* irony in Chapter 2 (Mrs. Bennet being unaware of her husband's visit to Bingley, which the reader knows).
12	**SKILL** Compare and Contrast			*Pride and Prejudice* Chapters 5–6	**LINK** to *Pride and Prejudice* – Students will have opportunities to practice the Compare and Contrast skill by comparing different pairs of characters in Chapters 5 and 6 (e.g., Bingley's open-heartedness vs. Darcy's aloofness; Jane's tolerance vs. Elizabeth's more judgmental nature; comparing Miss Bingley and Elizabeth, Charlotte and Elizabeth; and comparing what a single character truly feels with what he or she says).
13	**CLOSE READ** "The Masque of the Red Death" **BLAST** Fear Itself				

DAY	INSTRUCTIONAL PATH	EXTENDED WRITING PROJECT	RESEARCH PROJECT	FULL-TEXT STUDY	FULL-TEXT STUDY CONNECTIONS
14	**BRITISH LITERATURE & HISTORY** The Victorian Age (1837–1901) **FIRST READ** *Pride and Prejudice*			*Pride and Prejudice* Chapters 7–8 **COMPARE** to *How to Get a Rich Man*	**LINK** to *Pride and Prejudice* – Have students discuss as a class or in groups how events in chapters 7 and 8 advance Mrs. Bennet's hope to marry one of her daughters to Bingley (e.g., sending Jane to Netherfield) while also showing the obstacles working against her (the social snobbery of the Bingley sisters and, to a lesser degree, Darcy).
15	**SKILL** Character			*Pride and Prejudice* Chapters 9–12 **COMPARE** to *How to Get a Rich Man*	**LINK** to *Pride and Prejudice* –Have students meet in small groups to choose and discuss a character who is well-defined by action and speech in Chapters 9–12. Have them write and present a character sketch based on their discussion and textual evidence. Likely candidates might be Darcy, Elizabeth, Miss Bingley and Mrs. Bennet. Ask students to explain the character's importance in the novel so far.
16	**CLOSE READ** *Pride and Prejudice*			*Pride and Prejudice* Chapters 13–17	**LINK** to *Pride and Prejudice* – Invite students to discuss how the new character of William Collins relates to the themes introduced in Chapters 13–17. Discuss the necessity of social climbing through marriage (in entailed estates); the automatic respect accorded those of wealth and title (Bingley, Sir William, Darcy, Lady Catherine); the shallowness of those who pursue it (Collins, Mrs. Bennet), and the smugness or defiance of those who don't (Elizabeth, Mr. Bennet).

DAY	INSTRUCTIONAL PATH	EXTENDED WRITING PROJECT	RESEARCH PROJECT	FULL-TEXT STUDY	FULL-TEXT STUDY CONNECTIONS
17	**FIRST READ** *The Glass Menagerie*			*Pride and Prejudice* Chapters 18–23 **COMPARE** to *Bridget Jones's Diary*	**LINK** to *Pride and Prejudice* – Ask students to compare the scene from *The Glass Menagerie* with the scene of the Netherfield ball played out in Chapter 18 of *Pride and Prejudice*. Ask students how characters' goals or desires in the two texts are alike and dissimila (for example, Amanda and Mrs Bennet), and to compare how the characters strategize attaining those goals.
18	**SKILL** Media			*Pride and Prejudice* Chapters 24–26	**LINK** to *Pride and Prejudice* – The 1995 miniseries of *Pride and Prejudice*, episode three of which can be found on YouTube here, presents a good opportunity to use the Media Skill, noting how the screen version compares to the novel, whether at the point corresponding to Chapters 24–26 (starting at around 3:00 minutes) or at any other point before or after. Students might discuss how the film is faithful or departs from the novel and what is gained or lost and why.

DAY	INSTRUCTIONAL PATH	EXTENDED WRITING PROJECT	RESEARCH PROJECT	FULL-TEXT STUDY	FULL-TEXT STUDY CONNECTIONS
19	**CLOSE READ** *The Glass Menagerie*			*Pride and Prejudice* Chapters 27–31 **COMPARE** to *The Fatal Shore*	**LINK** to *Pride and Prejudice* – In this section of *Pride and Prejudice*, Elizabeth encounters the formidable Lady Catherine at Rosings and is subjected to an intense grilling by Her Ladyship, Ask students to contrast Lady Catherine with Amanda in *The Glass Menagerie*, taking into account the characters' objectives, styles, and interactions with others. Do the two women have anything in common?
20	**FIRST READ** *Wuthering Heights*			*Pride and Prejudice* Chapters 32–36	**LINK** to *Pride and Prejudice* – The central events of this section, and arguably the turning point of the novel, spans Darcy's proposal, Elizabeth's refusal, and Darcy's letter to Elizabeth justifying his actions and his history with Wickham. The excerpts from *Wuthering Heights* also describe a path of attempted reconciliation. Have students compare the two texts in terms of the part played by a misunderstanding; the character of the couples; and the reasons behind the success or failure of the reconciliation.

DAY	INSTRUCTIONAL PATH	EXTENDED WRITING PROJECT	RESEARCH PROJECT	FULL-TEXT STUDY	FULL-TEXT STUDY CONNECTIONS
21	**SKILL** Theme			*Pride and Prejudice* Chapters 37–42	**LINK** to *Pride and Prejudice* – These chapters lay out the factors leading to the elopement between Wickham and Lydia, Challenge students to determine one or more themes based on what characters did or failed to do. For example, Elizabeth and Jane keeping Wickham's past misdeeds a secret, and Mr. Bennet trusting Lydia to the supervision of others while she was in Brighton, might suggest the theme of family responsibility.
22	**CLOSE READ** *Wuthering Heights*			*Pride and Prejudice* Chapters 43–45	**LINK** to *Pride and Prejudice* – Passion, fate, and death collide in the excerpts from *Wuthering Heights*. Have students compare the intensity of emotion and the theme of fate vs. free will in *Wuthering Heights* and in Chapters 43–45 of *Pride and Prejudice*. How free are the two couples to "break the rules" and express their feelings to one another? Ask students to determine what accounts for that freedom or its lack, and what conclusion(s) they can draw from it about society and the individual.

DAY	INSTRUCTIONAL PATH	EXTENDED WRITING PROJECT	RESEARCH PROJECT	FULL-TEXT STUDY	FULL-TEXT STUDY CONNECTIONS
23	**FIRST READ** *The House of Mirth*			*Pride and Prejudice* Chapters 46–49	**LINK** to *Pride and Prejudice* – Chapters 46–49 focus on the elopement of Wickham and Lydia Bennet and the ripples of scandal it creates in Lydia's family. Have students compare the role family has played in the life of Lily Bart in *The House of Mirth* with the role of family in Lydia's life. Encourage them to draw on textual evidence in comparing or contrasting the family influence. Prompt discussion with the topics of wealth management, parental support, and family priorities.
24	**SKILL** Character			*Pride and Prejudice* Chapters 50–53	**LINK** to *Pride and Prejudice* – This section of *Pride and Prejudice* offers a good opportunity to revisit characters and consider how they have changed—possibly more than once—since students' character studies in Chapters 9–12. Among the characters worthy of "development assessment" are Darcy (conquering pride), Elizabeth (conquering prejudice), Bingley (taking charge), and, maybe, Mr. and Mrs Bennet (reacting to circumstance). Characters who resist changing might include Lydia and Wickham, and students should discuss why (both like to live on the edge).

DAY	INSTRUCTIONAL PATH	EXTENDED WRITING PROJECT	RESEARCH PROJECT	FULL-TEXT STUDY	FULL-TEXT STUDY CONNECTIONS
25	**CLOSE READ** *The House of Mirth*			*Pride and Prejudice* Chapters 54–57 **COMPARE** to "How to Marry Well"	**LINK** to *Pride and Prejudice* – Have students discuss the importance of a worthy enemy in the situations faced by Elizabeth and Lily Bart. What was the impact of Lady Catherine's attempted smackdown of Elizabeth on both Elizabeth and Darcy? Might a similar test of values have helped Lily Bart in her struggle to gain social standing? Why or why not? Did Elizabeth's childhood make her better equipped to attain her goals than Lily's childhood did? Why?
26	**BLAST** I Don't			*Pride and Prejudice* Chapters 58–61	**LINK** to *Pride and Prejudice* – From its opening ("a single man ... in want of a wife") to its last words ("... uniting them"), *Pride and Prejudice* seems to stake out marriage as its main theme or concept. But on what terms? Overcoming what obstacles? And defined by—or defining—which characters? Have students choose one or more marriages from the novel, analyze it, and compare it with marriage in American society today, as outlined in the Blast "I Don't." What lesson emerges from the Bennets' marriage? The Collinses'? The Bingleys'? The Wickhams'? The Darcys'? Does marriage still lend the same values or validation to partnerships today? Explain.

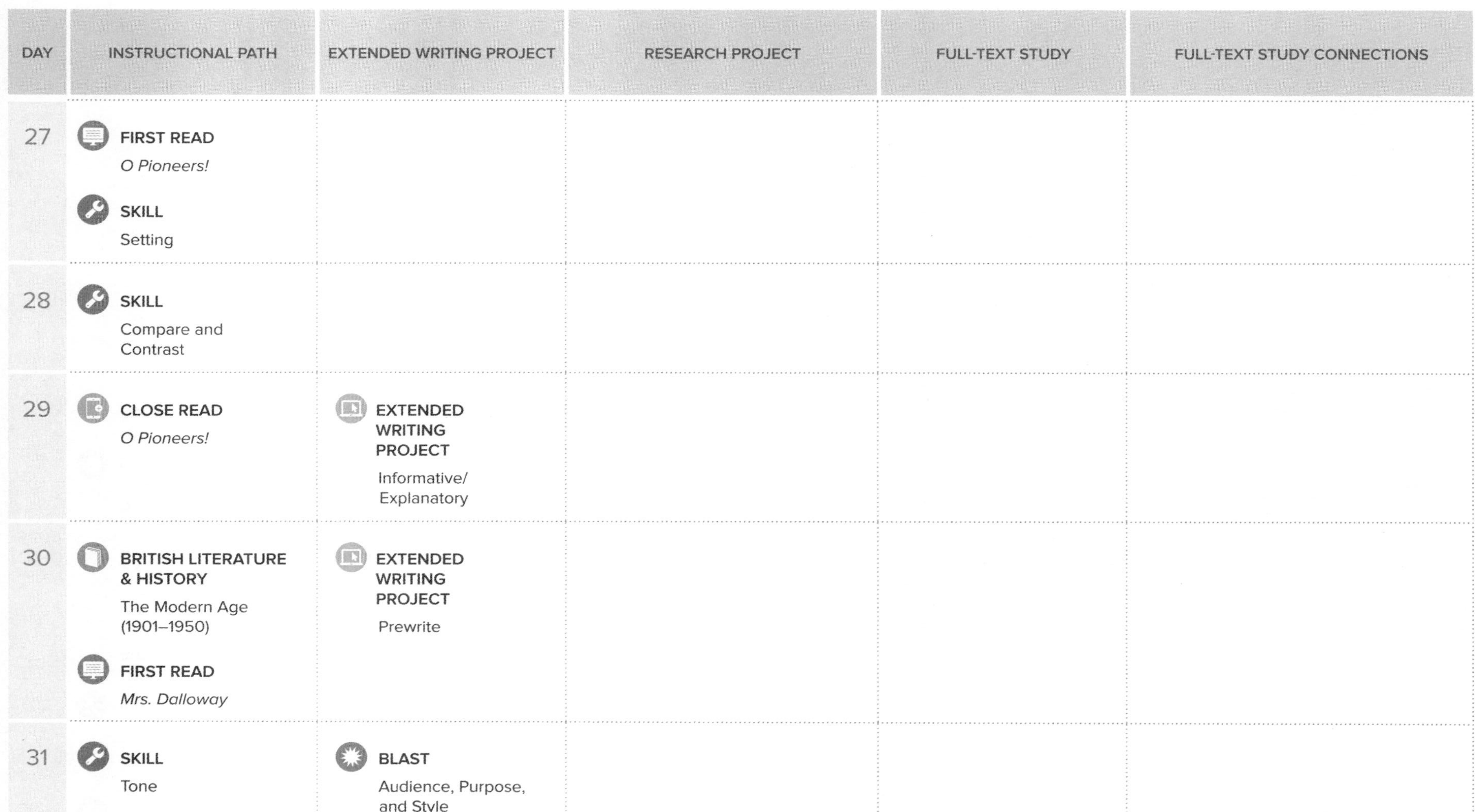

DAY	INSTRUCTIONAL PATH	EXTENDED WRITING PROJECT	RESEARCH PROJECT	FULL-TEXT STUDY	FULL-TEXT STUDY CONNECTIONS
27	**FIRST READ** *O Pioneers!* **SKILL** Setting				
28	**SKILL** Compare and Contrast				
29	**CLOSE READ** *O Pioneers!*	**EXTENDED WRITING PROJECT** Informative/ Explanatory			
30	**BRITISH LITERATURE & HISTORY** The Modern Age (1901–1950) **FIRST READ** *Mrs. Dalloway*	**EXTENDED WRITING PROJECT** Prewrite			
31	**SKILL** Tone	**BLAST** Audience, Purpose, and Style			

DAY	INSTRUCTIONAL PATH	EXTENDED WRITING PROJECT	RESEARCH PROJECT	FULL-TEXT STUDY	FULL-TEXT STUDY CONNECTIONS
32	**CLOSE READ** *Mrs. Dalloway*	**SKILL** Research and Note-Taking			
33	**FIRST READ** "The Star-Spangled Banner"	**SKILL** Thesis Statement			
34	**SKILL** Author's Purpose and Author's Point of View	**SKILL** Organize Informative Writing			
35	**CLOSE READ** "The Star-Spangled Banner" **BLAST** What So Proudly We Hailed	**SKILL** Supporting Details			

DAY	INSTRUCTIONAL PATH	EXTENDED WRITING PROJECT	RESEARCH PROJECT	FULL-TEXT STUDY	FULL-TEXT STUDY CONNECTIONS
36	**BLAST** Reaching the Masses **FIRST READ** "Be Ye Men of Valour"	**EXTENDED WRITING PROJECT** Plan			
37	**SKILL** Author's Purpose and Author's Point of View	**SKILL** Introductions and Conclusions			
38	**CLOSE READ** "Be Ye Men of Valour"	**SKILL** Body Paragraphs and Transitions			
39	**FIRST READ** "D-Day Prayer"	**EXTENDED WRITING PROJECT** Draft			
40	**SKILL** Connotation and Denotation				
41	**SKILL** Compare and Contrast	**SKILL** Sources and Citations			

DAY	INSTRUCTIONAL PATH	EXTENDED WRITING PROJECT	RESEARCH PROJECT	FULL-TEXT STUDY	FULL-TEXT STUDY CONNECTIONS
42	**CLOSE READ** "D-Day Prayer"	**EXTENDED WRITING PROJECT** Revise			
43	**BLAST** That's Entertainment!	**EXTENDED WRITING PROJECT** Edit, Proofread, Publish			
44	**ASSESSMENT** StudySync Grade 12 Unit 4 Assessment				
45	**ASSESSMENT** StudySync Grade 12 Unit 4 Assessment				

SHORTCUTS AND ADDITIONAL ACTIVITIES

Shortcuts

In a perfect world, teachers would have time to cover everything, but most teachers feel as though they are in a race against the bell. There is never enough time to cover everything. If you find yourself short on time, there are places where you can trim a StudySync Unit to ensure you are covering the most important parts. Here are some suggestions for how you can shorten this unit to fit in the time you have.

1. **Replace the Research Project with a Crowdsourcing Activity:** Instead of a 9-day research project, you can make the research component of this unit an informal exploration using a crowdsourcing activity. To facilitate a crowdsourcing assignment, break students into groups, give each group a question or research topic, and allow them time to research using computers or devices to generate information about their topic. Then allow them to share what they have learned with the class by writing their information on the board or posting it to a shared Padlet Wall (or other online collaborative space).
2. **Eliminate Repeated Tone, Setting, Compare & Contrast, Character, and/or Author's Purpose and Author's Point of View Skill Lessons:** Each unit focuses on developing specific skills. Some of these skills are repeated throughout the unit to ensure students have plenty of practice with those skills. As the old adage says, "practice makes perfect!" That said, if you are in a rush and looking to cut some of the content in a unit, you can eliminate one or two of these skill lessons and feel confident your students will still be exposed to the information they need about author's purpose and point of view.
3. **Content Cuts:** There are several different types of texts presented in a unit—excerpts from novels, nonfiction readings, short stories, and poems. If you are running out of time, you may want to eliminate a StudySync selection that focuses on a similar type of text as a previous lesson. For example, the unit contains several novel excerpts—*Wuthering Heights, The House of Mirth, O Pioneers!,* and *Mrs. Dalloway.*

Suggestions for Integrated and Multidisciplinary Lessons

The Thematic Unit, "Emotional Currents," draws on sweeping changes in society, reflected in its literature. The featured texts in the unit make key historical stops along the way, beginning with a trio of texts characterizing both British and American literary movements—*The Triumph of the Romantic Age (1750-1837); The Victorian Age (1837-1901);* and *The Modern Age (1901-1950)*—in the context of important historical events and cultural changes. Two featured works of fiction cast a revealing light on American society particular to their settings: Nathaniel Hawthorne's "Young Goodman Brown" captures the devil-obsessed Puritan mores of Salem, Massachusetts, in the 17th century, while Willa Cather's *O Pioneers!* brings the reader into the bleak landscape of the Nebraska prairie in the late 1800s, a patchwork of far-flung farming communities. Three texts focus on war in related purpose, but distinctive styles. "The Star-Spangled Banner" celebrates in full-blown bombastic rhetoric the endurance of a national symbol during a battle of The War of 1812. Winston Churchill's speech "Be Ye Men of Valour," delivered in May of 1940, rallies the British people to keep their resolve in a dark period for the Allies in World War II. Four years later, Franklin D. Roosevelt strikes a fervently religious tone on the eve of the Normandy invasion in his "D-Day Prayer."

Several Blasts offer diverting and thought-provoking visits to topics in history, popular culture, and science. The opening Blast of the Thematic Unit, "Emotional Currents," immerses students in the social and cultural ripples of romanticism, realism, and modernism, including links to subsets such as American transcendentalism and "hysterical realism" in the over-the-top literature of the 21st century. The Blast "Fear Itself" analyzes fear from a scientific perspective in links to articles about brain chemistry ("The Science of the Scream") and psychology ("Why Our Brains Love Horror Movies"). The history and cultural impact of our national anthem forms the basis of the Blast "What So Proudly We Hailed." Two concluding Blasts in the unit take a broader view of the overlap of popular culture and history. "Over the Airwaves" starts with the history of the medium of radio and through a variety of links mixes in politics, mass media, and social media. "That's

Entertainment" examines the historic underpinnings of the literary movements the unit began with, from the industrial revolution to World War I, and then locates the resulting social changes in movies, television today.

The Full-text Unit focusing on *Pride and Prejudice* mirrors the meeting of history, culture, and science represented in the texts and Blasts of the Thematic Unit. An excerpt from *Jane Austen: A Life* provides a window on the dawn of the 19th century in England. *The Fatal Shore* widens that view to show how the squalor of Georgian England and resulting crime led to such social developments as transportation of criminals to Australia. The social mores of love and marriage garner two views, modern American and Victorian British, in passages from *How to Get a Rich Man* and *How to Marry Well;* and *The Science of Love* seeks to bridge the gap between love's biological bases and its "psychological, social, historical, and evolutionary contexts." Finally, returning to Georgian England of 1789, Richard Price's sermon "A Discourse on the Love of Country" praises the French Revolution and constitutes another sign of antiaristocratic change in the air.

Suggestions for Further and Independent Reading

Both units anchored by *Pride and Prejudice* offer compelling choices for further reading. Students can read in entirety the four other classic novels excerpted in the Thematic Unit: Emily Bronte's *Wuthering Heights*, Virginia Woolf's *Mrs. Dalloway*, Edith Wharton's *House of Mirth*, and Willa Cather's *O Pioneers!* From the Full-text Unit, students may wish to learn more about Jane Austen in Claire Tomalin's biography, *Jane Austen: A Life*, or about the desperate underclass of England during Austen's lifetime in Richard Hughes's *The Fatal Shore: The Epic of Australia's Founding*. Students may also enjoy reading the book that gave momentum to the resurgent popularity of *Pride and Prejudice* of the 1990s: Helen Fielding's Austen-inspired *Bridget Jones's Diary*.

Reading outside the units presents a variety of options. *Pride and Prejudice* has inspired a bookcase of authors to continue, retell, update, or otherwise mess with, the immortal saga of Elizabeth Bennet, Mr. Darcy, and their entourages. Spinoffs include *Longbourn* by Jo Baker, which retells *Pride and Prejudice* from the point of view of the house staff, and a sequel, *Mr. and Mrs. Darcy: Two Shall Become One* by Sharon Lathan. Darcy's story is fully represented in a trilogy by Pamela Aidan: *An Assembly Such as This, Duty and Desire,* and *These Three Remain*. Other treatments and departures range from a high-school setting (*Prom and Prejudice* by Elizabeth Eulberg) to mystery (*Death Comes to Pemberley* by P. D. James) to horror (*Pride and Prejudice and Zombies*, coauthored by Seth Graham-Smith and Jane Austen). Of course Austen enthusiasts should pursue other titles from her shelf: *Sense and Sensibility, Mansfield Park, Emma, Northanger Abbey,* and *Persuasion*.

Difficult Concepts

Irony deals in the unexpected, the absurd, the counterintuitive. By its very nature it aims to confuse or surprise. However, irony is so well woven into everyday conversation and pop-culture situations, especially for the sake of humor, that the concept is probably best taught through familiar examples. Indeed, for some students the wording of the relevant standard will be (to use an ironical idiom) as clear as mud: "Analyze a case in which grasping a point of view requires distinguishing what is directly stated in a text from what is really meant (e.g., irony)" (RL 11-12.6). Examples of sarcasm, understatement, and misstatement to make a point will go far to clarify the difference between an actual statement and its meaning. Direct statement: (after a disaster) "That went well!" Real meaning: "That didn't go well at all." Understatement: "Oops." Real meaning: "Sorry for burning down the house." Sarcasm (misstatement with a barb): "Thanks so much for helping me with the groceries." Real meaning: "I'm angry with you for not helping." Familiarity with verbal irony can help clarify *situational* irony, an event that runs counter to expectation (the puniest player coming off the bench and scoring the winning basket; or Casey, the slugger, striking out in "Casey at the Bat." In the Thematic Unit skill lesson on irony, the situation is illustrated by "The Masque of the Red Death" in the unexpected appearance of the Red Death in a supposedly plague-proof fortress. Note that if the reader had previously observed Death making its entrance unbeknownst to the courtiers, the tension between the characters' expectation (immunity) and what the reader knows to be true (imminent death) is *dramatic* irony.

Knowing an author's purpose and point of view is an asset in reading comprehension. Understanding that the author's purpose in *Pride and Prejudice* is, perhaps, to point out how venal members of the British middle class are when it comes to plotting marriage into nobility might cause a reader to read the novel as a satire—being more aware of a humorous tone and less inclined to take what some characters say at face value. The value of the skill, then, is not just to identify the purpose and point of view but to recognize how the author supports them, or to cite the standard: "Determine an author's point of view or purpose in a text in which the rhetoric is particularly effective, analyzing how style and content contribute to the power, persuasiveness, or beauty of the text" (RI.11-12.6). That this concept is often applied to informational texts does not nullify its relevance to literary texts. In the Thematic Unit, the skill is modeled through a song, "The Star-Spangled Banner." It may be easier to identify the purpose and viewpoint of the author of an informational text—to inform, persuade, argue, reveal—but the process of identifying is the same in literature: study the style and content, notice how the use of language contributes to a prevailing point of view or goal on the part of the author. How are the characters presented—through wit, emotion, explanatory speeches? Is the plot mainly in service to a serious idea or historic event, or to the development of characters? The end is reflected by the means, and if the novel is written well, that purpose does not overshadow the narrative.

Read Aloud Selection

The opening chapter of *Pride and Prejudice* is an ideal read-aloud section of the novel, as well as a thematic clarion call highlighting the more personally revealing prose of the romantic movement in literature. The chapter introduces Jane Austen's knowing, ironic tone right from the famous opening sentence with its blunt, concluding alliteration—*It is a truth universally acknowledged, that a single man in possession of a good fortune, must be in want of a wife*. It will immediately make any reader sound both worldly-wise and tongue-in-cheek. Furthermore, Chapter 1 is a brilliant introduction to the Bennet family, beginning with the domestic comedy of Mrs. and Mr. Bennet, affording excellent opportunities for expressive reading through their verbal dueling. The brief chapter efficiently brings in the five Bennet daughters by reference, deftly singling out Elizabeth, the apple of her father's eye, and setting in motion the all-important Mr. Bingley plot. But Chapter 1 makes it clear that this will be a plot driven by characters, as well as the plight of the middle class in England (see Mrs. Bennet's envy toward the titled Lucases) at the beginning of the 19th century.

Instructional Path

Emotional Currents

BLAST:
Emotional Currents

OVERVIEW

To develop a focus for this unit, students will learn about three literary movements: romanticism, realism, and modernism. Students will explore research links that show how these three movements continue to influence us today. Then students will make their first attempt at responding to the unit's driving question.

OBJECTIVES

1. Explore background information about the literary movements known as romanticism, realism, and modernism.
2. Research using hyperlinks to a range of information about these movements and their influence on contemporary American culture.

ELA Common Core Standards:
Reading: Informational Text - RI.11-12.1
Writing - W.11-12.1.A, W.11-12.1.B, W.11-12.2.A, W.11-12.2.B; W.11-12.5, W.11-12.6
Speaking & Listening - SL.11-12.1.A, SL.11-12.1.C, SL.11-12.1.D

RESOURCES

Access 1 handout (Beginner)
Access 2 handout (Intermediate)
Access 4 handout (Approaching)

TITLE/DRIVING QUESTION

Core Path	Access Path
Discuss. As a class, read aloud the title and driving question for this Blast. These correspond to the driving question for the unit as a whole. Ask students what they already know about romanticism, realism, and modernism. When did these movements happen, and how do they relate to each other? What texts do students know that fit in these movements? Taking into account ideas generated by their classmates, do they have a sense of how these literary movements affect us today? Remind students that they'll be returning to this question and responding after they've read the Background and some of the Research Links.	**English Learners All Levels** **Discuss a Visual.** Have students view a page from the "Humans of New York" project, such as the one at http://tinyurl.com/oqkjrpk. Discuss how the image is an example of real people living their real lives, prompting students with questions such as: • What is the focus of this photo? What do readers know about these children? • What are the children doing? Does it remind you of any children you know? • What is the boy pretending to be? What does that make you think of?
Draft. In their notebooks or on scrap paper, have students draft their initial responses to the driving question. This will provide them with a baseline response that they will be altering as they gain more information about the topic in the Background and Research Links sections of the assignment.	**Beginner & Intermediate** **Draft with Sentence Frame.** When drafting their initial response to the driving question, have students refer to this Blast sentence frame on their Access 1 and 2 handouts: • Literary movements have affected us by/ because ____________________. Point out these two key features of the sentence frame: 1. The introductory clause "Literary movements have affected us" borrows language directly from the Blast driving question to provide a response. 2. Ask students to make special note of the choice between "by" and "because," which invites them to list a way that or reason why the literary movements of the past two centuries have affected us.

BACKGROUND

Core Path	Access Path
Read. Have students read the Blast background to provide context for the driving question.	**Beginner & Intermediate** **Read with Support.** Have students read the Blast background to provide context for the driving question. When they encounter unfamiliar words or phrases, have students refer to the glossary on their Access 1 and 2 handouts. If there are unfamiliar words that are not included in their glossary, encourage students to check a dictionary or online reference tool, such as http://dictionary.reference.com. **Approaching** **Read and Summarize.** Have students read the Blast background to provide context for the driving question. As they read, ask students to complete the fill-in-the-blanks summary of the background provided on their Access 4 handout. When they encounter unfamiliar words or phrases, have students refer to the glossary on their Access 4 handout.
Discuss. Pair students and have them discuss the following questions: 1. What is romanticism? (a movement that focused on nature, emotions, folklore, and the mysterious/supernatural) How are the elements of romanticism related? What do they have in common? (e.g., A focus on emotion over reason could lead a writer to explore the supernatural and fear. Folklore is often closely tied to nature and the environment of the writer.) 2. What is realism? (a movement that focused on real, everyday people and their lives) How is realism different from romanticism? (Realism is less emotional, drops the exotic and supernatural, and focuses on contemporary stories.)	**Beginner** **Discuss.** Pair Beginning with Advanced (or Beyond) students and have them use the dialogue starter on their Access 1 handout to discuss the topic. Advise them to return to the dialogue and switch roles if they get stuck. **Intermediate** **Discuss.** Pair Intermediate with Advanced (or Beyond) students and have them use the dialogue starter on their Access 2 handout to discuss the topic. Advise them to return to the dialogue and switch roles if they get stuck. If their conversation is progressing smoothly, encourage them to continue the discussion beyond the dialogue starter sheet. They can expand their conversations to discuss other examples of ways these literary movements have influenced the books, movies, and television shows they know.

Core Path	Access Path
3. What is modernism? (a movement characterized by disillusionment and a rejection of Victorian morals) What texts have you read that contain modernist elements, such as stream of consciousness or nonlinear storytelling? (e.g., "The Love Song of J. Alfred Prufrock," *Catch-22, Slaughterhouse Five*) 4. The Blast lists a few examples of fairy tale- and medieval-inspired TV shows. Can you think of other examples of those elements in pop culture? (e.g., recent movies: *Maleficent, Into the Woods, Jack the Giant Slayer, Snow White and the Huntsman, Beastly;* other TV shows: *Grimm, Sleepy Hollow, The Quest*)	
Brainstorm. Remind students about the driving question for this Blast: How have the literary movements of the last two centuries affected us? In their notebooks, ask students to make three columns: one for romanticism, one for realism, and one for modernism. Have them fill in the examples that the Blast suggests reflect each literary movement. Then, have them make a list of other movies, books, or TV shows they know that reflect these elements. Students may wish to work in pairs or groups for this activity. Here's a short of example of how this might look.	

Romanticism	Realism	Modernism
• *The Social Network* • *Lincoln* • *Game of Thrones* • *Twilight* • *Teen Wolf* • *The Walking Dead*	• "Humans of New York" • *There Will Be Blood* • *Precious* • *Winter's Bone*	• *Fight Club* • *Into the Wild* • *Memento* • *Kill Bill* • "The Love Song of J. Alfred Prufrock"

RESEARCH LINKS

Core Path	Access Path
Examine and Explore. Use these questions to guide students' exploration of the research links. 1. Have students explore "American Literary Movements," including the time line and the descriptions of each movement. Then ask, What surprised you about the time line of literary movements? (e.g., the overlaps between them, the length of each movement) According to the romanticism section, why is romanticism crucial to American thought? (The creation of the United States fulfills romantic ideals.) Who were some key writers of American realism? (Mark Twain, Theodore Dreiser, and Sinclair Lewis) How did different modernist writers react to the large changes at the beginning of the twentieth century? (Some, like T. S. Eliot, expressed loss and despair. Others thought the role of the artist and writer was to explain the world in the way that religion once did.) 2. Have students read the article "Defining a Contemporary Movement." Tell students that they need to read only Parts I and II. Then ask, How does the author define "hysterical realism"? (Hysterical realism takes realism a step further. It is overworked and seems "evasive of reality" rather than being unreal.) According to the author, what have contemporary authors learned from the realist Charles Dickens? (Dickens's characters are "flat" but vivid. As the author says, "Dickens makes caricature respectable for an age in which, for various reasons, it has become hard to create character.") 3. Ask students to look at "About Transcendentalism." How was transcendentalism related to romanticism? (Transcendentalism was an American version of romanticism. The movement was optimistic and idealistic.) As a class, discuss where you see the influence of transcendentalism in American society, pop culture, and cultural beliefs today.	

Core Path	Access Path
	Extend **Research, Discuss and Present.** 1. Assign each group one link to explore in depth. 2. Ask them to discuss the information: a. What are the key points? b. What inferences did you make as you read? c. What did you learn about this "big idea" from reading this research? d. How did this help you to better understand the topic? e. What questions does your group have after exploring this link? 3. Allow students time to informally present what they learned.
	Extend **Tech Infusion** **Create a Web.** As students explore the links, have them create a web to visually show connections between the movements and contemporary ideas using Google Drawing or another graphic organizer tool. Students should start with three center circles, one for each major movement of the last two centuries. As they read, they should add circles to the web for contemporary ideas, authors, and works influenced by the three movements. Draw lines to connect each new circle to the circle containing the movement (or movements) that influenced it. Remind students that some ideas can be connected to more than one movement. When groups have finished their web, they should present it to the class.

NUMBER CRUNCH

Core Path	Access Path
Participate. Answer the poll question. Have students use information from the background and research links to explain their answers.	

QUIKPOLL

Core Path	Access Path
Predict, Discuss, and Click. Before students click on the number, break them into pairs and have them make predictions about what they think the number is related to. After they've clicked the number, ask students if they are surprised by the revealed information.	

CREATE YOUR BLAST

Core Path	Access Path
Blast. Ask students to write their Blast response in 140 characters or less.	**Beginner** **Blast with Support.** Have students refer to the sentence frame on their Access 1 handout that they used to create their original Blast draft. Ask them to use this frame to write and enter their final Blast. **Intermediate** **Blast with Support.** Have students attempt to draft their Blast without the sentence frame on their Access 2 handout. If students struggle to compose their Blast draft without the sentence frame, remind them to reference it for support.

Core Path	Access Path
	Beyond **Write a Claim.** Ask students to use their answer to the poll question to write a strong claim that could be used as the foundation for a piece of argumentative writing. Once students have written their claims, ask them to read the claims to a small group of their peers. This activity will provide them practice writing claims, as well as expose them to claims written by their peers.
Review. After students have completed their own Blasts, ask them to review the Blasts of their peers and provide feedback.	
	Extend **Discuss.** As a whole class or in groups, identify a few strong Blasts and discuss what made those responses so powerful. As a group, analyze and discuss what characteristics make a Blast interesting or effective.
	Extend **Revise.** Resend a second version of this Blast assignment to your students and have them submit revised versions of their original Blasts. Do the same responses make the Top 10? How have the answers improved from the first submissions?

FIRST READ:
"The Rime of the Ancient Mariner"

OVERVIEW

"The Rime of the Ancient Mariner," by Samuel Taylor Coleridge, is an early example of British romanticism. The poem explores what happens to a mariner and his ship after a storm blows them to Antarctica. The First Read gives students the opportunity to experience the text with a limited context.

OBJECTIVES

1. Perform an initial reading of a text and demonstrate comprehension by responding to short analysis and inference questions with textual evidence.
2. Practice defining vocabulary words using context.
3. Participate effectively in a range of conversations and collaborations to express ideas and build upon the ideas of others.
4. Practice acquiring and using academic vocabulary correctly.

ELA Common Core Standards:
Reading: Literature - RL.11-12.1, RL.11-12.2, RL.11-12.4, RL.11-12.10
Writing - W.11-12.7
Speaking & Listening - SL.11-12.1.A, SL.11-12.1.B, SL.11-12.1.C, SL.11-12.1.D, SL.11-12.2
Language - L.11-12.4.A, L.11-12.4.C, L.11-12.6

RESOURCES

Access 1 handout (Beginner)
Access 2 handout (Intermediate)
Access 3 handout (Advanced)
Access 4 handout (Approaching)

ACCESS COMPLEX TEXT

"The Rime of the Ancient Mariner" is a long lyrical poem. The poem is the story of an ancient mariner who relates the story of his ship's harrowing voyage to Antarctica, where the rest of the crew dies after the mariner shoots an albatross. The crew's death is only the beginning of a series of supernatural events, such as spirits conversing and dead sailors helping to steer the ship home. Upon returning home, the mariner is condemned to walk the earth telling his story to those who need to hear a tale of redemption. To help students understand the mariner's tale, use the following ideas to provide scaffolded instruction for a first reading of the more complex features of this text:

- **Organization** - The poem uses a framing device. The mariner is telling his tale to an anonymous wedding guest, who occasionally interjects into the story. Readers may also be unfamiliar with the use of dialogue in a poem and should watch for quotation marks to help guide their reading.
- **Sentence Structure** - The poem contains some inverted sentences that may present a challenge to some readers. Students need to follow sentences across lines and pay attention to punctuation.
- **Specific Vocabulary** - Some archaic vocabulary such as *eftsoons*, *kirk*, and *wist* may present a challenge to readers.
- **Prior Knowledge** - The poem contains a nautical setting and references (*mast*, *prow*, *sails*, *fathom*) that will be unfamiliar to some readers.

1. INTRODUCTION

Core Path	Access Path
Read. Individually or as a class, read the introduction for "The Rime of the Ancient Mariner." The introduction provides context for the poem.	**English Learners All Levels & Approaching** **Read and Listen.** Ask students to read and listen to the introduction for "The Rime of the Ancient Mariner." Have them refer to the "Introduction Glossary" on their Access 1, 2, 3, and 4 handouts for definitions of key vocabulary terms. If there are unfamiliar words that are not included in their glossary, encourage students to check a dictionary or online reference tool, like http://dictionary.reference.com.

Core Path	Access Path
Build Background. In pairs or small groups, ask students to use devices to research the poetic and artistic movement of romanticism. Assign each group a topic to investigate: • Elements of romantic literature • Romanticism and nationalism in Europe • The supernatural and mystic aspects of romanticism • Romanticism in painting and visual art If you are in a low-tech classroom, you can provide photocopies of articles about romanticism for students to read and discuss.	**English Learners All Levels & Approaching** **Build Background.** Instead of having students conduct independent research on different topics involving romanticism, have students read "British Literature & History: The Triumph of Romanticism" from earlier in this unit. As they read, have students complete the chart on the Access 1, 2, 3, and 4 handouts. Sample answers appear at the end of the lesson plan online. When students have finished, have them discuss their responses with a partner. Based on this information about romanticism, what do they expect to find in "The Rime of the Ancient Mariner"?
	Extend **Discuss the Title and Introduction.** Explain to students that "rime" is an archaic spelling of "rhyme." It also can mean a type of frost that forms on objects in a fog. After reading the introduction, use the information provided to facilitate a prereading discussion to get students thinking about the events and themes in "The Rime of the Ancient Mariner." 1. What mood does the title impart on a reader? What does an archaic spelling of a word say to a reader? 2. What does romanticism mean to you? What qualities would you expect of a poem written during this time period? 3. With what omens and superstitions are you familiar? What superstitions would you expect of sailors who spend most of their lives on the sea?

2. READ

Core Path	Access Path
Preteach Special Vocabulary. "The Rime of the Ancient Mariner" was written in 1798, but the poem uses archaic language that was already old-fashioned at the time for effect. Have students use print or online resources to determine the meaning of each word below. Then ask students to find a modern synonym for the word. eftsoons = soon after kirk = a church (chiefly Scottish) ken = see averred = declared wist = know unslaked = not hydrated; thirsty drouth = drought weal = well-being hoary = extremely old, especially having white hair swound = swoon or faint As students read the poem, ask them to consider what effect these archaic terms have on the poem.	
Make Predictions about Vocabulary. There are five bold vocabulary words in the text. As students read the text, ask them to make predictions about what they think each bold vocabulary word means based on the context clues in the sentence. Have students use the annotation tool to make their predictions. It might be helpful to model this for students before they begin reading. Either using the board or projecting the actual text, focus in on the sentence that uses the word "albatross": • At length did cross an albatross Thorough the fog it came; As if it had been a Christian soul, We hailed it in God's name.	**Note:** This exercise, which extends vocabulary instruction, should be completed when the class shifts from whole group instruction to individual work during the "Read and Annotate" exercise. **Beginner, Intermediate & Approaching Pair Practice.** 1. Pair students with more proficient readers. 2. Give them an additional sentence that contains a new vocabulary word. 3. Ask the students to complete a Think Aloud using the teacher-led Make Predictions about Vocabulary activity as a model, while the proficient student actively listens.

Core Path	Access Path
Model for the class how to use these context clues to guess the meaning of the word: 1. When I look at the stanza containing the word *albatross*, I can see right away that it's preceded by the article "an," and so I can tell that it's a noun, which makes it a person, place, thing, or idea. 2. I can tell from the second line that it came "through the fog," which means it wasn't on the ship to begin with. But since the ship was on the ocean, the men on it were surrounded by water and sky. This tells me that an albatross might be a fish or bird of some sort. 3. To figure that out, I'll look at the last line, where the speaker says the men on the ship "hailed it in God's name." Hailing something in God's name reminds me of angels somehow, so that makes me think it's a bird. 4. My guess that an albatross is a bird is confirmed by the next stanza, where the speaker says that the albatross "flew."	4. The student should use the context clues in the sentence to try to determine the meaning of the new vocabulary word. 5. After the student has completed the Think Aloud and made a prediction about the word's meaning, allow time for the proficient reader to add his/her own thoughts and clarify any points of confusion. 6. Once they've completed this Think Aloud, encourage them to use a dictionary to confirm the definition of the new vocabulary word. Have them refer to the "Text Glossary" on their Access 1, 2, and 4 handouts for definitions of key vocabulary terms in the text. Encourage them to add any additional vocabulary words or idioms they find in the text and look up definitions for those words and idioms online or in a dictionary.
Model Reading Comprehension Strategy. Before students begin reading, model the reading comprehension strategy of summarizing by using this Think Aloud that talks students through the first stanzas of the poem. First explain to your students that summarizing is: *a process in which students select, organize, and synthesize the most important elements in a text* Model for students how summarizing will help them better comprehend the selection and help drive their discussions. • In the first line, we're introduced to a character: an ancient mariner. The action of the first stanza is a little confusing. We meet the mariner, who "stoppeth one of three." This means that the mariner stops one of a group of three. We don't know why the mariner chose the person he chose, but the fact that he did seems like key information.	**Note:** This exercise, which extends instruction around reading comprehension strategies, should be completed when the class shifts from whole group instruction to individual work during the "Read and Annotate" exercise. **Beginner, Intermediate & Approaching Apply Reading Comprehension Strategy.** 1. In small groups, have students read or listen to the audio of Part I of "The Rime of the Ancient Mariner." 2. Ask groups to summarize stanzas 5–8 using their own words. Encourage students to talk out the details and events that happen in these lines. Ask students to record their summaries in the Summarizing Chart on the Access 1, 2, and 4 handouts. Sample answers appear at the end of the lesson plan online.

Core Path	Access Path
• Then in the second stanza, the "one of three" explains why he can't stop. He is going to a wedding and is "kin" of the bridegroom. That seems like key information. • The fourth stanza confirms that the person who was stopped was a "wedding-guest." He is eager to go to the wedding, but the mariner's gaze manages to hold him there. There's a large contrast between the "merry din" of the wedding and the tense interplay between the mariner and the wedding guest outside. In my summary, it is important to note that the mariner manages to hold the wedding-guest against his will. • My full summary of the first four stanzas: "An ancient mariner stopped a man going into a wedding with his friends. The man is unable to stop listening to the mariner, and sits to hear his story."	3. Allow time for groups to continue the reading comprehension strategy of summarizing until they complete the Part I Summarizing Chart. Check groups' understanding of the strategy by circling around and asking questions. 4. Have students use the second Summarizing Chart to record their summaries as they read the rest of the poem independently.
Read and Annotate. Have students independently read and annotate the poem. Ask students to use the annotation tool as they read to: 1. use context clues to analyze and determine the meaning of the bolded vocabulary terms 2. ask questions about passages of the text that may be unclear or unresolved 3. identify key information, events, characters, and connections between them 4. note unfamiliar vocabulary	**Beginner** **Coach the Reading.** While other students read, annotate, and discuss the text independently, work with Beginning students, listening to the audio of the text and pausing periodically or when any student has a question. Coach students in articulating their questions for the group and in highlighting and annotating the text. Have students use the Annotation Guide on the Access 1 handout to support them as they highlight and annotate the text. For further support, ask questions about the text such as: • Is there anything about the poem that you don't understand? • What was the mariner's message to the wedding guest? Why does he have to tell his tale? • What do you think will happen to the mariner? the wedding guest?

Core Path	Access Path
	Intermediate **Listen to the Audio.** Have these students listen to the audio of the text and use the Text Glossary on the Access 2 handout to help them with words or idioms that may be unfamiliar. If students need help with annotating the text, have them use the Annotation Guide on the Access 2 handout. After working with the Beginning students, you may wish to check this group's progress and provide support as needed. **Advanced** **Pair with Proficient Peers.** Have Advanced students work with English-proficient peers to read, annotate, and discuss the text. Have students use the Annotation Guide in the Access 3 handout to support them as they highlight and annotate the text. Encourage them to listen to the audio of the text if needed. **Approaching** **Use the Annotation Guide.** Have students use the Annotation Guide on the Access 4 handout to support them as they highlight and annotate the text.
Discuss. In small groups or pairs, have students discuss the questions and inferences they made while reading. To help facilitate discussions, refer to Collaborative Discussions in the Speaking & Listening Handbook. 1. What happens to the ancient mariner's ship? Where does it go, and what happens there? Briefly summarize the plot of the poem. (The mariner's ship is sailing south. It gets stuck in Antarctica, and the mariner shoots an albatross. The crew is stranded and dies, but the mariner survives through many supernatural events. He returns home, condemned to tell his story to those who need to hear it.) 2. Why does the mariner shoot the albatross? Does this action make sense to you? Why or why not? (Answers will vary.)	**English Learners All Levels & Approaching** Use the extra time while on- and beyond-grade-level students are discussing their first reads of the text to work individually and in small groups with Approaching readers and English Learners as outlined above. Should those students complete their first reads quickly, integrate them into the on- and beyond-grade-level discussion groups. Otherwise, English Learners and Approaching readers will be given an opportunity to participate in text discussions with their peers later in the lesson.

Core Path	Access Path
3. What is the role of angels and spirits in the poem? Do they serve a positive or negative purpose? (Some spirits, like the one that pushes the ship home or the angels that inhabit the sailor's bodies, serve a positive purpose. Some, like Death and Life-in-Death, bring destruction. Some, like the voices the mariner hears, are neutral.) 4. What penance does the mariner have to do for shooting the albatross? What did he learn from the experience? (He has an intense urge to tell his story to others who are like he was before the experience. He needs to share his message of love and reverence for all God's creatures.) 5. In Part IV, what things does the mariner describe as beautiful? Why is this important? (The mariner describes the dead men as beautiful in contrast to the water snakes, the "thousand thousand slimy things." Later, however, the mariner notices the water snakes' beauty: "No tongue / Their beauty might declare." At this point in the poem, the curse begins to lift: the albatross falls from the marine's neck.) 6. Summarize the poem to a partner. Did your partner leave out any key information, or include any minor details that don't belong in a summary? Work together to create a clear and concise summary of the poem.	**Beyond** **Write.** Have students imagine that they are the wedding guest who listens to the ancient mariner's story. What is the guest like? Why did the ancient mariner stop him? Ask students to write two short journal entries: one from before the wedding and one from the next morning when the wedding guest wakes up as a "sadder and a wiser man." Tell students to be creative but remain consistent with information in the poem. Allow time for students to share their journal entries with the class.
	Extend **Tech Infusion** **Examine Illustrations.** The famous illustrator Gustave Doré created a popular illustrated version of "The Rime of the Ancient Mariner" in 1875. The illustrations are available online at http://tinyurl.com/o88ndlx. Project the illustrations or have students view them on devices. Then discuss what the illustrations contribute to the poem. 1. What mood do the illustrations have? Does this mood match the poem overall? Why or why not? 2. How do the illustrations enhance the poem? Do they clarify any sections of the poem for you?

Core Path	Access Path
	3. Do any of the illustrations contradict your own visualizations of the events described? How does this contradiction change your understanding of the poem? 4. Do the illustrations ever add details that aren't in the poem? Should an illustrator have license to add details, or should an illustrator stay faithful to only what is in the text?

3. THINK

Core Path	Access Path
Answer and Discuss. Have students complete the Think questions and then use the peer review instructions and rubric to complete two peer reviews. Refer to the sample answers at the end of the lesson plan online to discuss responses with your students.	**Beginner & Intermediate** **Sentence Frames.** Have students use the sentence frames on the Access 1 and 2 handouts to support their responses to the Think questions. If necessary, distribute sentence frames to Advanced students as well. **Approaching** **Find the Evidence.** Have students use Find the Evidence on the Access 4 handout to help them identify the evidence needed to answer the questions.
	Extend **Tech Infusion** **Organize.** Have students use Prezi (http://prezi.com/) to create a time line of the mariner's story. Students should add images for each point on the mariner's journey. When students are finished, have them share their time line with a partner. Partners should check that no major events are missing or included in error.

SKILL:
Tone

OVERVIEW

In a long, complex poem such as "The Rime of the Ancient Mariner," understanding a poet's tone can help students move toward uncovering the poem's meaning. This lesson plan provides follow-up questions and useful enrichments to help teachers guide students toward a usable, repeatable method for analyzing tone.

OBJECTIVES

1. Learn the definition of tone.
2. Practice using concrete strategies for analyzing tone in a poem.
3. Participate effectively in a range of conversations and collaborations to express ideas and build upon the ideas of others.

ELA Common Core Standards:
Reading: Literature - RL.11-12.1, RL.11-12.4
Speaking & Listening - SL.11-12.1.A, SL.11-12.1.C, SL.11-12.2

RESOURCES

Access 1 handout (Beginner)
Access 2 handout (Intermediate)
Access 3 handout (Advanced)
Access 4 handout (Approaching)

1. DEFINE

Core Path	Access Path
Watch. Watch the Concept Definition video on tone with your students. Have your students write down the definition of tone as it is stated in the video. Also, make sure they understand the different strategies for determining an author's tone. Pause the video at these key moments to discuss the information with your students: 1. 0:28 – Do all literary or informational texts contain a certain tone? Do you think it's possible for an author to remove tone from his or her writing? Why or why not? 2. 0:48 – Does an author always make his or her tone explicitly clear? Why is inference an important skill for determining an author's tone? 3. 0:58 – Why would an author choose a tone at odds with the subject being portrayed? What effect might this have on a literary text? What effect might it have on an informational text?	**English Learners All Levels & Approaching** **Complete the Sentences.** Have students complete the sentences on the Access 1, 2, 3, and 4 handouts as they watch the video. Answers are located at the end of the lesson plan online.
Read and Discuss. After watching the Concept Definition video, have students read the definition of tone. Either in small groups or as a whole class, use these questions to engage students in a discussion about tone. 1. How do you identify a speaker's "tone of voice" during a conversation? (You listen for stresses on certain words or phrases.) Why is tone of voice important to understanding what a person is saying? (It helps you understand the author's attitude toward a subject, a character (or person), or an audience.) 2. The definition says informational texts use an objective tone to prove they are credible sources. Why might a fiction writer create a nonobjective tone? (It allows them to better communicate the feelings of a character or a description of a place.)	**Beginner & Approaching** **Complete a Chart.** To prepare students to participate in the discussion, have them complete the chart on the Access 1 and 4 handouts as they read the definition. The correct answers are located at the end of the lesson plan online. **Intermediate & Advanced** **Discuss Prompts.** To help these students participate in the discussion, prompt them with questions that can be answered with a few words, such as: • What do we call it when a person stresses certain words or phrases? (tone of voice) • What do writers use to convey tone in poetry, stories, or informational texts? (elements such as word choice, sentence structure, or figures of speech) • What are connotations? (the emotions associated with certain words)

Core Path	Access Path
3. Why does "Jan cowered in a corner" suggest fear better than "Jan hid in a corner"? (The word "cowered" connotes the emotion of fear better than the word "hid.") How else could you change that sentence to better create a tense or ominous tone? (You might add a phrase to the sentence, such as "shaking like a leaf.")	**Beyond** **Pair and Share.** Give students an objective sentence, such as "Tucker was late for school because he missed the bus." Challenge pairs to rewrite the sentence in several different tones. Tell students that they can change the wording of the sentence as much as they want, as long as the basic idea remains the same. When students have finished, allow time for them to share with the class.
	Extend **Freewrite.** After watching the video, ask students to write a short (one paragraph) story on a topic of their choosing in an objective tone. Then have students rewrite the story in an ironic or humorous tone. Finally, have students rewrite the story in an emotional tone. When students are finished, have them discuss with a partner what changed and what stayed the same in their stories.

2. MODEL

Core Path	Access Path
Read and Annotate. Have students independently read the Model section. As they read, ask students to use the annotation tool to: • highlight key points • ask questions • identify places where the Model applies the strategies laid out in the Identification and Application section • comment on the effect that tone has on the text's meaning	**Note:** During this portion of the lesson, instruction shifts from whole group to individual work. Use this time to work one-on-one or in small groups with Beginning, Intermediate, Advanced, and Approaching students. **Beginner & Intermediate** **Coach the Reading.** Work with these students (either individually or in small groups) to fill out the guided reading questions on the Access 1 and 2 handouts. Have Beginning students refer to the glossary on the Access 1 handout to help them determine the meaning of difficult words (note: provide the Access 1 handout glossary to Intermediate students if necessary). Let students know they'll use these answers to help participate in the discussion about the Model. Sample answers for this exercise are located at the end of the lesson plan online.

Core Path	Access Path
	Advanced **Identify Evidence.** Ask Advanced students to complete the identifying evidence exercise on the Access 3 handout. Let students know that they'll use these answers to help participate in the discussion about the Model. Sample answers for this exercise are located at the end of the lesson plan online. **Approaching** **Guided Reading.** Have students complete the guided reading questions on the Access 4 handout as they read. Let them know that they'll use these answers to help participate in the discussion about the Model. Sample answers for this exercise are located at the end of the lesson plan online.
Discuss. After students read the Model text, use these questions to facilitate a whole group discussion that helps students understand how to determine and analyze the tone of the poem: 1. Why does the Model mention the verb tense of the first stanza? (The tense orients the reader to the time context of the poem's setting.) Is the archaic language of the first stanza appropriate for the time period when this poem was written? Why would Coleridge have used archaic language? (The language was archaic even in 1798. Coleridge's use of archaic language gives the poem an old-fashioned and formal tone.) 2. The Model mentions the connotation of the word "loon." What connection might the use of the word "loon" have to the rest of the poem? (All the ancient mariner's problems resulted from his decision to shoot an albatross, another waterbird. Here the mariner is compared to a waterbird himself.) 3. When does the tone of the ancient mariner's story change? (when he describes the storm that hit his ship) How does Coleridge express this change? (with personification of the storm as a frightening being that chases the ship)	

Core Path	Access Path
	Extend **Figures of Speech.** The Model identifies the personification of the storm and explains the effect of that choice. Pair students and have them return to the poem and look for other examples of personification. Then have students discuss how this figure of speech affects the poem.

3. YOUR TURN

Core Path	Access Path
Assess and Explain. Have students answer the comprehension questions to test for understanding. Share the explanations for Parts A and B (located online) with your students.	
	Extend **Revisit the Text.** Divide students into seven groups and assign each group one of the poem's parts. Have each group determine the tone or tones of their part and identify words and phrases that contribute to the tone. When groups have finished, discuss the overall tone of the poem. • Which parts have similar tones? Does Coleridge use similar words and phrases in each part? • Which parts include a change in tone? How is the change expressed? • What is the overall tone of the poem?

CLOSE READ: "The Rime of the Ancient Mariner"

OVERVIEW

Samuel Taylor Coleridge's poem "The Rime of the Ancient Mariner" describes a mariner's horrific trip to Antarctica and home again. The Close Read gives students the opportunity to analyze the poem's tone.

OBJECTIVES

1. Complete a close reading of a poem.
2. Practice and apply concrete strategies for analyzing tone in "The Rime of the Ancient Mariner."
3. Participate effectively in a range of conversations and collaborations to express ideas and build upon the ideas of others.
4. Prewrite, plan, and produce clear and coherent writing in response to a prompt.

ELA Common Core Standards:
Reading: Literature - RL.11-12.1, RL.11-12.2, RL.11-12.4, RL.11-12.5
Writing - W.11-12.4, W.11-12.5, W.11-12.6, W.11-12.9.A, W.11-12.10
Speaking & Listening - SL.11-12.1.A, SL.11-12.1.B, SL.11-12.1.C, SL.11-12.1.D, SL.11-12.6
Language - L.11-12.4.A, L.11-12.4.C, L.11-12.4.D, L.11-12.5.A

RESOURCES

"The Rime of the Ancient Mariner" Vocabulary handout
Access 1 handout (Beginner)
Access 2 handout (Intermediate)
Access 3 handout (Advanced)
Access 4 handout (Approaching)

1. INTRODUCTION

Core Path	Access Path
Define and Compare. Project the vocabulary words and definitions onto the board or provide students with handouts, so they can copy the vocabulary into their notebooks. Suggest that students consult general and specialized reference materials, both print and digital, to compare the precise meaning of a specific word with their initial vocabulary predictions from the First Read. Review words that students defined incorrectly to understand why they were unable to use context clues or other tools to develop usable definitions.	**Beginner & Intermediate** **Complete a Chart.** Have students complete the chart on the Access 1 and 2 handouts by writing the correct word for each of the definitions. **Advanced & Beyond** **Write in Journals.** Have students write a journal entry using all of their vocabulary words. Remind them to write sentences that communicate the meaning of the words they are using. **Approaching** **Graphic Organizer.** To support students in comparing their predictions with the correct meanings, have them complete the graphic organizer on the Access 4 handout to record the vocabulary words, their initial analysis, and the definitions. Then have them write sentences using the words.
Review. Have students complete the fill-in-the-blanks vocabulary worksheet attached to the lesson plan online. Answers for the worksheet are listed at the end of the lesson plan online	
	Extend **Create.** Have students create vocabulary flashcards. Students should write the word on one side of an index card and the part of speech and definition on the other. Students should use these flashcards to review and memorize the words.

2. READ

Core Path	Access Path
Model Close Reading. Project the text onto the board and model a close reading of the first six stanzas using the annotation strategies mentioned below. While modeling annotation strategies, make notes that tie the text to the focus skill and demonstrate what students are looking for as they read. Some guidance for you as you annotate for your students: • As the Skills lesson that precedes this text explains, Coleridge's word choice in various parts of the poem creates a variety of tones. • The question at the end of the first stanza, "Now wherefore stoppest thou me?" creates a mysterious tone from the beginning. I'll highlight that and add an annotation that explains the mysterious tone it creates by presenting questions before the speaker gives us any answers. • In the second stanza, we learn that the ancient mariner has stopped a wedding guest from going into a wedding. He is related to the groom ("I am next of kin") and does not know the ancient mariner. I'll highlight this because while it gives us some information, it still doesn't tell us why the mariner stopped that person. • The mysterious tone is continued when the wedding guest reacts by saying "unhand me, grey-beard loon!" This shows us that he doesn't know the mariner, and creates even more mystery about what we're about to read.	
Read and Annotate. Read the Skills Focus questions as a class, so your students know what they should pay close attention to as they read. Then have students read and annotate the poem. Ask students to use the annotation tool as they read to 1. respond to the Skills Focus section 2. make connections between the author's word choices and the poem's tone	**Note:** While on-grade-level students are reading and annotating, work one-on-one or in small groups with Beginning, Intermediate, Advanced, and Approaching students to support them as they read and annotate the text.

Core Path	Access Path
3. ask questions about how the author's tone affects the poem's meaning 4. note any unfamiliar vocabulary 5. capture their reaction to the language, the images, and the themes in the text As they reread the text, remind students to use the comprehension strategy of summarizing that they learned in the First Read.	**Beginner & Intermediate** **Summarize and Analyze the Text.** Work with these students to complete the sentence frames on the Access 1 and 2 handouts (note: the sentence frames for Intermediate students on the Access 2 handout contain fewer scaffolds). They will then use the completed sentence frames to help them analyze and annotate the text by completing the Skills Focus questions. Refer to the sample Skills Focus answers to help them complete the sentence frames and annotate the text. **Advanced** **Work in Pairs.** Pair these students with more proficient English speakers to work together on analyzing and annotating the text to complete the Skills Focus questions. If these students need more support, have them use the sentence frames on the Access 3 handout as they work with their more proficient peers. **Approaching** **Summarize the Text.** Have these students discuss and complete the text summary on the Access 4 handout and use their summary to help them analyze and annotate the text by completing the Skills Focus questions. Correct answers for the summary are at the end of the lesson plan online. Also refer to the sample Skills Focus answers to aid students with their annotations.
Discuss. After students have read the text, use the sample responses to the Skills Focus questions at the bottom of the lesson plan online to discuss the reading and the process of analyzing the poem's tone. Make sure that students have acquired and accurately use academic-specific words and phrases related to the skill and demonstrate a command of formal English appropriate to the discussion. To help facilitate discussions, refer to Collaborative Discussions in the Speaking & Listening Handbook.	**Extend** **Pair and Share.** In small, heterogeneous groups or pairs, ask students to share and discuss their annotations with a focus on the narrative in the poem.

Core Path	Access Path
	You can provide students with these questions to guide their discussion: 1. In Part II, after the albatross is shot, what kinds of words and phrases does the author use to describe the ocean? ("The very deeps did rot," "The water, like a witch's oils, / Burnt green, and blue and white.") What images do these words and phrases give to the reader? (The ocean itself is rotting and looks green, blue, and white like "witch's oils." None of these descriptions are typical for a description of the ocean. The description is unreal and prepares the reader for the supernatural elements soon to appear in the story.) 2. At the end of Part V and the beginning of Part VI, what information do the "two voices" share? What role do they serve in the narrative? (The two voices explain how the ship is moving and who is controlling it. The voices reveal the role of the moon in the events.) How are the two voices different, and why is that difference important? (The first voice asks questions, which the second answers. The first voice is angry and thinks the mariner should be punished for killing the albatross. The second voice is soft and calm and reveals that the mariner will do his "penance" for killing the albatross.) Who do you think the two voices are? Do the voices represent someone or something? (Student responses will vary.) 3. What role does the hermit play in the poem? Cite textual evidence to support your answer. (The hermit gives the mariner hope for peace. He also encourages the pilot to continue out to the ghost ship and is the first person to whom the mariner feels the need to tell his tale.)

Core Path	Access Path
	Extend **Research and Discuss.** Ask students what they think life was like for sailors in the late eighteenth century. From where do they get their mental images of sailors at this time? Then have students read about what sailing and life at sea was really like. (This article is a good starting point: http://tinyurl.com/yswcxo.) As students read, remind them to keep this context in mind.

3. WRITE

Core Path	Access Path
Prewrite and Plan. Read the prompt as a class and ask students to brainstorm about the tone in "The Rime of the Ancient Mariner." Remind your students to look at the excerpt and their annotations to find textual evidence to support their ideas.	**Beginner & Intermediate** **Plan and Organize.** Have students complete the prewriting activity on the Access 1 and 2 handouts and then explain their ideas to a partner before they write. Explain to students that they need to choose details, examples, or quotes from the text that support their ideas and then explain how those details support their statements. For example, students could include the lines, "Forthwith this frame of mine was wrenched / With a woeful agony, / Which forced me to begin my tale; / And then it left me free," which shows the mariner's pain ("wrenched," "agony") and the relief he feels after the retelling ("it left me free"). **Approaching** **Plan and Organize.** Have students complete the prewriting activity on the Access 4 handout to organize their thoughts before they write.

Core Path	Access Path
Discuss. Project these instructions for the peer review onto the board and review them with your class, so they know what they are looking for when they begin to provide their classmates with feedback: • How has this essay helped you understand how the mariner's reasons for retelling his story? How has the essay helped you better understand the poet's use of tone? • Did the writer explain the role of the wedding guest in supporting reader understanding? Does that explanation make sense? • What sort of evidence did the writer use from the text to support his or her writing? • How well does the writer explain how that evidence supports his or her ideas? • Does the writer write using standard grammar and punctuation? Are there any weak spots? • What specific suggestions can you make to help the writer improve the response? • What thing(s) does this paper do especially well? • Be sure to tell the writer what he or she did well and what he or she needs to work on. After you've looked at the peer review instructions, review the rubric with students before they begin writing. Allow time for students briefly to pose and discuss any questions they may have about the peer review instructions and the rubric. Tell students how many peer reviews they will need to complete once they submit their writing.	
Write. Ask students to complete the writing assignment using textual evidence to support their answers. Once they have completed their writing, they should click "Submit."	

Core Path	Access Path
	Extend **Organize.** Encourage students to create a Four Circles graphic organizer to organize their ideas before they type their responses. Have students write the word "Tone" in a center circle, and then draw four circles around it. Students can use the outer ring of circles to collect textual evidence for their response.
	Extend **Critique.** Project a writing sample on the board and ask the class to identify any claims the writer makes. Highlight or underline these claims. Then ask students to identify the textual evidence that supports each claim. As a class, discuss whether the evidence presented is the strongest piece of evidence the writer could have chosen, or if there is something better. Discuss constructive ways to offer feedback on an essay's textual evidence.
Review. Once students complete their writing assignment, they should submit substantive feedback to two peers. Students should use their peers' feedback to improve their writing.	

BLAST:
Modern Day Albatross

OVERVIEW

To further their study of "The Rime of the Ancient Mariner," students will learn about the hole in the ozone layer and what has been done to try and reverse it. They will explore how human behavior has impacted the stratosphere over time and how humans have played a role—both negative and positive—in the changes. Research links explore NASA data regarding the hole in the ozone layer.

OBJECTIVES

1. Explore background information about the ozone layer to consider how previous generations' actions have impacted people today.
2. Research using the hyperlinks to learn about the ozone layer and the steps being taken to protect it.

ELA Common Core Standards:
Reading: Science & Technical Subjects - RST.11-12.1, RST.11-12.7, RST.11-12.8
Writing: Science & Technical Subjects - WHST.11-12.1.A, WHST.11-12.1.B, WHST.11-12.5, WHST.11-12.6
Speaking & Listening - SL.11-12.1.A, SL.11-12.1.C, SL.11-12.1.D

RESOURCES

Access 1 handout (Beginner)
Access 2 handout (Intermediate)
Access 4 handout (Approaching)

TITLE/DRIVING QUESTION

Core Path	Access Path
Discuss. As a class, read aloud the title and driving question for this Blast. Ask students what they know about Antarctica or the ozone already. What happened to the ozone layer, and why? What other problems exist today because of actions from previous generations? Remind students that they should not immediately reply to this question. They'll be returning to this question and responding after they've read the Background and some of the Research Links.	**English Learners All Levels** **Discuss a Visual.** Have students view a diagram of how the ozone layer works, such as the one found here: http://tinyurl.com/mn3sldo. Encourage students to look at how the two different types of UV rays interact with the ozone layer. Discuss the image, prompting students with questions such as: • What do you see in this diagram? • What are the two types of UV rays? What does the ozone layer do to them? • What do you think would happen if more UVB rays got through the ozone layer?
Draft. In their notebooks or on scrap paper, have students draft their initial responses to the driving question. This will provide them with a baseline response that they will be altering as they gain more information about the topic in the Background and Research Links sections of the assignment.	**Beginner & Intermediate** **Draft with Sentence Frame.** When drafting their initial response to the driving question, have students refer to this Blast sentence frame on their Access 1 and 2 handouts: • We are still paying the price for ____________________. Point out these two key features of the sentence frame: 1. The introductory clause "We are still paying the price" borrows language directly from the Blast driving question to provide a response. 2. Ask students to make special note of the word "for" that prompts them to give an example of a current problem that stems from decisions in the past.

BACKGROUND

Core Path	Access Path
Read. Have students read the Blast background to provide context for the driving question.	**Beginner & Intermediate** **Read with Support.** Have students read the Blast background to provide context for the driving question. When they encounter unfamiliar words or phrases, have students refer to the glossary on their Access 1 and 2 handouts. If there are unfamiliar words that are not included in their glossary, encourage students to check a dictionary or online reference tool, like http://dictionary.reference.com. **Approaching** **Read and Summarize.** Have students read the Blast background to provide context for the driving question. As they read, ask students to complete the fill-in-the-blanks summary of the background provided on their Access 4 handout. When they encounter unfamiliar words or phrases, have students refer to the glossary on their Access 4 handout.
Discuss. Pair students and have them discuss the following questions: 1. When was the hole in the ozone first discovered? What caused it to increase? (Scientists first discovered the hole in the early 1980s. The hole was increasing because of an interaction caused by the CFCs reaching the stratosphere.) 2. Why did people start using CFCs? (In the 1920s, people began using them as a safer alternative to the toxic refrigerants of the time—they were the only ones allowed in many cities because they were so safe. Over time, people began using them in more ways—like aerosol sprays and car air conditioning.)	**Beginner** **Discuss.** Pair Beginning with Advanced (or Beyond) students and have them use the dialogue starter on their Access 1 handout to discuss the topic. Advise them to return to the dialogue and switch roles if they get stuck. **Intermediate** **Discuss.** Pair Intermediate with Advanced (or Beyond) students and have them use the dialogue starter on their Access 2 handout to discuss the topic. Advise them to return to the dialogue and switch roles if they get stuck. If their conversation is progressing smoothly, encourage them to continue the discussion beyond the dialogue starter sheet. They can expand their conversations to discuss other problems we face today that began in the past.

Core Path	Access Path
3. Why is the hole in the ozone layer a cause for concern? (The ozone layer protects us from the sun's damaging ultraviolet light, and a hole lets those rays through. It's also concerning because it's evidence that humans can negatively impact the earth, if we're not careful.) 4. What has been done to repair the damage to the ozone layer? (Twenty-seven countries signed the Montreal Treaty in 1987 to reduce the use the CFCs, and many nations have banned the use of them completely.)	
Brainstorm. Remind students about the driving question for this Blast: What mistakes from previous generations are we still paying the price for today? In their notebooks, ask students to make two columns. They should label one column "Problems Caused by Previous Generations," and the other "Things We're Doing to Make Up for Those Mistakes." Start with the Background and have them fill in the two columns. After they've finished that, have them brainstorm other issues that we currently face because of decisions made in the past.	

Problems Caused by Previous Generations	Things We're Doing to Make Up for Those Mistakes
The use of CFCs caused the hole in the ozone to increase a dangerous amount. Doctors over-prescribed penicillin in the 20th century and many bacteria are resistant to it.	Countries have agreed to reduce or eliminate the use of CFCs to help the ozone recover. Researchers are creating new drugs that will fight the drug-resistant bacteria.

RESEARCH LINKS

Core Path	Access Path
Examine and Explore. Use these questions to guide students' exploration of the research links: 1. Ask students to look at "Changes to the Ozone." What does the series of images show about how the ozone layer has changed over time? (The hole has gotten larger and deeper over time.) What does the accompanying article suggest is the reason for these changes? (The text explains that chlorofluorocarbons (CFCs) catalyzed ozone depletion.) 2. Ask students to look at "Ozone Depletion." What are some of the dangers associated with the hole in the ozone? (Increased UVB rays can cause skin cancer and cataracts in humans, and is believed to affect the reproductive rates of phytoplankton, fish, shrimp, crabs, frogs, and salamanders.) When is the level of chlorine in the ozone expected to recover? (It may take another 50 years to return to natural levels.) 3. Ask students to look at "Exploring Ozone." Why does the scientist called ozone "natural sunscreen"? (because ozone blocks out radiation from the sun) What are the three ingredients necessary for an ozone hole? (high levels of chlorine and bromine, very cold temperatures, and sunlight) When do scientists expect the ozone layer to get back to the size it was in 1980? (by about 2070)	
	Extend **Research, Discuss, and Present.** 1. Assign each group one link to explore in depth. 2. Ask them to discuss the information: a. What are the key points? b. What inferences did you make as you read? c. What did you learn about this driving question from reading this research?

Core Path	Access Path
	d. How did this help you to better understand the topic? e. What questions does your group have after exploring this link? 3. Allow students time to informally present what they learned.

QUIKPOLL

Core Path	Access Path
Participate. Answer the poll question. Have students use information from the background and research links to explain their answers.	

NUMBER CRUNCH

Core Path	Access Path
Predict, Discuss, and Click. Before students click on the number, break them into pairs and have them make predictions about what they think the number is related to. After they've clicked the number, ask students if they are surprised by the revealed information.	

CREATE YOUR BLAST

Core Path	Access Path
Blast. Ask students to write their Blast response in 140 characters or less.	**Beginner** **Blast with Support.** Have students refer back to the sentence frame on their Access 1 handout that they used to create their original Blast draft. Ask them to use this frame to write and enter their final Blast.

Core Path	Access Path
	Intermediate **Blast with Support.** Have students attempt to draft their Blast without the sentence frame on their Access 2 handout. If students struggle to compose their Blast draft without the sentence frame, remind them to reference it for support. **Beyond** **Write a Claim.** Ask students to use their answer to the poll question to write a strong claim that could be used as the foundation for a piece of argumentative writing. Once students have written their claims, ask them to read the claims to a small group of their peers. This activity will provide them practice writing claims, as well as expose them to claims written by their peers.
Review. After students have completed their own Blasts, ask them to review the Blasts of their peers and provide feedback.	
	Extend **Discuss.** As a whole class or in groups, identify a few strong Blasts and discuss what made those responses so powerful. As a group, analyze and discuss what characteristics make a Blast interesting or effective.
	Extend **Revise.** Resend a second version of this Blast assignment to your students and have them submit revised versions of their original Blasts. Do the same responses make the Top 10? How have the answers improved from the first submissions?

FIRST READ:
Young Goodman Brown

OVERVIEW

The story "Young Goodman Brown" by Nathaniel Hawthorne examines evil in the Puritan community of Salem, Massachusetts, in colonial times. The First Read gives students the opportunity to experience the text with a limited context.

OBJECTIVES

1. Perform an initial reading of a text and demonstrate comprehension by responding to short analysis and inference questions with textual evidence.
2. Practice defining vocabulary words using context.
3. Participate effectively in a range of conversations and collaborations to express ideas and build upon the ideas of others.
4. Practice acquiring and using academic vocabulary correctly.

ELA Common Core Standards:
Reading: Literature - RL.11-12.1, RL.11-12.4, RL.11-12.10
Speaking & Listening - SL.11-12.1.A, SL.11-12.1.B, SL.11-12.1.C, SL.11-12.1.D, SL.11-12.2
Language - L.11-12.4.A, L.11-12.4.B, L.11-12.6

RESOURCES

Access 1 handout (Beginner)
Access 2 handout (Intermediate)
Access 3 handout (Advanced)
Access 4 handout (Approaching)

ACCESS COMPLEX TEXT

"Young Goodman Brown" concerns the battle between good and evil in the mind of a young man in colonial Massachusetts. Brown sets out on a nighttime journey to meet with the devil. During the journey he learns that the spiritual leaders of his community embrace evil, and he has a crisis of faith. To help students understand Young Goodman Brown's mental crisis, use the following ideas to provide scaffolded instruction for a first reading of the more complex features of this text:

- **Genre** - Elements of fantasy in this work of Gothic fiction may confuse readers, as the story begins with a realistic setting and then moves into the dark and foreboding forest, which symbolizes the realm of evil. Hawthorne never clearly reveals whether the events that take place in this gloomy landscape are real or imagined.
- **Sentence Structure** - Long, involved sentences with nonstandard punctuation may be difficult for some students to follow. Students may benefit from breaking longer sentences into smaller pieces to better understand the story.
- **Specific Vocabulary** - Difficult vocabulary, including archaic terms such as *prithee*, *fain*, and *verily*, may present a challenge to some readers. Students may benefit from rereading sentences with these terms and replacing them with contemporary language.
- **Prior Knowledge** - The historical context, including the Salem witch trials of 1692, may be unfamiliar to some readers. You may wish to point out that the author uses the names of two women who were executed in Salem on charges of witchcraft for characters' names in the story: Goody Cloyse and Martha Carrier.

1. INTRODUCTION

Core Path	Access Path
Read. Individually or as a class, read the introduction to "Young Goodman Brown." The introduction provides context for the story.	**English Learners All Levels & Approaching** **Read and Listen.** Ask students to read and listen to the introduction for *Young Goodman Brown*. Have them refer to the "Introduction Glossary" on their Access 1, 2, 3, and 4 handouts for definitions of key vocabulary terms. If there are unfamiliar words that are not included in their glossary, encourage students to check a dictionary or online reference tool, like http://dictionary.reference.com.

Core Path	Access Path
Access Prior Knowledge. Find out what your students already know about colonial Massachusetts or the Puritans. 1. First, divide your students into small groups. 2. Ask each group to generate a list (on the board or on paper) of the information and previous knowledge your students have about colonial Massachusetts. 3. After compiling their lists, ask students to share with the class where their previous knowledge came from—a drama, a class, a documentary, or a book? Discuss.	**Beginner & Approaching** **Access Prior Knowledge.** Have students create a concept map to show what they know about colonial Massachusetts, including the Salem witch trials. Then, as a class, discuss the challenges a member of such a community might have faced, such as showing one's piety and the importance of maintaining a good reputation. Discuss the importance of gossip during this time period and how a rumor could lead to a person's downfall. **Intermediate & Advanced** **Access Prior Knowledge.** Have students create a concept map to show what they know about colonial Massachusetts, including the Salem witch trials. In groups, ask students to discuss the challenges a member of such a community might have faced. Prompt students with such questions as: • What were the Puritans' religious beliefs? How did their religious beliefs impact their daily lives? • Why was it important to maintain a good reputation during this time? • What famous trials took place in the late 1600s in Salem? What role did gossip play in these trials?
	Extend **Discuss the Introduction.** After reading the introduction, use the information provided to facilitate a prereading discussion to get students thinking about the events and themes in "Young Goodman Brown." 1. Why might a forest be considered "the domain of the devil"? 2. How might a "serpentine walking stick" be a symbol of evil? 3. Why might people who are "above reproach" be willing to meet with the devil?

2. READ

Core Path	Access Path
Preteach Special Vocabulary. "Young Goodman Brown" includes a number of archaic and specialized expressions that might interfere with student comprehension. Before students read the text, explain the meaning of the following words: Goodman = a title similar to *Mr.* used for a man not of the upper class prithee = variation of "pray thee" used to make a request, similar to the word *please* 'twixt = a contraction of *betwixt,* meaning *between* return whence I came = return to the place from which I came wot = know fain = gladly verily = truly husbandman = farmer e'en = even catechism = course of religious instruction gossip = good friend smallage = wild celery cinquefoil = flowering plant of the rose family, also called potentilla wolf's bane = poisonous flowering plant related to the buttercup, often called *aconitum* Egyptian magi = Egyptian holy men thither = to that place durst = dare aught = nothing proselytes = persons newly converted to a religion or cult polluted = morally impure lattice = gate	
Make Predictions about Vocabulary. There are ten bold vocabulary words in the text. As students read the text, ask them to make predictions about what they think each bold vocabulary word means based on the context clues in the sentence. Have students use the annotation tool to make their predictions.	**Note:** This exercise, which extends vocabulary instruction, should be completed when the class shifts from whole group instruction to individual work during the "Read and Annotate" exercise.

Core Path	Access Path
It might be helpful to model this for students before they begin reading. Either using the board or projecting the actual text, focus in on the sentence that uses the word "unfathomable": • Unfathomable to mere mortals is the lore of fiends. Model for the class how to use these context clues to guess the meanings of the words: 1. When I first look at this sentence, I can see that its structure is different from what I am used to seeing. 2. I think that to understand the sentence, I will need to change its word order into one I am familiar with. I try changing the order to "The lore of fiends is unfathomable to mere mortals." 3. If this change is a correct one, "unfathomable" looks like it is a describing word for "lore of fiends." I am not sure what "lore" means, but it is now in the subject position in the sentence. 4. The sentence before the one containing "unfathomable" describes the verse of a hymn that is slow and mournful and "joined to words" like "sin, and darkly hinted at." These references make me think that "lore" might be a song or a story, and the words "sin," "darkly," and "fiends" make me think of something that is evil. 5. If "lore of fiends" refers to a tale that is sung or told, then I think it is a tale of evil. 6. I know that "mortals" refer to humans who will one day die, and so the context of the sentence seems to mean that the evil song is something humans have trouble understanding. 7. Therefore, I guess that "unfathomable" may mean something like "hard to understand." 8. I will check my inference in a print or online dictionary to see if I am correct.	**Beginner, Intermediate & Approaching Pair Practice.** 1. Pair students with more proficient readers. 2. Give them an additional sentence that contains a new vocabulary word. 3. Ask the students to complete a Think Aloud using the teacher-led Make Predictions about Vocabulary activity as a model, while the proficient student actively listens. 4. The student should use the context clues in the sentence to try to determine the meaning of the new vocabulary word. 5. After the student has completed the Think Aloud and made a prediction about the word's meaning, allow time for the proficient reader to add his/her own thoughts and clarify any points of confusion. 6. Once they've completed this Think Aloud, encourage them to use a dictionary to confirm the definition of the new vocabulary word. Have them refer to the "Text Glossary" on their Access 1, 2, and 4 handouts for definitions of key vocabulary terms in the text. Encourage them to add any additional vocabulary words or idioms they find in the text and look up definitions for those words and idioms online or in a dictionary.

Core Path	Access Path
In addition, point out to students that word part analysis can help them reinforce their understanding of word meanings. For example, tell students that "fathom" is a verb that means "to understand." Then ask students to identify the prefix and the suffix in the word and to explain how those affixes change the word's meaning and part of speech. (The prefix "un-" means "not" and reverses the meaning of the word. The suffix "-able" means "capable of" and turns the word into an adjective. Therefore, adding those affixes changes the word's part of speech to an adjective and the meaning to "not capable of being understood.") Have students think of other words that have the "un-" prefix and the "-able" suffix and explain the definitions of those words (such as, *unmanageable, unreliable, unacceptable*). Finally, have students apply word part analysis to the vocabulary word "irrepressible" and have them analyze other words with similar word parts, such as *irresponsible, irreplaceable,* and *irrecoverable.*	
Model Reading Comprehension Strategy. Before students begin reading, model the reading comprehension strategy of making, revising, and confirming predictions by using this Think Aloud that talks students through the first paragraph of text. First explain to your students that making, revising, and confirming predictions can assist readers in becoming more active by helping them to set a purpose for reading. When students make predictions before or during reading, they are also making inferences, or using available information and prior knowledge to construct meaning. Model for students how making, revising, and confirming predictions will help them better comprehend the selection and help drive their discussions. • When I read the first two paragraphs, I learn that a young man is setting off on a journey, and he is leaving his wife at home in Salem village. What kind of journey will he be making?	**Note:** This exercise, which extends instruction around reading comprehension strategies, should be completed when the class shifts from whole group instruction to individual work during the "Read and Annotate" exercise. **Beginner, Intermediate & Approaching** **Apply Reading Comprehension Strategy.** 1. Have students listen to the audio version of "Young Goodman Brown." As they listen to the audio, pause the recording after paragraph 6. Instruct them to write one sentence predicting whether Goodman Brown will turn back or continue on his journey. 2. Resume the audio, pausing periodically to allow students to write a new sentence underneath, refining their previous predictions. Offer guidance to help them notice clues in the events, descriptions, and dialogue.

Core Path	Access Path
• I predict that he is going on a trip involving some sort of business and that he will go to another town or a city with a market. • When I read the third paragraph, I realize I need to revise my prediction. The young man will travel at night and be back by sunrise. What kind of journey takes place over a single night? I guess that he is going to some sort of secret meeting, and I will look for details and information to either confirm my prediction or revise it to something else.	3. Once they have finished listening to the audio, have them write one final sentence, summarizing the text. 4. Pair students with more proficient readers and ask them to discuss the differences between their initial predictions and their final summaries. Which predictions changed and which stayed the same? What clues were the most important? Encourage groups to share their findings with the class, and point out strategies that may have used without realizing it.
Read and Annotate. Have students independently read and annotate the story. Ask students to use the annotation tool as they read to: 1. use context clues to analyze and determine the meaning of the bolded vocabulary terms 2. ask questions about passages of the text that may be unclear or unresolved 3. identify key information, events, characters, and connections between them 4. note unfamiliar vocabulary 5. make, confirm, and revise predictions	**Beginner** **Coach the Reading.** While other students read, annotate, and discuss the text independently, work with Beginning students, listening to the audio of the text and pausing periodically or when any student has a question. Coach students in articulating their questions for the group and in highlighting and annotating the text. Have students use the Annotation Guide on the Access 1 handout to support them as they highlight and annotate the text. For further support, ask questions about the text such as: • Is there anything about the story that you don't understand? • Do you think Goodman Brown dreamed about the night in the forest or really experienced it? • Do you think Goodman Brown should have treated his family and townspeople the way he did after his encounter with the devil? Why or why not?

Core Path	Access Path
	Intermediate **Listen to the Audio.** Have these students listen to the audio of the text and use the Text Glossary on the Access 2 handout to help them with words or idioms that may be unfamiliar. If students need help with annotating the text, have them use the Annotation Guide on the Access 2 handout. After working with the Beginning students, you may wish to check this group's progress and provide support as needed. **Advanced** **Pair with Proficient Peers.** Have Advanced students work with English-proficient peers to read, annotate, and discuss the text. Have students use the Annotation Guide in the Access 3 handout to support them as they highlight and annotate the text. Encourage them to listen to the audio of the text if needed. **Approaching** **Use the Annotation Guide.** Have students use the Annotation Guide on the Access 4 handout to support them as they highlight and annotate the text.
Discuss. In small groups or pairs, have students discuss the questions and inferences they made while reading. To help facilitate discussions, refer to Collaborative Discussions in the Speaking & Listening Handbook. 1. What is the reason for Young Goodman Brown's journey to the wooded area? (He has an "evil purpose"; he may be thinking of doing something wrong.) Why might the devil be dressed in "decent attire" when he meets Brown? (He probably wants to look respectable to make Brown feel comfortable when talking to him.)	**English Learners All Levels & Approaching** Use the extra time while on- and beyond-grade-level students are discussing their first reads of the text to work individually and in small groups with Approaching readers and English Learners as outlined above. Should those students complete their first reads quickly, integrate them into the on- and beyond-grade-level discussion groups. Otherwise, English Learners and Approaching readers will be given an opportunity to participate in text discussions with their peers later in the lesson.

Core Path	Access Path
2. How does the devil weaken Brown's resistance to evil? (He shows the evil side of people that Brown respects.) At what point is Brown finally able to resist the devil's temptation? (as the devil is preparing to "baptize" him and Faith) 3. If you stop reading three paragraphs before the end of the story, what information can help you predict how the night in the woods will change Young Goodman Brown? (He has seen his catechism teacher, his pastor, and his wife with the devil, so he probably will change to become less trusting of people and expect the worst from them.)	**Beyond** **Tech Infusion** **Write.** Pair students and ask them to write a short dialogue that might take place between Goodman Brown and the devil a year after their encounter in the forest. Students should mimic Hawthorne's style, using dialogue in the story as a model. Students who have access to a collaborative tool such as Google Docs should use it to create and share their dialogues.
	Extend **Perform.** Have small groups create comic sketches that use some of the archaic vocabulary words in "Young Goodman Brown." The sketches should involve a contemporary setting for heightened effect. Ask groups to perform their sketches for the class

3. THINK

Core Path	Access Path
Answer and Discuss. Have students complete the Think questions and then use the peer review instructions and rubric to complete two peer reviews. Refer to the sample answers at the end of the lesson plan online to discuss responses with your students.	**Beginner & Intermediate** **Sentence Frames.** Have students use the sentence frames on the Access 1 and 2 handouts to support their responses to the Think questions. If necessary, distribute sentence frames to Advanced students as well. **Approaching** **Find the Evidence.** Have students use Find the Evidence on the Access 4 handout to help them identify the evidence needed to answer the questions.

Core Path	Access Path
	Extend **Debate.** Present students with an issue from the text that can be debated. Allow students to debate the issue as a class or in smaller groups. Debate prompt: Is Young Goodman Brown imagining or dreaming some parts of the story? If so, how much? If not, why not? Use evidence from the text to support your opinion.

SKILL:
Setting

OVERVIEW

The setting tells the where and when of a story. Setting can play a key role in setting the mood of a story. It can also strongly influence what the characters say and do. This lesson plan provides follow-up questions and enrichments to help teachers guide students toward a usable, repeatable method for understanding setting.

OBJECTIVES

1. Learn the definition of setting.
2. Practice using concrete strategies for analyzing setting.
3. Participate effectively in a range of conversations and collaborations to express ideas and build upon the ideas of others.

ELA Common Core Standards:
Reading: Literature - RL.11-12.1, RL.11-12.3, RL.11-12.4
Speaking & Listening - SL.11-12.1.A, SL.11-12.1.C, SL.11-12.2

RESOURCES

Access 1 handout (Beginner)
Access 2 handout (Intermediate)
Access 3 handout (Advanced)
Access 4 handout (Approaching)

1. DEFINE

Core Path	Access Path
Watch. Watch the Concept Definition video on setting with your students. Have your students write down the definition of setting and what it encompasses, and make sure they understand how a story's setting can influence its plot, character(s), and theme(s). Pause the video at these key moments to discuss the information with your students: 1. 0:30 – How might the "emotional conditions" of a setting influence a story? Give an example or two of a setting that contains certain emotional conditions that affect either characters or plot. 2. 1:04 – Think of another simple plot like the example given in the video. Now, think of two different settings where it could take place: one that would benefit its characters, and another that would lead to conflict. Which of the two settings sounds like it would make for a more interesting story? Why? 3. 1:22 – How does your own setting influence you? Imagine yourself in a place that would lead to more conflict, as well as one that would lessen the conflict. How would these different settings change your day-to-day life?	**English Learners All Levels & Approaching** **Match.** Have students complete the matching exercise on the Access 1, 2, 3, and 4 handouts as they watch the video. Answers are located at the end of the lesson plan online.
Read and Discuss. After watching the Concept Definition video, have students read the definition of setting. Either in small groups or as a whole class, use these questions to engage students in a discussion about setting: 1. What are some interesting settings you've read about in other stories or novels? What made the setting interesting? (Answers will vary, but students may reference details of setting that made them feel a certain emotion.)	**Beginner & Approaching** **Fill in the Blanks.** To prepare students to participate in the discussion, have them complete the fill-in-the-blanks activity on the Access 1 and 4 handouts as they read the definition. The correct answers are located at the end of the lesson plan online.

Core Path	Access Path
2. In what kind of story would more than one setting be needed? (stories with more than one plot, stories taking place over several years, stories with action occurring in different places) 3. Setting consists of both time and place. Which of these two do you think is more important in a story? Why? (Some students may say that place is more important because readers can really visualize it. Others may say that time is more important because a time period can tell readers a lot about its people, history, and culture.)	**Intermediate & Advanced** **Discuss Prompts.** To help these students participate in the discussion, prompt them with questions that can be answered with a few words, such as: • What two elements make up the setting? (time and place) • What mood does a deserted house create? a raging blizzard? (sample answers: scary, eerie; suspenseful, dangerous) • How can setting affect a character's actions? (Answers will vary.) **Beyond** **Discuss.** Have students select a book they've read and describe its setting. Compile a list of examples that includes both times and places. Have students discuss how the setting of each work affects the mood, characters, and plot. How would the story change if the time setting were different, such as moving the story to the distant past or to the future?
	Extend **Brainstorm.** After watching the video, ask students to think of movies and television shows they have seen that have interesting settings. Using a whiteboard or projector, compile a list of what makes a setting interesting.

2. MODEL

Core Path	Access Path
Read and Annotate. Have students independently read the Model section. As they read, ask students to use the annotation tool to: • highlight key points • ask questions	**Note:** During this portion of the lesson, instruction shifts from whole group to individual work. Use this time to work one-on-one or in small groups with Beginning, Intermediate, Advanced, and Approaching students.

Core Path	Access Path
• identify places where the Model applies the strategies laid out in the Identification and Application section • comment on the effect the setting has on the text's meaning	**Beginner & Intermediate** **Coach the Reading.** Work with these students (either individually or in small groups) to fill out the guided reading questions on the Access 1 and 2 handouts. Have Beginning students refer to the glossary on the Access 1 handout to help them determine the meaning of difficult words (note: provide the Access 1 handout glossary to Intermediate students if necessary). Let students know they'll use these answers to help participate in the discussion about the Model. Sample answers for this exercise are located at the end of the lesson plan online. **Advanced** **Identify Evidence.** Ask Advanced students to complete the identifying evidence exercise on the Access 3 handout. Let students know that they'll use these answers to help participate in the discussion about the Model. Sample answers for this exercise are located at the end of the lesson plan online. **Approaching** **Guided Reading.** Have students complete the guided reading questions on the Access 4 handout as they read. Let them know that they'll use these answers to help participate in the discussion about the Model. Sample answers for this exercise are located at the end of the lesson plan online.
Discuss. After students read the Model text, use these questions to facilitate a whole group discussion that helps students understand how to determine and analyze the setting of the story: 1. How does the Model analyze the impact of the setting on the mood of the story? (It examines the connotations of the adjectives that describe where the story is taking place.) 2. Aside from the mood of the story, what else does the Model say may be affected by the sinister setting? (the resolve or mind of the main character, Goodman Brown)	

Core Path	Access Path
3. In the second part of the Model, what type of imagery is discussed as it relates to the description of the setting? (fire imagery, which represents candles but also perhaps the fires of the underworld) 4. Based on the points made in the Model, what can you infer is an unusual element of the setting in "Young Goodman Brown"? (The setting includes supernatural elements, such as the way the living pine trees burn like candles.)	
	Extend **Tech Infusion** **Create.** On slips of paper, write one-word descriptions of different types of story moods, such as suspenseful, comic, combative, terrifying, and happy. Assign small groups and give each group a slip of paper. Have groups discuss how the setting could help create the mood that has been assigned to them. Then have groups use Prezi (prezi.com) to create a presentation that walks through how an author could use setting to build that mood.

3. YOUR TURN

Core Path	Access Path
Assess and Explain. Have students answer the comprehension questions to test for understanding. Share the explanations for Parts A and B (located online) with your students.	
	Extend **Create an Image.** Ask students to create an image that reflects the elements of the setting mentioned in the sample passage. Students might draw the dark cloud and the forest, or they might make a collage out of images collected from Internet sources.

CLOSE READ:
Young Goodman Brown

OVERVIEW

The story "Young Goodman Brown" by Nathaniel Hawthorne examines evil in the community of Salem, Massachusetts, in colonial times. The Close Read gives students the opportunity to analyze the setting of the story.

OBJECTIVES

1. Complete a close reading of a short story.
2. Practice and apply concrete strategies for analyzing setting in an excerpt from "Young Goodman Brown."
3. Participate effectively in a range of conversations and collaborations to express ideas and build upon the ideas of others.
4. Prewrite, plan, and produce clear and coherent writing in response to a prompt.

ELA Common Core Standards:
Reading: Literature - RL.11-12.1, RL.11-12.3, RL.11-12.4, RL.11-12.9
Writing - W.11-12.4, W.11-12.5, W.11-12.6, W.11-12.9.A, W.11-12.10
Speaking & Listening - SL.11-12.1.A, SL.11-12.1.B, SL.11-12.1.C, SL.11-12.1.D, SL.11-12.6
Language - L.11-12.4.A, L.11-12.4.C, L.11-12.4.D

RESOURCES

"Young Goodman Brown" Vocabulary handout
Access 1 handout (Beginner)
Access 2 handout (Intermediate)
Access 3 handout (Advanced)
Access 4 handout (Approaching)

1. INTRODUCTION

Core Path	Access Path
Define and Compare. Project the vocabulary words and definitions onto the board or provide students with handouts so they can copy the vocabulary into their notebooks. Suggest that students consult general and specialized reference materials, both print and digital, to compare the precise meaning of a specific word with their initial vocabulary predictions from the First Read. Review words that students defined incorrectly to understand why they were unable to use context clues to develop usable definitions.	**Beginner & Intermediate** **Complete a Chart.** Have students complete the chart on the Access 1 and 2 handouts by writing the correct word for each of the definitions. **Advanced & Beyond** **Write in Journals.** Have students write a journal entry using all of their vocabulary words. Remind them to write sentences that communicate the meaning of the words they are using. **Approaching** **Graphic Organizer.** To support students in comparing their predictions with the correct meanings, have them complete the graphic organizer on the Access 4 handout to record the vocabulary words, their initial analysis, and the definitions. Then have them write sentences using the words.
Review. Have students complete the fill-in-the-blanks vocabulary worksheet attached to the lesson plan online. Answers for the worksheet are listed at the end of the lesson plan online.	
	Extend **Tech Infusion** **Create.** Assign students to small groups and ask them to create an animated story using three words from the vocabulary list. Have them use an animation website such as Powtoon (http://www.powtoon.com/) or an iPad or Android app like StickDraw.

2. READ

Core Path	Access Path
Model Close Reading. Project the text onto the board and model a close reading of the first six paragraphs using the annotation strategies mentioned below. While modeling annotation strategies, make notes that tie the text to the focus skill and demonstrate what students are looking for as they read. Some guidance for you as you annotate for your students: • Recall from the Skills lesson that precedes this story that settings tell both the where and the when of a story. • In the first paragraph, we learn that it is sunset as Young Goodman Brown gives his wife a "parting kiss." It seems unusual for a husband to be leaving his house, and wife, at the end of the day rather than in the morning. The wife, Faith, is described as being "aptly named," which is also interesting. • In the third paragraph, we learn that Brown's journey will be completed before sunrise. An all-night journey seems especially unusual. We also learn that this is the only such journey that Brown will be making during the year. It sounds important. • In the eighth paragraph, we learn that Brown's journey has an "evil purpose." He admits that knowing the purpose of his journey would kill his wife. This makes us wonder what kind of person he might be. The setting turns gloomy and lonely; the story is taking on a dark mood.	
Read and Annotate. Read the Skills Focus questions as a class, so your students know what they should pay close attention to as they read. Then have students read and annotate the story. Ask students to use the annotation tool as they read to 1. respond to the Skills Focus section 2. ask questions about how setting influences other story elements, such as character and plot	**Note:** While on-grade-level students are reading and annotating, work one-on-one or in small groups with Beginning, Intermediate, Advanced, and Approaching students to support them as they read and annotate the text.

Core Path	Access Path
3. make connections between the setting and the themes in the story 4. identify key characters, events, and descriptions 5. note unfamiliar vocabulary 6. capture their reaction to the ideas and examples in the text As they reread the text, remind students to use the comprehension strategy of making, revising, and confirming predictions that they learned in the First Read.	**Beginner & Intermediate** **Summarize and Analyze the Text.** Work with these students to complete the sentence frames on the Access 1 and 2 handouts (note: the sentence frames for Intermediate students on the Access 2 handout contain fewer scaffolds). They will then use the completed sentence frames to help them analyze and annotate the text by completing the Skills Focus questions. Refer to the sample Skills Focus answers to help them complete the sentence frames and annotate the text. **Advanced** **Work in Pairs.** Pair these students with more proficient English speakers to work together on analyzing and annotating the text to complete the Skills Focus questions. If these students need more support, have them use the sentence frames on the Access 3 handout as they work with their more proficient peers. **Approaching** **Summarize the Text.** Have these students discuss and complete the text summary on the Access 4 handout and use their summary to help them analyze and annotate the text by completing the Skills Focus questions. Correct answers for the summary are at the end of the lesson plan online. Also refer to the sample Skills Focus answers to aid students with their annotations.
Discuss. After students have read the text, use the sample responses to the Skills Focus questions at the bottom of the lesson plan online to discuss the reading and the process of analyzing how setting affects other elements in a story.	**Extend** **Pair and Share.** In small, heterogeneous groups or pairs, ask students to share and discuss their annotations with a focus on the setting.

Core Path	Access Path
Make sure that students have acquired and accurately use academic-specific words and phrases related to the skill and demonstrate a command of formal English appropriate to the discussion. To help facilitate discussions, refer to Collaborative Discussions in the Speaking & Listening Handbook.	You can provide students with questions to guide their discussion: 1. The story begins in the village, continues into the forest, and then concludes in the village again. How are these changes in setting related to the plot? Cite specific textual evidence to support your statements. (The village represents civilization, where people's behavior seems to be under control. The forest represents wildness and evil. Brown leaves the village to test his faith and returns to the village a changed man who sees evil everywhere.) 2. Discuss the descriptions of the forest path or road. How does it change during Brown's journey? Cite specific textual evidence to support your statements. (Brown enters the forest on a narrow path. He meets the Devil after a "crook in the road." As Brown approaches the clearing in the forest, the path grows "wilder and drearier and more faintly traced, and vanished at length.") 3. The climax of the story occurs at midnight in a clearing in the forest. List some phrases from the story that describe this setting. (Student responses will vary but may include "lurid blaze," "benighted wilderness pealing," "dark wall," "an altar or a pulpit," and "fitfully illuminating.") What feeling do these phrases give the reader? (A feeling of foreboding, fear or terror)
	Extend **Research.** Ask small groups to research the Salem witch trials of the early 1600s, which took place in the same village where Goodman Brown lives. Assign groups different topics, such as the types of activities that were labeled witchcraft, the judges at the trial, who was executed and how, and what led to the end of the trials. Ask a representative from each group to present their findings to the class.

3. WRITE

Core Path	Access Path
Prewrite and Plan. Read the prompt as a class and ask students to brainstorm about the setting in "Young Goodman Brown." Remind your students to look at the story and their annotations to find textual evidence to support their ideas.	**Beginner & Intermediate** **Plan and Organize.** Have students complete the prewriting activity on the Access 1 and 2 handouts and then explain their ideas to a partner before they write. Explain to students that they need to choose details, examples, or quotes from the text that support their ideas and then explain how those details support their statements. For example, students could include the line, "He had taken a dreary road, darkened by all the gloomiest trees of the forest, which barely stood aside to let the narrow path creep through, and closed immediately behind," which describes the dark and scary environment that Goodman Brown encounters as he begins his journey through the forest. **Approaching** **Plan and Organize.** Have students complete the prewriting activity on the Access 4 handout to organize their thoughts before they write.
Discuss. Project these instructions for the peer review onto the board and review them with your class, so they know what they are looking for when they begin to provide their classmates with feedback: • How has this essay helped you understand how the story's descriptions of setting create a frightening mood in the story? • How clearly did the writer show that the mood became increasingly frightening over the course of the story? • What five pieces of evidence from the text did the writer use to support his or her writing? • How well does the writer explain how that evidence supports his or her arguments? • Does the writer write using standard grammar and punctuation? Are there any weak spots?	

Core Path	Access Path
• What specific suggestions can you make to help the writer improve the response? • What thing(s) does this paper do especially well? After you've looked at the peer review instructions, review the rubric with students before they begin writing. Allow time for students briefly to pose and discuss any questions they may have about the peer review instructions and the rubric. Tell students how many peer reviews they will need to complete once they submit their writing.	
Write. Ask students to complete the writing assignment using textual evidence to support their answers. Once they have completed their writing, they should click "Submit."	
	Extend **Critique.** Project a writing sample on the board and ask the class to identify the elements of writing that are strong, as well as those that are weak or in need of improvement. Alternatively, you can put students in small groups and give them photocopies of a writing sample to collaboratively evaluate. After students have had an opportunity to evaluate student samples, work as a class to generate strategies students can use as they complete their peer reviews to ensure they are substantive.
Review. Once students complete their writing assignment, they should submit substantive feedback to two peers.	

First Read: The Masque of the Red Death

OVERVIEW

The story "The Masque of the Red Death" by Edgar Allan Poe is a Gothic tale about the efforts of a wealthy prince to protect himself and his friends from a deadly plague. The First Read gives students the opportunity to experience the text with a limited context.

OBJECTIVES

1. Perform an initial reading of a text and demonstrate comprehension by responding to short analysis and inference questions with textual evidence.
2. Practice defining vocabulary words using context.
3. Learn and practice strategies for varying the length and complexity of phrases, clauses, and sentences.
4. Participate effectively in a range of conversations and collaborations to express ideas and build upon the ideas of others.
5. Practice acquiring and using academic vocabulary correctly.

ELA Common Core Standards:
Reading: Literature - RL.11-12.1, RL.11-12.2, RL.11-12.4, RL.11-12.5, RL.11-12.10
Writing - W.11-12.7
Speaking & Listening - SL.11-12.1.A, SL.11-12.1.B, SL.11-12.1.C, SL.11-12.1.D, SL.11-12.2
Language - L.11-12.3.A, L.11-12.4.C, L.11-12.4.D, L.11-12.4.A, L.11-12.6

RESOURCES

Grammar handout: Syntax
Access 1 handout (Beginner)
Access 2 handout (Intermediate)
Access 3 handout (Advanced)
Access 4 handout (Approaching)

ACCESS COMPLEX TEXT

"The Masque of the Red Death" describes a prince in the Middle Ages who seals himself and a thousand friends into an abbey to avoid the Red Death, which was a devastating plague. During a masked ball, a ghostly figure arrives and spreads the pestilence throughout the abbey, killing everyone. To help students understand the surreal mood and allegorical elements of the story, use the following ideas to provide scaffolded instruction for a first reading of the more complex features of this text:

- **Genre** - The sudden appearance of a ghostlike figure and other elements of fantasy in this work of Gothic fiction may confuse readers. Discuss with students the elements of Gothic fiction (supernatural beings, spooky settings, and so on), and give recent examples such as movies about Dracula or other classic monsters.
- **Connection of Ideas** - Allegorical elements link ideas in the text and may be difficult for some students to follow. For example, students may not initially consider the significance of the room colors: all are colorful and cheerful except for the final room, which serves as an allegory of death. As students read, encourage them to consider the significance of each item or description in the story beyond its literal meaning.
- **Specific Vocabulary** - Some difficult vocabulary, such as *depopulated*, *voluptuous*, and *grotesque* may present a challenge to readers.
- **Prior Knowledge** - A situation involving a medieval plague may be unfamiliar to some readers. Build background with students by explaining how the plague greatly affected the population of Europe during the Middle Ages. It might also be helpful to discuss modern medical epidemics such as ebola or other rapidly spreading deadly diseases.

1. INTRODUCTION

Core Path	Access Path
Read. Individually or as a class, read the introduction for "The Masque of the Red Death." The introduction provides context for the story.	**English Learners All Levels & Approaching** **Read and Listen.** Ask students to read and listen to the introduction for "The Masque of the Red Death." Have them refer to the "Introduction Glossary" on their Access 1, 2, 3, and 4 handouts for definitions of key vocabulary terms. If there are unfamiliar words that are not included in their glossary, encourage students to check a dictionary or online reference tool, like http://dictionary.reference.com.

Core Path	Access Path
Build Background. In pairs or small groups, ask students to use devices to research different aspects of the plagues that affected medieval Europe. Assign each group a topic to investigate. Remind students to include relevant facts, definitions, and concrete details in their research: • The Black Death of the 1300s • Italy in the 1300s • Medieval medical practices • Depictions of the plague in literature If you are in a low-tech classroom, you can provide photocopies of information about medieval plagues for students to read and discuss. Have students present their findings.	**English Learners All Levels** **Build Background.** Pair Beginning and Intermediate students with more proficient (Beyond) readers to research one of the four suggested topics. Ask Beginning students to think about these questions to guide their research. • The Black Death of the 1300s 1. What were some reasons that the plague spread so rapidly? 2. What were the consequences of this plague in Europe and elsewhere? • Italy in the 1300s 1. What was life like for the average person? 2. What was life like for a wealthy person or a person of noble birth? • Medieval medical practices 1. What is one medieval medical practice that you might be willing to try? 2. What practice seems the most unusual to you? Do you think it was effective? • Depictions of the plague in literature 1. How was the plague depicted in nonfiction? What was the purpose of these writings? 2. How was the plague depicted in fiction?
	Extend **Analyze and Discuss a Quotation.** "A short story must have a single mood and every sentence must build towards it." (Edgar Allan Poe) 1. What must an author do to create mood in a story? 2. Why might a short story benefit from having a single mood?

Core Path	Access Path
	3. How would you classify the mood of "The Masque of the Red Death"? Why?

2. READ

Core Path	Access Path
Preteach Special Vocabulary. "The Masque of the Red Death" includes a number of archaic and specialized expressions that might interfere with student comprehension. Before students read the text, explain the meaning of the following words: his castellated abbeys = large residences that have the features of castles and were formerly the home of religious communities but now belong to the prince courtiers = friends and advisers to a monarch ingress ... egress = entrance ... exit buffoons = clowns *improvisatori* = Italian poets who create original spoken poetry masked ball = a ball at which people disguise themselves in costumes, also called a masquerade disposed = arranged casement = the framework of a window brazier = a pan that contains burning coals stricken = struck harken = listen perforce = as a result of circumstances evolutions = circular movements disconcert = confusion fête = a French word meaning *party* or *ball* phantasm = illusion "Hernani" = a play by the French author Victor Hugo, which is famous for its elaborate costumes and set design anon = at once habiliments = clothes mummer = a person disguised in a costume cerements = shrouds that are used to clothe the dead untenanted = unoccupied	

Core Path	Access Path

Core Path

Make Predictions about Vocabulary. There are six bold vocabulary words in the text. As students read the text, ask them to make predictions about what they think each bold vocabulary word means based on the context clues in the sentence. Have students use the annotation tool to make their predictions.

It might be helpful to model this for students before they begin reading. Either using the board or projecting the actual text, focus in on the sentence that uses the word "pestilence":

- No pestilence had ever been so fatal, or so hideous.

Model for the class how to use these context clues to guess the meaning of the word:

1. I can tell right away from the sentence that pestilence is a bad thing because the sentence says that it's more "fatal" and "hideous" than those before.
2. If something is fatal, it results in someone's death, so I can tell that a pestilence could kill someone.
3. It's also hideous, so I can guess that means that it's gross, and that the death resulting from it causes something to happen to its victim.
4. Two sentences later, I see the words "pains," "dizziness," and "bleeding," which explains the word "hideous," and also tells me that this is probably some sort of a disease or plague.

Finally, remind students that they can verify their preliminary determination of the meaning of a word by checking in a dictionary. Have students practice this by working in small groups to use a digital or print dictionary to look up "pestilence" and to answer these questions about the word's meaning, part of speech, pronunciation, and etymology (the word's origin or history).

Access Path

Note: This exercise, which extends vocabulary instruction, should be completed when the class shifts from whole group instruction to individual work during the "Read and Annotate" exercise.

Beginner, Intermediate & Approaching Pair Practice.

1. Pair students with more proficient readers.
2. Give them an additional sentence that contains a new vocabulary word.
3. Ask the students to complete a Think Aloud using the teacher-led Make Predictions about Vocabulary activity as a model, while the proficient student actively listens.
4. The student should use the context clues in the sentence to try to determine the meaning of the new vocabulary word.
5. After the student has completed the Think Aloud and made a prediction about the word's meaning, allow time for the proficient reader to add his/her own thoughts and clarify any points of confusion.
6. Once they've completed this Think Aloud, encourage them to use a dictionary to confirm the definition of the new vocabulary word. Have them refer to the "Text Glossary" on their Access 1, 2, and 4 handouts for definitions of key vocabulary terms in the text. Encourage them to add any additional vocabulary words or idioms they find in the text and look up definitions for those words and idioms online or in a dictionary.

Core Path	Access Path
1. What is the dictionary definition of "pestilence"? How closely does the inferred meaning match up with the dictionary definition? (The dictionary definition of "pestilence" is "a fatal epidemic disease." The inferred meaning is a close match because it expresses the idea that the disease is fatal but it also goes beyond the dictionary definition to define it as something "gross.") 2. Does "pestilence" have another possible part of speech or meaning? Explain ("Pestilence" can be used only as a noun and has only one meaning.) 3. Is there more than one way to pronounce "pestilence"? Some words have variant pronunciations. (No, "pestilence" has only one pronunciation.) 4. What is the etymology of the word "pestilence"? How does the etymology of the word relate to its current meaning? ("Pestilence" derives from the Latin *pestis*, meaning "a plague." This directly relates to its current meaning because a plague is a deadly and highly contagious disease.)	
Model Reading Comprehension Strategy. Before students begin reading, model the reading comprehension strategy of summarizing by using this Think Aloud that talks students through the first two paragraphs of the story. First explain to your students that summarizing is: *a process in which students select, organize, and synthesize the most important elements in a text* Model for students how summarizing will help them better comprehend the selection and help drive their discussions. • As I read the first paragraph, I learn that the "Red Death" is killing many people in a country. Then there is a description of the disease; the most important fact seems to be that the disease can kill a person within 30 minutes.	**Note:** This exercise, which extends instruction around reading comprehension strategies, should be completed when the class shifts from whole group instruction to individual work during the "Read and Annotate" exercise. **Beginner, Intermediate & Approaching Model Reading Comprehension Strategy.** 1. Have students make notes in the Summarizing Chart about paragraphs 1–2 as they listen to you model the strategy for the whole class. 2. Then, divide Beginning, Intermediate, and Approaching students in small groups and have them read paragraphs 3–7 of "The Masque of the Red Death."

Core Path

- The second paragraph tells about a prince. He must be the main character. He invites many friends to one of his homes. It seems important that they are trying to avoid the disease. The descriptions of the building seem less important. I wouldn't include those descriptions in a summary.
- Thinking of the most important facts in the first two paragraphs, I wonder if the people will manage to avoid the terrible disease.
- As I continue to read, I will note details that seem important to add to a summary of the story.

Access Path

3. Ask groups to summarize the paragraphs using their own words. Encourage students to talk out the details and events that happen in these paragraphs. Ask students to record their summaries in the Summarizing Chart on the Access 1, 2, and 4 handouts.
4. Have groups repeat these steps for paragraphs 8–11 and paragraphs 12–14.
5. When students have completed their charts, have them share their notes with another group and compare their summaries. Did they include the same details? Did they leave out any details the other group included? Encourage them to add any significant details they missed to their charts.

Core Path

Read and Annotate. Have students independently read and annotate the story. Ask students to use the annotation tool as they read to:

1. use context clues to analyze and determine the meaning of the bolded vocabulary terms
2. ask questions about passages of the text that may be unclear or unresolved
3. identify key information, events, characters, and connections between them
4. note unfamiliar vocabulary

Access Path

Beginner
Coach the Reading. While other students read, annotate, and discuss the text independently, work with Beginning students, listening to the audio of the text and pausing periodically or when any student has a question. Coach students in articulating their questions for the group and in highlighting and annotating the text. Have students use the Annotation Guide on the Access 1 handout to support them as they highlight and annotate the text.

For further support, ask questions about the text such as:

- Is there anything about the story that you don't understand?
- What type of people did the prince invite to his castle? What type of people was excluded? Why is this important?
- How does the setting affect the story?

Core Path	Access Path
	Intermediate **Listen to the Audio.** Have these students listen to the audio of the text and use the Text Glossary on the Access 2 handout to help them with words or idioms that may be unfamiliar. If students need help with annotating the text, have them use the Annotation Guide on the Access 2 handout. After working with the Beginning students, you may wish to check this group's progress and provide support as needed. **Advanced** **Pair with Proficient Peers.** Have Advanced students work with English-proficient peers to read, annotate, and discuss the text. Have students use the Annotation Guide in the Access 3 handout to support them as they highlight and annotate the text. Encourage them to listen to the audio of the text if needed. **Approaching** **Use the Annotation Guide.** Have students use the Annotation Guide on the Access 4 handout to support them as they highlight and annotate the text.
Discuss Text Structure. Tell students that Poe's short story is structured to create a sense of fear and dread in the reader. The fear is evoked right from start and ebbs and flows throughout the story until its conclusion. In small groups or pairs, have students apply the comprehension strategy of summarizing as they discuss the following questions about text structure and how text structure can contribute to meaning and aesthetic impact.	**English Learners All Levels & Approaching** Use the extra time while on- and beyond-grade-level students are discussing their first reads of the text to work individually and in small groups with Approaching readers and English Learners as outlined above. Should those students complete their first reads quickly, integrate them into the on- and beyond-grade-level discussion groups. Otherwise, English Learners and Approaching readers will be given an opportunity to participate in text discussions with their peers later in the lesson.

Core Path	Access Path
To help facilitate discussions, refer to Collaborative Discussions in the Speaking & Listening Handbook. 1. What details from the first paragraph evoke feelings of fear and dread in the reader? (Possible response: The first paragraph describes how deadly the disease is and how "hideous" the death is, emphasizing "the horror of blood" and the "profuse bleeding" caused by the disease.) 2. As you continue reading the story, explain how certain events and descriptions help to build or lessen the sense of fear and dread? (Possible response: As the story progresses, there is some relief from the feelings of fear and dread, with the idea that Prince Prospero and his friends can escape the Red Death through seclusion in his abbey. However, the feeling of fear is always present, given the bizarre setting and atmosphere. For example, in paragraph 4, the description of the "deep blood colour" of the windows of the seventh suite is highly suggestive that the Red Death will infect the abbey.) 3. What lesson might a reader take away about fear from the story's tragic ending? (Possible response: Rich and selfish people might fear death and try to escape it, but ultimately, they cannot control their own destiny.)	**Beyond** **Tech Infusion** **Brainstorm.** Pair students and ask them to brainstorm how the story might be different if it were set in modern times. What kind of person might the main character be? A politician? A celebrity? What type of plague would be happening? How might the setting be different? If students have access to Google Docs or another word processing app, encourage them to compile and share their notes electronically.
(G) **Grammar, Usage, and Mechanics.** Distribute the StudySync grammar handout on syntax and discuss the instruction provided on the handout with students. Have students respond individually to the questions on the handout and then discuss their responses as a class. Possible responses to the questions appear at the end of this document.	**Beginner & Intermediate** **Work with the Teacher.** Remind these students that syntax is the way words are put together in clauses, phrases, and sentences. Point out that Poe uses complex sentences in order to show action, to add important details, to create the mood and heighten tension, and to drive the reader forward through the text (pacing).

Core Path	Access Path
	Write the following sentence from the story on the board: *Then, summoning the wild courage of despair, a throng of the revellers at once threw themselves into the black apartment, and, seizing the mummer, whose tall figure stood erect and motionless within the shadow of the ebony clock, gasped in unutterable horror at finding the grave cerements and corpse-like mask, which they handled with so violent a rudeness, untenanted by any tangible form.* Ask: *What are the main actions in this sentence?* (The revellers enter the apartment and seize the mummer, only to discover that the specter has no form to it.) *What additional information do we learn in the sentence?* (the emotions of the revellers; how the mummer looked) Discuss with students which specific phrases or words of the sentence show action, add details, create the mood or heighten tension, or drive the pace of the story. For example, Poe could have begun a new sentence after the revellers entered the apartment. Instead, he continues the action using "and," which creates a quicker pace. **Advanced & Beyond** **Extend the Search.** Challenge these students to work in pairs or small groups to find one or more complex sentences in the text, and to note how each phrase shows action, adds details, creates the mood or heightens tension, or drives the pace of the story. **Approaching** **Analyze an Example.** If students need more support understanding syntax, call their attention to the sentence you wrote on the board for Beginning and Intermediate students. Ask pairs or small groups to analyze each phrase and tell what purpose it serves: to show action, add details, create the mood or heighten tension, or drive the pace of the story. Encourage students to discuss how each phrase builds meaning in the sentence.

3. THINK

Core Path	Access Path
Answer and Discuss. Have students complete the Think questions and then use the peer review instructions and rubric to complete two peer reviews. Refer to the sample answers at the end of the lesson plan online to discuss responses with your students.	**Beginner & Intermediate** **Sentence Frames.** Have students use the sentence frames on the Access 1 and 2 handouts to support their responses to the Think questions. If necessary, distribute sentence frames to Advanced students as well. **Approaching** **Find the Evidence.** Have students use Find the Evidence on the Access 4 handout to help them identify the evidence needed to answer the questions.
	Extend **Debate.** Present students with an issue from the text that can be debated. Allow students to debate the issue as a class or in smaller groups. Debate prompt: Did the people in the abbey get what they deserved? Why or why not?

SKILL:
Irony

OVERVIEW

There are three types of irony: verbal irony, situational irony, and dramatic irony. Situational irony is an important part of Edgar Allan Poe's "The Masque of the Red Death." This lesson plan provides follow-up questions and enrichments to help teachers guide students toward a usable, repeatable method for analyzing irony.

OBJECTIVES

1. Learn the definition of irony.
2. Practice using concrete strategies for analyzing irony.
3. Participate effectively in a range of conversations and collaborations to express ideas and build upon the ideas of others.

ELA Common Core Standards:
Reading: Literature - RL.11-12.1, RL.11-12.6
Speaking & Listening - SL.11-12.1.A, SL.11-12.1.C, SL.11-12.2

RESOURCES

Access 1 handout (Beginner)
Access 2 handout (Intermediate)
Access 3 handout (Advanced)
Access 4 handout (Approaching)

1. DEFINE

Core Path	Access Path
Watch. Watch the Concept Definition video on irony with your students. Ask students to write the definition of each type and the key evidence they can examine to determine irony in their notes. Pause the video at these key moments to discuss the information with your students: 1. 0:21 – Ben and Christina's first interchange demonstrates what type of irony? 2. 1:27 – What is the difference between verbal irony and situational irony? How do they express different attitudes? 3. 2:06 – Tell about an example of dramatic irony that you have seen in a TV show or a movie. What was the purpose of the irony?	**English Learners All Levels & Approaching** **Match.** Have students complete the matching exercise on the Access 1, 2, 3, and 4 handouts as they watch the video. Answers are located at the end of the lesson plan online.
Read and Discuss. After watching the Concept Definition video, have students read the definition of irony. Either in small groups or as a whole class, use these questions to engage students in a discussion about irony. 1. If someone says that an explanation is "clear as mud," how is that an example of verbal irony? (Because mud isn't clear at all, the expression shows a contrast between what is said and what is meant by the words a speaker uses.) 2. Can a story or novel have both situational irony and dramatic irony? Why or why not? (Yes. The author may surprise a reader by confronting a reader's expectations of action with a twist or surprise event that they weren't expecting. Then, later, the author might share a secret with readers that will surprise characters in the story.)	**Beginner & Approaching** **Complete a Chart.** To prepare students to participate in the discussion, have them complete the chart on the Access 1 and 4 handouts as they read the definition. The correct answers are located at the end of the lesson plan online. **Intermediate & Advanced** **Discuss Prompts.** To help these students participate in the discussion, prompt them with questions that can be answered with a few words, such as: • What kind of irony is sarcasm? (verbal irony) • Who knows more in dramatic irony, the audience or the characters? (the audience) • If a policeman got pulled over for speeding, what kind of irony would this be? (situational irony)

Core Path	Access Path
3. What are some examples of verbal irony that you have heard recently, either in everyday conversation or on a TV show? (Answers will vary. Students may give an example of verbal irony from a conversation with a friend, or an example of situational irony from a movie or television program.)	**Beyond** **Discuss.** Have students think of movies or books that use irony. Compile a list of examples. Have students identify the type(s) of irony used in each example. How does the irony enhance the movie or book? What would the movie or book be like if it did not include irony?
	Extend **Tech Infusion** **Create.** Have small groups create comedy sketches that include examples of at least two types of irony. Remind students that they can choose from the following options: verbal irony, situational irony, and dramatic irony. Record the groups' performances and post the videos to a class YouTube channel.

2. MODEL

Core Path	Access Path
Read and Annotate. Have students independently read the Model section. As they read, ask students to use the annotation tool to: • highlight key points • ask questions • identify places where the Model applies the strategies laid out in the Identification and Application section • comment on the effect that irony has on the text's meaning	**Note:** During this portion of the lesson, instruction shifts from whole group to individual work. Use this time to work one-on-one or in small groups with Beginning, Intermediate, Advanced, and Approaching students. **Beginner & Intermediate** **Coach the Reading.** Work with these students (either individually or in small groups) to fill out the guided reading questions on the Access 1 and 2 handouts. Have Beginning students refer to the glossary on the Access 1 handout to help them determine the meaning of difficult words (note: provide the Access 1 handout glossary to Intermediate students if necessary). Let students know they'll use these answers to help participate in the discussion about the Model. Sample answers for this exercise are located at the end of the lesson plan online.

Core Path	Access Path
	Advanced **Identify Evidence.** Ask Advanced students to complete the identifying evidence exercise on the Access 3 handout. Let students know that they'll use these answers to help participate in the discussion about the Model. Sample answers for this exercise are located at the end of the lesson plan online. **Approaching** **Guided Reading.** Have students complete the guided reading questions on the Access 4 handout as they read. Let them know that they'll use these answers to help participate in the discussion about the Model. Sample answers for this exercise are located at the end of the lesson plan online.
Discuss. After students read the Model text, use these questions to facilitate a whole group discussion that helps students understand how to determine and analyze the author's use of irony within the passage: 1. Which type of irony does the Model focus on? (situational irony) What is the definition of this type of irony? (a contrast between what the reader expects to happen and what actually occurs) 2. In the story "The Masque of the Red Death," what expectation does the author set up for readers, and what actually occurs? (Readers likely expect that the people will be safe from the Red Death because they are sealed away in an abbey. However, the Red Death gets into the abbey and kills all of the people anyway.) 3. How does the narrator emphasize the irony of the story's ending? (The narrator focuses on the dagger hitting the floor after Prospero's death to emphasize that he is unable to save his own life, despite the precautions he has taken.)	

Core Path	Access Path
	Extend **Talk Together.** Pair students and have them discuss the passages from the story that are included in the Model. Ask them to explain how the first passage builds readers' expectations and how the second passage upends those expectations. If they were not surprised by the story's ending, have them explain the textual evidence they used to build their own expectations.

3. YOUR TURN

Core Path	Access Path
Assess and Explain. Have students answer the comprehension questions to test for understanding. Share the explanations for Parts A and B (located online) with your students.	
	Extend **Tech Infusion** **Create.** Have students work in pairs to create a visual representation of the Red Death as it is described in the story. Offer them the choice of creating it on paper or using an art app such as AWW (https://awwapp.com/). Then have them share these images with another pair of students and discuss each pair's visual interpretation.

SKILL:
Compare and Contrast

OVERVIEW

Comparing and contrasting is a useful skill for examining two works of literature. It can often provide additional insights that might not be apparent when studying the works separately. This lesson plan provides follow-up questions and enrichments to help teachers guide students toward a usable, repeatable method for comparing and contrasting two works of literature.

OBJECTIVES

1. Learn the definition of compare and contrast.
2. Practice using concrete strategies for comparing and contrasting.
3. Participate effectively in a range of conversations and collaborations to express ideas and build upon the ideas of others.

ELA Common Core Standards:
Reading: Literature - RL.11-12.1, RL.11-12.9
Speaking & Listening - SL.11-12.1.A, SL.11-12.1.C, SL.11-12.2

RESOURCES

Access 1 handout (Beginner)
Access 2 handout (Intermediate)
Access 3 handout (Advanced)
Access 4 handout (Approaching)

1. DEFINE

Core Path	Access Path
Watch. Watch the Concept Definition video on compare and contrast with your students. Make sure your students understand the difference between comparing and contrasting, and how it can help to unlock meaning in a given text. Pause the video at these key moments to discuss the information with your students: 1. 0:16 – In addition to the example in the video, what are some other things you can compare and contrast? Why do you think people like to compare and contrast things? 2. 1:34 – When is it helpful to compare and contrast two (or more) different texts, or characters within a text? How does this help to make you a more active reader? 3. 1:58 – What do you think we gain by comparing a character's actions or choices to our own? How do you respond differently to a character who has more in common with you, versus a character who is more different?	**English Learners All Levels & Approaching** **Match.** Have students complete the matching exercise on the Access 1, 2, 3, and 4 handouts as they watch the video. Answers are located at the end of the lesson plan online.
Read and Discuss. After watching the Concept Definition video, have students read the definition of compare and contrast. Use these questions to engage students in a discussion, either in small groups or as a whole class, about compare and contrast. 1. Which other story in this unit would it be interesting to compare and contrast with "The Masque of the Red Death"? (Students might say that, since "Young Goodman Brown" was written during the same time period, comparing the two stories could show some interesting similarities and differences in style, themes, and content.)	**Beginner & Approaching** **Complete the Sentences.** To prepare students to participate in the discussion, have them complete the sentences on the Access 1 and 4 handouts as they read the definition. The correct answers are located at the end of the lesson plan online. **Intermediate & Advanced** **Discuss Prompts.** To help these students participate in the discussion, prompt them with questions that can be answered with a few words, such as: • What do we do when we compare and contrast? (distinguish between two or more things)

Core Path	Access Path
2. Which horror movies does "The Masque of the Red Death" remind you of? Why? (Answers will vary, but students should come up with the title of a movie that has elements of surprise and horror and can be compared and contrasted to the story.) 3. Can you think of a time when you compared and contrasted things in your everyday life? What strategies did you use? (Students may remember comparing themselves with their friends or contrasting their attributes, behaviors, and family acceptance with those of their siblings.)	• What is one way we compare and contrast every day? (choosing what to wear, what to buy, or where to go) • What is something you will need to compare and contrast in the future? (Answers will vary, but examples may include jobs, cars, and colleges.) **Beyond** **Discuss.** Have students select a book they've read that has been turned into a movie. Compile a list of examples. Have students discuss how the books and films are similar and different. What parts remained the same? What parts were changed or added? Why do you think the filmmakers made these changes? Which did you enjoy more: the book or the film? Why?
	Extend **Tech Infusion** **Create.** Have partners use Google Drawing to create a flowchart telling how to compare and contrast two pieces of literature. Students should base their charts on the information in the Definition and the Identification and Application sections of the student text.

2. MODEL

Core Path	Access Path
Read and Annotate. Have students independently read the Model section. As they read, ask students to use the annotation tool to: • highlight key points • ask questions	**Note:** During this portion of the lesson, instruction shifts from whole group to individual work. Use this time to work one-on-one or in small groups with Beginning, Intermediate, Advanced, and Approaching students.

Core Path	Access Path
• identify places where the Model applies the strategies laid out in the Identification and Application section • comment on the similarities and differences they see in the two stories mentioned in the Model	**Beginner & Intermediate** **Coach the Reading.** Work with these students (either individually or in small groups) to fill out the guided reading questions on the Access 1 and 2 handouts. Have Beginning students refer to the glossary on the Access 1 handout to help them determine the meaning of difficult words (note: provide the Access 1 handout glossary to Intermediate students if necessary). Let students know they'll use these answers to help participate in the discussion about the Model. Sample answers for this exercise are located at the end of the lesson plan online. **Advanced** **Identify Evidence.** Ask Advanced students to complete the identifying evidence exercise on the Access 3 handout. Let students know that they'll use these answers to help participate in the discussion about the Model. Sample answers for this exercise are located at the end of the lesson plan online. **Approaching** **Guided Reading.** Have students complete the guided reading questions on the Access 4 handout as they read. Let them know that they'll use these answers to help participate in the discussion about the Model. Sample answers for this exercise are located at the end of the lesson plan online.
Discuss. After students read the Model text, use these questions to facilitate a whole group discussion that helps students understand how to compare and contrast elements of two stories: 1. What does the compare-and-contrast analysis focus on? (how the two authors turn realistic situations into nightmares) 2. How are "The Masque of the Red Death" and "Young Goodman Brown" similar? (They are both works of Gothic American fiction; they both have the same theme; they both use description to develop theme.) How are "The Masque of the Red Death" and "Young Goodman Brown" different? (Their settings are very different.)	

Core Path	Access Path
3. What are primordial symbols? (universal symbols that trigger something in the unconscious) What other symbols do "The Masque of the Red Death" and "Young Goodman Brown" use to develop their themes? ("Masque" uses a chiming clock to symbolize the inevitability of death. "Goodman Brown" uses fire to represent a revelation and pink to represent innocence.)	
	Extend **Practice.** Have small groups choose two other passages from the stories and do a compare-and-contrast analysis similar to the one shown in the Model. Students can focus either on reality versus the supernatural or on another characteristic of Gothic fiction. Have each group share their findings with another group.

3. YOUR TURN

Core Path	Access Path
Assess and Explain. Have students answer the comprehension questions to test for understanding. Share the explanations for Parts A and B (located online) with your students.	
	Extend **Tech Infusion** **Share and Discuss.** Have students complete the Your Turn section in class. Poll students about their responses and as a class discuss the different strategies they used to determine the correct answers. Ask students which aspects of the questions they found hard and what strategies they used to overcome the difficulty. Conduct your poll by asking your students to complete a handout with questions or use Poll Everywhere (www.polleverywhere.com) or Socrative (www.socrative.com).

CLOSE READ:
The Masque of the Red Death

OVERVIEW

Edgar Allan Poe's "The Masque of the Red Death" is set in medieval Europe and tells the story of Prince Prospero's failed efforts to save himself and his wealthy friends from a plague called the Red Death. The Close Read gives students the opportunity to analyze a foundational work of American literature, identify themes, and analyze irony.

OBJECTIVES

1. Complete a close reading of a passage of literature.
2. Practice and apply concrete strategies for identifying irony and comparing and contrasting elements in "The Masque of the Red Death."
3. Participate effectively in a range of conversations and collaborations to express ideas and build upon the ideas of others.
4. Prewrite, plan, and produce clear and coherent writing in response to a prompt.

ELA Common Core Standards:
Reading: Literature - RL.11-12.1, RL.11-12.2, RL.11-12.4, RL.11-12.6, RL.11-12.9, RL.11-12.10
Writing - W.11-12.4, W.11-12.5, W.11-12.6, W.11-12.9.A, W.11-12.10
Speaking & Listening - SL.11-12.1.A, SL.11-12.1.B, SL.11-12.1.C, SL.11-12.1.D, SL.11-12.6
Language - L.11-12.4.A, L.11-12.4.C, L.11-12.4.D

RESOURCES

"The Masque of the Red Death" Vocabulary handout
Access 1 handout (Beginner)
Access 2 handout (Intermediate)
Access 3 handout (Advanced)
Access 4 handout (Approaching)

1. INTRODUCTION

Core Path	Access Path
Define and Compare. Project the vocabulary words and definitions onto the board or provide students with handouts, so they can copy the vocabulary into their notebooks. Suggest that students consult general and specialized reference materials, both print and digital, to compare the precise meaning of a specific word with their initial vocabulary predictions from the First Read. Review words that students defined incorrectly to understand why they were unable to use context clues or other tools to develop usable definitions.	**Beginner & Intermediate** **Complete a Chart.** Have students complete the chart on the Access 1 and 2 handouts by writing the correct word for each of the definitions. **Advanced & Beyond** **Write in Journals.** Have students write a journal entry using all of their vocabulary words. Remind them to write sentences that communicate the meaning of the words they are using. **Approaching** **Graphic Organizer.** To support students in comparing their predictions with the correct meanings, have them complete the graphic organizer on the Access 4 handout to record the vocabulary words, their initial analysis, and the definitions. Then have them write sentences using the words.
Review. Have students complete the fill-in-the-blanks vocabulary worksheet attached to the lesson plan online. Answers for the worksheet are listed at the end of the lesson plan online.	
	Extend **Tech Infusion** **Create.** Have partners create a crossword puzzle using the vocabulary words and a website such as Puzzle Maker (http://www.discoveryeducation.com/free-puzzlemaker/). Students should write clues in their own words rather than simply copying and pasting definitions. Pairs should exchange puzzles when finished and solve them.

2. READ

Core Path	Access Path
Model Close Reading. Project the text onto the board and model a close reading of the first three paragraphs using the annotation strategies mentioned below. While modeling annotation strategies, make notes that tie the text to the focus skill and demonstrate what students are looking for as they read. Some guidance for you as you annotate for your students: • As the Skills lesson on irony explains, there are three types of irony: verbal, situational, and dramatic. • In the first paragraph, I do not see any expressions that mean the opposite of their literal meaning, so there doesn't seem to be any verbal irony so far. • The narrator is not telling me anything that the characters do not know, such as what one of them is thinking or what will happen later. That means there is no dramatic irony because readers do not know something that the characters are unaware of. • So I will focus on situational irony. The second paragraph says that the prince and the courtiers seal themselves into an abbey because the Red Death is devastating the country. I read that "The abbey was amply provisioned," which makes me think the people will be safe in the abbey for a long time. I need to keep reading to see if the author includes situational irony to upend this expectation.	
Read and Annotate. Read the Skills Focus questions as a class so your students know what they should pay close attention to as they read. Then have students read and annotate the story. Ask students to use the annotation tool as they read to 1. respond to the Skills Focus section. 2. ask questions about how the author uses irony	**Note:** While on-grade-level students are reading and annotating, work one-on-one or in small groups with Beginning, Intermediate, Advanced, and Approaching students to support them as they read and annotate the text.

Core Path	Access Path
3. make connections between the author's use of irony and its relationship to the themes in the story. 4. identify key information, examples, and details that readers can use to compare and contrast this story with another story from this time period, such as "Young Goodman Brown." 5. note unfamiliar vocabulary 6. capture their reaction to the ideas and examples in the text As they reread the story, remind students to use the comprehension strategy of summarizing that they learned in the First Read.	**Beginner & Intermediate** **Summarize and Analyze the Text.** Work with these students to complete the sentence frames on the Access 1 and 2 handouts (note: the sentence frames for Intermediate students on the Access 2 handout contain fewer scaffolds). They will then use the completed sentence frames to help them analyze and annotate the text by completing the Skills Focus questions. Refer to the sample Skills Focus answers to help them complete the sentence frames and annotate the text. **Advanced** **Work in Pairs.** Pair these students with more proficient English speakers to work together on analyzing and annotating the text to complete the Skills Focus questions. If these students need more support, have them use the sentence frames on the Access 3 handout as they work with their more proficient peers. **Approaching** **Summarize the Text.** Have these students discuss and complete the text summary on the Access 4 handout and use their summary to help them analyze and annotate the text by completing the Skills Focus questions. Correct answers for the summary are at the end of the lesson plan online. Also refer to the sample Skills Focus answers to aid students with their annotations.
Discuss. After students have read the text, use the sample responses to the Skills Focus questions at the bottom of the lesson plan online to discuss the reading and the process of analyzing irony and identifying elements that can be compared and contrasted with other stories from this time period.	**Extend** **Pair and Share.** Ask students to share and discuss their annotations, in small groups or pairs, with a focus on irony.

Core Path	Access Path
Make sure that students have acquired and accurately use academic-specific words and phrases related to the skill and demonstrate a command of formal English appropriate to the discussion. To help facilitate discussions, refer to Collaborative Discussions in the Speaking & Listening Handbook.	You can provide students with questions to guide their discussion: 1. What is your expectation after reading the first three paragraphs? Cite specific textual evidence to support your statements. (I expect that the prince will be punished in some way for throwing a big party while "the pestilence raged most furiously abroad.") 2. What kind of mood does Poe create through his descriptions of the masquerade ball? (Poe creates a mood of uncontrolled celebration with words like "delirious" and "wanton.") How does this affect your expectations about what will happen? Cite specific textual evidence to support your statements. (This deepens my feeling that something bad might happen because such debauchery doesn't usually end well.) 3. Are there examples of verbal irony or dramatic irony anywhere in the story? (There is no verbal irony because there are not any sentences that mean the opposite of what they say. There are hints of dramatic irony because some readers may figure out who the Red Death is before he kills Prospero and his guests.)
	Extend **Read and Discuss.** The American author O. Henry (William Sydney Porter) is considered a master of situational irony. Have students locate one of his short stories online and read it as a class. Then, discuss how the story is ironic.

3. WRITE

Core Path	Access Path
Prewrite and Plan. Read the prompt as a class and ask students to brainstorm about allegory in "The Masque of the Red Death" and "Young Goodman Brown." Students can brainstorm together either as a class or in small groups to begin planning their responses. Remind your students to look at the stories and their annotations to find textual evidence to support their ideas.	**Beginner & Intermediate** **Plan and Organize.** Have students complete the prewriting activity on the Access 1 and 2 handouts and then explain their ideas to a partner before they write. Explain to students that they need to choose details, examples, or quotes from the text that support their ideas and then explain how those details support their statements. For example, students might note that when the revellers seized the uninvited guest, they found that he was "untenanted by any tangible form." This shows that the figure was not a flesh-and-blood human, unlike the other characters in the story. They may compare this figure with the devil in "Young Goodman Brown." **Approaching** **Plan and Organize.** Have students complete the prewriting activity on the Access 4 handout to organize their thoughts before they write.
Discuss. Project these instructions for the peer review onto the board and review them with your class, so they know what they are looking for when they begin to provide their classmates with feedback: • How does this essay help you understand how each story functions as an allegory? • Does the writer identify a message about human nature in each story? Does that explanation make sense? • How clear is the writer's comparison and contrast of the stories? Does the writer include information about symbols, settings, characters, and the authors' attitudes toward these elements? • What sort of evidence does the writer use from the text to support his or her writing? • How well does the writer explain how that evidence supports his or her arguments?	

Core Path	Access Path
• Does the writer write using standard grammar and punctuation? Are there any weak spots? • What specific suggestions can you make to help the writer improve the response? • What thing(s) does this paper do especially well? After you've looked at the peer review instructions, review the rubric with students before they begin writing. Allow time for students briefly to pose and discuss any questions they may have about the peer review instructions and the rubric. Tell students how many peer reviews they will need to complete once they submit their writing.	
Write. Ask students to complete the writing assignment using textual evidence to support their answers. Once they have completed their writing, they should click "Submit."	
	Extend **Brainstorm.** Ask students to reread the prompt and think about which parts might be hardest to address in their response. Then have them brainstorm additional questions focused on these specific parts of their responses to help guide their peer reviewers.
Review. Once students complete their writing assignment, they should submit substantive feedback to two peers. Students should use their peers' feedback to improve their writing.	

BLAST:
Fear Itself

OVERVIEW

To better understand the influence of Gothic fiction in their own lives, students will learn about the popularity of supernatural literature and consider why people enjoy it so much. Students will explore research links that connect them to the science of fear and the influence of the paranormal in popular culture.

OBJECTIVES

1. Explore background information about the popularity of supernatural fiction and why people love reading supernatural or scary stories.
2. Research using hyperlinks to a range of information about supernatural fiction and the human response to fear, including articles, an interview, and an overview of why paranormal literature is so popular among young adults.

ELA Common Core Standards:
Reading: Informational Text - RI.11-12.1
Writing - W.11-12.1.A, W.11-12.1.B, W.11-12.5, W.11-12.6
Speaking & Listening - SL.11-12.1.A, SL.11-12.1.C, SL.11-12.1.D

RESOURCES

Access 1 handout (Beginner)
Access 2 handout (Intermediate)
Access 4 handout (Approaching)

TITLE/DRIVING QUESTION

Core Path	Access Path
Discuss. As a class, read aloud the title and driving question for this Blast. Ask students why they like or dislike supernatural stories. What do they already know about the influence of the supernatural on literature and popular culture? Do they have a favorite supernatural book, movie, or television series? Do they have a favorite supernatural creature or character? Taking into account ideas generated by their classmates, do they have a sense of why people love supernatural stories? Remind students that they'll be returning to this question for their formal entries after they've written a draft and read and discussed the Background and some of the Research Links.	**English Learners All Levels** **Discuss a Visual.** Have students view an image of someone experiencing fear, such as the one at http://tinyurl.com/ozx5e7t. Discuss how the image depicts someone who is afraid but who also wants to see what will happen next, prompting students with questions such as: • What is happening in this photo? Why is the woman peeking through her fingers? • What are some reasons why someone might cover their eyes like this? • What emotions do you think the woman is feeling? • Do you think the woman is enjoying feeling this way? Why or why not?
Draft. In their notebooks or on scrap paper, have students draft their initial responses to the driving question. This will provide them with a baseline response that they will be altering as they gain more information about the topic in the Background and Research Links sections of the assignment.	**Beginner & Intermediate** **Draft with Sentence Frame.** When drafting their initial response to the driving question, have students refer to this Blast sentence frame on their Access 1 and 2 handouts: • People enjoy supernatural stories because ____________________. Point out these two key features of the sentence frame: 1. The introductory clause "People enjoy supernatural stories" borrows language directly from the Blast driving question to provide a response. 2. Ask students to make special note of the word "because," which invites them to list a reason or reasons why people enjoy supernatural stories.

BACKGROUND

Core Path	Access Path
Read. Have students read the Blast background to provide context for the driving question.	**Beginner & Intermediate** **Read with Support.** Have students read the Blast background to provide context for the driving question. When they encounter unfamiliar words or phrases, have students refer to the glossary on their Access 1 and 2 handouts. If there are unfamiliar words that are not included in their glossary, encourage students to check a dictionary or online reference tool, like http://dictionary.reference.com. **Approaching** **Read and Summarize.** Have students read the Blast background to provide context for the driving question. As they read, ask students to complete the fill-in-the-blanks summary of the background provided on their Access 4 handout. When they encounter unfamiliar words or phrases, have students refer to the glossary on their Access 4 handout.
Discuss. Pair students and have them discuss the following questions: 1. How have supernatural stories had a long-lasting effect on audiences? (The characters become a part of our "collective cultural consciousness," such as when people dress as Frankenstein's monster on Halloween.) 2. Why do some people like feeling scared? (The body releases dopamine and adrenaline when we're scared, but these chemicals also make us feel happy and excited.) 3. How can supernatural stories help us feel courageous? (They make it possible for us to imagine battling supernatural creatures, like vampires or zombies, that we can't fight in real life.)	**Beginner** **Discuss.** Pair Beginning with Advanced (or Beyond) students and have them use the dialogue starter on their Access 1 handout to discuss the topic. Advise them to return to the dialogue and switch roles if they get stuck. **Intermediate** **Discuss.** Pair Intermediate with Advanced (or Beyond) students and have them use the dialogue starter on their Access 2 handout to discuss the topic. Advise them to return to the dialogue and switch roles if they get stuck. If their conversation is progressing smoothly, encourage them to continue the discussion beyond the dialogue starter sheet. They can expand their conversations to discuss other reasons why people enjoy supernatural stories.

Core Path	Access Path
4. How many Americans believe in paranormal activities, and how does this belief relate to supernatural literature? (Almost 75 percent of Americans said they believe in the paranormal. This suggests that supernatural literature is so popular because a lot of people think supernatural events could happen in real life.) 5. Why do some people want to believe in ghosts or other supernatural creatures? (to explain unexplainable occurrences)	
Brainstorm. Remind students about the driving question for this Blast: Why do people enjoy supernatural stories? In their notebooks, ask students to make three columns and label them "Character/Creature," "Frightening," and "Fascinating." Start with the first column, and have students fill in the name of a specific supernatural character (e.g., Dracula) or a type of supernatural creature (e.g., vampires). Then have them list reasons why that creature is both frightening and fascinating. Here's a short example of how this might look:	

Character/ Creature	Frightening	Fascinating
vampires	They're deadly and hard to kill.	They're super strong and can live forever.

RESEARCH LINKS

Core Path	Access Path
Examine and Explore. Use these activities and questions to guide students' exploration of the Research Links: 1. The Background asks why people love supernatural scary stories. Which Research Link might provide an answer to this key question? ("Why We Like To Be Scared: The Science Behind the Scream" or "Why Do We Like To Be Scared?" These links likely explain why people like to feel fear.) 2. Ask students to look at "Why Our Brains Love Horror Movies." What does the writer say about why people go see horror films? (They seek the safe thrill as a way to escape their normal lives.) According to the writer, why are young people more likely to enjoy scary movies? (Young people are more likely to seek "intense experiences." Also, older people have had "scary" life experiences, so they no longer need to experience scary scenarios on a movie screen.) Although scary movies are popular at the box office, why don't people often list horror as their favorite genre? (Horror films often leave audiences feeling "nervous and unsettled," which may be fun in the moment but does not lead to fond memories.) 3. Have students explore "Where The Coolest Kids Are, Like, Undead" and "The Success of Paranormals." Given your understanding of these two pieces, why you think supernatural book series, movies, and TV shows are so popular among young adults? Discuss this in small groups or as a class.	

Core Path	Access Path
	Extend **Research, Discuss, and Present.** 1. Assign each group one link to explore in depth. 2. Ask them to discuss the information: a. What are the key points made in this resource? b. What inferences did you make as you read? c. What did you learn about this "big idea" from reading this research? d. How did this help you to better understand the topic? e. What questions does your group have after exploring this link? 3. Allow students time to informally present what they learned.
	Extend **Tech Infusion** **Share.** As students explore the links, encourage them to use an online poster and collage maker, such as Glogster (http://edu.glogster.com), to create an interactive poster about supernatural fiction. Students can combine text, music, photos, and videos that effectively explain why supernatural literature is so popular. Then they can share their posters with the class.

QUIKPOLL

Core Path	Access Path
Participate. Answer the poll question. Have students use information from the background and research links to explain their answers.	

NUMBER CRUNCH

Core Path	Access Path
Predict, Discuss, and Click. Before students click on the number, break them into pairs and have them make predictions about what they think the number is related to. After they've clicked the number, ask students if they are surprised by the revealed information.	

CREATE YOUR BLAST

Core Path	Access Path
Blast. Ask students to write their Blast response in 140 characters or less.	**Beginner** **Blast with Support.** Have students refer back to the sentence frame on their Access 1 handout that they used to create their original Blast draft. Ask them to use this frame to write and enter their final Blast. **Intermediate** **Blast with Support.** Have students attempt to draft their Blast without the sentence frame on their Access 2 handout. If students struggle to compose their Blast draft without the sentence frame, remind them to reference it for support. **Beyond** **Write a Claim.** Ask students to use their answer to the poll question to write a strong claim that could be used as the foundation for a piece of argumentative writing. Once students have written their claims, ask them to read the claims to a small group of their peers. This activity will provide them practice writing claims, as well as expose them to claims written by their peers.
Review. After students have completed their own Blasts, ask them to review the Blasts of their peers and provide feedback.	

Core Path	Access Path
	Extend **Discuss.** As a whole class or in groups, identify a few strong Blasts and discuss what made those responses so powerful. As a group, analyze and discuss what characteristics make a Blast interesting or effective.
	Extend **Revise.** Resend a second version of this Blast assignment to your students and have them submit revised versions of their original Blasts. Do the same responses make the Top 10? How have the answers improved from the first submissions?

FIRST READ:
Pride and Prejudice

OVERVIEW

Jane Austen's classic novel *Pride and Prejudice* examines the upper class of Regency Britain and exposes its fascination with marriage and money through the love story of Elizabeth Bennet. The First Read gives students the opportunity to experience the text with a limited context.

OBJECTIVES

1. Perform an initial reading of a text and demonstrate comprehension by responding to short analysis and inference questions with textual evidence.
2. Practice defining vocabulary words using context.
3. Participate effectively in a range of conversations and collaborations to express ideas and build upon the ideas of others.
4. Practice acquiring and using academic vocabulary correctly.

ELA Common Core Standards:
Reading: Literature - RL.11-12.1, RL.11-12.4, RL.11-12.10
Writing - W.11-12.7
Speaking & Listening - SL.11-12.1.A, SL.11-12.1.B, SL.11-12.1.C, SL.11-12.1.D, SL.11-12.2, SL.11-12.3, SL.11-12.6
Language - L.11-12.4.A, L.11-12.4.D, L.11-12.6

RESOURCES

Access 1 handout (Beginner)
Access 2 handout (Intermediate)
Access 3 handout (Advanced)
Access 4 handout (Approaching)

ACCESS COMPLEX TEXT

This excerpt from *Pride and Prejudice* features Mr. and Mrs. Bennet discussing a new gentleman who has moved into the neighborhood. Their exchange is characteristic of Jane Austen's style, using witty dialogue to reveal characters and themes rather than relying mostly on a narrator. To help students understand the characters and the structure of the world they inhabit, use the following ideas to provide scaffolded instruction for a first reading of the more complex features of this text:

- **Connection of Ideas** - Jane Austen's writing, especially in the dialogue of Mr. Bennet, often features irony and satire, which may challenge some readers since what is said does not always reflect what is meant. Austen also leaves off dialogue tags in many instances, so struggling readers may have a hard time keeping track of who is speaking.
- **Prior Knowledge** - The Regency England setting and social norms will be unfamiliar to some readers. For example, readers may not understand Mrs. Bennet's preoccupation with finding a husband for her daughters or the social norms that require Mr. Bennet to make the first introductions.
- **Specific Vocabulary** - Some archaic vocabulary words and syntax, such as *must be in want of a wife* and *Netherfield Park is let at last*, may present a challenge to some readers.

1. INTRODUCTION

Core Path	Access Path
Watch. As a class, watch the video preview of *Pride and Prejudice*.	**English Learners All Levels** **Fill in the Blanks.** Ask students to use their Access 1, 2, and 3 handouts to fill in the blanks of the transcript for the preview's voiceover as they watch the preview along with their classmates. Answers are located at the end of the lesson plan online.
Read. Individually or as a class, read the introduction for *Pride and Prejudice*. The introduction provides context for the excerpt from Chapter 1.	**English Learners All Levels & Approaching** **Read and Listen.** Ask students to read and listen to the introduction for *Pride and Prejudice*. Have them refer to the "Introduction Glossary" on their Access 1, 2, 3, and 4 handouts for definitions of key vocabulary terms. If there are unfamiliar words that are not included in their glossary, encourage students to check a dictionary or online reference tool, like http://dictionary.reference.com.

Core Path	Access Path
Build Background. In pairs or small groups, ask students to use devices to research the British Regency period. Assign each group a topic to investigate. Remind students to include relevant facts, definitions, and concrete details in their research: • Politics in the Regency period • The novel as entertainment in the Regency period • The role of women in the Regency period • Society in the Regency period If you are in a low-tech classroom, you can provide photocopies of articles about the Regency period for students to read and discuss.	**Beginner & Intermediate** **Build Background.** Have groups of students view still images from a film adaptation of *Pride and Prejudice*. See, for example, http://tinyurl.com/ok3hvq8 and http://tinyurl.com/ogyy7np. Have students work in pairs and discuss what the images suggest about the characters and life in Regency society. **Approaching** **Build Background.** Have groups of students view still images from a film adaptation of *Pride and Prejudice*. See, for example, http://tinyurl.com/ok3hvq8 and http://tinyurl.com/ogyy7np. Have students work in pairs and discuss what the images suggest about the characters and life in Regency society. Ask them to think about these questions: • What are the characters doing in these scenes? What emotions do they show? • What can you infer about Regency society based on the costumes and sets? • Do you think it would be easy or difficult to succeed in society during this time? Why?
	Extend **Analyze and Discuss a Quote.** "[Austen was] a writer who believed the clash of personalities was as meaningful as—perhaps more meaningful than—the clash of sabers. For those of us who suspect that all the mysteries of life are contained in the microcosm of the family, that personal relationships prefigure all else, the work of Jane Austen is the Rosetta Stone of literature." (Anna Quindlen, http://tinyurl.com/ofve6sr)

Core Path	Access Path
	1. How would you restate this quote in your own words? 2. How might personal relationships help people to better understand their life experiences? 3. Do you agree with this quote? Why or why not? 4. Does this quote make you want to read more of Jane Austen's work? Why or why not?

2. READ

Core Path	Access Path
Make Predictions about Vocabulary. There are five bold vocabulary words in the text. As students read the text, ask them to make predictions about what they think each bold vocabulary word means based on the context clues in the sentence. Have students use the annotation tool to make their predictions. It might be helpful to model this for students before they begin reading. Either using the board or projecting the actual text, focus in on the sentence that uses the word "scrupulous": • "You are over-scrupulous surely. I dare say Mr. Bingley will be very glad to see you; and I will send a few lines by you to assure him of my hearty consent to his marrying whichever he chooses of the girls: though I must throw in a good word for my little Lizzy."	**Note:** This exercise, which extends vocabulary instruction, should be completed when the class shifts from whole group instruction to individual work during the "Read and Annotate" exercise. **Beginner, Intermediate & Approaching Pair Practice.** 1. Pair students with more proficient readers. 2. Give them an additional sentence that contains a new vocabulary word. 3. Ask the students to complete a Think Aloud using the teacher-led Make Predictions about Vocabulary activity as a model, while the proficient student actively listens.

Core Path	Access Path
Model for the class how to use the overall structure and meaning of the sentence and the sentences around it, the word's position, and other clues to define the unfamiliar vocabulary word. In this case, point out these context clues: 1. Read both sentences closely. Mr. Bennet is saying that Mrs. Bennet is "over-scrupulous," so he means that her actions are too scrupulous, more than is needed. We can start by asking what Mrs. Bennet has been doing excessively. 2. What were Mrs. Bennet's actions before this line? She has been refusing to go meet Mr. Bingley until Mr. Bennet does so first. She says, "it will be impossible for us to visit him if you do not." 3. Mrs. Bennet's refusal to visit Mr. Bingley before Mr. Bennet does looks to be a social norm. Women did not go visit new gentleman until their husbands (or fathers) had already done so. So Mrs. Bennet is very concerned with doing things "properly," and this insistence is what Mr. Bennet thinks is being "over-scrupulous." From this, I can infer that "scrupulous" means following norms or morals. 4. I'll check my inferred meaning in a dictionary to make sure I am correct.	4. The student should use the context clues in the sentence to try to determine the meaning of the new vocabulary word. 5. After the student has completed the Think Aloud and made a prediction about the word's meaning, allow time for the proficient reader to add his/her own thoughts and clarify any points of confusion. 6. Once they've completed this Think Aloud, encourage them to use a dictionary to confirm the definition of the new vocabulary word. Have them refer to the "Text Glossary" on their Access 1, 2, and 4 handouts for definitions of key vocabulary terms in the text. Encourage them to add any additional vocabulary words or idioms they find in the text and look up definitions for those words and idioms online or in a dictionary.
Model Reading Comprehension Strategy. Before students begin reading, model the reading comprehension strategy of rereading by using this Think Aloud to talk students through the first few paragraphs of the text. First, explain to your students that rereading is valuable because: *strong readers understand that they may miss important points during a first read of a poem or complex text*	**Note:** This exercise, which extends instruction around reading comprehension strategies, should be completed when the class shifts from whole group instruction to individual work during the "Read and Annotate" exercise.

Core Path	Access Path
Model for students how rereading will help them better comprehend the selection and help drive their discussions. • In the first two paragraphs, the narrator makes several general comments about society. She introduces the idea that when a man enters a neighborhood, he is looked at only as a prospective husband by local families, and she says this is "universally acknowledged." This tells us that everyone in the novel is going to share and understand this idea. • As the first chapter continues, we are entered into a conversation about a new man moving to the neighborhood. Now the first two paragraphs make more sense. I'll go back and reread them. • On the second read, I catch more of the irony in those lines. The feelings of the man himself are "little known." The "truth" is actually not that the man is "in want of a wife"—it's that the families with daughters are in want of, a wealthy husband. At first it seemed that Austen was serious, but on rereading we can see that she actually seems to be poking fun at this dynamic.	**Beginner, Intermediate & Approaching** **Apply Reading Comprehension Strategy.** 1. In small groups, have students read the text. Ask students to complete the first column in the First Read and Second Read Chart located on the Access 1, 2, and 4 handouts. 2. Then, have groups reread the text in order to complete the second column in the First Read and Second Read Chart. 3. Call on groups to discuss their initial answers and their answers after having reread the text.
Read and Annotate. Have students independently read and annotate the excerpt. Ask students to use the annotation tool as they read to: 1. use context clues to analyze and determine the meaning of the bolded vocabulary terms 2. ask questions about passages of the text that may be unclear or unresolved 3. identify key information, events, characters, and connections between them 4. note unfamiliar vocabulary	**Beginner** **Coach the Reading.** While other students read, annotate, and discuss the text independently, work with Beginning students, listening to the audio of the text and pausing periodically or when any student has a question. Coach students in articulating their questions for the group and in highlighting and annotating the text. Have students use the Annotation Guide on the Access 1 handout to support them as they highlight and annotate the text. For further support, ask questions about the text such as: • Is there anything about the story that you don't understand? • What do you think will happen to the Bennets? • Why do you think marriage is so important in this society?

Core Path	Access Path
	Intermediate **Listen to the Audio.** Have these students listen to the audio of the text and use the Text Glossary on the Access 2 handout to help them with words or idioms that may be unfamiliar. If students need help with annotating the text, have them use the Annotation Guide on the Access 2 handout. After working with the Beginning students, you may wish to check this group's progress and provide support as needed. **Advanced** **Pair with Proficient Peers.** Have Advanced students work with English-proficient peers to read, annotate, and discuss the text. Have students use the Annotation Guide in the Access 3 handout to support them as they highlight and annotate the text. Encourage them to listen to the audio of the text if needed. **Approaching** **Use the Annotation Guide.** Have students use the Annotation Guide on the Access 4 handout to support them as they highlight and annotate the text.
Discuss. In small groups or pairs, have students discuss the questions and inferences they made while reading. To help facilitate discussions, refer to Collaborative Discussions in the Speaking & Listening Handbook. 1. Paraphrase the first sentence. What does this sentence mean? (A rich bachelor is always looking for a wife, and everyone knows this.) How does this sentence set up the rest of the chapter? (The chapter is about Mrs. Bennet's plan to marry one of her daughters to Mr. Bingley. Because he is wealthy, she assumes that he's looking for a wife and she hopes arranging a marriage with him will help her family.)	**English Learners All Levels & Approaching** Use the extra time while on- and beyond-grade-level students are discussing their first reads of the text to work individually and in small groups with Approaching readers and English Learners as outlined above. Should those students complete their first reads quickly, integrate them into the on- and beyond-grade-level discussion groups. Otherwise, English Learners and Approaching readers will be given an opportunity to participate in text discussions with their peers later in the lesson.

Core Path	Access Path
2. Why is Mrs. Bennet annoyed with her husband? (He shows little interest in trying to arrange a match between one of their daughters and Mr. Bingley, but she needs him to introduce the family.) What does this interaction suggest about English society at the time? (This suggests that men and women did not have the same concerns and that women were dependent on men for many things.) 3. Reread the descriptions of Mr. and Mrs. Bennet in the last paragraph. What evidence can you find to support these descriptions in the dialogue? (e.g., Mr. Bennet's sarcastic humor: "I have a high respect for your nerves. They are my old friends." Mrs. Bennet fancied herself nervous: "You have no compassion on my poor nerves.")	**Beyond** **Tech Infusion** **Brainstorm.** Pair students and ask them to brainstorm a list of qualities that they think an ideal man or woman would possess during this time period. Then have them discuss these qualities. How are the qualities for women and men similar? How are they different? How are they similar to the qualities that are valued in today's society? Encourage students to compose their lists in a Google Doc so they can share them with the class.

3. SYNCTV

Core Path	Access Path
Watch. As a class, watch the SyncTV video on *Pride and Prejudice*. Pause the video at these key moments to discuss the information with your students: 1. 4:32 – Why do the students discuss the Regency period in British history? How does this history support their discussion of the text? What information is irrelevant?	**Beginner & Intermediate** **Analyze the Discussion.** Have students use the "Analyze the Discussion" guide on the Access 1 and 2 handouts to identify key points in the discussion and the evidence the students use to determine those points. Sample answers are at the end of the lesson plan online.

Core Path	Access Path
2. 7:21 – What is the purpose of the discussion of romanticism? Does this topic support the students' assigned prompt? What evidence from the text could you add to this discussion to make it more relevant? 3. 8:41 – The students discuss the "subtext" of Austen's dialogue as being more than merely funny. What other examples of humorous subtext can you find in the chapter? Is Austen's purpose to entertain or is it more, as the students think? Support your answer with evidence from the excerpt.	**Advanced** **Analyze Regency England.** Have students discuss and complete the "Regency England" chart on the Access 3 handout, referring back to the SyncTV video as needed to clarify their answers. Sample answers appear at the end of the lesson plan online. **Approaching** **Analyze the Discussion.** Have students complete the chart on the Access 4 handout by listing textual evidence cited by the students in the video. Sample answers are at the end of the lesson plan online.

4. THINK

Core Path	Access Path
Answer and Discuss. Have students complete the Think questions and then use the peer review instructions and rubric to complete two peer reviews. Refer to the sample answers at the end of the lesson plan online to discuss responses with your students.	**Beginner & Intermediate** **Sentence Frames.** Have students use the sentence frames on the Access 1 and 2 handouts to support their responses to the Think questions. If necessary, distribute sentence frames to Advanced students as well. **Approaching** **Find the Evidence.** Have students use Find the Evidence on the Access 4 handout to help them identify the evidence needed to answer the questions.
SyncTV Style Discussion. Put students into heterogeneous small groups and give them a prompt to discuss. Remind them to model their discussions after the SyncTV episodes they have seen. Stress the importance of using both academic language and formal English correctly and citing textual evidence in their conversations to support their ideas.	**Beginner & Intermediate** **Use Sentence Frames.** Have these students use the sentence frames on the Access 1 and 2 handouts to help them participate in the discussion.

Core Path	Access Path
To help students prepare for, strategize, and evaluate their discussions, refer to the Collaborative Discussions section of the Speaking & Listening Handbook. Discussion prompt options: 1. Why does Mr. Bennet comment on Mrs. Bennet's appearance during their conversation? What does this show about Mr. Bennet? 2. What role does marriage play in the Bennets' lives? What inferences can you make about British society at this time based on this role? Have students review the key ideas expressed, demonstrating an understanding of multiple perspectives through reflection and paraphrasing. You may wish to have students create a video or audio recording of their SyncTV style discussion.	**Approaching** **Use Think Questions.** Remind these students to refer back to their answers to the Think questions to help them participate in the group discussion.
	Extend **Tech Infusion** **Write.** Ask students to imagine that they are one of the Bennet daughters they know about so far: Jane, Lizzy, or Lydia. Have them write a journal entry as that daughter, describing her parents' relationship with each other and with her, and discussing the arrival of Mr. Bingley in town. Tell students they can add their own ideas, but everything they add must be consistent with Austen's text. When students have finished, consider posting the journal entries on a Bennet diary blog using Blogger (https://blogger.com/) or Weebly (https://education.weebly.com/).

SKILL:
Character

OVERVIEW

Characters are a key narrative element. Students should be able to analyze characters in a novel excerpt by examining both direct and indirect characterization, as in the excerpt from *Pride and Prejudice*. This lesson plan provides follow-up questions and useful enrichments to help teachers guide students toward a usable, repeatable method for analyzing characters.

OBJECTIVES

1. Learn the definition of character.
2. Practice using concrete strategies for analyzing characters.
3. Participate effectively in a range of conversations and collaborations to express ideas and build upon the ideas of others.

ELA Common Core Standards:
Reading: Literature - RL.11-12.1, RL.11-12.3
Speaking & Listening - SL.11-12.1.A, SL.11-12.1.C, SL.11-12.2

RESOURCES

Access 1 handout (Beginner)
Access 2 handout (Intermediate)
Access 3 handout (Advanced)
Access 4 handout (Approaching)

1. DEFINE

Core Path	Access Path
Watch. Watch the Concept Definition video on character with your students. Make sure students write down and understand the definition of character traits, focusing in particular on how these traits may change or evolve over the course of a story's plot. Pause the video at these key moments to discuss the information with your students: 1. 0:18 – Who are some of your favorite characters from literary works you've read? Share a few of your favorite characters and discuss what it is about these characters that make them interesting or likable 2. 0:35 – Can you think of any other ways to understand character traits, aside from dialogue and action? How does a story's point of view determine how character traits are revealed? 3. 0:51 – Why might some characters in a story change or evolve over the course of a story's plot, and why might other characters not? Which characters in a story are most likely to change, and why?	**English Learners All Levels & Approaching** **Match.** Have students complete the matching exercise on the Access 1, 2, 3, and 4 handouts as they watch the video. Answers are located at the end of the lesson plan online.
Read and Discuss. After watching the Concept Definition video, have students read the definition of character. Either in small groups or as a whole class, use these questions to engage students in a discussion about characters. 1. The definition says that characters are "inseparable from the plot." What does that mean? (Without characters, you couldn't have a plot because characters' thoughts, feelings, actions, and reactions drive the plot.) Do you agree, or do you think characters are a separate element? (Answers may vary.)	**Beginner & Approaching** **Complete a Chart.** To prepare students to participate in the discussion, have them complete the chart on the Access 1 and 4 handouts as they read the definition. The correct answers are located at the end of the lesson plan online. **Intermediate & Advanced** **Discuss Prompts.** To help these students participate in the discussion, prompt them with questions that can be answered with a few words, such as: • How do characters drive the plot? (through thoughts, feelings, actions, and reactions) • How do authors construct characters? (through description, dialogue, and situations that reveal their personalities and traits)

Core Path	Access Path
2. Usually, some characters in a story are better developed than others. Why might an author choose to leave a character vague or underdeveloped? (The author may choose to reveal more about the character later in the story. He or she may also provide fewer details for less important characters who only play a small part in the story's plot.) When is strong development best? (Strong development is essential for main characters, such as the protagonist and the antagonist. Without character development, it is hard to find the characters interesting or believable.) 3. Can you think of any stories, novels, or movies in which a minor character was the most memorable character for you? Why was that? Did it hurt the quality of the story overall? (Answers will vary.)	• Which kind of character do you find more compelling: the protagonist or the antagonist? Why? (Answers will vary.) **Beyond** **Discuss.** Have students select a book they've read with a memorable antagonist. Compile a list of examples. Have students discuss how the antagonist affected the protagonist and the overall plot of the story. What motivated the antagonist? Why was the antagonist an interesting character? Do they ever root for the antagonist to win? Why or why not?
	Extend **Brainstorm.** After watching the video, ask students to think about their favorite character from the works you've read so far in class. Have students write a short alternate ending for that literary work, imagining that the character changed in one minor way. (For example, if Hamlet is someone's favorite character, the alternate ending could be that Hamlet stopped being indecisive, took initiative, and killed Claudius while he was at prayer.) Ask volunteers to share their alternate endings with the class and discuss the relationship between character traits and plot.

2. MODEL

Core Path	Access Path
Watch. Ask students to take notes on the SkillsTV video on characters in *Pride and Prejudice* as you watch together. Remind students to listen for the way the students use academic vocabulary related to the definition of character during their discussion. Pause the video at these key moments to discuss the information with your students: 1. 1:08 – What inferences do the students make about Mr. and Mrs. Bennet based on the excerpt Michael reads? What evidence from the text could be used to support these inferences? 2. 1:44 – How do the students use Mr. Bennet's reactions to characterize Mrs. Bennet? Is their conclusion supported by the rest of the excerpt? Why or why not? 3. 2:59 – Does Ian provide sufficient support for his statement that Mrs. Bennet's gossiping makes her childish? What evidence could he have provided? What other characteristics does Mrs. Bennet have that make her seem childlike?	**Beginner, Intermediate & Approaching** **Analyze the Discussion.** Have students watch the video again and complete the chart on the Access 1, 2, and 4 handouts as they watch the video. Sample answers for this exercise are located at the end of the lesson plan online. **Advanced** **Journals.** Have students note in their journals the strategies the students in the SkillsTV video use to analyze character.
Read and Annotate. Have students independently read the Model section. As they read, ask students to use the annotation tool to: • highlight key points • ask questions • identify places where the Model applies the strategies laid out in the Identification and Application section • comment on the effect that characters have on the plot and other story elements	**Note:** During this portion of the lesson, instruction shifts from whole group to individual work. Use this time to work one-on-one or in small groups with Beginning, Intermediate, Advanced, and Approaching students.

Core Path	Access Path
	Beginner & Intermediate **Coach the Reading.** Work with these students (either individually or in small groups) to fill out the guided reading questions on the Access 1 and 2 handouts. Have Beginning students refer to the glossary on the Access 1 handout to help them determine the meaning of difficult words (note: provide the Access 1 handout glossary to Intermediate students if necessary). Let students know they'll use these answers to help participate in the discussion about the Model. Sample answers for this exercise are located at the end of the lesson plan online. **Advanced** **Identify Evidence.** Ask Advanced students to complete the identifying evidence exercise on the Access 3 handout. Let students know that they'll use these answers to help participate in the discussion about the Model. Sample answers for this exercise are located at the end of the lesson plan online. **Approaching** **Guided Reading.** Have students complete the guided reading questions on the Access 4 handout as they read. Let them know that they'll use these answers to help participate in the discussion about the Model. Sample answers for this exercise are located at the end of the lesson plan online.

Core Path	Access Path
Discuss. After students read the Model text, use these questions to facilitate a whole group discussion that helps students understand how to analyze characters in the excerpt: 1. What is the difference between direct and indirect characterization? (Direct characterization is when an author describes a character's personality directly. Indirect characterization is when the character's personality is expressed through his or her own dialogue or actions.) Which form of characterization is more prevalent in the first section of *Pride and Prejudice* that the Model analyzes? (indirect characterization) 2. Which of Mrs. Bennet's character traits is first revealed? (She is a gossip.) What evidence does the Model provide for this trait? (Her friend Mrs. Long has just left their house—"has just been here"—and Mrs. Bennet immediately and "impatiently" goes to tell her husband the news.) 3. How does the direct characterization later in the excerpt support Mrs. Bennet's indirect characterization as a gossip? (The narrator says outright that the "solace" of Mrs. Bennet's life is "visiting and news.") 4. The narrator says of Mr. Bennet that "the experience of three-and-twenty years had been insufficient to make his wife understand his character." How does this statement reveal something about both characters? (This statement reveals that Mr. Bennet is somewhat complicated and hard to know; it also reveals that Mrs. Bennet has either failed to learn much about her husband, or she hasn't tried very hard.)	

Core Path	Access Path
	Extend **Write.** To further student understanding of indirect characterization, have students write a character analysis for a character from a popular television show or movie. Point out that since these types of media don't directly tell us what characters are like, viewers have to base their analysis on things the character says or does or how others respond to the character. Have students work in pairs to complete their analyses.

3. YOUR TURN

Core Path	Access Path
Assess and Explain. Have students answer the comprehension questions to test for understanding. Share the explanations for Parts A and B (located online) with your students.	
	Extend **Tech Infusion** **Blog the Characters.** Have students post blog entries for Mr. and Mrs. Bennet, in those characters' voices and in keeping with their character traits, on a class or personal blog. Encourage students to use the kind of informal, personal voice that bloggers often use. Students may wish to work in pairs.

CLOSE READ:
Pride and Prejudice

OVERVIEW

Pride and Prejudice is Jane Austen's classic novel of manners. Austen is famous for her use of witty dialogue to develop her characters. The Close Read gives students the opportunity to analyze Austen's dialogue in order to better understand the characters of Mr. and Mrs. Bennet.

OBJECTIVES

1. Complete a close reading of a passage of literature.
2. Practice and apply concrete strategies for analyzing characters and irony in an excerpt from *Pride and Prejudice*.
3. Participate effectively in a range of conversations and collaborations to express ideas and build upon the ideas of others.
4. Prewrite, plan, and produce clear and coherent writing in response to a prompt.

ELA Common Core Standards:
Reading: Literature - RL.11-12.1, RL.11-12.3, RL.11-12.4, RL.11-12.6
Writing - W.11-12.4, W.11-12.5, W.11-12.6, W.11-12.9.A, W.11-12.10
Speaking & Listening - SL.11-12.1.A, SL.11-12.1.B, SL.11-12.1.C, SL.11-12.1.D, SL.11-12.6
Language - L.11-12.4.A, L.11-12.4.C, L.11-12.4.D

RESOURCES

Pride and Prejudice Vocabulary handout
Pride and Prejudice Three-Column Chart
Access 1 handout (Beginner)
Access 2 handout (Intermediate)
Access 3 handout (Advanced)
Access 4 handout (Approaching)

1. INTRODUCTION

Core Path	Access Path
Define and Compare. Project the vocabulary words and definitions onto the board or provide students with handouts, so they can copy the vocabulary into their notebooks. Suggest that students consult general and specialized reference materials, both print and digital, to compare the precise meaning of a specific word with their initial vocabulary predictions from the First Read. Review words that students defined incorrectly to understand why they were unable to use context clues or other tools to develop usable definitions.	**Beginner & Intermediate** **Complete a Chart.** Have students complete the chart on the Access 1 and 2 handouts by writing the correct word for each of the definitions. **Advanced & Beyond** **Write in Journals.** Have students write a journal entry using all of their vocabulary words. Remind them to write sentences that communicate the meaning of the words they are using. **Approaching** **Graphic Organizer.** To support students in comparing their predictions with the correct meanings, have them complete the graphic organizer on the Access 4 handout to record the vocabulary words, their initial analysis, and the definitions. Then have them write sentences using the words.
Review. Have students complete the fill-in-the-blanks vocabulary worksheet attached to the lesson plan online. Answers for the worksheet are listed at the end of the lesson plan online.	
	Extend **Write.** Have students write a short, one-paragraph story that uses all the vocabulary words from *Pride and Prejudice*. Challenge students to make sure the meaning of each word is clear from the context. When students have finished their writing, have them trade papers with another student and check that each word is used correctly.

2. READ

Core Path	Access Path
Model Close Reading. Project the text onto the board and model a close reading of the first two paragraphs using the annotation strategies mentioned on the next page. While modeling annotation strategies, make notes that tie the text to the focus skill and demonstrate what students are looking for as they read. Some guidance for you as you annotate for your students: • The book opens with a famous first line: "It is a truth universally acknowledged that a single man in possession of a good fortune must be in want of a wife." This is a clear statement. But at the same time, I'm left with questions. Universally acknowledged by whom? It seems to me that people want many different things, and that not all wealthy men necessarily want a wife. • The second paragraph begins with "However little known the feelings or views of such a man may be." That's a clue that this paragraph might contradict that first sentence, since it says that actually, people don't know what the "single man" is thinking or feeling. • In a way, it does. The second sentence admits that it is not the wealthy man who wants a wife. It is the people around him who know this "truth" about him. • At the end of the second paragraph, the wealthy man is referred to as the "rightful property" of his neighbors' daughters. This phrase is ironic because if one of their daughters did marry this man, she would legally become his property, not the other way around. And the phrase "someone or other of their daughters" is humorous in this context, since we often think of marriage as needing to be a good match—not just any two people. We can see from these opening sentences that Austen sees these views as worthy of ridicule.	

Core Path	Access Path
• Further reading will undoubtedly expose more of Austen's views through the words she chooses and the meanings she assigns to those words. We can look for irony not only in situations but also in the dialogue she uses to reveal traits about her characters.	
Read and Annotate. Read the Skills Focus questions as a class, so your students know what they should pay close attention to as they read. Then have students read and annotate the excerpt. Ask students to use the annotation tool as they read to 1. respond to the Skills Focus section 2. ask questions about how Austen's attitudes are relayed through the dialogue of her characters 3. make connections between Austen's characters and the dialogue they use 4. identify key information, examples, and dialogue that characterizes some of the characters 5. note unfamiliar vocabulary 6. capture their reaction to the ideas and examples in the text As they read the text, remind students to use the comprehension strategy of rereading that they learned in the First Read.	**Note:** While on-grade-level students are reading and annotating, work one-on-one or in small groups with Beginning, Intermediate, Advanced, and Approaching students to support them as they read and annotate the text. **Beginner & Intermediate** **Summarize and Analyze the Text.** Work with these students to complete the sentence frames on the Access 1 and 2 handouts (note: the sentence frames for Intermediate students on the Access 2 handout contain fewer scaffolds). They will then use the completed sentence frames to help them analyze and annotate the text by completing the Skills Focus questions. Refer to the sample Skills Focus answers to help them complete the sentence frames and annotate the text. **Advanced** **Work in Pairs.** Pair these students with more proficient English speakers to work together on analyzing and annotating the text to complete the Skills Focus questions. If these students need more support, have them use the sentence frames on the Access 3 handout as they work with their more proficient peers. **Approaching** **Summarize the Text.** Have these students discuss and complete the text summary on the Access 4 handout and use their summary to help them analyze and annotate the text by completing the Skills Focus questions. Correct answers for the summary are at the end of the lesson plan online. Also refer to the sample Skills Focus answers to aid students with their annotations.

Core Path	Access Path
Discuss. After students have read the text, use the sample responses to the Skills Focus questions at the bottom of the lesson plan online to discuss the reading and the process of searching for the ways the author develops her characters. Make sure that students have acquired and accurately use academic-specific words and phrases related to the skill and demonstrate a command of formal English appropriate to the discussion. To help facilitate discussions, refer to Collaborative Discussions in the Speaking & Listening Handbook.	**Extend** **Pair and Share.** In small, heterogeneous groups or pairs, ask students to share and discuss their annotations with a focus on the characters presented in the selection. You can provide students with these questions to guide their discussion: 1. Why does Mrs. Bennet bring up the neighbors Sir William and Lady Lucas? What does this reveal about Mrs. Bennet? (Mrs. Bennet mentions the Lucases to convince her husband that other neighbors with daughters are going to visit Mr. Bingley. This shows that Mrs. Bennet is concerned that her neighbors will "beat" her in marrying their daughter to Mr. Bingley and helps demonstrate how marrying off her daughters really is a "business" to her.) 2. Do you think Mr. and Mrs. Bennet are well-matched? Cite specific textual evidence to support your opinion. (Answers will vary. Some students may respond that the Bennets are not well-matched because they do not share Mrs. Bennet's love of gossip and Mr. Bennet seems reluctant to help his wife. Others may respond that they are well-matched because Mr. Bennet's teasing is playful and he indulges his wife's need to gossip even though he is not interested in what she has to say.) 3. What is the role of marriage in the Bennets' world? How is that role different from today? (In the Bennets' world, a good marriage to a wealthy man is the one option for a good life for a young woman. Mrs. Bennet needs to focus on marrying off her daughters to provide for their futures. Today, women can have their own careers and don't need to marry for stability.)

Core Path	Access Path
	Extend **Tech Infusion** **View and Connect.** As a class, watch the first episode of The Lizzie Bennet Diaries, a YouTube vlog and modern-day reinterpretation of *Pride and Prejudice* (available here: http://youtu.be/KisuGP2lcPs/). In this episode, Lizzie recreates the dialogue between her parents from the first chapter of the novel. After watching the clip, discuss the interpretation as a class. What obvious changes did you notice? What works? What doesn't? Then have students create their own modern versions of the dialogue between Mr. and Mrs. Bennet. Allow students to record a video version of the dialogue if they wish.

3. WRITE

Core Path	Access Path
Prewrite and Plan. Read the prompt as a class and ask students to brainstorm about characterization in the excerpt from *Pride and Prejudice*. Students can brainstorm together either as a class or in small groups to begin planning their responses. Remind your students to look at the excerpt and their annotations to find textual evidence to support their ideas.	**Beginner & Intermediate** **Plan and Organize.** Have students complete the prewriting activity on the Access 1 and 2 handouts and then explain their ideas to a partner before they write. Explain to students that they need to choose details, examples, or quotes from the text that support their ideas and then explain how those details support their statements. For example, students could include the line, "Mr. Bennet was so odd a mixture of quick parts, sarcastic humour, reserve, and caprice, that the experience of three-and-twenty years had been insufficient to make his wife understand his character," which uses direct characterization to suggest that Mr. Bennet is a complex character.

Core Path	Access Path
	Approaching **Plan and Organize.** Have students complete the prewriting activity on the Access 4 handout to organize their thoughts before they write.
Discuss. Project these instructions for the peer review onto the board and review them with your class, so they know what they are looking for when they begin to provide their classmates with feedback: • Has this essay helped you understand how Jane Austen uses dialogue and irony to characterize Mr. and Mrs. Bennet? • Does the writer explain the use of indirect characterization in the excerpt? Does that explanation make sense? • How clear is the writer's explanation of how Austen uses irony to develop character traits? • What sort of evidence does the writer use from the text to support his or her writing? • How well does the writer explain how that evidence supports his or her ideas? • Does the writer write using standard grammar and punctuation? Are there any weak spots? • What specific suggestions can you make to help the writer improve the response? • What thing(s) does this paper do especially well? • Be sure to tell the writer what he or she does well and what he or she needs to improve. After you've looked at the peer review instructions, review the rubric with students before they begin writing. Allow time for students briefly to pose and discuss any questions they may have about the peer review instructions and the rubric. Tell students how many peer reviews they will need to complete once they submit their writing.	
Write. Ask students to complete the writing assignment using textual evidence to support their answers. Once they have completed their writing, they should click "Submit."	

Core Path	Access Path
	Extend **Organize.** Encourage students to complete a graphic organizer, such as a three-column chart, to organize their ideas before they type their responses.
	Extend **Critique.** Remind students that a comma splice is a form of run-on sentence in which two independent clauses are joined by a comma. Remind students that independent clauses should be either separated into two sentences, joined by a semicolon, or joined by a comma and a conjunction. Display an example sentence: Let me know if you can make it on Saturday, I need to know how much pizza to order. Ask students how this sentence could be corrected. Some examples: Let me know if you can make it on Saturday. I need to know how much pizza to order. Let me know if you can make it on Saturday; I need to know how much pizza to order. Let me know if you can make it on Saturday, because I need to know how much pizza to order. Tell students to watch for comma splices in their peers' essays and to make suggestions for ways to fix the error.
Review. Once students complete their writing assignment, they should submit substantive feedback to two peers. Students should use their peers' feedback to improve their writing.	

FIRST READ:
The Glass Menagerie

OVERVIEW

The play *The Glass Menagerie,* by Tennessee Williams, explores a mother's desperate attempt to find a husband for her shy daughter and relive her "glory days" as a southern belle in the process. The First Read gives students the opportunity to experience the text with limited context.

OBJECTIVES

1. Perform an initial reading of a text and demonstrate comprehension by responding to short analysis and inference questions with textual evidence.
2. Practice defining vocabulary words using context.
3. Participate effectively in a range of conversations and collaborations to express ideas and build upon the ideas of others.
4. Practice acquiring and using academic vocabulary correctly.

ELA Common Core Standards:
Reading: Literature - RL.11-12.1, RL.11-12.4, RL.11-12.10
Speaking & Listening - SL.11-12.1.A, SL.11-12.1.B, SL.11-12.1.C, SL.11-12.1.D, SL.11-12.2
Language - L.11-12.4.A, L.11-12.6

RESOURCES

Access 1 handout (Beginner)
Access 2 handout (Intermediate)
Access 3 handout (Advanced)
Access 4 handout (Approaching)

1. INTRODUCTION

Core Path	Access Path
Read. Individually or as a class, read the introduction for *The Glass Menagerie*. The introduction provides context for the excerpt from scene five.	**English Learners All Levels & Approaching** **Read and Listen.** Ask students to read and listen to the introduction for *The Glass Menagerie*. Have them refer to the "Introduction Glossary" on their Access 1, 2, 3, and 4 handouts for definitions of key vocabulary terms. If there are unfamiliar words that are not included in their glossary, encourage students to check a dictionary or online reference tool, such as http://dictionary.reference.com.
Access Prior Knowledge. Find out what your students already know about gender roles in the early 20th century. Have a class discussion about women in the early part of the century through the Great Depression. Prompt students with questions such as: 1. What were the expectations for women in the early 20th century? Were they different in different parts of the country (the South, urban areas, etc.)? 2. What was dating like during this time period? How did men and women meet? What role did parents play in arrangements? 3. What would have happened to a family without a father in the 1930s? After students share their ideas, ask them to think about possible conflicts that could arise from these gender roles.	**English Learners All Levels** **Complete and Discuss the Chart.** Create mixed-proficiency pairs and have students complete "The Role of Parents" chart on the Access 1, 2, and 3 handouts. When pairs have finished, have them discuss their answers with another pair. Have students focus on differences in their responses. **Approaching** **Discuss.** Before joining the class discussion on gender roles in the early 20th century, have Approaching students share their ideas with a partner. Encourage them to write down the answers to the discussion questions. Allow students to use their notes to participate in the class discussion.

Core Path	Access Path
	Extend **Analyze and Discuss a Quote.** "The straight realistic play with its genuine Frigidaire and authentic ice-cubes, its characters that speak exactly as its audience speaks, corresponds to the academic landscape and has the same virtue of a photographic likeness. Everyone should know nowadays the unimportance of the photographic in art: that truth, life, or reality is an organic thing which the poetic imagination can represent or suggest, in essence, only through transformation, through changing into other forms than those which were merely present in appearance." (Tennessee Williams, from "The Author's Production Notes" for *The Glass Menagerie*) Lead students in a discussion of the quote. 1. What do you think this quotation means? 2. How does this quotation affect your expectations of the play you will read? 3. Should a play try to be perfectly realistic? Why or why not?

2. READ

Core Path	Access Path
Make Predictions about Vocabulary. There are six bold vocabulary words in the text. As students read the text, ask them to make predictions about what they think each bold vocabulary word means based on the context clues in the sentence. Have students use the annotation tool to make their predictions. It might be helpful to model this for students before they begin reading. Either using the board or projecting the actual text, focus in on the line that uses the word "sphinx": • TOM: You're not a sphinx	**Note:** This exercise, which extends vocabulary instruction, should be completed when the class shifts from whole-group instruction to individual work during the "Read and Annotate" exercise.

Core Path	Access Path
Model for the class how to use these context clues to guess the meaning of the word: 1. Look at the structure of the sentence. What part of speech is the word "sphinx"? (noun) Knowing a sphinx is a person, place, or thing allows us to begin to figure out what it means. 2. In the lines before this one, Tom tells Amanda that he knows what she wished for on the moon. In reply, Amanda says, "Is my head so transparent?" After Tom says she is not a "sphinx," she replies, "No, I don't have secrets." That tells me that a sphinx is something not transparent and possibly that has secrets. 3. I also know the word "sphinx" from the famous structure in Egypt. That sphinx is a lion with a man's head. That makes me think that the sphinx is a mythological creature that keeps secrets. 4. I can confirm this guess with a dictionary. The sphinx was a creature in ancient Greek and Egyptian mythology. It told riddles to travelers and killed anyone who could not come up with the answer. Tom is telling Amanda that she is not secretive like that creature.	**Beginner, Intermediate & Approaching Pair Practice.** 1. Pair students with more proficient readers. 2. Give them an additional sentence that contains a new vocabulary word. 3. Ask the students to complete a Think Aloud using the teacher-led Make Predictions about Vocabulary activity as a model, while the proficient student actively listens. 4. The student should use the context clues in the sentence to try to determine the meaning of the new vocabulary word. 5. After the student has completed the Think Aloud and made a prediction about the word's meaning, allow time for the proficient reader to add his/her own thoughts and clarify any points of confusion. 6. Once they've completed this Think Aloud, encourage them to use a dictionary to confirm the definition of the new vocabulary word. Have them refer to the "Text Glossary" on their Access 1, 2, and 4 handouts for definitions of key vocabulary terms in the text. Encourage them to add any additional vocabulary words or idioms they find in the text and look up definitions for those words and idioms online or in a dictionary.

Core Path	Access Path
Model Reading Comprehension Strategy. Before students begin reading, model the reading comprehension strategy of visualizing by using this Think Aloud that talks students through the first paragraph of text. First explain to your students that visualizing is: *forming a mental picture of something as you read and using new details from the text to add to or change the mental images you have created* Model for students how visualizing will help them better comprehend the selection and help drive their discussions. • *The Glass Menagerie* is a play, so instead of detailed descriptive paragraphs, we get stage directions. Tennessee Williams includes some very detailed stage directions, such as at the beginning of scene five. • In that first group of stage directions, we learn the time of day and year: a spring evening. Amanda and Laura are described as "pale and silent as moths." That helps me picture their movements. It makes them seem delicate and quiet. • I can picture Tom standing up, not offering to help his mother or sister with the dishes, and moving out to the fire escape for a cigarette. I can use my prior knowledge of apartment buildings with metal fire escapes to envision where he sits. • I will use the details in the play to create a picture of Tom and Amanda's actions in my mind.	**Note:** This exercise, which extends instruction around reading comprehension strategies, should be completed when the class shifts from whole-group instruction to individual work during the "Read and Annotate" exercise. **Beginner, Intermediate & Approaching** **Apply Reading Comprehension Strategy.** In small groups, have students read or listen to the audio of the excerpt from *The Glass Menagerie.* After taking turns reading in groups, ask students to draw or sketch a picture that shows the mood of the scene. They can use different colors to highlight words or phrases, or draw simple illustrations of images on the screen, such as "A caller with a bouquet" and the apartment. The drawings can be moody and abstract. Call on students to describe what they drew and why. • What overall mood does the scene have? Why? • Why did they include particular images and/or colors? • How did they "paint" the emotions and feelings of the scene?

Core Path	Access Path
Read and Annotate. Have students independently read and annotate the excerpt. Ask students to use the annotation tool as they read to: 1. use context clues to analyze and determine the meaning of the bolded vocabulary terms 2. ask questions about passages of the text that may be unclear or unresolved 3. identify key details, events, characters, and connections between them 4. note unfamiliar vocabulary	**Beginner** **Coach the Reading.** While other students read, annotate, and discuss the text independently, work with Beginning students, listening to the audio of the text and pausing periodically or when any student has a question. Coach students in articulating their questions for the group and in highlighting and annotating the text. Have students use the Annotation Guide on the Access 1 handout to support them as they highlight and annotate the text. For further support, ask questions about the text such as: • Is there anything about the play that you don't understand? • How do Tom and Amanda treat Laura? What does that tell you about Laura's character? • What do you think will happen when James comes for dinner? **Intermediate** **Listen to the Audio.** Have these students listen to the audio of the text and use the Text Glossary on the Access 2 handout to help them with words or idioms that may be unfamiliar. If students need help with annotating the text, have them use the Annotation Guide on the Access 2 handout. After working with the Beginning students, you may wish to check this group's progress and provide support as needed. **Advanced** **Pair with Proficient Peers.** Have Advanced students work with English-proficient peers to read, annotate, and discuss the text. Have students use the Annotation Guide in the Access 3 handout to support them as they highlight and annotate the text. Encourage them to listen to the audio of the text if needed. **Approaching** **Use the Annotation Guide.** Have students use the Annotation Guide on the Access 4 handout to support them as they highlight and annotate the text.

Core Path	Access Path
Discuss. In small groups or pairs, have students discuss the questions and inferences they made while reading. To help facilitate discussions, refer to Collaborative Discussions in the Speaking & Listening Handbook. 1. What announcement does Tom make in this excerpt? How does Amanda respond? (Tom has invited a friend from work over for dinner. Amanda makes a big "fuss" because she wants to marry Laura to the "gentleman caller.") 2. What do readers learn about Tom and Laura's father in this excerpt? (Their father is not around and is always referred to in past tense. He drank but was attractive and charming. Amanda's marriage was a "tragic mistake.") 3. How does Tom describe Laura? How does Amanda respond? (Tom calls Laura "peculiar" and "crippled," which are both terms that Amanda rejects. Tom thinks Laura is "very different" from other girls and that they should not expect too much of her when James comes over.) 4. How did visualizing the Wingfield apartment help you understand Tom and Amanda's conversation? (Answers will vary.)	**English Learners All Levels & Approaching** Use the extra time while on- and beyond-grade-level students are discussing their first reads of the text to work individually and in small groups with Approaching readers and English learners as outlined on the previous page. Should those students complete their first reads quickly, integrate them into the on- and beyond-grade-level discussion groups. Otherwise, English learners and Approaching readers will be given an opportunity to participate in text discussions with their peers later in the lesson. **Beyond** **Perform.** Pair students and ask them to perform a short excerpt from scene five. Students should include some props and setting details, such as an interactive whiteboard as the screen behind the stage. Have students film their performances to share with the class. If available, post the videos on a class YouTube channel.

3. THINK

Core Path	Access Path
Answer and Discuss. Have students complete the Think questions and then use the peer review instructions and rubric to complete two peer reviews. Refer to the sample answers at the end of the lesson plan online to discuss responses with your students.	**Beginner & Intermediate** **Sentence Frames.** Have students use the sentence frames on the Access 1 and 2 handouts to support their responses to the Think questions. If necessary, distribute sentence frames to Advanced students as well.

Core Path	Access Path
	Approaching **Find the Evidence.** Have students use Find the Evidence on the Access 4 handout to help them identify the evidence needed to answer the questions.
	Extend **Understand an Allusion.** Have students use devices to explain the allusion in the word "Annunciation" on the screen at the beginning of the scene. (The Annunciation was the announcement by the angel Gabriel to Mary that she was pregnant with Jesus, the Son of God.) Once students have explained the allusion, have them discuss what it adds to the scene. • Why might Williams have used the word "annunciation" rather than "announcement"? • What effect does it have on Tom's announcement? • What does the allusion make viewers or readers of the play think will happen?
	Extend **Reflection.** Ask students to imagine that Laura was eavesdropping on Tom and Amanda's whole conversation. Have them write a diary entry from Laura's perspective about the conversation and James's impending visit. Make sure students keep the tone and content consistent with what they know about Laura. If available, have students share their diary entries on a class blog.

SKILL:
Media

OVERVIEW

Analyzing multiple performances of a drama is a key way to help students understand both the author's intention and the role of a director. This lesson plan provides follow-up questions and enrichments to help teachers guide students toward a usable, repeatable method for analyzing dramatic media.

OBJECTIVES

1. Learn the definition of media.
2. Practice using concrete strategies for analyzing media.
3. Participate effectively in a range of conversations and collaborations to express ideas and build upon the ideas of others.

ELA Common Core Standards:
Reading: Literature - RL.11-12.1, RL.11-12.7
Speaking & Listening - SL.11-12.1.A, SL.11-12.2

RESOURCES

Access 1 handout (Beginner)
Access 2 handout (Intermediate)
Access 3 handout (Advanced)
Access 4 handout (Approaching)

1. DEFINE

Core Path	Access Path
Watch. Watch the Concept Definition video on media with your students. Have your students write down the definition of "media" and consider the many different kinds of media, as well as the role of technology in the dissemination of information. Pause the video at these key moments to discuss the information with your students: 1. 0:30 – "Media" refers to methods of communication, but what do we mean when we say "the media"? What does this term encompass? From which forms of media do you get most of your news, entertainment, etc.? 2. 0:36 – How has technology influenced the three basic forms of communication (spoken, written, visual)? Does all communication still fall into these three basic categories, or are there new forms that have been created? 3. 0:43 – Think about modern forms of media, including Twitter, Facebook, Instagram, etc. How are language, form, and audience experience different for each? Discuss.	**English Learners All Levels & Approaching** **Fill in the Blanks.** Have students complete the fill-in-the-blanks exercise on the Access 1, 2, 3, and 4 handouts as they watch the video. Answers are located at the end of the lesson plan online.
Read and Discuss. After watching the Concept Definition video, have students read the definition of media. Either in small groups or as a whole class, use these questions to engage students in a discussion about media. 1. How did media change at the end of the 19th century, and why? (New technology and inventions, such as photography, the telegraph, and the telephone, gave people new ways to communicate with each other.) 2. How is the "language" of Twitter different than the language of film? Of YouTube? Why? (Answers will vary.) 3. Why do people like to reinvent old stories in new media? Can you think of any examples? (New interpretations of a story tend to reflect the objectives, ideas, and values of a particular time period.)	**Beginner & Approaching** **Complete the Chart.** To prepare students to participate in the discussion, have them complete the chart on the Access 1 and 4 handouts as they read the definition. The correct answers are located at the end of the lesson plan online. **Intermediate & Advanced** **Discuss Prompts.** To help these students participate in the discussion, prompt them with questions that can be answered with a few words, such as: • What is a medium? (a means of sending a communication to an intended audience) • When did media options expand beyond speech, drawing, and writing? (the middle of the 19th century) • What medium do you use most often? Explain a distinctive feature of that medium. (Answers will vary.)

Core Path	Access Path
	Beyond **Discuss.** Have students select a movie they have seen that was based on a book that they read. Have them create a list of ways the book and movie were similar and different. In what ways was the book better? What about the movie? Why do you think the director or screenwriter make those different choices?
	Extend **Write.** Have students choose a medium they use on a daily basis (suggest Twitter, YouTube, Reddit, texting, or Snapchat). Have them write a "guidebook" explaining the language, form, and audience experience a user of their chosen medium would encounter. Students should include examples. Allow time for students to share their guidebooks with the class.

2. MODEL

Core Path	Access Path
Read and Annotate. Have students independently read the Model section. As they read, ask students to use the annotation tool to: • highlight key points • ask questions • identify places where the Model applies the strategies laid out in the Identification and Application section • comment on the effect that multiple interpretations of a drama have on a reader	**Note:** During this portion of the lesson, instruction shifts from whole-group to individual work. Use this time to work one-on-one or in small groups with Beginning, Intermediate, Advanced, and Approaching students. **Beginner & Intermediate** **Coach the Reading.** Work with these students (either individually or in small groups) to fill out the guided reading questions on the Access 1 and 2 handouts. Have Beginning students refer to the glossary on the Access 1 handout to help them determine the meaning of difficult words (note: provide the Access 1 handout glossary to Intermediate students if necessary). Let students know they'll use these answers to help participate in the discussion about the Model. Sample answers for this exercise are located at the end of the lesson plan online.

Core Path	Access Path
	Advanced **Identify Evidence.** Ask Advanced students to complete the identifying evidence exercise on the Access 3 handout. Let students know that they'll use these answers to help participate in the discussion about the Model. Sample answers for this exercise are located at the end of the lesson plan online. **Approaching** **Guided Reading.** Have students complete the guided reading questions on the Access 4 handout as they read. Let them know that they'll use these answers to help participate in the discussion about the Model. Sample answers for this exercise are located at the end of the lesson plan online.
Discuss. After students read the Model text, use these questions to facilitate a whole-group discussion that helps students understand how to determine and analyze the different interpretations of the play: 1. How does a written version of a drama differ from a movie adaptation? (In a written version of a drama, the reader uses dialogue, stage directions, and his own her own imagination to guess how actors might move or speak. In a movie, actors will use their voices, facial expressions, and body language to communicate what they think are the appropriate emotions.) 2. What are some questions to ask yourself when analyzing different versions of a text? (What medium is being used? What are the main similarities and the differences between the versions? Are the characters and events portrayed similarly or differently?) 3. What does the Model say readers can infer about Tom and Amanda from the play? (The characters have a playful relationship. Tom enjoys teasing his mother, but he is also somewhat disrespectful.)	

Core Path	Access Path
4. What evidence does the Model present to support the inference that Tom is disrespectful to Amanda? Which movie version highlights this trait? (He dismisses her feelings about the apartment, saying, "I don't see why you have to think at all" and "Mother, this boy is no one to make a fuss over!" The 1987 version shows Tom's disrespect.) 5. How does watching the film clips change your understanding of the scene? (The film clips make it easy to see Tom and Amanda's relationship. The films show Amanda's flurry to get ready and Tom's hesitance regarding Laura.) 6. Which version of the scene do you think is most faithful to Williams's script? Why? (Answers will vary, but students should support their answers with evidence from the text and film clips.)	
	Extend **Annotate.** Have half the students in the class watch the 1973 version again, and have the other half watch the 1987 version again. As they watch, have students follow along in the text and mark any changes the film makes. Students should strike through lines that were cut and note any lines that were changed. After they have made their annotations, have students decide whether the change makes a difference in how they interpreted that line. Students should mark the annotations as "effect" or "no effect." When they have finished, pair a 1973 student with a 1987 student and have them compare their annotations and notes.
	Extend **Create a List.** Pair students and have them create a list of points of comparison between the text and movie versions of a drama. Once students have their lists, post them on a class blog or in the classroom to help students analyze *The Glass Menagerie.*

3. YOUR TURN

Core Path	Access Path
Assess and Explain. Have students answer the comprehension questions to test for understanding. Share the explanations for Parts A and B (located online) with your students.	
	Extend **Write.** Have students choose a medium other than film. Then ask them to adapt scene five from *The Glass Menagerie* into that medium. Encourage students to be creative. (You may want to show students an excerpt from *Texts from Jane Eyre* to show how a novel can be adapted into the texting medium: http://tinyurl.com/prahqlj). When students have finished their adaptations, allow time for volunteers to share their writing. Discuss as a class the choices the volunteer made to fit the story to the chosen medium.

CLOSE READ:
The Glass Menagerie

OVERVIEW

Tennessee Williams's classic American drama *The Glass Menagerie* explores a mother's changing relationships with her two children. Amanda struggles to find an appropriate husband for her shy daughter and clashes with a son who would rather write than help provide for the family. The Close Read gives students the opportunity to more deeply analyze the author's development of these characters and their situation, and to consider how an actor's choices affects a viewer's experience of Williams's well-known text.

OBJECTIVES

1. Complete a close reading of a passage of literature.
2. Practice and apply concrete strategies for comparing and contrasting elements of *The Glass Menagerie* as portrayed in two film adaptations of the text.
3. Participate effectively in a range of conversations and collaborations to express ideas and build upon the ideas of others.
4. Prewrite, plan, and produce clear and coherent writing in response to a prompt.

ELA Common Core Standards:
Reading: Literature - RL.11-12.1, RL.11-12.4, RL.11-12.7
Writing - W.11-12.1.A, W.11-12.1.B, W.11-12.4, W.11-12.5, W.11-12.6, W.11-12.9.A, W.11-12.10
Speaking & Listening - SL.11-12.1.A, SL.11-12.1.B, SL.11-12.1.C, SL.11-12.1.D, SL.11-12.6
Language - L.11-12.4.A, L.11-12.4.C, L.11-12.4.D

RESOURCES

The Glass Menagerie Vocabulary handout
Access 1 handout (Beginner)
Access 2 handout (Intermediate)
Access 3 handout (Advanced)
Access 4 handout (Approaching)

1. INTRODUCTION

Core Path	Access Path
Define and Compare. Project the vocabulary words and definitions onto the board or provide students with handouts so they can copy the vocabulary into their notebooks. Suggest that students consult general and specialized reference materials, both print and digital, to compare the precise meaning of a specific word with their initial vocabulary predictions from the First Read. Review words that students defined incorrectly to understand why they were unable to use context clues to develop usable definitions.	**Beginner & Intermediate** **Complete the Chart.** Have students complete the chart on the Access 1 and 2 handouts by writing the correct word for each of the definitions. **Advanced & Beyond** **Write in Journals.** Have students write a journal entry using all of their vocabulary words. Remind them to write sentences that communicate the meaning of the words they are using. **Approaching** **Graphic Organizer.** To support students in comparing their predictions with the correct meanings, have them complete the graphic organizer on the Access 4 handout to record the vocabulary words, their initial analysis, and the definitions. Then have them write sentences using the words.
Review. Have students complete the fill-in-the-blanks vocabulary worksheet attached to the lesson plan online. Answers for the worksheet are listed at the end of the lesson plan online.	
	Extend **Create.** Ask students to use an app such as Quizlet (http://quizlet.com) or StudyBlue (www.studyblue.com) to make a set of online flashcards showing each vocabulary word, its part of speech on one side and the definition on the other. Have them use the flashcards to review and remember the words.

Core Path	Access Path
	Extend **Write a Scene.** Ask pairs or small groups of students to write a short dialogue or brief scene using all of the vocabulary words. Encourage students to include context clues that would help people infer the meaning of each word. If there is enough time, have groups perform their scenes for the class, omitting the vocab words as they read and allowing volunteers from the audience to guess which word would fill each blank in the scene.

2. READ

Core Path	Access Path
Model Close Reading. Project the text of Tom's memories of the Paradise Dance Hall from scene five onto the board and access the corresponding video clips from the 1973 made-for-television film version at http://tinyurl.com/poc3ypn and the 1987 film version at http://tinyurl.com/nr42kjz. Use the text and video to model a close reading/viewing using the annotation strategies mentioned on the next page. While modeling annotation strategies, make notes that tie the text to the focus skill and demonstrate what students are looking for as they read and view. Here is some guidance for you as you annotate for your students: • As the Skills lesson that precedes this text makes clear, different media use different techniques to convey story elements and themes. Consider, for example, the way the text introduces Tom's reflections and memories.	

Core Path	Access Path
• In the text, Williams makes it clear that this long piece of dialogue consists of Tom's recollections and reflections on his past. To signal to the reader that this section is separate from the ongoing conversation Tom is having with Amanda, Williams adds a music cue, [*Dance music: "The World Is Waiting for the Sunrise!"*], and includes stage directions that tell readers that Tom is speaking directly to the audience. • In the 1973 adaptation, the director sets up Tom's reverie apart from the rest of the text in another way. In this version, Tom's memories are introduced as a voice-over, so viewers know that Tom is lost in his own thoughts and not speaking directly to another character. • The 1987 film version follows Williams's stage directions, playing music over the actor's words as he speaks directly to the audience. Tom remains lost in thought until Amanda calls his name from inside the apartment, causing the character to snap back to reality.	
Read and Annotate. Read the Skills Focus questions as a class, so your students know what they should pay close attention to as they read. Then have students read and annotate the excerpt. Ask students to use the annotation tool as they read to: 1. respond to the Skills Focus section 2. ask questions about how the text develops characters and key themes 3. analyze the author's purpose, and how it shapes the story; remember that people choose certain types of media over others, depending on which one best suits their purpose 4. evaluate the advantages and disadvantages of using different mediums, such as print and film, to present a particular topic or idea	**Note:** While on-grade-level students are reading and annotating, work one-on-one or in small groups with Beginning, Intermediate, Advanced, and Approaching students to support them as they read and annotate the text. **Beginner & Intermediate** **Summarize and Analyze the Text.** Work with these students to complete the sentence frames on the Access 1 and 2 handouts (note: the sentence frames for Intermediate students on the Access 2 handout contain fewer scaffolds). They will then use the completed sentence frames to help them analyze and annotate the text by completing the Skills Focus questions. Refer to the sample Skills Focus answers to help them complete the sentence frames and annotate the text.

Core Path	Access Path
5. note any unfamiliar vocabulary 6. capture their reaction to the ideas and examples in the text and films As they reread the text, remind students to use the comprehension strategy of Visualizing that they learned in the First Read.	**Advanced** **Work in Pairs.** Pair these students with more proficient English speakers to work together on analyzing and annotating the text to complete the Skills Focus questions. If these students need more support, have them use the sentence frames on the Access 3 handout as they work with their more proficient peers. **Approaching** **Summarize the Text.** Have these students discuss and complete the text summary on the Access 4 handout and use their summary to help them analyze and annotate the text by completing the Skills Focus questions. Correct answers for the summary are at the end of the lesson plan online. Also refer to the sample Skills Focus answers to aid students with their annotations.
Discuss. After students have read the text, use the sample responses to the Skills Focus questions at the bottom of the lesson plan online to discuss the reading and the process of searching for the ways to compare and contrast different versions of the same text. Make sure that students have acquired and accurately use academic-specific words and phrases related to the skill and demonstrate a command of formal English appropriate to the discussion. To help facilitate discussions, refer to Collaborative Discussions in the Speaking & Listening Handbook.	**Extend** **Pair and Share.** In small, heterogeneous groups or pairs, ask students to share and discuss their annotations with a focus on comparing and contrasting media formats used to tell the story. You can provide students with these questions to guide their discussion: 1. Neither film adaptation uses the projection screens Williams includes in the text of the play. What role do these projections play in Williams's text? How does the choice to omit them affect the audience's understanding of the text? Cite specific textual evidence to support your statements. (Williams uses the projections to highlight key points in the scene. As the scene begins, the word "Annunciation" appears on the screen, signaling to audiences that a formal announcement is going to happen. Without this projection, this foreshadowing is eliminated. Later in the scene, a projection of a gentleman caller appears to represent Amanda's hopes for Laura's future. The omission of this projection affects the audience less because the dialogue also highlights this key idea.)

Core Path	Access Path
	2. Directors of film adaptations usually make changes as they bring a story to life. Note one key change in one of the film adaptations from Williams's original text. Why might the director have made that choice? How does it affect the overall themes of the text? Cite specific textual evidence to support your answer. (Student responses will vary, but may include that both versions cut the beginning of the scene, in which Amanda asks Tom to comb his hair. This part was likely cut due to time constraints, and its omission does not affect the scene's focus on appearances because much of the dialogue that develops themes relating to appearances has been retained.) 3. Imagine that you are making a film adaptation of *The Glass Menagerie*. Whom would you cast as Tom, Amanda, and Laura, and why? What qualities of each character would you want to focus on in your adaptation? (Student responses will vary, but may include a focus on Amanda's vanity and desperation, Tom's disillusionment and protectiveness, and Laura's inability to connect with people outside her family)
	Extend **Tech Infusion** **Create.** Ask student groups to use Glogster (http://edu.glogster.com) or Google Drawing to create electronic collages using images and clips from three different versions of *The Glass Menagerie*. Invite student groups to present their collages to the class, explaining why they selected particular images, text, and audio clips.

3. WRITE

Core Path	Access Path
Prewrite and Plan. Read the writing prompt as a class and ask students to brainstorm about the techniques used in the three versions of *The Glass Menagerie*. Students can brainstorm together either as a class or in small groups to begin planning their responses. Remind your students to look at the excerpt and their annotations to find textual evidence to support their ideas.	**Beginner & Intermediate** **Plan and Organize.** Have students complete the prewriting activity on the Access 1 and 2 handouts and then explain their ideas to a partner before they write. Explain to students that they need to choose details, examples, or quotes from the text that support their ideas and then explain how those details support their statements. For example, students could include a description of how Malkovich speaks Tom's lines about the Paradise Dance Hall aloud to the audience, which emphasizes his role as the narrator in addition to being one of the characters in the play. **Approaching** **Plan and Organize.** Have students complete the prewriting activity on the Access 4 handout to organize their thoughts before they write.
Discuss. Project these instructions for the peer review onto the board and review them with your class, so they know what they are looking for when they begin to provide their classmates with feedback: • Did the writer choose a clear position and argue for it coherently? • What theme did the writer identify? How clear was the writer's explanation of why one version developed that theme better than the other version? • How well did the writer address the ways the film version used character, setting, and dialogue to develop the theme of the scene? • What sort of evidence did the writer use from the text to support his or her writing? • How well does the writer explain how that evidence supports his or her arguments? • Does the writer write using standard grammar and punctuation? Are there any weak spots?	

Core Path	Access Path
• What specific suggestions can you make to help the writer improve the response? • What thing(s) does this paper do especially well? After you've looked at the peer review instructions, review the rubric with students before they begin writing. Allow time for students briefly to pose and discuss any questions they may have about the peer review instructions and the rubric. Tell students how many peer reviews they will need to complete once they submit their writing.	
Write. Ask students to complete the writing assignment using textual evidence to support their answers. Once they have completed their writing, they should click "Submit."	
	Extend **Evaluate a Writing Sample.** Project a writing sample on the board and have students identify the elements of writing that are strong, as well as those that are weak or in need of improvement. Alternatively, you can give students photocopies of a writing sample to collaboratively evaluate. After students have had an opportunity to evaluate student samples, have them generate and share with the class strategies to use as they complete their peer reviews to ensure they are substantive.
Review. Once students complete their writing assignment, they should submit substantive feedback to two peers. Students should use their peers' feedback to improve their writing.	

FIRST READ:
Wuthering Heights

OVERVIEW

The novel *Wuthering Heights*, by Emily Brontë, tells the tragic love story of Catherine and Heathcliff, who, despite their deep love for each other, cannot marry because of the difference in their status. The First Read gives students the opportunity to experience the text with a limited context.

OBJECTIVES

1. Perform an initial reading of a text and demonstrate comprehension by responding to short analysis and inference questions with textual evidence.
2. Practice defining vocabulary words using context.
3. Learn and practice strategies for determining when to use italics.
4. Participate effectively in a range of conversations and collaborations to express ideas and build upon the ideas of others.
5. Practice acquiring and using academic vocabulary correctly.

ELA Common Core Standards:
Reading: Literature - RL.11-12.1, RL.11-12.4, RL.11-12.10
Writing - W.11-12.7
Speaking & Listening - SL.11-12.1.A, SL.11-12.1.B, SL.11-12.1.C, SL.11-12.1.D, SL.11-12.2, SL.11-12.3, SL.11-12.6
Language - L.11-12.2, L.11-12.4.A, L.11-12.6

RESOURCES

Grammar handout: Italics
Access 1 handout (Beginner)
Access 2 handout (Intermediate)
Access 3 handout (Advanced)
Access 4 handout (Approaching)

ACCESS COMPLEX TEXT

This excerpt from *Wuthering Heights*, spanning three chapters across the novel, captures the misunderstandings, impassioned love, and tragedy that characterizes Heathcliff and Catherine's relationship. To help students understand the complexity of their relationship and the range of emotions it inspires in readers, use the following ideas to provide scaffolded instruction for a first reading of the more complex features of this text:

- **Organization** - The excerpt contains selections from Chapters 9, 15, and 16. Students may need guidance connecting the plot events described in the excerpt. In Chapter 9, Catherine confesses to Nelly that she plans to marry Edgar Linton even though she is in love with Heathcliff. Heathcliff overhears the beginning of their conversation and leaves before hearing Catherine profess her love for him. In Chapter 15, we see the ramifications of Catherine's decision as the two former lovers quarrel and reconcile before her death. In Chapter 16, Heathcliff grieves for Catherine after she has passed away.

- **Connection of Ideas** - Characterization may be difficult for students to trace because of the brevity of the selection and the characters' extreme emotions. Explain that *Wuthering Heights* is an example of romanticism, a movement that rejected the Enlightenment's emphasis on reason and instead embraced emotion and passion. The novel also includes elements of Gothic literature, such as the manor, extreme melancholy, darkness, and cruelty.

- **Sentence Structure** - Brontë's style includes some long sentences and nonstandard punctuation. Struggling readers may benefit from paraphrasing as they read or breaking more difficult sentences into smaller pieces.

- **Specific Vocabulary** - Some difficult and archaic vocabulary, such as *ere*, *bade*, and *scintillating*, may present a challenge to some readers.

1. INTRODUCTION

Core Path	Access Path
Watch. As a class, watch the video preview of *Wuthering Heights*.	**English Learners All Levels** **Fill in the Blanks.** Ask students to use their Access 1, 2, and 3 handouts to fill in the blanks of the transcript for the preview's voiceover as they watch the preview along with their classmates. Answers are located at the end of the lesson plan online.

Core Path	Access Path
Read. Individually or as a class, read the introduction for *Wuthering Heights*. The introduction provides context for the excerpts taken from Chapters 9, 15, and 16.	**English Learners All Levels & Approaching** **Read and Listen.** Ask students to read and listen to the introduction for *Wuthering Heights*. Have them refer to the "Introduction Glossary" on their Access 1, 2, 3, and 4 handouts for definitions of key vocabulary terms. If there are unfamiliar words that are not included in their glossary, encourage students to check a dictionary or online reference tool, like http://dictionary.reference.com.
Build Background. In pairs or small groups, ask students to use devices to research the lives and works of Emily Brontë and her sisters. Assign each group a topic to investigate. Remind students to include relevant facts, definitions, and concrete details in their research: • their biographies • their works • their literary influences • the time period in which they lived If you are in a low-tech classroom, you can provide photocopies of articles about the Brontës for students to read and discuss. Have students present their findings.	**English Learners All Levels & Approaching** **Research.** Pair students and provide them with a short, credible online biography of the Brontë sisters, such as the one at http://tinyurl.com/labllek. Have students read the short biography and use the facts they've learned to help them complete the Build Background sentence frames on the Access 1, 2, 3, and 4 handouts. Sample answers for this activity can be found at the end of the lesson plan online.
	Extend **Make Predictions.** Based on the introduction, ask students to make predictions about the central ideas they would expect to encounter in this text. Does the plot, as summarized in the introduction, remind them of any other works of literature they have read? How does the plot affect the students' predictions?

2. READ

Core Path

Make Predictions about Vocabulary. There are five bold vocabulary words in the text. As students read the text, ask them to make predictions about what they think each bold vocabulary word means based on the context clues in the sentence. Have students use the annotation tool to make their predictions.

It might be helpful to model this for students before they begin reading. Either using the board or projecting the actual text, focus in on the sentence that uses the word "countenance":

- Her present countenance had a wild vindictiveness in its white cheek, and a bloodless lip and scintillating eye; and she retained in her closed fingers a portion of the locks she had been grasping.

Model for the class how to use these context clues to guess the meaning of the word:

1. I read the passage and see that this is two complete sentences joined by a semicolon. The word "countenance" appears in the first sentence, so I will focus on that part: "Her present countenance had a wild vindictiveness in its white cheek, and a bloodless lip and scintillating eye."
2. I see that "countenance" appears in the subject position of this sentence, so I can infer that the rest of the words and phrases in the sentence are describing it.
3. I see the phrases "white cheek," "bloodless lip," and "scintillating eye." I know that "scintillating" means "lively." These are all parts of a face, so I can determine that "countenance" means "face."

Access Path

Note: This exercise, which extends vocabulary instruction, should be completed when the class shifts from whole group instruction to individual work during the "Read and Annotate" exercise.

Beginner, Intermediate & Approaching Pair Practice.

1. Pair students with more proficient readers.
2. Give them an additional sentence that contains a new vocabulary word.
3. Ask the students to complete a Think Aloud using the teacher-led Make Predictions about Vocabulary activity as a model, while the proficient student actively listens.
4. The student should use the context clues in the sentence to try to determine the meaning of the new vocabulary word.
5. After the student has completed the Think Aloud and made a prediction about the word's meaning, allow time for the proficient reader to add his/her own thoughts and clarify any points of confusion.
6. Once they've completed this Think Aloud, encourage them to use a dictionary to confirm the definition of the new vocabulary word. Have them refer to the "Text Glossary" on their Access 1, 2, and 4 handouts for definitions of key vocabulary terms in the text. Encourage them to add any additional vocabulary words or idioms they find in the text and look up definitions for those words and idioms online or in a dictionary.

Core Path

Model Reading Comprehension Strategy. Before students begin reading, model the reading comprehension strategy of asking and answering questions by using this Think Aloud that talks students through the first few lines of the excerpt. First, explain to your students that:

proficient readers ask themselves questions before, during, and after they read to facilitate understanding. Good readers approach a text with questions and ask new questions as they read

Model for students how asking and answering questions will help them better comprehend the text and help drive their discussions.

- The excerpt begins in Chapter 9, so a lot has happened in the novel already. I begin by asking myself, Who are these characters? What are they talking about?
- I scan the excerpt from Chapter 9 and see that characters named Nelly and Catherine are having a conversation. I notice that Nelly calls the other woman "Miss Catherine," so this helps me figure out that Catherine must be in a higher social position.
- Next, I try to figure out who the other characters are. I focus on the sentence in which Catherine names both men: "I've no more business to marry Edgar Linton than I have to be in heaven; and if the wicked [Hindley] had not brought Heathcliff so low, I shouldn't have thought of it." From this sentence, I can understand that Linton is the man Catherine will marry, but Heathcliff is the man she wants to marry. Because of this conflict, I ask myself, Why can't Catherine marry whom she wants?

Access Path

Note: This exercise, which extends instruction around reading comprehension strategies, should be completed when the class shifts from whole group instruction to individual work during the "Read and Annotate" exercise.

Beginner, Intermediate & Approaching
Apply Reading Comprehension Strategy.

1. Explain to students the reasons why readers should ask questions during all stages of reading:
   - Before Reading: Asking questions helps readers connect to the text and set a purpose for reading.
   - During Reading: Asking questions helps readers monitor their understanding and stay engaged with the text.
   - After Reading: Asking questions helps readers determine how well they understood the text and how well they can remember and summarize it.
2. Group students in pairs or small groups. On their Access 1, 2, and 4 handouts, have students write in their "Reading Strategy Chart" one question they have before reading the text. If students struggle to come up with one, prompt them by referring to the Introduction and asking: *Why does Catherine's plan fail? Why don't Catherine and Heathcliff run away together?*
3. Then have students listen to the audio version of the excerpt from *Wuthering Heights* and follow along in the text. In their "Reading Strategy Chart" have students write down at least one question they have during reading. Remind students that they can ask questions about parts of the text that are not clear, such as a particular sentence, a character's words or actions, or an unfamiliar word.

Core Path	Access Path
• I keep reading Catherine's dialogue: "It would degrade me to marry Heathcliff now." Based on this line, and the inference I made earlier about Catherine's social class, I can infer that Heathcliff would be a disadvantageous match for Catherine and that Linton must be close to her in status.	4. Once students have listened to the audio version, have them write down one more question in their charts after reading. 5. Then have students discuss the questions in their charts. Give students time to explain why they asked the questions and how they found the answers to them when they read or listened to the story again.
Read and Annotate. Have students independently read and annotate the excerpt. Ask students to use the annotation tool as they read to: 1. use context clues to analyze and determine the meaning of the bolded vocabulary terms 2. ask questions about passages of the text that may be unclear or unresolved 3. identify key information, events, characters, and connections between them 4. note unfamiliar vocabulary	**Beginner** **Coach the Reading.** While other students read, annotate, and discuss the text independently, work with Beginning students, listening to the audio of the text and pausing periodically or when any student has a question. Coach students in articulating their questions for the group and in highlighting and annotating the text. Have students use the Annotation Guide on the Access 1 handout to support them as they highlight and annotate the text. For further support, ask questions about the text such as: • How does Catherine feel about Heathcliff? • How does Heathcliff think Catherine feels about him? • Do you think this story will have a happy ending? Why or why not? **Intermediate** **Listen to the Audio.** Have these students listen to the audio of the text and use the Text Glossary on the Access 2 handout to help them with words or idioms that may be unfamiliar. If students need help with annotating the text, have them use the Annotation Guide on the Access 2 handout. After working with the Beginning students, you may wish to check this group's progress and provide support as needed.

Core Path	Access Path
	Advanced **Pair with Proficient Peers.** Have Advanced students work with English-proficient peers to read, annotate, and discuss the text. Have students use the Annotation Guide in the Access 3 handout to support them as they highlight and annotate the text. Encourage them to listen to the audio of the text if needed. **Approaching** **Use the Annotation Guide.** Have students use the Annotation Guide on the Access 4 handout to support them as they highlight and annotate the text.
Discuss. In small groups or pairs, have students discuss the questions and inferences they made while reading. To help facilitate discussions, refer to Collaborative Discussions in the Speaking & Listening Handbook. 1. In Chapter 9, why does Heathcliff quietly leave the room? (He overhears Catherine telling Nelly that she plans to marry someone else.) What inference do you think he makes based on what he overhears? 2. How would you describe the reunion between Catherine and Heathcliff in Chapter 15? (Possible answers: passionate, frightening, emotional, romantic, violent) What questions and answers could help readers understand the complex emotions the two characters feel for each other? 3. What questions did you have before reading the excerpt from Chapter 16? Did the text provide the answers you needed? Why or why not? (Answers may vary.)	**English Learners All Levels & Approaching** Use the extra time while on- and beyond-grade-level students are discussing their first reads of the text to work individually and in small groups with Approaching readers and English Learners as outlined above. Should those students complete their first reads quickly, integrate them into the on- and beyond-grade-level discussion groups. Otherwise, English Learners and Approaching readers will be given an opportunity to participate in text discussions with their peers later in the lesson. **Beyond** **Tech Infusion** **Write.** What might have happened if Catherine hadn't died? Have students write an alternate ending to the last chapter, drawing inspiration from the characterization and tone of *Wuthering Heights*. Have students share their endings by publishing them on Pen.io. (http://pen.io). Pair students and have them compare and contrast the narrative choices they made.

Core Path	Access Path
Grammar, Usage, and Mechanics. Distribute the StudySync grammar handout on italics and discuss the instruction provided on the handout with students. Have students respond individually to the questions on the handout and then discuss their responses as a class. Answers to the questions appear at the end of the lesson plan online.	**Beginner & Intermediate** **Work with the Teacher.** Remind students that italics have uses beyond setting off book and movie titles. Authors sometimes use italics to emphasize certain words in a text. Explain: *Italics draw attention to a specific word. Italics can add a certain emotion to the word, such as anger or surprise, depending on the context of the sentence.* Write the following statements on the board: A. How can you say that? B. How can *you* say that? Ask: *Which sentence has italics?* (B) *Which word does the italics emphasize?* (the word "you") Read both statements aloud, emphasizing the *you* in Sentence B. *How does the italic* you *affect the meaning of the sentence?* (By emphasizing "you," the focus of the sentence is on the person who said something. It emphasizes a mismatch (an irony or hypocrisy) between the person's character or experience and his or her words.) Encourage students to write the own sentence pairs, providing support as needed. Allow time for students to share their sentences. Then have these students participate in the short lesson above with Approaching students. Then work with them to complete the Italics Handout. **Advanced & Beyond** **Extend the Search.** Challenge these students to work in pairs or small groups to find different examples of italics in the text, and to note their purpose and effect.

Core Path	Access Path
	Approaching **Analyze an Example.** If students need more support identifying the purpose and effect of italics, call their attention to these words in Chapter 15: "I love *my* murderer—but *yours!* How can I?" Ask: *Who says these words?* (Heathcliff) *To whom is he referring when he says "my murderer"?* (Catherine) *Why does he call her his murderer?* (because she hurt him) *To whom is he referring when he says "but yours"?* (Catherine) *If Catherine is both of their murderers, why does he make a distinction between "my murder" and "yours"?* (He can forgive Catherine for hurting him, but he can't forgive her for hurting herself.) Then have students complete the Italics Handout.
	Extend **Tech Infusion** **Poll.** Use Poll Everywhere (www.polleverywhere.com) to allow students to vote "Catherine," "Heathcliff," or "Someone Else" in response to the following question: "Who do you think is to blame for the tragic ending to the love story between Catherine and Heathcliff?" Students can respond using cell phones, tablets, or laptops. If students voted "someone else," ask them who or what is to blame. Share the poll results with the class and discuss why students voted the way they did.

3. SYNCTV

Core Path	Access Path
Watch. As a class, watch the SyncTV video on *Wuthering Heights*. Remind students to listen for the way the students use academic vocabulary during their discussion. Pause the video at these key moments to discuss the information with your students: 1. 1:51 – Describe the tone and word choice Troy uses to talk about his superstitious aunt. Considering the characters' beliefs in the text, is this a fair representation of having a belief in the supernatural? Why or why not? 2. 4:19 – Ellie says that *Wuthering Heights* "sounds more like a horror story" than a love story. How well does she support her claim? Do you agree with her? Why or why not? 3. 7:26 – Ellie calls Heathcliff "brutal." Is this description supported by the text? Why or why not? Consider the textual evidence cited by each member of the group.	**Beginner & Intermediate** **Analyze the Discussion.** Have students use the "Analyze the Discussion" guide on the Access 1 and 2 handouts to identify key points in the discussion and the evidence the students use to determine those points. Sample answers are at the end of the lesson plan online. **Advanced** **Emotional Currents.** Have students discuss and complete the "Emotional Currents" chart on the Access 3 handout, referring back to the SyncTV video as needed to clarify their answers. Sample answers appear at the end of the lesson plan online. **Approaching** **Analyze the Discussion.** Have students complete the chart on the Access 4 handout by listing textual evidence cited by the students in the video. Sample answers are at the end of the lesson plan online.

4. THINK

Core Path	Access Path
Answer and Discuss. Have students complete the Think questions and then use the peer review instructions and rubric to complete two peer reviews. Refer to the sample answers at the end of the lesson plan online to discuss responses with your students.	**Beginner & Intermediate** **Sentence Frames.** Have students use the sentence frames on the Access 1 and 2 handouts to support their responses to the Think questions. If necessary, distribute sentence frames to Advanced students as well. **Approaching** **Find the Evidence.** Have students use Find the Evidence on the Access 4 handout to help them identify the evidence needed to answer the questions.

Core Path	Access Path
SyncTV Style Discussion. Put students into small groups and give them a prompt to discuss. Remind them to model their discussions after the SyncTV episodes they have seen. Stress the importance of using both academic language and formal English correctly and citing textual evidence in their conversations to support their ideas. To help students prepare for, strategize, and evaluate their discussions, refer to the Collaborative Discussions section of the Speaking & Listening Handbook. Discussion prompt options: 1. Do you think *Wuthering Heights* presents a timeless romantic love story? Why or why not? Use textual evidence to support your stance. 2. What effect did romanticism have on the text? Remind students to review the notes they took during the Build Background activity before they read the text.	**Beginner & Intermediate** **Use Sentence Frames.** Have these students use the sentence frames on the Access 1 and 2 handouts to help them participate in the discussion. **Approaching** **Use Think Questions.** Remind these students to refer back to their answers to the Think questions to help them participate in the group discussion.
	Extend **Tech Infusion** **Record.** Ask one student in each group to record their conversation on video. They can upload their videos to YouTube, share them via Google Drive, or e-mail them to you for review. They can also play the video and critique their own conversations to continually improve.
	Extend **Freewrite.** Ask students to trace the references to dreams that are made throughout the excerpts from the novel. Then have them freewrite for two minutes about the role dreams play in the text.

SKILL:

Theme

OVERVIEW

Determining and analyzing theme is vital to understanding a work of literature. This is especially true for a long and complex novel like Emily Brontë's *Wuthering Heights*. This lesson plan provides follow-up questions and useful enrichments to help teachers guide students toward a usable, repeatable method for analyzing theme.

OBJECTIVES

1. Learn the definition of theme.
2. Practice using concrete strategies for analyzing theme.
3. Participate effectively in a range of conversations and collaborations to express ideas and build upon the ideas of others.

ELA Common Core Standards:
Reading: Literature - RL.11-12.1, RL.11-12.2
Speaking & Listening - SL.11-12.1.A, SL.11-12.1.C, SL.11-12.2

RESOURCES

Access 1 handout (Beginner)
Access 2 handout (Intermediate)
Access 3 handout (Advanced)
Access 4 handout (Approaching)

1. DEFINE

Core Path	Access Path
Watch. Watch the Concept Definition video on theme with your students. Ask students to write the definitions and the key evidence they can examine to determine theme in their notes. Pause the video at these key moments to discuss the information with your students: 1. 1:00 – Why would authors choose to have readers infer stories' themes? Why don't all authors just come out and state the theme like they do in fables? 2. 1:25 – What are some other real-life examples of when inference skills are important? 3. 2:37 – Can you think of any evidence that might help a reader identify theme that the students in the video don't mention? Are some pieces of evidence more important for determining theme?	**English Learners All Levels & Approaching** **Fill in the Blanks.** Have students complete the fill-in-the-blanks activity on the Access 1, 2, 3, and 4 handouts as they watch the video. Answers are located at the end of the lesson plan online.
Read and Discuss. After watching the Concept Definition video, have students read the definition of theme. Either in small groups or as a whole class, use these questions to engage students in a discussion about theme. 1. Why do fables often state the theme at the end of the text? (The moral that states the main idea, or theme, is used to sum up the lesson taught in the fable.) How are fables different from novels? (In fables, themes are stated directly, and there is usually one clear theme. In novels, there are many themes, and often, readers must infer them because they are not stated directly.) 2. How can analyzing the structure of a text help you determine its theme? (The structure itself carries clues to discerning its theme or themes. For example, in a cause-and-effect text structure, readers can study the pattern of consequences resulting from certain actions and events. Through this, they can watch as themes develop through the course of the story.)	**Beginner & Approaching** **Complete a Chart.** To prepare students to participate in the discussion, have them complete the chart on the Access 1 and 4 handouts as they read the definition. The correct answers are located at the end of the lesson plan online. **Intermediate & Advanced** **Discuss Prompts.** To help these students participate in the discussion, prompt them with questions that can be answered with a few words, such as: • How do authors sometimes state theme? (through a title, the words of a character, or a descriptive line) • How is a topic different from theme? (A topic can be stated in a word or two. A theme is stated in a sentence.) • What was the theme of your favorite book? How do you know? (Answers will vary.)

Core Path	Access Path
3. When is it important to rely on textual evidence to determine theme? (when the theme must be inferred, because it is not stated directly) 4. Think about another text you have read in this class. Ask yourself, What is the text really about? What factors help you determine the answer to this question? (Answers may vary, but students should refer to ways that story elements, such as characters, plot, and setting, can help unfold the theme or themes in a story.)	**Beyond** **Discuss.** Challenge students to come up with a list of topics and themes for a story they'd like to write. Then have them discuss how they would develop that theme using story elements. Would they directly state the theme through the title, the characters' dialogue, or a descriptive line? Why or why not?
	Extend **Write.** Ask students to write one sentence that expresses a possible theme of *Wuthering Heights.* Then collect students' responses and choose a few at random to read aloud. As a class, discuss evidence students could use to support the suggested theme.

2. MODEL

Core Path	Access Path
Read and Annotate. Have students independently read the Model section. As they read, ask students to use the annotation tool to: • highlight key points • ask questions • identify places where the Model applies the strategies laid out in the Identification and Application section • comment on the effect that authors achieve when they state a theme directly and when they leave readers to infer the theme or themes	**Note:** During this portion of the lesson, instruction shifts from whole group to individual work. Use this time to work one-on-one or in small groups with Beginning, Intermediate, Advanced, and Approaching students. **Beginner & Intermediate** **Coach the Reading.** Work with these students (either individually or in small groups) to fill out the guided reading questions on the Access 1 and 2 handouts. Have Beginning students refer to the glossary on the Access 1 handout to help them determine the meaning of difficult words (note: provide the Access 1 handout glossary to Intermediate students if necessary). Let students know they'll use these answers to help participate in the discussion about the Model. Sample answers for this exercise are located at the end of the lesson plan online.

Core Path	Access Path
	Advanced **Identify Evidence.** Ask Advanced students to complete the identifying evidence exercise on the Access 3 handout. Let students know that they'll use these answers to help participate in the discussion about the Model. Sample answers for this exercise are located at the end of the lesson plan online. **Approaching** **Guided Reading.** Have students complete the guided reading questions on the Access 4 handout as they read. Let them know that they'll use these answers to help participate in the discussion about the Model. Sample answers for this exercise are located at the end of the lesson plan online.
Discuss. After students read the Model text, use these questions to facilitate a whole group discussion that helps students understand how to determine and analyze the theme of the passage: 1. How does the Model for this passage start to go about finding the theme? (It traces references to dreams throughout the excerpt.) 2. How does the Model use dialogue to make inferences about theme? (First, the Model compares what Catherine and Nelly each believe about dreams to infer that dreams can have a strong effect on reality in the text. Their dialogue reveals each woman's point of view. Then, it shows how Nelly's use of dream imagery to tell of Catherine's death does not lessen Heathcliff's grief.) 3. How has the theme developed and changed by the end of the excerpt? (The Model says that the strong connection between dreams and reality is "tested and disproved" by the end of the excerpt because Heathcliff's grief highlights the unavoidable realities of death.)	

Core Path	Access Path
	Extend **Evaluate.** Remind students that the Model essay gives just one interpretation of *Wuthering Heights*. Divide students into small groups and ask them to evaluate the Model's explanation. To aid in their evaluations, ask students: • Do you agree with what the Model writer has written? • Can you use the textual evidence listed in the Model to support another theme? • Can you think of any textual evidence that contradicts the Model's claims?

3. YOUR TURN

Core Path	Access Path
Assess and Explain. Have students answer the comprehension questions to test for understanding. Share the explanations for Parts A and B (located online) with your students.	
	Extend **Discuss.** Have students compare the themes identified in the Model and in the Your Turn exercises. Ask students: • What do these themes have in common? • How are these themes different? • How do these themes interact and build on each other in the text?

CLOSE READ:
Wuthering Heights

OVERVIEW

Wuthering Heights is a complex novel that uses the doomed love story of Catherine and Heathcliff to explore themes relating to clashes between fate and personal choice, dreams and reality, and love and selfishness. The Close Read gives students the opportunity to identify the themes of *Wuthering Heights* and analyze how the author develops these themes throughout the text.

OBJECTIVES

1. Complete a close reading of a passage of literature.
2. Practice and apply concrete strategies for determining and analyzing theme in an excerpt from *Wuthering Heights.*
3. Participate effectively in a range of conversations and collaborations to express ideas and build upon the ideas of others.
4. Prewrite, plan, and produce clear and coherent writing in response to a prompt.

ELA Common Core Standards:
Reading: Literature - RL.11-12.1, RL.11-12.2, RL.11-12.3, RL.11-12.4, RL.11-12.10
Writing - W.11-12.4, W.11-12.5, W.11-12.6, W.11-12.9.A, W.11-12.10
Speaking & Listening - SL.11-12.1.A, SL.11-12.1.B, SL.11-12.1.C, SL.11-12.1.D, SL.11-12.6
Language - L.11-12.4.A, L.11-12.4.C, L.11-12.4.D

RESOURCES

Wuthering Heights Vocabulary handout
Six Circles Graphic Organizer
Access 1 handout (Beginner)
Access 2 handout (Intermediate)
Access 3 handout (Advanced)
Access 4 handout (Approaching)

1. INTRODUCTION

Core Path	Access Path
Define and Compare. Project the vocabulary words and definitions onto the board or provide students with handouts, so they can copy the vocabulary into their notebooks. Suggest that students consult general and specialized reference materials, both print and digital, to compare the precise meaning of a specific word with their initial vocabulary predictions from the First Read. Review words that students defined incorrectly to understand why they were unable to use context clues or other tools to develop usable definitions.	**Beginner & Intermediate** **Complete a Chart.** Have students complete the chart on the Access 1 and 2 handouts by writing the correct word for each of the definitions. **Advanced & Beyond** **Write in Journals.** Have students write a journal entry using all of their vocabulary words. Remind them to write sentences that communicate the meaning of the words they are using. **Approaching** **Graphic Organizer.** To support students in comparing their predictions with the correct meanings, have them complete the graphic organizer on the Access 4 handout to record the vocabulary words, their initial analysis, and the definitions. Then have them write sentences using the words.
Review. Have students complete the fill-in-the-blanks vocabulary worksheet attached to the lesson plan online. Answers for the worksheet are listed at the end of the lesson plan online.	
	Extend **Draw.** Ask pairs of students to draw a picture or comic that conveys the meaning of each vocabulary word. Students may use paper and other art supplies or an online tool, such as Google Drawings or Make Belief Comix (http://www.makebeliefscomix.com). When they are finished, have them share and discuss their word representations with their partner.

Core Path	Access Path
	Extend **Write.** Break students into pairs and have them write a short narrative based in the world of *Wuthering Heights* using each of the vocabulary words. They may rewrite the events as they appear in the novel or imagine a new scenario featuring Catherine, Heathcliff, and Nelly, or some combination of the three. Make sure students write new sentences for each of the vocabulary words and do not plagiarize Brontë's text.

2. READ

Core Path	Access Path
Model Close Reading. Project the text onto the board and model a close reading of the first excerpt using the annotation strategies mentioned on the next page. While modeling annotation strategies, make notes that tie the text to the focus skill and demonstrate what students are looking for as they read. Here is some guidance for you as you annotate for your students: • As the Skills lesson that precedes this text explains, theme is the central idea or message of a text. • I scan the excerpt from Chapter 9 and see that Catherine is recounting a dream she has had, and Nelly doesn't want to hear it. I reread the dialogue and ask, What is this conversation *really* about? • I begin by looking closely at Catherine's dream. She dreamt she was in heaven and that she was miserable there. This seems strange because one would think that being in heaven would bring Catherine happiness and peace.	

Core Path	Access Path
• I keep reading and see that Catherine compares heaven to marrying Linton: "I've no more business to marry Edgar Linton than I have to be in heaven; and if the wicked [Hindley] had not brought Heathcliff so low, I shouldn't have thought of it." Based on this, I can infer that Catherine thinks marrying Linton would raise her status, but she does not think it would make her happy. I can also infer that Catherine wants to marry Heathcliff, but she won't do it because it would lower her social status. This helps me figure out that one of the themes of this novel has to do with choosing between love and selfishness.	
Read and Annotate. Read the Skills Focus questions as a class, so your students know what they should pay close attention to as they read. Then have students read and annotate the excerpt. Ask students to use the annotation tool as they read to 1. respond to the Skills Focus section 2. ask questions about which story elements might help to convey the theme or themes 3. make connections between story elements, such as setting, characters, and plot, and themes in the story 4. identify key information, examples, and themes 5. note unfamiliar vocabulary 6. capture their reaction to the ideas and examples in the text As they reread the text, remind students to use the comprehension strategy of asking and answering questions that they learned in the First Read.	**Note:** While on-grade-level students are reading and annotating, work one-on-one or in small groups with Beginning, Intermediate, Advanced, and Approaching students to support them as they read and annotate the text. **Beginner & Intermediate** **Summarize and Analyze the Text.** Work with these students to complete the sentence frames on the Access 1 and 2 handouts (note: the sentence frames for Intermediate students on the Access 2 handout contain fewer scaffolds). They will then use the completed sentence frames to help them analyze and annotate the text by completing the Skills Focus questions. Refer to the sample Skills Focus answers to help them complete the sentence frames and annotate the text. **Advanced** **Work in Pairs.** Pair these students with more proficient English speakers to work together on analyzing and annotating the text to complete the Skills Focus questions. If these students need more support, have them use the sentence frames on the Access 3 handout as they work with their more proficient peers.

Core Path	Access Path
	Approaching **Summarize the Text.** Have these students discuss and complete the text summary on the Access 4 handout and use their summary to help them analyze and annotate the text by completing the Skills Focus questions. Correct answers for the summary are at the end of the lesson plan online. Also refer to the sample Skills Focus answers to aid students with their annotations.
Discuss. After students have read the text, use the sample responses to the Skills Focus questions at the bottom of the lesson plan online to discuss the reading and the process of determining and analyzing theme. Make sure that students have acquired and accurately use academic-specific words and phrases related to the skill and demonstrate a command of formal English appropriate to the discussion. To help facilitate discussions, refer to Collaborative Discussions in the Speaking & Listening Handbook.	**Extend** **Pair and Share.** In small, heterogeneous groups or pairs, ask students to share and discuss their annotations with a focus on the theme of the selection. You can provide students with these questions to guide their discussion: 1. How does Nelly and Catherine's conversation about dreams help develop the theme of the text? Cite specific textual evidence to support your statements. (Nelly's "superstitious" feelings about dreams suggests that one theme is that one cannot escape her own fate. Catherine's statement that dreams have changed her ["I've dreamt in my life dreams that have stayed with me ever after, and changed my ideas: they've gone through and through me, like wine through water, and altered the colour of my mind"] supports this theme.)

Core Path	Access Path
	2. What does Catherine's choice of husband suggest about the novel's portrayal of marriage, and how does it relate to the theme of the text? Cite specific textual evidence to support your answer. (Catherine chooses to marry Linton, even though she is madly in love with Heathcliff. She says, "[Heathcliff is] more myself than I am. Whatever our souls are made of, his and mine are the same; and Linton's is as different as a moonbeam from lightning, or frost from fire." This suggests that romantic love is much less important in a marriage than financial stability, which helps develop the theme that Catherine is trapped by her own selfishness and life circumstances.) 3. Heathcliff quietly leaves after hearing Catherine's plan and does not confront her until several years later. How do these actions help develop the theme of the text? (Heathcliff's actions suggest that a possible theme of the text is that people are victims not of fate but, rather, of their own decisions. His relationship with Catherine might have turned out differently if he had acted sooner instead of waiting until years after the fact.)
	Extend **Compare and Contrast.** The excerpt from *Wuthering Heights* focuses on the love story between Catherine and Heathcliff. Ask students to define love and identify a real-life couple who they believe to have a strong relationship. Then have students create a Venn diagram to compare and contrast the couple they chose with Catherine and Heathcliff. Lastly, have students share their Venn diagrams with a peer and discuss how love is represented in the novel and brainstorm how love relates to the themes of the novel.

3. WRITE

Core Path	Access Path
Prewrite and Plan. Read the prompt as a class and ask students to brainstorm about the themes of *Wuthering Heights.* Students can brainstorm together either as a class or in small groups to begin planning their responses. Remind your students to look at the excerpt and their annotations to find textual evidence to support their ideas.	**Beginner & Intermediate** **Plan and Organize.** Have students complete the prewriting activity on the Access 1 and 2 handouts and then explain their ideas to a partner before they write. Explain to students that they need to choose details, examples, or quotes from the text that support their ideas and then explain how those details support their statements. For example, students could include Catherine's question, "... did it never strike you that if Heathcliff and I married, we should be beggars?" which shows the theme of the destructiveness of social status. **Approaching** **Plan and Organize.** Have students complete the prewriting activity on the Access 4 handout to organize their thoughts before they write.
Discuss. Project these instructions for the peer review onto the board and review them with your class, so they know what they are looking for when they begin to provide their classmates with feedback: • How has this essay helped you understand how characterization and dialogue develop theme in the text? • How well does the writer describe the characterization of Catherine, Heathcliff, or Nelly? • How well does the writer analyze the characters' dialogue? • What themes does the writer identify? How clear is the writer's explanation of how the themes interact and build on each other? • What sort of evidence does the writer use from the text to support his or her writing? • How well does the writer explain how that evidence supports his or her ideas?	

Core Path	Access Path
• Does the writer write using standard grammar and punctuation? Are there any weak spots? • What specific suggestions can you make to help the writer improve the response? • What thing(s) does this paper do especially well? After you've looked at the peer review instructions, review the rubric with students before they begin writing. Allow time for students briefly to pose and discuss any questions they may have about the peer review instructions and the rubric. Tell students how many peer reviews they will need to complete once they submit their writing.	
Write. Ask students to complete the writing assignment using textual evidence to support their answers. Once they have completed their writing, they should click "Submit."	
	Extend **Organize.** Distribute copies of the Six Circles Graphic Organizer to students. Ask them to write a theme in the large center circle and to list supporting ideas and details in the smaller circles. Ask them to include at least one direct quotation as support.
	Extend **Give Feedback.** After students have completed their Six Circles Graphic Organizer but before they begin writing, divide them into pairs and have them trade organizers. Begin by having students compare the themes they have identified, and then ask them to evaluate the textual evidence chosen as support. Ask: • Has the student included evidence that relates to the theme? • Do you believe the student provided a sufficient amount of textual evidence to support the theme? • If the theme requires more support, ask your partner to identify additional textual evidence.

Core Path	Access Path
Review. Once students complete their writing assignment, they should submit substantive feedback to two peers. Students should use their peers' feedback to improve their writing.	

FIRST READ:
The House of Mirth

OVERVIEW

The novel *The House of Mirth*, by Edith Wharton, describes the struggles of Lily Bart to find a rich husband in New York society after her family has lost their money. The First Read gives students the opportunity to experience the text with limited context.

OBJECTIVES

1. Perform an initial reading of a text and demonstrate comprehension by responding to short analysis and inference questions with textual evidence.
2. Practice defining vocabulary words using context.
3. Participate effectively in a range of conversations and collaborations to express ideas and build upon the ideas of others.
4. Practice acquiring and using academic vocabulary correctly.

ELA Common Core Standards:
Reading: Literature - RL.11-12.1, RL.11-12.4, RL.11-12.10
Writing - W.11-12.7
Speaking & Listening - SL.11-12.1.A, SL.11-12.1.B, SL.11-12.1.C, SL.11-12.1.D, SL.11-12.2
Language - L.11-12.4.A, L.11-12.6

RESOURCES

Access 1 handout (Beginner)
Access 2 handout (Intermediate)
Access 3 handout (Advanced)
Access 4 handout (Approaching)

ACCESS COMPLEX TEXT

This excerpt from *The House of Mirth* describes Lily Bart's stress over her need to get married. She then thinks back on her childhood and how she got into her current situation. To help students understand the main character of Lily, and the internal and external conflicts she faces, use the following ideas to provide scaffolded instruction for a first reading of the more complex features of this text:

- **Organization** - The excerpt's focus is on Lily's remembrances of her mother and childhood before her family lost their money. Some readers may struggle to follow the jumps in time. Point out to students that Lily's childhood memories begin in paragraph 10, preceded by a more current memory in paragraph 9 of her mother's vindictive demand of her upon the loss of the family's wealth.

- **Connection of Ideas** - Because the excerpt is from Chapter III of the novel, some readers may not understand Lily's motivations or references. You may wish to provide students with summaries of the previous chapters as well as the chapter itself.

- **Prior Knowledge** - Upper-class New York society in the 1890s and its social customs will be unfamiliar to some readers. Explain to students that this period in American history is often referred to as the "Gilded Age," which lasted from the 1870s to about 1900. The Gilded Age was an era of rapid economic growth, especially in the North and the West, and higher wages attracted millions of immigrants. However, it was also an era of poverty and inequality as very poor European immigrants poured in and wealth became highly concentrated among the few. In New York City, social classes became increasingly stratified and customs among the upper classes more rigid and complex.

1. INTRODUCTION

Core Path	Access Path
Read. Individually or as a class, read the introduction for *The House of Mirth*. The introduction provides context for the excerpt from Chapter III.	**English Learners All Levels & Approaching** **Read and Listen.** Ask students to read and listen to the introduction for *The House of Mirth*. Have them refer to the "Introduction Glossary" on their Access 1, 2, 3, and 4 handouts for definitions of key vocabulary terms. If there are unfamiliar words that are not included in their glossary, encourage students to check a dictionary or online reference tool, like http://dictionary.reference.com.

Core Path	Access Path
Build Background. In pairs or small groups, ask students to use devices to research New York high society of the late nineteenth century. Assign each group a topic to investigate. Remind students to include relevant facts, definitions, and concrete details in their research: • Business and wealth in the Gilded Age • Role of women and marriage in the upper classes at the end of the nineteenth century • Growth and changes in New York City at the end of the nineteenth century • Early industrialists and financiers (John D. Rockefeller, Andrew Carnegie, J. P. Morgan, etc.) If you are in a low-tech classroom, you can provide photocopies of articles about the Gilded Age for students to read and discuss. Have students present their findings.	**Beginner** **Build Background.** To focus their research when building background, ask students to complete the specified Targeted Background Research Chart about early industrialists and financiers as they work in small groups. These charts are on the Access 1 handouts. Sample answers are provided at the end of the lesson plan online. **Intermediate & Advanced** **Build Background.** To focus the research when building background, ask students to complete the specified Targeted Background Research Chart about women and marriage as they work in small groups. These charts are on the Access 2 and 3 handouts. Sample answers are provided at the end of the lesson plan online. **Approaching** **Build Background.** To focus the research when building background, ask students to complete the specified Targeted Background Research Chart about business and wealth in the Gilded Age as they work in small groups. These charts are on the Access 4 handouts. Sample answers are provided at the end of the lesson plan online.
	Extend **Analyze and Discuss a Quote.** "What is the chief end of man?—to get rich. In what way?—dishonestly if we can; honestly if we must." (Mark Twain) Lead students in a discussion of this quote. 1. What do you think this quote means? 2. How would you define the "chief end of man?" Has that changed over time? 3. Do you agree with this quote? Why or why not?

2. READ

Core Path	Access Path
Make Predictions about Vocabulary. There are six bold vocabulary words in the text. As students read the text, ask them to make predictions about what they think each bold vocabulary word means based on the context clues in the sentence. Have students use the annotation tool to make their predictions. It might be helpful to model this for students before they begin reading. Either using the board or projecting the actual text, focus in on the sentence that uses the word "desiccating": • Her ambitions had shrunk gradually in the desiccating air of failure. Model for the class how to use these context clues to guess the meanings of the words: 1. Look at the structure of the sentence. What part of speech is the word "desiccating"? (adjective) Knowing that "desiccating" describes the word "air" allows us to begin to figure out what it means. 2. If we look at the beginning of the sentence, we see that Lily is describing her ambitions as having shrunk in the "desiccating air of failure." "Desiccating" air must cause things to shrink. 3. I'll think about my prior knowledge of what could cause things to shrink. I think of wilting plants, dried leaves, or old fruit. These things all shrink because of a lack of water. 4. If "desiccating air" caused Lily's ambitions to shrink, then I think "desiccating" means "drying." 5. I will check my preliminary determination of the meaning in a dictionary to make sure I have it right before I move on.	**Note:** This exercise, which extends vocabulary instruction, should be completed when the class shifts from whole group instruction to individual work during the "Read and Annotate" exercise. **Beginner, Intermediate & Approaching Pair Practice.** 1. Pair students with more proficient readers. 2. Give them an additional sentence that contains a new vocabulary word. 3. Ask the students to complete a Think Aloud using the teacher-led Make Predictions about Vocabulary activity as a model, while the proficient student actively listens. 4. The student should use the context clues in the sentence to try to determine the meaning of the new vocabulary word. 5. After the student has completed the Think Aloud and made a prediction about the word's meaning, allow time for the proficient reader to add his/her own thoughts and clarify any points of confusion. 6. Once they've completed this Think Aloud, encourage them to use a dictionary to confirm the definition of the new vocabulary word. Have them refer to the "Text Glossary" on their Access 1, 2, and 4 handouts for definitions of key vocabulary terms in the text. Encourage them to add any additional vocabulary words or idioms they find in the text and look up definitions for those words and idioms online or in a dictionary.

Core Path	Access Path
Model Reading Comprehension Strategy. Before students begin reading, model the reading comprehension strategy of asking and answering questions by using this Think Aloud that talks students through the first several paragraphs of text. First explain to your students that: *strong readers ask themselves questions before, during, and after reading—not just about surface meaning, but also about big ideas and themes—to check and enhance their understanding* Model for students how asking and answering questions will help them better comprehend the selection and help drive their discussions. • In the Introduction, I learn that Lily Bart is struggling with the expectations of society. Then I see in the first sentence of the excerpt that Lily is feeling this pressure: "A world in which such things could be seemed a miserable place to Lily Bart." I ask myself, What "such things" worry Lily? • In the next paragraph, we learn that Lily begins to get ready for bed without the help of her maid. That tells me that it is expected in this society that maids help wealthy women undress and get ready. Then Lily describes herself as "long enough in bondage to other people's pleasure." I ask myself, is this feeling of "bondage" the thing that worries Lily? It might answer my question. • I read on. I don't get an immediate answer to my questions, but we learn that Lily is very concerned about her appearance and looking older or stressed. Her appearance must be important to making herself less miserable.	**Note:** This exercise, which extends instruction around reading comprehension strategies, should be completed when the class shifts from whole group instruction to individual work during the "Read and Annotate" exercise. **Beginner, Intermediate & Approaching Apply Reading Comprehension Strategy.** 1. To practice asking and answering questions, have students listen to the audio version of the excerpt from *The House of Mirth* paired with the written text. As they listen to the audio recording, ask them to draw a question mark next to portions of the text where they have a question. Next have them underline words in the text that they understand. Encourage them to use what they know to both ask questions and draw conclusions about the text. If students struggle to come up with questions, you might prompt them with some, such as What does Lily look like? How does Lily remember her parents? What was their home like? What are the main differences between Lily's life before and after her family lost their money? 2. Once they have listened to the audio version and created annotated areas where they have questions and understandings, pair Beginning and Intermediate students with more proficient readers and ask them to describe what they underlined and why. What words, descriptions, and ideas are familiar to them? 3. Allow pairs time to discuss the question-marked sections. Were there any details from the text that might help in their understanding? If so, encourage them to make inferences.
Read and Annotate. Have students independently read and annotate the excerpt. Ask students to use the annotation tool as they read to: 1. use context clues to analyze and determine the meaning of the bolded vocabulary terms	

Core Path	Access Path
2. ask questions about passages of the text that may be unclear or unresolved 3. identify key details, events, characters, and connections between them 4. note unfamiliar vocabulary	**Beginner** **Coach the Reading.** While other students read, annotate, and discuss the text independently, work with Beginning students, listening to the audio of the text and pausing periodically or when any student has a question. Coach students in articulating their questions for the group and in highlighting and annotating the text. Have students use the Annotation Guide on the Access 1 handout to support them as they highlight and annotate the text. For further support, ask questions about the text such as: • Is there anything about the excerpt that you don't understand? • What did you learn about high society in 19th century America from this excerpt? • If you were in Lily's position, how would you respond? Is Lily justified in her reaction to her situation? Why or why not? **Intermediate** **Listen to the Audio.** Have these students listen to the audio of the text and use the definitions on the Access 2 handout to help them with words or idioms that may be unfamiliar. If students need help with annotating the text, have them use the Annotation Guide on the Access 2 handout. After working with the Beginning students, you may wish to check this group's progress and provide support as needed. **Advanced** **Pair with Proficient Peers.** Have Advanced students work with English-proficient peers to read, annotate, and discuss the text. Have students use the Annotation Guide in the Access 3 handout to support them as they highlight and annotate the text. Encourage them to listen to the audio of the text if needed. **Approaching** **Use the Annotation Guide.** Have students use the Annotation Guide on the Access 4 handout to support them as they highlight and annotate the text.

Core Path	Access Path
Discuss. In small groups or pairs, have students discuss the questions and inferences they made while reading. To help facilitate discussions, refer to Collaborative Discussions in the Speaking & Listening Handbook. 1. What comparison does Lily make between herself and her maid? (Lily says she is in the same position as her maid because she is also "in bondage to other people's pleasure.") What does this tell you about the role of women in Lily's society? (That comparison tells me that women do not have much agency, or power, in Lily's society.) 2. How does Lily remember her father? (He worked all the time. He was distant and silent and appeared very old to Lily.) How is this different from Lily's memories of her mother? (In Lily's mind, Mrs. Bart is a "vigorous and determined figure." Her mother took her to Europe and summers away, and imparted to Lily ideas of what is proper for keeping up appearances.) 3. What questions did you have while reading? Were any left unanswered by the end of the excerpt? (Answers will vary.)	**English Learners All Levels & Approaching** Use the extra time while on- and beyond-grade-level students are discussing their first reads of the text to work individually and in small groups with Approaching readers and English Learners as outlined on the previous page. Should those students complete their first reads quickly, integrate them into the on- and beyond-grade-level discussion groups. Otherwise, English Learners and Approaching readers will be given an opportunity to participate in text discussions with their peers later in the lesson. **Beyond** **Tech Infusion** **Record.** Use a voice recording app (Voice Memo on the iPhone or Smart Voice Recorder for Androids) or VoiceThread (https://voicethread.com) to capture each group's ideas.

3. THINK

Core Path	Access Path
Answer and Discuss. Have students complete the Think questions and then use the peer review instructions and rubric to complete two peer reviews. Refer to the sample answers at the end of the lesson plan online to discuss responses with your students.	**Beginner & Intermediate** **Sentence Frames.** Have students use the sentence frames on the Access 1 and 2 handouts to support their responses to the Think questions. If necessary, distribute sentence frames to Advanced students as well. **Approaching** **Find the Evidence.** Have students use Find the Evidence on the Access 4 handout to help them identify the evidence needed to answer the questions.

Core Path	Access Path
	Extend **Tech Infusion** **Reflection.** Lily Bart is worried about her own future, but her thoughts of her situation circle back to pressure from her mother to marry well and regain the family's wealth. Have students write a short reflection on the role parental pressure can play in a young person's life. What kinds of pressure do they feel from parents or other family members? How is that pressure similar to or different from what Lily feels? Allow them to reflect on paper or using an online journaling tool like Penzu (www.penzu.com).

SKILL:
Character

OVERVIEW

Characters are a key part of what makes a story worth reading. Lily Bart in *The House of Mirth* is a memorable and tragic heroine. This lesson plan provides follow-up questions and enrichments to help teachers guide students toward a usable, repeatable method for analyzing characters in a work of fiction.

OBJECTIVES

1. Learn the definition of character.
2. Practice using concrete strategies for analyzing characters in a novel.
3. Participate effectively in a range of conversations and collaborations to express ideas and build upon the ideas of others.

ELA Common Core Standards:
Reading: Literature - RL.11-12.1, RL.11-12.3
Speaking & Listening - SL.11-12.1.A, SL.11-12.1.C, SL.11-12.2

RESOURCES

Access 1 handout (Beginner)
Access 2 handout (Intermediate)
Access 3 handout (Advanced)
Access 4 handout (Approaching)

1. DEFINE

Core Path	Access Path
Watch. Watch the Concept Definition video on character with your students. Make sure students write down and understand the definition of character, focusing in particular on how character traits may change or evolve over the course of a story's plot. Pause the video at these key moments to discuss the information with your students: 1. 0:36 – Ben says that character traits are developed through dialogue and actions. What are the advantages and disadvantages of each method of developing characters? 2. 0:45 – Why do characters typically change over the course of a story? What attracts people to stories of a person changing? Why might that be interesting to read? 3. 0:57 – What is the relationship between characters and plot? How do these elements impact each other?	**English Learners All Levels & Approaching** **Fill in the Blanks.** Have students complete the fill-in-the-blanks exercise on the Access 1, 2, 3, and 4 handouts as they watch the video. Answers are located at the end of the lesson plan online.
Read and Discuss. After watching the Concept Definition video, have students read the definition of character. Either in small groups or as a whole class, use these questions to engage students in a discussion about characters: 1. How are nonhuman characters developed differently from human characters? (An author may or may not give nonhumans the ability to think or communicate. Instead, he or she might develop nonhuman characters through a description of their physical characteristics and special abilities. Most humans, on the other hand, would be characterized through their dialogue, actions, and behaviors, as well as the reactions of other characters.) Why might an author choose to use nonhuman characters in a story? (He or she might create a setting that requires them, such as in a magical world or in a myth.) Can you think of any examples? (Answers will vary.)	**Beginner & Approaching** **Complete a Chart.** To prepare students to participate in the discussion, have them complete the chart on the Access 1 and 4 handouts as they read the definition. The correct answers are located at the end of the lesson plan online. **Intermediate & Advanced** **Discuss Prompts.** To help these students participate in the discussion, prompt them with questions that can be answered with a few words, such as: • How do authors reveal their characters' personalities and traits in a work of fiction? (through description, dialogue, and situations) • What is the main difference between main characters and minor characters? (The story revolves around the main character or characters. Minor characters support the main characters, helping to reveal aspects of their personalities.)

Core Path	Access Path
2. What is the relationship between character traits and how realistic a character seems to a reader? (Character traits motivate actions, and characters' actions move the plot forward. We all have character traits that motivate us, so characters driven by their traits will seem realistic) 3. What's the difference between a protagonist and an antagonist? (The protagonist is usually the character that the story revolves around. The antagonist is the character that works against the protagonist.) Does a story always need both? (Yes, because the tension between their motivations provide the conflict of the plot.) 4. What is the role of minor characters? (They help to reveal aspects of the protagonist and antagonist in the story.)	• How is the plot of a work of fiction like an engine and the protagonist like the person behind the steering wheel? (The protagonist's thoughts, feelings, actions, and reactions drive the plot and move it forward.) **Beyond** **Discuss.** Have students think of another novel or short story they've read and describe how the characters' traits drive the story's plot. Then have students discuss the strengths and weaknesses of the protagonists in each story. What kind of protagonists do they enjoy reading about most? Why?
	Extend **Write.** 1. Ask students to choose one character from a book or story they've read in class this year. Have students start by writing a short paragraph describing the character's traits, including appearance and behavior. 2. Then have students choose one trait that was most important to the plot or the character's development in the story (Hamlet's indecisiveness, for example). Have students write a short paragraph explaining why this trait was so important and how changing it would have affected the rest of the character's story. 3. Use these paragraphs as a starting point for a discussion of the impact of characters on other story elements.

2. MODEL

Core Path	Access Path
Read and Annotate. Have students independently read the Model section. As they read, ask students to use the annotation tool to: • highlight key points • ask questions • identify places where the Model applies the strategies laid out in the Identification and Application section • comment on the effect that characters have on the plot	**Note:** During this portion of the lesson, instruction shifts from whole group to individual work. Use this time to work one-on-one or in small groups with Beginning, Intermediate, Advanced, and Approaching students. **Beginner & Intermediate** **Coach the Reading.** Work with these students (either individually or in small groups) to fill out the guided reading questions on the Access 1 and 2 handouts. Have Beginning students refer to the glossary on the Access 1 handout to help them determine the meaning of difficult words (note: provide the Access 1 handout glossary to Intermediate students if necessary). Let students know they'll use these answers to help participate in the discussion about the Model. Sample answers for this exercise are located at the end of the lesson plan online. **Advanced** **Identify Evidence.** Ask Advanced students to complete the identifying evidence exercise on the Access 3 handout. Let students know that they'll use these answers to help participate in the discussion about the Model. Sample answers for this exercise are located at the end of the lesson plan online. **Approaching** **Guided Reading.** Have students complete the guided reading questions on the Access 4 handout as they read. Let them know that they'll use these answers to help participate in the discussion about the Model. Sample answers for this exercise are located at the end of the lesson plan online.

Core Path	Access Path
Discuss. After students read the Model text, use these questions to facilitate a whole-group discussion that helps students understand how to analyze characters in the excerpt: 1. According to the Model, what do readers learn about Lily from direct characterization in this excerpt? (She is considerate toward servants.) What traits do readers learn from indirect characterization? (Lily is intelligent and observant, and she thinks highly of herself.) 2. How is Mr. Bart's character described? ("hazy," "neutral-tinted," "bald and slightly stooping") What clues does this description suggest about Mr. Bart's relationship with Lily? (Lily and her father are not close. She barely recognizes him as more important than the butler.) 3. What is Mrs. Bart's role in Lily's life? (She was the one around when Lily was young. She taught Lily the importance of "dressing well" and keeping up appearances.) How is Lily's mother still influencing her today? (Lily thinks of her mother when she is worried about her chances of "landing" Percy Gryce.) 4. In what ways may Mrs. Bart and Lily be considered archetypes? (Mrs. Bart is the overbearing mother. Lily is the woman using her looks to get ahead.)	
	Extend **Brainstorm.** As a class, brainstorm other examples of the bad mother archetype, such as Cassiopeia from Greek mythology (and the movie *Clash of the Titans*), who declared that her daughter Andromeda was more beautiful than a goddess and had to sacrifice her to a sea monster—until she was saved by Perseus. When the class has a good list, discuss what effect these mothers have on their children. Have students make predictions for Lily based on her experience with her mother.

Core Path	Access Path
	Extend **Tech Infusion** **Poll.** Using Poll Everywhere (http://www.polleverywhere.com/), ask students to submit their favorite character from literature. It can be a character from this class or an outside reading. Then conduct a second poll in which students submit a key trait that makes characters interesting or memorable. Discuss the results as a class.

3. YOUR TURN

Core Path	Access Path
Assess and Explain. Have students answer the comprehension questions to test for understanding. Share the explanations for Parts A and B (located online) with your students.	
	Extend **Write and Perform.** Pair students and have them revisit the excerpt from *The House of Mirth*. Ask them to imagine the conversations Mr. and Mrs. Bart have about money. Staying true to the character traits in the excerpt, ask students to write a dialogue in which Mrs. Bart asks Mr. Bart for money. When students are finished, ask volunteers to perform their dialogues for the class.

CLOSE READ:
The House of Mirth

OVERVIEW

Edith Wharton's *The House of Mirth* is the story of Lily Bart, a young woman whose family lost everything and who tries to find a suitable husband while struggling with the expectations of high society. The Close Read gives students the opportunity to more deeply analyze the characterization of Lily and her parents and how these characters influence one another.

OBJECTIVES

1. Complete a close reading of a passage of literature.
2. Practice and apply concrete strategies for analyzing characters.
3. Participate effectively in a range of conversations and collaborations to express ideas and build upon the ideas of others.
4. Prewrite, plan, and produce clear and coherent writing in response to a prompt.

ELA Common Core Standards:
Reading: Literature - RL.11-12.1, RL.11-12.2, RL.11-12.3, RL.11-12.4, RL.11-12.6, RL.11-12.10
Writing - W.11-12.1.A, W.11-12.1.B, W.11-12.4, W.11-12.5, W.11-12.6, W.11-12.9.A, W.11-12.10
Speaking & Listening - SL.11-12.1.A, SL.11-12.1.B, SL.11-12.1.C, SL.11-12.1.D, SL.11-12.6
Language - L.11-12.4.A, L.11-12.4.C, L.11-12.4.D

RESOURCES

The House of Mirth Vocabulary handout
Access 1 handout (Beginner)
Access 2 handout (Intermediate)
Access 3 handout (Advanced)
Access 4 handout (Approaching)

1. INTRODUCTION

Core Path	Access Path
Define and Compare. Project the vocabulary words and definitions onto the board or provide students with handouts, so they can copy the vocabulary into their notebooks. Suggest that students consult general and specialized reference materials, both print and digital, to compare the precise meaning of a specific word with their initial vocabulary predictions from the First Read. Review words that students defined incorrectly to understand why they were unable to use context clues or other tools to develop usable definitions.	**Beginner & Intermediate** **Complete a Chart.** Have students complete the chart on the Access 1 and 2 handouts by writing the correct word for each of the definitions. **Advanced & Beyond** **Write in Journals.** Have students write a journal entry using all of their vocabulary words. Remind them to write sentences that communicate the meaning of the words they are using. **Approaching** **Graphic Organizer.** To support students in comparing their predictions with the correct meanings, have them complete the graphic organizer on the Access 4 handout to record the vocabulary words, their initial analysis, and the definitions. Then have them write sentences using the words.
Review. Have students complete the fill-in-the-blanks vocabulary worksheet attached to the lesson plan online. Answers for the worksheet are listed at the end of the lesson plan online.	
	Extend **Create.** Ask students to use an app such as Quizlet (http://quizlet.com) or StudyBlue (www.studyblue.com) to make a set of online flashcards showing each vocabulary word, its part of speech on one side and the definition on the other. Have them use the flashcards to review and remember the words.

Core Path	Access Path
	Extend **Discuss the Title.** Ask pairs or small groups to use devices to research the allusion in the title of the book. (It's a reference to a line in Ecclesiastes 7:4 in the Hebrew Bible: *The heart of the wise is in the house of mourning; but the heart of fools is in the house of mirth.*) As a class, discuss what that line means. As they read, have students think about how this line might apply to Lily's situation.

2. READ

Core Path	Access Path
Model Close Reading. Project the text onto the board and model a close reading of the first two paragraphs using the annotation strategies mentioned on the next page. While modeling annotation strategies, make notes that tie the text to the focus skill and demonstrate what students are looking for as they read. Some guidance for you as you annotate for your students: • This excerpt is from Chapter III, so we know as readers that we have already missed some important plot elements and the introduction of the characters. But we can still learn a lot about the main character in this section. • Point out that the main character of the novel, Lily Bart, is introduced in the first sentence. Our first impression of Lily is that she is self-centered: "she had never been able to understand the laws of a universe which was so ready to leave her out of its calculations."	

Core Path	Access Path
• Then in the next sentence, Lily becomes a more complex character. She may seem self-centered, but we would not expect a self-centered character to think about her maid's feelings. She surprises us by not calling for her maid. Lily may think that the world is unfair, but she is observant enough to be considerate toward servants. We also learn that Lily considers herself to be "in bondage to other people's pleasure," so she must not be an independent woman. We'll have to read on to learn why.	
Read and Annotate. Read the Skills Focus questions as a class, so your students know what they should pay close attention to as they read. Then have students read and annotate the excerpt. Ask students to use the annotation tool as they read to 1. respond to the Skills Focus section 2. ask questions about the ways the author characterizes the characters 3. make connections between character traits and character actions 4. identify key information, examples, and themes 5. note unfamiliar vocabulary 6. capture their reaction to the ideas and examples in the text As they reread the text, remind students to use the comprehension strategy of asking and answering questions that they learned in the First Read.	**Note:** While on-grade-level students are reading and annotating, work one-on-one or in small groups with Beginning, Intermediate, Advanced, and Approaching students to support them as they read and annotate the text. **Beginner & Intermediate** **Summarize and Analyze the Text.** Work with these students to complete the sentence frames on the Access 1 and 2 handouts (note: the sentence frames for Intermediate students on the Access 2 handout contain fewer scaffolds). They will then use the completed sentence frames to help them analyze and annotate the text by completing the Skills Focus questions. Refer to the sample Skills Focus answers to help them complete the sentence frames and annotate the text. **Advanced** **Work in Pairs.** Pair these students with more proficient English speakers to work together on analyzing and annotating the text to complete the Skills Focus questions. If these students need more support, have them use the sentence frames on the Access 3 handout as they work with their more proficient peers.

Core Path	Access Path
	Approaching **Summarize the Text.** Have these students discuss and complete the text summary on the Access 4 handout and use their summary to help them analyze and annotate the text by completing the Skills Focus questions. Correct answers for the summary are at the end of the lesson plan online. Also refer to the sample Skills Focus answers to aid students with their annotations.
Discuss. After students have read the text, use the sample responses to the Skills Focus questions at the bottom of the lesson plan online to discuss the reading and the process of analyzing the characters. Make sure that students have acquired and accurately use academic-specific words and phrases related to the skill and demonstrate a command of formal English appropriate to the discussion. To help facilitate discussions, refer to Collaborative Discussions in the Speaking & Listening Handbook.	**Extend** **Pair and Share.** In small, heterogeneous groups or pairs, ask students to share and discuss their annotations with a focus on the characters presented in the selection. You can provide students with these questions to guide their discussion: 1. What kind of childhood did Lily Bart have? What words and phrases does the author use to describe it? Cite specific textual evidence to support your statements. (Lily's childhood is described as "chaos," "an equally changing dynasty," with "quarrels" and a "turbulent element." These words make her childhood seem frantic and possibly unstable. The family never had enough money, but they spent lavishly.) 2. What, to Lily and her mother, do people do to "live like pigs"? Cite specific textual evidence to support your answer. (According to Lily and her mother, these people "lived like pigs" lived in "dingy" houses with cheap engravings on the wall and had "slatternly" maids. The worst part for Lily was that these people were wealthy. For Lily and her mother, wealth did not create class.) Is their definition what you expected? Why or why not? (Answers will vary.)

Core Path	Access Path
	3. What tone does the narrator have toward the Barts? How does that affect your reading of the excerpt? Cite specific textual evidence to support your answer. (Examples may vary. The narrator's tone is often neutral but occasionally is critical or points out hypocrisy. For example, "Lily could not recall the time when there had been money enough, and in some vague way her father seemed always to blame for the deficiency. It could certainly not be the fault of Mrs. Bart, who was spoken of by her friends as a 'wonderful manager.'")
	Extend **Connect.** In Lily's mind, people who "lived like pigs" had engravings of Cole's Voyage of Life hanging on the walls. As a class or in small groups, find images of these paintings. Discuss this question: Why might these paintings have seemed so déclassé, or tasteless, to Lily and Mrs. Bart?

3. WRITE

Core Path	Access Path
Prewrite and Plan. Read the prompt as a class and ask students to brainstorm about Lily's motivations in *The House of Mirth*. Students can brainstorm together either as a class or in small groups to begin planning their responses. Remind your students to look at the excerpt and their annotations to find textual evidence to support their ideas.	**Beginner & Intermediate** **Plan and Organize.** Have students complete the prewriting activity on the Access 1 and 2 handouts and then explain their ideas to a partner before they write. Explain to students that they need to choose details, examples, or quotes from the text that support their opinions and then explain how those details support their statements. For example, in the second paragraph, students could include the line, "She had been long enough in bondage to other

Core Path	Access Path
	people's pleasure ... and in her bitter moods it sometimes struck her that she and her maid were in the same position, except that the latter received her wages more regularly," which demonstrates that Lily feels a deep resentment about her position in life. She seems to envy her own servant for receiving regular payment for her daily work, indicating she may not feel her own struggle to gain wealth is worth it. **Approaching** **Plan and Organize.** Have students complete the prewriting activity on the Access 4 handout to organize their thoughts before they write.
Discuss. Project these peer review instructions onto the board and review them with your class, so they know what they are looking for when they begin to provide their classmates with feedback: • How has this essay helped you understand Lily's attitudes toward marriage and wealth? • Does the writer explain how Lily's character is influenced by her childhood and her society? Does that explanation make sense? • What sort of evidence does the writer use from the text to support his or her writing? • How well does the writer explain how that evidence supports his or her arguments? • Does the writer write using standard grammar and punctuation? Are there any weak spots? • What specific suggestions can you make to help the writer improve the response?	

Core Path	Access Path
• What thing(s) does this paper do especially well? • Be sure to tell the writer what he or she did well and what he or she needs to work on. After you've looked at the peer review instructions, review the rubric with students before they begin writing. Allow time for students briefly to pose and discuss any questions they may have about the peer review instructions and the rubric. Tell students how many peer reviews they will need to complete once they submit their writing.	
Write. Ask students to complete the writing assignment using textual evidence to support their answers. Once they have completed their writing, they should click "Submit."	
	Extend **Critique.** As students read their peers' essays, remind them that a strong literary analysis contains a thesis supported by evidence. Discuss these common errors in literary analysis essays: • the essay summarizes the plot without providing analysis • the essay presents ideas that are not supported by evidence from the text • the essay repeats the same idea multiple times in different words After students have had the chance to look over each other's essays, generate and brainstorm with the class some strategies for correcting these common errors in their writing.
Review. Once students complete their writing assignment, they should submit substantive feedback to two peers. Students should use their peers' feedback to improve their writing.	

BLAST:
I Don't

OVERVIEW

To better understand the role of marriage in texts like *Wuthering Heights*, *Pride and Prejudice*, and *The House of Mirth*, students will consider the role marriage plays in their own world. Students will explore research links that connect them to the declining marriage rates in the United States today and reasons both for and against entering into a marriage.

OBJECTIVES

1. Explore background information about marriage as a social institution.
2. Research using hyperlinks to a range of information about changes in attitudes toward marriage over time, including statistics, polls, and opinion articles.

ELA Common Core Standards:
Reading: Informational Text - RI.11-12.1
Writing - W.11-12.1.A, W.11-12.1.B, W.11-12.5, W.11-12.6
Speaking & Listening - SL.11-12.1.A, SL.11-12.1.C, SL.11-12.1.D

RESOURCES

Access 1 handout (Beginner)
Access 2 handout (Intermediate)
Access 4 handout (Approaching)

TITLE/DRIVING QUESTION

Core Path	Access Path
Discuss. As a class, read aloud the title and driving question for this Blast. Ask students what they think about marriage. What do they know about the history of marriage as a social and cultural institution? Do they want to get married someday? Why or why not? Taking into account ideas generated by their classmates, do they have a sense of the current state of marriage in the United States? Remind students that they'll be returning to this question for their formal entries after they've read the Background and some of the Research Links.	**English Learners All Levels** **Discuss a Visual.** Have students view a chart or graph depicting marriage rates in the United States, such as the one at http://tinyurl.com/qzbn8cw. Discuss how the image shows a decline in marriage rates over time, prompting students with questions such as: • When was the marriage rate among women the highest, and what percentage was it? • Why do you think the marriage rate was so high at that time? • When was the marriage rate among women the lowest, and what percentage was it? • What happened in society between these dates? Why do you think the marriage rate fell so much?
Draft. In their notebooks or on scrap paper, have students draft their initial responses to the driving question. This will provide them with a baseline response that they will be altering as they gain more information about the topic in the Background and Research Links sections of the assignment.	**Beginner & Intermediate** **Draft with Sentence Frame.** When drafting their initial response to the driving question, have students refer to this Blast sentence frame on their Access 1 and 2 handouts: • Today, marriage is ______________ because _________________. Point out these two key features of the sentence frame: 1. The introductory clause "Today, marriage is" borrows language directly from the Blast driving question to invite students to give a word or phrase that describes the state of marriage in the United States today. 2. Ask students to make special note of the word "because," which invites them to list a reason or reasons why marriage is this way.

BACKGROUND

Core Path	Access Path
Read. Have students read the Blast background to provide context for the driving question.	**Beginner & Intermediate** **Read with Support.** Have students read the Blast background to provide context for the driving question. When they encounter unfamiliar words or phrases, have students refer to the glossary on their Access 1 and 2 handouts. If there are unfamiliar words that are not included in their glossary, encourage students to check a dictionary or online reference tool, like http://dictionary.reference.com. **Approaching** **Read and Summarize.** Have students read the Blast background to provide context for the driving question. As they read, ask students to complete the fill-in-the-blanks summary of the background provided on their Access 4 handout. When they encounter unfamiliar words or phrases, have students refer to the glossary on their Access 4 handout.
Discuss. Pair students and have them discuss the following questions: 1. Why is marriage often considered the "bedrock of society"? (Strong marriages have historically led to stability, power, wealth, and heirs.) 2. Why did attitudes toward marriage begin to shift in the 1970s? (Because of feminism and the ability to support themselves financially, women began to be empowered. Marriage was no longer viewed as necessary for stability.) 3. Why are marriage rates so low today? (Some millennials are getting married later in life, and others reject marriage as an outdated and unnecessary institution.) 4. If marriage is no longer necessary, why do some people still get married? (There are numerous rights that come along with marriage. Married people are happier and healthier than single people. Children who are raised by married couples are more successful.)	**Beginner** **Discuss.** Pair Beginning with Advanced (or Beyond) students and have them use the dialogue starter on their Access 1 handout to discuss the topic. Advise them to return to the dialogue and switch roles if they get stuck. **Intermediate** **Discuss.** Pair Intermediate with Advanced (or Beyond) students and have them use the dialogue starter on their Access 2 handout to discuss the topic. Advise them to return to the dialogue and switch roles if they get stuck. If their conversation is progressing smoothly, encourage them to continue the discussion beyond the dialogue starter sheet. They can expand their conversations to discuss other reasons why fewer people are getting married in the United States today.

Core Path	Access Path
Brainstorm. Remind students about the driving question for this Blast: What is the state of marriage in the United States today? In their notebooks, ask students to make three columns. They should label one column "Why People Get Married," another "Why People Don't Get Married," and the last "My Opinion." Start with the Background and have them fill in reasons for the first two columns. After they've finished that, have them ask themselves whether or not they plan to get married and the reasons why or why not. Have them write their answer in the third column. Here's a short of example of how this might look:	

Why People Get Married	Why People Don't Get Married	My Opinion
They want to raise a family in a financially secure home.	People want to be financially independent on their own before getting married.	I'd like to get married some day because I want a partner for life, not because I need one for stability.

RESEARCH LINKS

Core Path	Access Path
Examine and Explore. Use these questions to guide students' exploration of the Research Links: 1. Have students read "Record Share of Americans Have Never Married." Then ask, Which statistics in the poll surprised you? Do you see these trends reflected in your own community? Why or why not?	

Core Path	Access Path
2. Ask students to look at "The Beta Marriage: How Millennials Approach 'I Do.'" What connection does the writer draw between millennials' attitudes toward commitment and technology? (Millennials like to test things out before they commit to them, like the way they'd run a beta test on a new technology.) Why are millennials interested in "beta marriages"? (Millennials are used to thinking about life as a constantly changing work in progress, so it makes sense to "beta test" a marriage to determine if it works well.) According to the article, why might "beta marriages" lead to stronger relationships over time? (Beta marriages allow people to test their relationship and work out the kinks before truly committing. This gives people the opportunity to find better long-term matches and to "strategize for future romantic success.") 3. Have students explore "Why Marriage Makes People Happy" and "The Disestablishment of Marriage." Then ask, Given your understanding of these two pieces, do you think marriage will always be an important part of American society? Debate this in small groups or as a class.	
	Extend **Research, Discuss, and Present.** 1. Assign each group one link to explore in depth. 2. Ask them to discuss the information: a. What are the key points made in this resource? b. What inferences did you make as you read? c. What did you learn about this "big idea" from reading this research? d. How did this help you to better understand the topic? e. What questions does your group have after exploring this link? 3. Allow students time to informally present what they learned.

Core Path	Access Path
	Extend **Tech Infusion** **Annotate.** As students explore the links, encourage them to use online tools, such as Diigo (http://www.diigo.com), to highlight and annotate as they read. When students have finished annotating, have them use Google Docs to compile their notes, including their own observations and any images or graphs they think might be helpful. Last, have students share and discuss their findings with a partner.

QUIKPOLL

Core Path	Access Path
Participate. Answer the poll question. Have students use information from the background and research links to explain their answers.	

NUMBER CRUNCH

Core Path	Access Path
Predict, Discuss, and Click. Before students click on the number, break them into pairs and have them make predictions about what they think the number is related to. After they've clicked the number, ask students if they are surprised by the revealed information.	

CREATE YOUR BLAST

Core Path	Access Path
Blast. Ask students to write their Blast response in 140 characters or less.	**Beginner** **Blast with Support.** Have students refer back to the sentence frame on their Access 1 handout that they used to create their original Blast draft. Ask them to use this frame to write and enter their final Blast. **Intermediate** **Blast with Support.** Have students attempt to draft their Blast without the sentence frame on their Access 2 handout. If students struggle to compose their Blast draft without the sentence frame, remind them to reference it for support. **Beyond** **Write a Claim.** Ask students to use their answer to the poll question to write a strong claim that could be used as the foundation for a piece of argumentative writing. Once students have written their claims, ask them to read the claims to a small group of their peers. This activity will provide them practice writing claims, as well as expose them to claims written by their peers.
Review. After students have completed their own Blasts, ask them to review the Blasts of their peers and provide feedback.	
	Extend **Discuss.** As a whole class or in groups, identify a few strong Blasts and discuss what made those responses so powerful. As a group, discuss and analyze what characteristics make a Blast interesting or effective.
	Extend **Revise.** Resend a second version of this Blast assignment to your students and have them submit revised versions of their original Blasts. Do the same responses make the Top 10? How have the answers improved from the first submissions?

FIRST READ:
O Pioneers!

OVERVIEW

The novel *O Pioneers!* by Willa Cather depicts the struggles of settlers trying to survive on the harsh Nebraska prairie at the end of the 19th century. The First Read gives students the opportunity to experience the text with a limited context.

OBJECTIVES

1. Perform an initial reading of a text and demonstrate comprehension by responding to short analysis and inference questions with textual evidence.
2. Practice defining vocabulary words using context.
3. Participate effectively in a range of conversations and collaborations to express ideas and build upon the ideas of others.
4. Practice acquiring and using academic vocabulary correctly.

ELA Common Core Standards:
Reading: Literature - RL.11-12.1, RL.11-12.4, RL.11-12.10
Speaking & Listening - SL.11-12.1.A, SL.11-12.1.B, SL.11-12.1.C, SL.11-12.1.D, SL.11-12.2, SL.11-12.3, SL.11-12.6
Language - L.11-12.4.A, L.11-12.6

RESOURCES

Access 1 handout (Beginner)
Access 2 handout (Intermediate)
Access 3 handout (Advanced)
Access 4 handout (Approaching)

ACCESS COMPLEX TEXT

This excerpt from *O Pioneers!* is broken into two parts. A short excerpt from Part I, Chapter IV establishes the lifestyle and beliefs the narrator attributes to pioneers. An excerpt from Part II, Chapter V introduces some of the principal characters of the novel. To help students understand the characters, setting, and, historical context of *O Pioneers!,* use the following ideas to provide scaffolded instruction for a first reading of the more complex features of this text:

- **Connection of Ideas** - This excerpt is taken from two different parts of the novel and depicts different characters and situations, so readers may struggle to draw connections between the two passages in order to draw conclusions about the themes of the novel. A brief summary of the novel's plot may be beneficial to these students. For instance, tell students that Carl, Alexandra, and her brothers, the Bergson boys, are second-generation pioneers struggling to maintain the farms established by their parents.

- **Prior Knowledge** - The harsh conditions faced by settlers in the American West in the 19th century may be unfamiliar to some readers. You might begin by explaining the Homestead Act of 1862 and how it enabled many American to move west and establish farms, even if they had no experience with farming or the climate of the Great Plains. Knowledge about the droughts that plagued the area at the turn of the century would also be beneficial.

- **Specific Vocabulary** - Some terms relating to nature—such as "ironweed," "snow-on-the-mountain," and "plumage"—may present a challenge to some readers.

1. INTRODUCTION

Core Path	Access Path
Watch. As a class, watch the video preview of *O Pioneers!*	**English Learners All Levels** **Fill in the Blanks.** Ask students to use their Access 1, 2, and 3 handouts to fill in the blanks of the transcript for the preview's voiceover as they watch the preview along with their classmates. Answers are located at the end of the lesson plan online.

Core Path	Access Path
Read. Individually or as a class, read the introduction for *O Pioneers!*. The introduction provides context for the excerpts from Part I, Chapter IV and Part II, Chapter V.	**English Learners All Levels & Approaching** **Read and Listen.** Ask students to read and listen to the introduction for *O Pioneers!*. Have them refer to the "Introduction Glossary" on their Access 1, 2, 3, and 4 handouts for definitions of key vocabulary terms. If there are unfamiliar words that are not included in their glossary, encourage students to check a dictionary or online reference tool, such as http://dictionary.reference.com.
Access Prior Knowledge. Find out what your students already know about pioneer settlements in the West in the early 1900s. 1. First, divide your students into small groups. 2. Ask each group to generate a list of information about pioneers and ask students to share where their previous knowledge came from. 3. Then discuss ways in which the media (songs, movies, books, magazines, video games) impacts the way we think about pioneers. Discuss if and how those depictions glorify or romanticize the pioneer as a classic American figure.	**English Learners All Levels & Approaching** **Discuss a Visual.** Have students view images of life for 19th-century pioneers on the prairie, such as the ones found on the following website: http://tinyurl.com/qz33m59. Discuss how the pioneers pictured had to build their homes from the ground up and work to sustain them over time, prompting students with questions such as: • What are some challenges the pioneers likely faced? • What do you think life on the prairie was like? • Why do you think so many people migrated west during this time? • Do you think you would have joined the homesteaders? Why or why not?
	Extend **Analyze and Discuss a Quote.** "I decided not to 'write' at all,—simply to give myself up to the pleasure of recapturing in memory people and places I'd forgotten." (Willa Cather, in an interview about writing *O Pioneers!*) Lead students in a discussion of this quote. 1. What do you think this quote means? 2. Cather says that instead of writing, she "gives herself up." What does this imply about writing and the writing process? Have you ever had a writing experience that felt like "giving yourself up?"

Core Path	Access Path
	3. What does this quote suggest about the relationship between writing, loving, and memory?

2. READ

Core Path	Access Path

Core Path

Make Predictions about Vocabulary. There are six bold vocabulary words in the text. As students read the text, ask them to make predictions about what they think each bold vocabulary word means based on the context clues in the sentence. Have students use the annotation tool to make their predictions.

It might be helpful to model this for students before they begin reading. Either using the board or projecting the actual text, focus in on the sentence that uses the word "habitable":

- The settlers sat about on the wooden sidewalks in the little town and told each other that the country was never meant for men to live in; the thing to do was to get back to Iowa, to Illinois, to any place that had been proved habitable.

Model for the class how to use these context clues to guess the meanings of the words:

1. Because of its word ending, I know "habitable" is an adjective. The word appears at the end of the sentence, so I work backwards to see what it is describing.
2. Iowa and Illinois are described as places that are "habitable." I keep scanning backward and see that the narrator says settlers should "get back" to those places because "the country was never meant for men to live in."
3. Based on these clues, I can infer that "habitable" must mean "suitable for living."

Access Path

Note: This exercise, which extends vocabulary instruction, should be completed when the class shifts from whole-group instruction to individual work during the "Read and Annotate" exercise.

Beginner, Intermediate & Approaching Pair Practice.

1. Pair students with more proficient readers.
2. Give them an additional sentence that contains a new vocabulary word.
3. Ask the students to complete a Think Aloud using the teacher-led Make Predictions about Vocabulary activity as a model, while the proficient student actively listens.
4. The student should use the context clues in the sentence to try to determine the meaning of the new vocabulary word.
5. After the student has completed the Think Aloud and made a prediction about the word's meaning, allow time for the proficient reader to add his/her own thoughts and clarify any points of confusion.
6. Once they've completed this Think Aloud, encourage them to use a dictionary to confirm the definition of the new vocabulary word. Have them refer to the "Text Glossary" on their Access 1, 2, and 4 handouts for definitions of key vocabulary terms in the text. Encourage them to add any additional vocabulary words or idioms they find in the text and look up definitions for those words and idioms online or in a dictionary.

Core Path	Access Path
Model Reading Comprehension Strategy. Before students begin reading, model the reading comprehension strategy of visualizing by using this think aloud that talks students through the first paragraph of Part II, Chapter V. First explain to your students that visualizing is: *forming a mental picture of something as you read, and using new details from the text to add to or change the mental images you have created* Model for students how visualizing will help them better comprehend the selection and help drive their discussions. • The paragraph begins with the phrase "The dawn in the east," which is a basic identifier. Then the sentence continues with a rich simile: "[it] looked like the light from some great fire that was burning under the edge of the world." This gives a powerful image that suggests the majesty of the place in the morning. • I keep reading: "The color was reflected in the globules of dew that sheathed the short gray pasture grass." This image extends the previous one—it shows the power of the sunrise and how the sun connects to the land. • Then, the text jumps to Carl's memories of Alexandra: "Even as a boy he used to feel, when he saw her coming with her step, her upright head and calm shoulders, that she looked as if she had walked straight out the morning itself." This image suggests to me that, to Carl, Alexandra is like the dawn, a figure of hope and beauty.	**Note:** This exercise, which extends instruction around reading comprehension strategies, should be completed when the class shifts from whole-group instruction to individual work during the "Read and Annotate" exercise. **Beginner, Intermediate & Approaching Apply Reading Comprehension Strategy.** 1. Have Beginning and Intermediate students listen to the audio version of *O Pioneers!* As they listen to the audio recording, ask them to work in pairs to list words that come to mind as they listen. Encourage them to include as many descriptive or sensory words as possible. Words can be categorized under the senses—seeing, hearing, feeling, smelling, and touching. Some students may want to draw pictures of what they "see" instead of listing words. 2. Once they have listened to the audio version and created a list or pictures based on what they heard, pair Beginning and Intermediate students with more proficient readers and ask them to tell why they listed the words or drew those pictures. Why did they include particular words? How are the words sensory? Do the drawings match words? 3. Allow pairs time to discuss the lists and drawings. Are there any words they would like to add? If so, encourage them to add words based on their conversations.

Core Path	Access Path
Read and Annotate. Have students independently read and annotate the excerpt. Ask students to use the annotation tool as they read to: 1. use context clues to analyze and determine the meaning of the bolded vocabulary terms 2. ask questions about passages of the text that may be unclear or unresolved 3. identify key information, events, characters, and connections between them 4. note unfamiliar vocabulary	**Beginner** **Coach the Reading.** While other students read, annotate, and discuss the text independently, work with Beginning students, listening to the audio of the text and pausing periodically or when any student has a question. Coach students in articulating their questions for the group and in highlighting and annotating the text. Have students use the Annotation Guide on the Access 1 handout to support them as they highlight and annotate the text. For further support, ask questions about the text such as: • Is there anything about the story that you don't understand? • What do you think will happen to Alexandra and Carl? • Why do you think *O Pioneers!* is the title of the novel? **Intermediate** **Listen to the Audio.** Have these students listen to the audio of the text and use the Text Glossary on the Access 2 handout to help them with words or idioms that may be unfamiliar. If students need help with annotating the text, have them use the Annotation Guide on the Access 2 handout. After working with the Beginning students, you may wish to check this group's progress and provide support as needed. **Advanced** **Pair with Proficient Peers.** Have Advanced students work with English-proficient peers to read, annotate, and discuss the text. Have students use the Annotation Guide in the Access 3 handout to support them as they highlight and annotate the text. Encourage them to listen to the audio of the text if needed. **Approaching** **Use the Annotation Guide.** Have students use the Annotation Guide on the Access 4 handout to support them as they highlight and annotate the text.

Core Path	Access Path
Discuss. In small groups or pairs, have students discuss the questions and inferences they made while reading. To help facilitate discussions, refer to Collaborative Discussions in the Speaking & Listening Handbook. 1. The section from Part I, Chapter IV mentions the "Bergson boys." What inference can readers make about second-generation settlers based on their example? (The children of settlers might not be as committed to the prairie or as hardy as the parents who brought them there.) 2. Compare and contrast the descriptions of the frontier in Part I, Chapter IV and Part II, Chapter V. (Part I, Chapter IV suggests that the prairie is a hard and forbidding place and that pioneers "should have imagination" to survive there. Part II, Chapter V suggests it is a beautiful place, bathed in sun and "globules of dew.") What inference can readers make based on this contrast? (The frontier is not for everyone, but it holds tremendous potential for the right people.) 3. Emil's shooting of the ducks bothers both Marie and Carl. What does this event suggest about the cycle of life evident on the farm? (Pain and loss—and even death—are part of the cycle, but life is also renewed, as shown by the sunrise and the dew that covers the prairie.)	**English Learners All Levels & Approaching** Use the extra time while on- and beyond-grade-level students are discussing their first reads of the text to work individually and in small groups with Approaching readers and English Learners as outlined on the previous page. Should those students complete their first reads quickly, integrate them into the on- and beyond-grade-level discussion groups. Otherwise, English Learners and Approaching readers will be given an opportunity to participate in text discussions with their peers later in the lesson. **Beyond** **Tech Infusion** **Brainstorm.** Pair students and ask them to brainstorm challenges pioneers might face on the prairie, both as they set up their homesteads and in the years that follow. Compare and contrast two likely challenges: building a farm from scratch versus rebuilding a farm after a significant drought. Which seems harder? Students who have access to a back-channel tool such as TodaysMeet (https://todaysmeet.com/) may enjoy brainstorming in that medium.

3. SYNCTV

Core Path	Access Path
Watch. As a class, watch the SyncTV video on *O Pioneers!* Remind students to listen for the way the students use academic vocabulary during their discussion. Pause the video at these key moments to discuss the information with your students: 1. 0:27 – Why does Sasha say that Willa Cather reminds her of a Girl Scout leader? What evidence from the text could Sasha use to support her point of view?	**Beginner & Intermediate** **Analyze the Discussion.** Have students use the "Analyze the Discussion" guide on the Access 1 and 2 handouts to identify key points in the discussion and the evidence the students use to determine those points. Sample answers are at the end of the lesson plan online.

Core Path	Access Path
2. 4:57 – What "lost dream" of Carl's do the students identify? How do they use reasoning and text evidence to draw this conclusion? 3. 6:38 – What conclusions do the students draw about the role sound plays in developing the setting? How well do they use text evidence and reasoning to make their points?	**Advanced** **Analyze Setting and Theme.** Have students discuss and complete the "Setting and Theme" chart on the Access 3 handout, referring to the SyncTV video as needed to clarify their answers. Sample answers appear at the end of the lesson plan online. **Approaching** **Analyze the Discussion.** Have students complete the chart on the Access 4 handout by listing textual evidence cited by the students in the video. Sample answers are at the end of the lesson plan online.

4. THINK

Core Path	Access Path
Answer and Discuss. Have students complete the Think questions and then use the peer review instructions and rubric to complete two peer reviews. Refer to the sample answers at the end of the lesson plan online to discuss responses with your students.	**Beginner & Intermediate** **Sentence Frames.** Have students use the sentence frames on the Access 1 and 2 handouts to support their responses to the Think questions. If necessary, distribute sentence frames to Advanced students as well. **Approaching** **Find the Evidence.** Have students use Find the Evidence on the Access 4 handout to help them identify the evidence needed to answer the questions.
SyncTV Style Discussion. Put students into heterogeneous small groups and give them a prompt to discuss. Remind them to model their discussions after the SyncTV episodes they have seen. Stress the importance of using both academic language and formal English correctly and citing textual evidence in their conversations to support their ideas.	**Beginner & Intermediate** **Use Sentence Frames.** Have these students use the sentence frames on the Access 1 and 2 handouts to help them participate in the discussion. **Approaching** **Use Think Questions.** Remind these students to refer to their answers to the Think questions to help them participate in the group discussion.

Core Path	Access Path
To help students prepare for, strategize, and evaluate their discussions, refer to the Collaborative Discussions section of the Speaking & Listening Handbook. Discussion prompt: 1. Is Carl suited for life on the Nebraska prairie? Why or why not? 2. Are Carl's memories more helpful or hurtful? Why? Have students review the key ideas expressed, demonstrating an understanding of multiple perspectives through reflection and paraphrasing. You may wish to have students create a video or audio recording of their SyncTV style discussion.	
	Extend **Dramatization.** Put students into groups and ask them to rewrite the excerpt from Part I, Chapter IV or a scene from Part II, Chapter V as a script, using only dialogue and stage directions. When groups complete their scripts, have them exchange their work with another group to discuss the challenges of writing in this form.

SKILL:

Setting

OVERVIEW

Setting is one of the most important parts of any story. It lays the foundation upon which the other narrative elements are built. This lesson plan provides follow-up questions and enrichments to help teachers guide students toward a usable, repeatable method for identifying and analyzing elements of setting in a novel.

OBJECTIVES

1. Learn the definition of setting.
2. Practice using concrete strategies for identifying elements of setting.
3. Participate effectively in a range of conversations and collaborations to express ideas and build upon the ideas of others.

ELA Common Core Standards:
Reading: Literature - RL.11-12.1, RL.11-12.3
Speaking & Listening - SL.11-12.1.A, SL.11-12.1.C, SL.11-12.2

RESOURCES

Access 1 handout (Beginner)
Access 2 handout (Intermediate)
Access 3 handout (Advanced)
Access 4 handout (Approaching)

1. DEFINE

Core Path	Access Path
Watch. Watch the Concept Definition video on setting with your students. Make sure students understand the different components of setting. Pause the video at these key moments to discuss the information with your students: 1. 0:43 – Christina says that setting can have a "huge effect on the events and characters in a story." Why? How does a story's setting affect other narrative elements? 2. 1:00 – What examples does Christina use to describe the influence setting can have on a story? Using these examples, discuss how the mood, plot, and even genre might change based on setting. 3. 1:12 – How does setting relate to theme? Which is more important in developing the theme of a story: setting or dialogue? Why?	**English Learners All Levels & Approaching** **Complete the Sentences.** Have students complete the sentences on the Access 1, 2, 3, and 4 handouts as they watch the video. Answers are located at the end of the lesson plan online.
Read and Discuss. After watching the Concept Definition video, have students read the definition of setting. Either in small groups or as a whole class, use these questions to engage students in a discussion about setting. 1. Why might an author choose to give a story an unfamiliar setting? What are some of the advantages and disadvantages of basing a story in an unfamiliar world? (In an unfamiliar setting, the author is free to make up any details he or she thinks will advance the plot or affect characterization.) 2. How does setting create mood? What kind of setting might create an ominous mood? A joyful mood? (Setting creates mood by evoking certain feelings. For example, the woods at night might create an ominous mood, while a parade or party might evoke a joyful mood.)	**Beginner & Approaching** **Complete the Chart.** To prepare students to participate in the discussion, have them complete the chart on the Access 1 and 4 handouts as they read the definition. Sample answers are located at the end of the lesson plan online. **Intermediate & Advanced** **Discuss Prompts.** To help these students participate in the discussion, prompt them with questions that can be answered with a few words, such as: • What is setting? (the time and place in which the events of the plot unfold) • What does an author often create through setting? (mood) • Why might an author choose to write a story in an unfamiliar setting? (Answers will vary.)

Core Path	Access Path
3. Does a story's setting always correlate with mood? Why or why not? (Not always. Sometimes a story's mood might be at odds with the setting, such as an ominous mood during a celebration that is supposed to be happy.) 4. Besides *The Wizard of Oz*, can you think of a story, novel, TV show, or movie in which the setting "is the problem a character confronts"? (In the novel and film *Lord of the Flies*, the deserted island setting is the problem the characters confront) What makes these stories particularly memorable? (Answers will vary.)	**Beyond** **Discuss.** Have students select two books they've read and describe their distinct settings. Compile a list of examples. Have students discuss how the books would be different if they swapped settings. What might happen, for example, if *Hamlet* were set in the world of *Beowulf*? How might a switch in setting affect not only the plot and the characters but also a reader's enjoyment of the story?
	Extend **Tech Infusion** **Write.** Create a Blast and ask students to "blast out" a description of the most interesting setting they can imagine. After they've completed the Blast, challenge students to write a scene from a short story set in a world imagined by one of their classmates. Students can use an online journaling tool such as Penzu (www.penzu.com) or a blogging tool such as Pen.io (http://pen.io.com) to write and share their narrative scenes.

2. MODEL

Core Path	Access Path
Watch. Ask students to take notes on the SkillsTV video on setting in *O Pioneers!* as you watch together. Remind students to listen for the way the students use academic vocabulary related to the definition of point of view during their discussion. Pause the video at these key moments to discuss the information with your students: 1. 1:40 – What inferences do the students make about the setting based on the excerpt Rebecca reads aloud? What evidence from the text could be used to support these inferences?	**Beginner, Intermediate & Approaching** **Analyze the Discussion.** Have students watch the video again and complete the chart on the Access 1, 2, and 4 handouts as they watch the video. Sample answers for this exercise are located at the end of the lesson plan online. **Advanced** **Journals.** Have students note in their journals the strategies the students in the SkillsTV video use to analyze the setting.

Core Path	Access Path
2. 2:01 – What information does Olivia find in an Internet search? Without this information, can readers understand the role setting plays in the novel? Why or why not? 3. 3:40 – What is the relationship between character and setting? Which details from the text support the inferences the students make about how characterization and setting are linked in the novel?	
Read and Annotate. Have students independently read the Model section. As they read, ask students to use the annotation tool to: • highlight key points • ask questions • identify places where the Model applies the strategies laid out in the Identification and Application section.	**Note:** During this portion of the lesson, instruction shifts from whole-group to individual work. Use this time to work one-on-one or in small groups with Beginning, Intermediate, Advanced, and Approaching students. **Beginner & Intermediate** **Coach the Reading.** Work with these students (either individually or in small groups) to fill out the guided reading questions on the Access 1 and 2 handouts. Have Beginning students refer to the glossary on the Access 1 handout to help them determine the meaning of difficult words (note: provide the Access 1 handout glossary to Intermediate students if necessary). Let students know they'll use these answers to help participate in the discussion about the Model. Sample answers for this exercise are located at the end of the lesson plan online. **Advanced** **Identify Evidence.** Ask Advanced students to complete the identifying evidence exercise on the Access 3 handout. Let students know that they'll use these answers to help participate in the discussion about the Model. Sample answers for this exercise are located at the end of the lesson plan online. **Approaching** **Guided Reading.** Have students complete the guided reading questions on the Access 4 handout as they read. Let them know that they'll use these answers to help participate in the discussion about the Model. Sample answers for this exercise are located at the end of the lesson plan online.

Core Path	Access Path
Discuss. After students read the Model text, use these questions to facilitate a whole-group discussion that helps students understand how to determine and analyze the setting of the novel: 1. What strategies does the Model recommend to find information about the setting of *O Pioneers!*? (reading the introduction and using online research) Why might such tactics be necessary to understand the setting of a work of fiction? (Possible answers include: Readers might not know anything about the time or place where a story is set; the author may not explicitly state where a story is set.) 2. What kinds of words and phrases does the Model point out from the description of the setting in the first passage? ("wooden sidewalks," "little town," "any place that had proved habitable," "wilderness") What inference can readers make based on this description? (The setting is rural and rugged.) 3. According to the Model, how does Cather use setting to provide cultural context? (The author shows the discouragement of the struggling settlers and uses the setting to create a mood of despair.) 4. According to the Model, how does Cather use setting to develop the main characters? (The author describes the harshness of the frontier and says that the Bergson boys "had been dragged into the wilderness." This suggests that the Bergson boys would not have chosen to live such a hard life as the frontier requires.)	
	Extend **Create a List.** Challenge students to list examples of stories, novels, TV shows, or movies in which the setting is like another character in the story (for example, Gotham City in the Batman movies or Oz in *The Wizard of Oz*.) Then have them discuss why that setting is so important to the development of the story and its characters.

3. YOUR TURN

Core Path	Access Path
Assess and Explain. Have students answer the comprehension questions to test for understanding. Share the explanations for Parts A and B (located online) with your students.	
	Extend **Pair and Share.** Pair students and have them choose another work of fiction that they have read this year. Then have them discuss how the setting of that story impacted the main character's development. For example, students may discuss how Hamlet was affected by life in the castle at Elsinore or how Gulliver was affected by his unfamiliar surroundings.

SKILL:
Compare and Contrast

OVERVIEW

Comparing and contrasting two works of literature that were written around the same time is a useful and interesting way for readers to learn more about that time period in history. This lesson plan provides follow-up questions and enrichments to help teachers guide students toward a usable, repeatable method for comparing and contrasting two foundational works of American literature.

OBJECTIVES

1. Learn the definition of compare and contrast.
2. Practice using concrete strategies for comparing and contrasting two novels.
3. Participate effectively in a range of conversations and collaborations to express ideas and build upon the ideas of others.

ELA Common Core Standards:
Reading: Literature - RL.11-12.1, RL.11-12.9
Speaking & Listening - SL.11-12.1.A, SL.11-12.1.C, SL.11-12.2

RESOURCES

Access 1 handout (Beginner)
Access 2 handout (Intermediate)
Access 3 handout (Advanced)
Access 4 handout (Approaching)

1. DEFINE

Core Path	Access Path
Watch. Watch the Concept Definition video on compare and contrast with your students. Make sure your students understand the difference between comparing and contrasting, and how this skill can help to unlock meaning in a given text. Pause the video at these key moments to discuss the information with your students: 1. 0:16 – Ben says that people often talk about apples and oranges when they talk about compare and contrast. What does that expression typically mean? How do people use it? 2. 1:08 – How can comparing and contrasting help you remember details and information? Can you think of any times you've used compare and contrast as a memory aid? 3. 1:35 – How can comparing and contrasting two texts give perspective on a character, situation, or event? What do two texts need to have in common to make them valuable to compare?	**English Learners All Levels & Approaching** **Finish the Sentences.** Have students complete the finish-the-sentences exercise on the Access 1, 2, 3, and 4 handouts as they watch the video. Answers are located at the end of the lesson plan online.
Read and Discuss. After watching the Concept Definition video, have students read the definition of compare and contrast. Either in small groups or as a whole class, use these questions to engage students in a discussion about compare and contrast: 1. If people compare and contrast so often in their everyday lives, why do we need to practice it as a reading skill? How is comparing and contrasting texts different from doing so in everyday life? (Comparing and contrasting texts can help you analyze and better understand the two texts.) 2. What do two texts need to have in common to make them valuable to compare and contrast? (Having a key similarity, such as a common topic, makes texts valuable to compare and contrast.) 3. Which do you learn more from—comparisons or contrasts? Why? (Answers will vary.)	**Beginner & Approaching** **Complete the Chart.** To prepare students to participate in the discussion, have them complete the chart on the Access 1 and 4 handouts as they read the definition. Sample answers are located at the end of the lesson plan online. **Intermediate & Advanced** **Discuss Prompts.** To help these students participate in the discussion, prompt them with questions that can be answered with a few words, such as: • What do we do when we compare and contrast? (distinguish between two or more things) • What can comparing and contrasting help us do when we read? (determine what two characters have in common or how differently two texts treat the same topic) • What were the last two things you compared and contrasted? (Answers will vary.)

Core Path	Access Path
	Beyond **Discuss.** Have students select another work they've read and describe its setting. How does that setting compare and contrast with the setting of *O Pioneers!*? Have students discuss the similarities and differences between the two settings. Which do they find more interesting? Why? Which poses more of a problem for the characters? Why?
	Extend **Pair and Share.** Pair students and have them compare and contrast two characters from texts in the unit, such as Mrs. Bennet and Mrs. Bart. Have pairs make a list of similarities and a list of differences. When they finish, have students discuss what they learned about each character from the exercise.

2. MODEL

Core Path	Access Path
Read and Annotate. Have students independently read the Model section. As they read, ask students to use the annotation tool to: • highlight key points • ask questions • identify places where the Model applies the strategies laid out in the Identification and Application section	**Note:** During this portion of the lesson, instruction shifts from whole-group to individual work. Use this time to work one-on-one or in small groups with Beginning, Intermediate, Advanced, and Approaching students. **Beginner & Intermediate** **Coach the Reading.** Work with these students (either individually or in small groups) to fill out the guided reading questions on the Access 1 and 2 handouts. Have Beginning students refer to the glossary on the Access 1 handout to help them determine the meaning of difficult words (note: provide the Access 1 handout glossary to Intermediate students if necessary). Let students know they'll use these answers to help participate in the discussion about the Model. Sample answers for this exercise are located at the end of the lesson plan online.

Core Path	Access Path
	Advanced **Identify Evidence.** Ask Advanced students to complete the identifying evidence exercise on the Access 3 handout. Let students know that they'll use these answers to help participate in the discussion about the Model. Sample answers for this exercise are located at the end of the lesson plan online. **Approaching** **Guided Reading.** Have students complete the guided reading questions on the Access 4 handout as they read. Let them know that they'll use these answers to help participate in the discussion about the Model. Sample answers for this exercise are located at the end of the lesson plan online.
Discuss. After students read the Model text, use these questions to facilitate a whole-group discussion that helps students understand how to compare and contrast two novels: 1. Why does the Model say *The House of Mirth* and *O Pioneers!* are worth comparing and contrasting? (Both are examples of American realism that take place at the turn of the 20th century.) 2. According to the Model, in what way are Lily's and Carl's childhood memories different? (Lily's childhood was frantic and included the trappings of wealth. Carl's memories are calm and focused on one person.) 3. What other comparisons or contrasts can you make between the first passages besides the ones the Model explained? (Unlike Lily's memories, Carl's childhood days always started the same way. Carl and Alexandra had to work as children, unlike Lily.) 4. How do the characters in *O Pioneers!* react differently than the Barts do to financial hardship? (In *O Pioneers!,* financial hardship is a community feeling. The Barts' struggles are individual.)	

Core Path	Access Path
5. How does the comparison with *The House of Mirth* help you understand the attitudes toward money expressed in *O Pioneers!*? (Sample answer: The community feeling in *O Pioneers!* didn't seem unusual at first, but comparing it to *The House of Mirth* reminded me that not everyone feels that way about money.)	
	Extend **Research.** Form small groups and have students read about what was happening in the United States at the turn of the 20th century. Have students focus on the economy and the role of women. Then have students apply this information to their comparison of *The House of Mirth* and *O Pioneers!* How does the historical background support the events in the novels? In what ways did the authors fictionalize, or alter, historical events?

3. YOUR TURN

Core Path	Access Path
Assess and Explain. Have students answer the comprehension questions to test for understanding. Share the explanations for Parts A and B (located online) with your students.	
	Extend **Compile.** Ask students to think of other pieces of literature they've read in class or in previous classes that deal with the theme of parental pressure. Make a list of those texts on the board. Then ask students to compare and contrast those texts with *The House of Mirth* and *O Pioneers!*

CLOSE READ:
O Pioneers!

OVERVIEW

The novel *O Pioneers!* by Willa Cather explores the lifestyle and beliefs of settlers on the Nebraska prairie at the end of the 19th century. The Close Read gives students the opportunity to analyze the setting and compare the text with *The House of Mirth*.

OBJECTIVES

1. Complete a close reading of a passage of literature.
2. Practice and apply concrete strategies for analyzing setting in *O Pioneers!*
3. Participate effectively in a range of conversations and collaborations to express ideas and build upon the ideas of others.
4. Prewrite, plan, and produce clear and coherent writing in response to a prompt.

ELA Common Core Standards:
Reading: Literature - RL.11-12.1, RL.11-12.3, RL.11-12.4, RL.11-12.9, RL.11-12.10
Writing - W.11-12.1.A, W.11-12.1.B, W.11-12.4, W.11-12.5, W.11-12.6, W.11-12.9.A, W.11-12.10
Speaking & Listening - SL.11-12.1.A, SL.11-12.1.B, SL.11-12.1.C, SL.11-12.1.D, SL.11-12.6
Language - L.11-12.4.A, L.11-12.4.C, L.11-12.4.D

RESOURCES

O Pioneers! Vocabulary handout
Access 1 handout (Beginner)
Access 2 handout (Intermediate)
Access 3 handout (Advanced)
Access 4 handout (Approaching)

1. INTRODUCTION

Core Path	Access Path
Define and Compare. Project the vocabulary words and definitions onto the board or provide students with a handout, so they can copy the vocabulary into their notebooks. Suggest that students consult general and specialized reference materials, both print and digital, to compare the precise meaning of a specific word with their initial vocabulary predictions from the First Read. Review words that students defined incorrectly to understand why they were unable to use context clues to develop usable definitions.	**Beginner & Intermediate** **Complete the Chart.** Have students complete the chart on the Access 1 and 2 handouts by writing the correct word for each of the definitions. **Advanced & Beyond** **Write in Journals.** Have students write a journal entry using all of their vocabulary words. Remind them to write sentences that communicate the meaning of the words they are using. **Approaching** **Graphic Organizer.** To support students in comparing their predictions with the correct meanings, have them complete the graphic organizer on the Access 4 handout to record the vocabulary words, their initial analysis, and the definitions. Then have them write sentences using the words.
Review. Have students complete the fill-in-the-blanks vocabulary worksheet attached to the lesson plan online. Answers for the worksheet are listed at the end of the lesson plan online.	
	Extend **Tech Infusion** **Act and Record.** Break students into small groups, assign each group a vocabulary word, and ask them to design a short skit to demonstrate the meaning of the word for their peers. If possible, record skits and post them to your class YouTube channel, so they can be reviewed.
	Extend **Write.** Living creatures other than humans—insects, birds, and so on—are important to the setting of *O Pioneers!* Have students write a paragraph about an animal from the selection using each of the vocabulary words.

2. READ

Core Path	Access Path
Model Close Reading. Project the text onto the board and model a close reading of the second paragraph from Part II, Chapter V using the annotation strategies mentioned below. While modeling annotation strategies, make notes that tie the text to the focus skill and demonstrate what students are looking for as they read. Some guidance for you as you annotate for your students: • We follow Carl in this paragraph, who is sitting in the prairie and "musing until the sun leaped up above the prairie." Around him an orchestral cacophony of life is heard: "Birds and insects without number began to chirp, to twitter, to snap and whistle, to make all manner of fresh shrill noises." The prairie sounds vibrant and alive. • Images follow that create an expansive picture of the prairie. Phrases such as "The pasture was flooded with light" and "the golden light seemed to be rippling like the tide racing in" make the prairie seem as vast as the ocean. • This relationship created between the landlocked prairie and the powerful ocean suggests that the prairie is a tremendous geographic feature that is a wellspring of life.	
Read and Annotate. Read the Skills Focus questions as a class, so your students know what they should pay close attention to as they read. Then have students read and annotate the excerpt. Ask students to use the annotation tool as they read to: 1. respond to the Skills Focus section 2. ask questions about setting, including its relationship to plot and theme as well as Cather's attitude toward it 3. find examples of sound imagery and analyze their meaning 4. evaluate the role of women in the text 5. note unfamiliar vocabulary	**Note:** While on-grade-level students are reading and annotating, work one-on-one or in small groups with Beginning, Intermediate, Advanced, and Approaching students to support them as they read and annotate the text. **Beginner & Intermediate** **Summarize and Analyze the Text.** Work with these students to complete the sentence frames on the Access 1 and 2 handouts (note: the sentence frames for Intermediate students on the Access 2 handout contain fewer scaffolds). They will then use the completed sentence frames to help them analyze and annotate the text by completing the Skills Focus questions. Refer to the sample Skills Focus answers to help them complete the sentence frames and annotate the text.

Core Path	Access Path
6. capture their reaction to the ideas and examples in the text As they reread the text, remind students to use the comprehension strategy of visualizing that they learned in the First Read.	**Advanced** **Work in Pairs.** Pair these students with more proficient English speakers to work together on analyzing and annotating the text to complete the Skills Focus questions. If these students need more support, have them use the sentence frames on the Access 3 handout as they work with their more proficient peers. **Approaching** **Summarize the Text.** Have these students discuss and complete the text summary on the Access 4 handout and use their summary to help them analyze and annotate the text by completing the Skills Focus questions. Correct answers for the summary are at the end of the lesson plan online. Also refer to the sample Skills Focus answers to aid students with their annotations.
Discuss. After students have read the text, use the sample responses to the Skills Focus questions at the bottom of the lesson plan online to discuss the reading and the process of analyzing the setting. Make sure that students have acquired and accurately use academic-specific words and phrases related to the skill and demonstrate a command of formal English appropriate to the discussion. To help facilitate discussions, refer to Collaborative Discussions in the Speaking & Listening Handbook.	**Extend** **Pair and Share.** In small, heterogeneous groups or pairs, ask students to share and discuss their annotations with a focus on the setting presented in the selection. You can provide students with these questions to guide their discussion: 1. How do outside forces affect the setting in *O Pioneers!*? Cite textual evidence in your response. (Foreclosures and economic difficulty made the prairie more difficult than it already was to inhabit.) 2. In Part II, Chapter V, how does the setting influence Carl's memories? (Carl's memories are triggered by place and time. The dawn on the pasture reminds him of milking cows with Alexandra. Seeing Emil and Marie hunting makes him mournful, suggesting another memory.)

Core Path	Access Path
	3. Lost dreams is one theme suggested by the setting and the characters' interactions with it. Does the text suggest that it is better not to adopt a pioneering dream or that it is better to dream a pioneering dream, even if it is lost? Support your response with textual evidence. (Answers will vary. Suggest students approach the question character by character.)

3. WRITE

Core Path	Access Path
Prewrite and Plan. Read the prompt as a class and ask students to brainstorm about the prairie setting in *O Pioneers!* Students can brainstorm together either as a class or in small groups to begin planning their responses. Remind your students to look at the excerpt and their annotations to find textual evidence to support their ideas.	**Beginner & Intermediate** **Plan and Organize.** Have students complete the prewriting activity on the Access 1 and 2 handouts and then explain their ideas to a partner before they write. Explain to students that they need to choose details, examples, or quotes from the text that support their ideas and then explain how those details support their statements. For example, students could include the line, "A pioneer should have imagination, should be able to enjoy the idea of things more than the things themselves" to support the opinion that the Bergson boys should leave Nebraska because they are not cut out to be pioneers. **Approaching** **Plan and Organize.** Have students complete the prewriting activity on the Access 4 handout to organize their thoughts before they write.
Discuss. Project these instructions for the peer review onto the board and review them with your class, so they know what they are looking for when they begin to provide their classmates with feedback:	

Core Path	Access Path
• Did the writer choose a clear position and argue for it coherently? • How well did the writer address the complexity of the issue of living as a pioneer? • What sort of evidence did the writer use from the text to support his or her writing? • How well does the writer explain how that evidence supports his or her arguments? • Does the writer write using standard grammar and punctuation? Are there any weak spots? • What specific suggestions can you make to help the writer improve the response? • What thing(s) does this paper do especially well? • Be sure to tell the writer what he or she did well and what he or she needs to work on. Remember that your comments are most useful when they are constructive. After you've looked at the peer review instructions, review the rubric with students before they begin writing. Tell students how many peer reviews they will need to complete once they submit their writing.	
Write. Ask students to complete the writing assignment using textual evidence to support their answers. Once they have completed their writing, they should click "Submit."	
	Extend **Evaluate a Writing Sample.** Project a writing sample on the board and have students identify the elements of writing that are strong, as well as those that are weak or in need of improvement. Alternatively, you can give students photocopies of a writing sample to collaboratively evaluate. After students have had an opportunity to evaluate student samples, have them generate and share with the class strategies to use as they complete their peer reviews to ensure they are substantive.

Core Path	Access Path
Review. Once students complete their writing assignment, they should submit substantive feedback to two peers. Students should use their peers' feedback to improve their writing.	

FIRST READ:
Mrs. Dalloway

OVERVIEW

The novel *Mrs. Dalloway,* by Virginia Woolf, follows the titular character as she walks through London and interacts with her neighbors before she hosts a party. The First Read gives students the opportunity to experience the text with a limited context.

OBJECTIVES

1. Perform an initial reading of a text and demonstrate comprehension by responding to short analysis and inference questions with textual evidence.
2. Practice defining vocabulary words using context.
3. Participate effectively in a range of conversations and collaborations to express ideas and build upon the ideas of others.
4. Practice acquiring and using academic vocabulary correctly.

ELA Common Core Standards:
Reading: Literature - RL.11-12.1, RL.11-12.4, RL.11-12.10
Writing - W.11-12.7
Speaking & Listening - SL.11-12.1, SL.11-12.1.A, SL.11-12.1.B, SL.11-12.1.C, SL.11-12.1.D, SL.11-12.2
Language - L.11-12.4.A, L.11-12.4.D, L.11-12.6

RESOURCES

Access 1 handout (Beginner)
Access 2 handout (Intermediate)
Access 3 handout (Advanced)
Access 4 handout (Approaching)

ACCESS COMPLEX TEXT

This excerpt from *Mrs. Dalloway* focuses on the thoughts and actions of Mrs. Dalloway as she walks through her neighborhood one morning. The narration, however, does not stay with this title character. Instead, the author uses a stream-of-consciousness technique to explore the thoughts and points of view of several characters. To help students understand Woolf's unique style and the characters and world she has created, use the following ideas to provide scaffolded instruction for a first reading of the more complex features of this text:

- **Organization** - At first glance, the text appears to be organized chronologically, but the excerpt includes flashbacks that may be hard to recognize. For example, point out that the parenthetical "for a girl of eighteen as she then was" preceding Peter Walsh's comment "Musing among the vegetables" is a clue that the event occurred earlier in time.
- **Sentence Structure** - Woolf depicts the inner consciousness of several characters, but she does not include quotation marks or other clues to signal to readers when she is shifting points of view. In addition, the sentences are very long and have phrases strung together. Suggest that students use the semicolons and dashes to separate the text into chunks that are easier to understand.
- **Specific Vocabulary** - Some difficult and British vocabulary may present a challenge to readers. Explain that some British words have slightly different spellings from the American English word, but students may be able to use context to recognize the word. For example, "aeroplane" is the British spelling for "airplane." Remind students to check a dictionary when a word interferes with their comprehension.

1. INTRODUCTION

Core Path	Access Path
Read. Individually or as a class, read the Introduction for *Mrs. Dalloway*. The introduction provides context for the excerpt taken from Chapter 1.	**English Learners All Levels & Approaching** **Read and Listen.** Ask students to read and listen to the introduction for *Mrs. Dalloway.* Have them refer to the "Introduction Glossary" on their Access 1, 2, 3, and 4 handouts for definitions of key vocabulary terms. If there are unfamiliar words that are not included in their glossary, encourage students to check a dictionary or online reference tool, such as http://dictionary.reference.com.

Core Path	Access Path
Build Background. In pairs or small groups, ask students to use devices to research different aspects of modernism. Assign each group a topic to investigate: • characteristics of modernism • modernism as a response to World War I • key modernist writers, including Virginia Woolf • other examples of modernist literature	**English Learners All Levels & Approaching** **Research Guide.** Pair students with more proficient readers and assign them one of the topics of modernism to research. Have students complete the sentence frames on the Access 1, 2, 3, and 4 handouts to guide their research. Sample answers for this activity can be found at the end of the lesson plan online. If students struggle to find credible online sources, provide them with the following websites: On modernism: http://tinyurl.com/8x4oten; On Virginia Woolf: http://tinyurl.com/ntuedfl.
	Extend **Tech Infusion** **Take Notes.** Create a shared Google Doc and ask students to compile their notes on modernism. Encourage students to include relevant images along with their notes. When students have completed their research, discuss their findings as a class.

2. READ

Core Path	Access Path
Make Predictions about Vocabulary. There are five bold vocabulary words in the text. As students read the text, ask them to make predictions about what they think each bold vocabulary word means based on the context clues in the sentence. Have students use the annotation tool to make their predictions. It might be helpful to model this for students before they begin reading. Either using the board or projecting the actual text, focus in on the sentence that uses the word "trudge":	**Note:** This exercise, which extends vocabulary instruction, should be completed when the class shifts from whole-group instruction to individual work during the "Read and Annotate" exercise. **Beginner, Intermediate & Approaching** **Pair Practice.** 1. Pair students with more proficient readers. 2. Give them an additional sentence that contains a new vocabulary word. 3. Ask the students to complete a Think Aloud using the teacher-led Make Predictions about Vocabulary activity as a model, while the proficient student actively listens.

Core Path	Access Path
• In people's eyes, in the swing, tramp, and trudge; in the bellow and the uproar; the carriages, motor cars, omnibuses, vans, sandwich men shuffling and swinging; brass bands; barrel organs; in the triumph and the jingle and the strange high singing of some aeroplane overhead was what she loved; life; London; this moment of June. Model for the class how to use these context clues to guess the meanings of the words: 1. This is a long, complex sentence, so I will start by looking for patterns. I see that Woolf has divided the sentence into smaller parts using semicolons. The part I need to focus on says " in the swing, tramp, and trudge." I'm not sure what these words have in common, so I'll compare this part with another long part of the sentence. 2. I read, "the carriages, motor cars, omnibuses, vans, sandwich men shuffling and swinging." These words all refer to transportation of some kind, but they are all different. 3. I look back at "in the swing, tramp, and trudge." I know that "swing" and "tramp" are types of movement, and based on what I've learned about the patterns in this sentence, I can infer that "trudge" refers to movement, too. 4. Then I think about the meanings of "swing" and "tramp." I know that "swing" refers to fast movement and "tramp" refers to steady movement, so "trudge" must mean "to walk slowly." 5. Because this is a complicated sentence, I'll check my preliminary definition in a dictionary to make sure I have the meaning correct before moving on.	4. The student should use the context clues in the sentence to try to determine the meaning of the new vocabulary word. 5. After the student has completed the Think Aloud and made a prediction about the word's meaning, allow time for the proficient reader to add his/her own thoughts and clarify any points of confusion. 6. Once they've completed this Think Aloud, encourage them to use a dictionary to confirm the definition of the new vocabulary word. Have them refer to the "Text Glossary" on their Access 1, 2, and 4 handouts for definitions of key vocabulary terms in the text. Encourage them to add any additional vocabulary words or idioms they find in the text and look up definitions for those words and idioms online or in a dictionary.

Core Path	Access Path
Model Reading Comprehension Strategy. Before students begin reading, model the reading comprehension strategy of visualizing by using this Think Aloud that talks students through the several paragraphs of text. First explain to your students that visualizing is: *forming a mental picture of something as you read and using new details from the text to add to or change the mental images you have created* Explain to students how visualizing will help them better comprehend the selection and help drive their discussions. • When I read the first sentence, I learn that a woman named Mrs. Dalloway is going to buy flowers. I don't know yet what she looks like or what her neighborhood looks like, so I keep reading. • In the third paragraph, I find more details that help my visualization. The text says, "she had burst open the French windows and plunged at Bourton into the open air. How fresh, how calm, stiller than this of course, the air was in the early morning; like the flap of a wave; the kiss of a wave; chill and sharp." This helps me imagine what Mrs. Dalloway's house looks like, the weather on that day, and how the wind would feel on her skin as she walked. • The fourth paragraph gives me clues about what Mrs. Dalloway herself looks like: "a touch of the bird about her, of the jay, blue-green, light, vivacious, though she was over fifty, and grown very white since her illness." This helps me imagine a thin, pale woman who, regardless of her illness, has a smile on her face. • As I read on, I will continue to pay attention to details that help me visualize the characters and events in the story.	**Note:** This exercise, which extends instruction around reading comprehension strategies, should be completed when the class shifts from whole-group instruction to individual work during the "Read and Annotate" exercise. **Beginner, Intermediate & Approaching** **Apply Reading Comprehension Strategy.** 1. Have students listen to the audio version of the excerpt from *Mrs. Dalloway.* As they listen to the audio recording, ask them to list phrases that describe images, such as "like the flap of a wave" and "Musing among the vegetables?" in the first column of the chart on the Access 1, 2, and 4 handouts. 2. Once they have listened to the audio version and created their lists based on what they heard, pair students with more proficient readers and ask them to discuss those phrases and the images and feelings they inspire in them as readers. As they conduct their discussions, have students take notes about their visualizations in the second column in the chart on their handouts. 3. Allow pairs time to discuss the lists. Students may want to compare and contrast the lists. If they discover phrases they didn't include but find particularly rich in imagery, encourage them to add to their lists based on their conversations.

Core Path	Access Path
Read and Annotate. Read and annotate the excerpt. Ask students to use the annotation tool as they read to: 1. use context clues to analyze and determine the meaning of the bolded vocabulary terms 2. ask questions about passages of the text that may be unclear or unresolved 3. identify key information, events, characters, and connections between them 4. note unfamiliar vocabulary	**Beginner** **Coach the Reading.** While other students read, annotate, and discuss the text independently, work with Beginning students, listening to the audio of the text and pausing periodically or when any student has a question. Coach students in articulating their questions for the group and in highlighting and annotating the text. Have students use the Annotation Guide on the Access 1 handout to support them as they highlight and annotate the text. For further support, ask questions about the text such as: • Is there anything about the excerpt that you don't understand? • How do other characters reveal information about Mrs. Dalloway? • What do you imagine Mrs. Dalloway's party will be like? **Intermediate** **Listen to the Audio.** Have these students listen to the audio of the text and use the Text Glossary on the Access 2 handout to help them with words or idioms that may be unfamiliar. If students need help with annotating the text, have them use the annotation Guide on the Access 2 handout. After working with the Beginning students, you may wish to check this group's progress and provide support as needed. **Advanced** **Pair with Proficient Peers.** Have Advanced students work with English-proficient peers to read, annotate, and discuss the text. Have students use the Annotation Guide in the Access 3 handout to support them as they highlight and annotate the text. Encourage them to listen to the audio of the text if needed. **Approaching** **Use the Annotation Guide.** Have students use the Annotation Guide on the Access 4 handout to support them as they highlight and annotate the text.

Core Path	Access Path
Discuss. In small groups or pairs, have students discuss the questions and inferences they made while reading. To help facilitate discussions, refer to Collaborative Discussions in the Speaking & Listening Handbook. 1. Who are Mrs. Dalloway's friends and neighbors? (Peter Walsh, Scrope Purvis, Hugh and Evelyn Whitbread) 2. From how many points of view does Woolf tell the story of *Mrs. Dalloway*, in this excerpt? (two: Mrs. Dalloway's and Scrope Purvis's) How can you tell when one point of view ends and another begins? (The narrator attributes the thoughts to the person thinking them. When narrating from Scrope Purvis's point of view, for example, the text says, "A charming woman, Scrope Purvis thought her ...") 3. How does Mrs. Dalloway interact with the world around her? (Mrs. Dalloway flits from one thing to another like a bird.) How does visualizing help you understand Mrs. Dalloway's perspective? (Visualizing helps you keep track of all the people and places Mrs. Dalloway is describing.)	**English Learners All Levels & Approaching** Use the extra time while on- and beyond-grade-level students are discussing their first reads of the text to work individually and in small groups with Approaching readers and English Learners as outlined on the previous page. Should those students complete their first reads quickly, integrate them into the on- and beyond-grade-level discussion groups. Otherwise, English Learners and Approaching readers will be given an opportunity to participate in text discussions with their peers later in the lesson. **Beyond** **Brainstorm.** Pair students and ask them to brainstorm what theme or themes may be developed in *Mrs. Dalloway* based on the details in this excerpt from Chapter 1. Students who have access to a backchannel tool such as TodaysMeet (https://todaysmeet.com/) may enjoy brainstorming in that medium.
	Extend **Reflect.** Ask students to imagine what would happen if they took a walk like Mrs. Dalloway's around their own neighborhood. What would they see? Who would they talk to? How would their experience be similar to Mrs. Dalloway's? How would it be different? Allow them to reflect in writing on paper or using an online journaling tool, such as Penzu (http://penzu.com) or Pen.io (http://pen.io/)

3. THINK

Core Path	Access Path
Answer and Discuss. Have students complete the Think questions and then use the peer review instructions and rubric to complete two peer reviews. Refer to the sample answers at the end of the lesson plan online to discuss responses with your students.	**Beginner & Intermediate** **Sentence Frames.** Have students use the sentence frames on the Access 1 and 2 handouts to support their responses to the Think questions. If necessary, distribute sentence frames to Advanced students as well. **Approaching** **Find the Evidence.** Have students use Find the Evidence on the Access 4 handout to help them identify the evidence needed to answer the questions.
	Extend **Research.** Put students into small groups and ask them to use devices to research the following: What was London like right after World War I? How might the social, economic, and political atmosphere affect a work of fiction written during this time? When students have completed their research, ask them to compare their notes to the text to determine how accurate the setting is. Then have students brainstorm why Woolf chose this time and place for the novel.

SKILL:
Tone

OVERVIEW

Analyzing tone is key to understanding any work of fiction. This is especially true when the tone changes as quickly and seamlessly it does in Virginia Woolf's *Mrs. Dalloway*. This lesson plan provides follow-up questions and useful enrichments to help teachers guide students toward a usable, repeatable method for tracing and analyzing tone.

OBJECTIVES

1. Learn the definition of tone.
2. Practice using concrete strategies for analyzing tone.
3. Participate effectively in a range of conversations and collaborations to express ideas and build upon the ideas of others.

ELA Common Core Standards:
Reading: Literature - RL.11-12.1, RL.11-12.3, RL.11-12.4
Speaking & Listening - SL.11-12.1.A, SL.11-12.1.C, SL.11-12.2

RESOURCES

Access 1 handout (Beginner)
Access 2 handout (Intermediate)
Access 3 handout (Advanced)
Access 4 handout (Approaching)

1. DEFINE

Core Path	Access Path
Watch. Watch the Concept Definition video on tone with your students. Have your students write down the definition of tone as it is stated in the video. Also, make sure they understand the different strategies for determining an author's tone. Pause the video at these key moments to discuss the information with your students: 1. 0:13 – When speaking, how do you express attitude? What cues do texts have that reveal the author's or the narrator's attitude? 2. 0:47 – How would the same text be different if the tone changed from formal to informal? Or from serious to sarcastic? 3. 0:53 – What other examples can you think of in which the tone might be at odds with the subject matter? What effect does that have?	**English Learners All Levels & Approaching** **Fill in the Blanks.** Have students complete the fill-in-the-blanks exercise on the Access 1, 2, 3, and 4 handouts as they watch the video. Answers are located at the end of the lesson plan online.
Read and Discuss. After watching the Concept Definition video, have students read the definition of tone. Either in small groups or as a whole class, use these questions to engage students in a discussion about tone. 1. What cues should you examine to determine the tone of a text? (an author's choice of words and point of view) 2. How does tone function differently in a work of fiction than it does in an informational text? (Answers will vary. Possible answer: The tone of a work of fiction helps to develop plot or characterization, while the tone of an informational text might give you clues to an author's purpose or point of view.) 3. Besides the addition of exclamation marks, how could a writer use punctuation to communicate tone in a written text? (Answers will vary. Possible answer: An author might use numerous apostrophes in contractions to convey a conversational tone using informal language.)	**Beginner & Approaching** **Complete the Sentences.** To prepare students to participate in the discussion, have them complete the sentences on the Access 1 and 4 handouts as they read the definition. The correct answers are located at the end of the lesson plan online. **Intermediate & Advanced** **Discuss Prompts.** To help these students participate in the discussion, prompt them with questions that can be answered with a few words, such as: • What does tone express? (the author's attitude) • How does connotation show tone? (through emotions associated with the word) • How can punctuation express tone? (It can stress a point.)

Core Path	Access Path
	Beyond **Discuss.** Have students select a poem or a story they've read and describe its tone. Compile a list of examples. Have students discuss how the tone of each work affects the mood. How might changing the words chosen, sentence structures, or figures of speech affect the tone and the way readers feel about the subject or theme?
	Extend **Brainstorm.** After reading the definition of tone, have students brainstorm a list of words that describe tone. You might begin by reminding students of the tones listed in the definition (sympathy, rage, irony, sadness, bitterness, humor, and seriousness). Compile a list on the board. Then discuss how a writer could express these tones in a written work.

2. MODEL

Core Path	Access Path
Read and Annotate. Have students independently read the Model section. As they read, ask students to use the annotation tool to: • highlight key points • ask questions • identify places where the Model applies the strategies laid out in the Identification and Application section • comment on the effect the tone has on the text's meaning	**Note:** During this portion of the lesson, instruction shifts from whole-group to individual work. Use this time to work one-on-one or in small groups with Beginning, Intermediate, Advanced, and Approaching students. **Beginner & Intermediate** **Coach the Reading.** Work with these students (either individually or in small groups) to fill out the guided reading questions on the Access 1 and 2 handouts. Have Beginning students refer to the glossary on the Access 1 handout to help them determine the meaning of difficult words (note: provide the Access 1 handout glossary to Intermediate students if necessary). Let students know they'll use these answers to help participate in the discussion about the Model. Sample answers for this exercise are located at the end of the lesson plan online.

Core Path	Access Path
	Advanced **Identify Evidence.** Ask Advanced students to complete the identifying evidence exercise on the Access 3 handout. Let students know that they'll use these answers to help participate in the discussion about the Model. Sample answers for this exercise are located at the end of the lesson plan online. **Approaching** **Guided Reading.** Have students complete the guided reading questions on the Access 4 handout as they read. Let them know that they'll use these answers to help participate in the discussion about the Model. Sample answers for this exercise are located at the end of the lesson plan online.
Discuss. After students read the Model text, use these questions to facilitate a whole-group discussion that helps students understand how to determine the tone of the passage: 1. How does the Model for this passage go about finding the tone of *Mrs. Dalloway*? (The Model looks closely at Woolf's word choice and figurative language.) 2. How does the writer of the Model describe the tone of the beginning of Chapter 1 of *Mrs. Dalloway?* (as light and breezy) How does the tone change in this paragraph? (Woolf includes the word "solemn" and hints that "something awful was about to happen.") 3. What does the tone suggest about Mrs. Dalloway's character? (The tone seems light at first but then turns heavy. This suggests that Mrs. Dalloway herself seems cheerful on the surface, but she might not be as happy as she seems.) 4. What does the tone suggest about the city of London? (The Model suggests that the quickly shifting tone reflects the multiple layers of the city.)	

Core Path	Access Path
	Extend **Read Aloud.** Ask for volunteers to read the excerpt from *Mrs. Dalloway* aloud, one paragraph at a time. Encourage volunteers to change the tone of their voice as they read to match the tone of the story. As they listen, ask students to take notes describing the tone of each paragraph. Then discuss how the tone affects the meaning of the text.

3. YOUR TURN

Core Path	Access Path
Assess and Explain. Have students answer the comprehension questions to test for understanding. Share the explanations for Parts A and B (located online) with your students.	
	Extend **Share and Discuss.** Have students write their own Your Turn questions about a different passage of *Mrs. Dalloway*. Then have them swap papers with a classmate and answer their peer's question. Last, encourage each pair to discuss the strategies they used to write their questions and give their responses.

CLOSE READ:
Mrs. Dalloway

OVERVIEW

Virginia Woolf's *Mrs. Dalloway* is a complex novel that uses a stream-of-consciousness style of writing to follow the titular character during a single day in post-World War I London. The Close Read gives students the opportunity to analyze the tone and characterization within the text.

OBJECTIVES

1. Complete a close reading of a passage of literature.
2. Practice and apply concrete strategies for analyzing tone in an excerpt from *Mrs. Dalloway.*
3. Participate effectively in a range of conversations and collaborations to express ideas and build upon the ideas of others.
4. Prewrite, plan, and produce clear and coherent writing in response to a prompt.

ELA Common Core Standards:
Reading: Literature - RL.11-12.1, RL.11-12.3, RL.11-12.4, RL.11-12.10
Writing - W.11-12.2.A, W.11-12.2.B, W.11-12.4, W.11-12.5, W.11-12.6, W.11-12.9.A, W.11-12.10
Speaking & Listening - SL.11-12.1.A, SL.11-12.1.B, SL.11-12.1.C, SL.11-12.1.D, SL.11-12.6
Language - L.11-12.4.A, L.11-12.4.C, L.11-12.4.D

RESOURCES

Mrs. Dalloway Vocabulary Review
Access 1 handout (Beginner)
Access 2 handout (Intermediate)
Access 3 handout (Advanced)
Access 4 handout (Approaching)

1. INTRODUCTION

Core Path	Access Path
Define and Compare. Project the vocabulary words and definitions onto the board or provide students with handouts so they can copy the vocabulary into their notebooks. Suggest that students consult general and specialized reference materials, both print and digital, to compare the precise meaning of a specific word with their initial vocabulary predictions from the First Read. Review words that students defined incorrectly to understand why they were unable to use context clues to develop usable definitions.	**Beginner & Intermediate** **Complete the Chart.** Have students complete the chart on the Access 1 and 2 handouts by writing the correct word for each of the definitions. **Advanced & Beyond** **Write in Journals.** Have students write a journal entry using all of their vocabulary words. Remind them to write sentences that communicate the meaning of the words they are using. **Approaching** **Graphic Organizer.** To support students in comparing their predictions with the correct meanings, have them complete the graphic organizer on the Access 4 handout to record the vocabulary words, their initial analysis, and the definitions. Then have them write sentences using the words.
Review. Have students complete the fill-in-the-blanks vocabulary worksheet attached to the lesson plan online. Answers for the worksheet are listed at the end of the lesson plan online.	
	Extend **Create.** Have students create their own flashcards for the vocabulary words. Challenge them to write a new definition in their own words, and have them use a print or online dictionary to find the word's exact pronunciation and, if available, its etymology. Use these flashcards to review and memorize the words.

2. READ

Core Path	Access Path
Model Close Reading. Project the text onto the board and model a close reading of the first three paragraphs using the annotation strategies mentioned on the next page. While modeling annotation strategies, make notes that tie the text to the focus skill and demonstrate what students are looking for as they read. Here is some guidance for you as you annotate for your students: • Recall from the Skills lesson that precedes this text that tone is the attitude of an author toward a subject, a character or person, or even an audience. • I read the first sentence: "Mrs. Dalloway said she would buy the flowers herself." This is a matter-of-fact statement. I keep reading to see if the next paragraph uses this same straightforward tone. • At the end of the next paragraph, I read, "And then, thought Clarissa Dalloway, what a morning—fresh as if issued to children on a beach." Based on the matter-of-fact tone of the first paragraph, I have no reason to think the second one is sarcastic, so I can infer that Mrs. Dalloway is a cheerful woman who is glad to be outside. • The next paragraph continues Mrs. Dalloway's positive thoughts: "What a lark! What a plunge!... How fresh, how calm, stiller than this of course, the air was in the early morning; like the flap of a wave; the kiss of a wave." These thoughts maintain the light, matter-of-fact tone of the text. • However, as the text goes on, I notice darker imagery: "the trees with the smoke winding off them and the rooks rising, falling." This is less positive than what came before, so I know the tone of the text must shift here. I'll have to keep reading to determine why the tone shifts and what that could mean.	

Core Path	Access Path
Read and Annotate. Read the Skills Focus questions as a class, so your students know what they should pay close attention to as they read. Then have students read and annotate the excerpt. Ask students to use the annotation tool as they read to: 1. respond to the Skills Focus section 2. examine sentence structure, especially as it relates to tone 3. identify examples of particularly fresh, engaging, or beautiful language and note their impact on meaning and tone 4. note descriptions of London and analyze Mrs. Dalloway's relationship with her city 5. examine the use of dialogue in the story 6. note unfamiliar vocabulary 7. capture their reaction to the ideas and examples in the text As they reread the text, remind students to use the comprehension strategy of visualizing that they learned in the First Read.	**Note:** While on-grade-level students are reading and annotating, work one-on-one or in small groups with Beginning, Intermediate, Advanced, and Approaching students to support them as they read and annotate the text. **Beginner & Intermediate** **Summarize and Analyze the Text.** Work with these students to complete the sentence frames on the Access 1 and 2 handouts (note: the sentence frames for Intermediate students on the Access 2 handout contain fewer scaffolds). They will then use the completed sentence frames to help them analyze and annotate the text by completing the Skills Focus questions. Refer to the sample Skills Focus answers to help them complete the sentence frames and annotate the text. **Advanced** **Work in Pairs.** Pair these students with more proficient English speakers to work together on analyzing and annotating the text to complete the Skills Focus questions. If these students need more support, have them use the sentence frames on the Access 3 handout as they work with their more proficient peers. **Approaching** **Summarize the Text.** Have these students discuss and complete the text summary on the Access 4 handout and use their summary to help them analyze and annotate the text by completing the Skills Focus questions. Correct answers for the summary are at the end of the lesson plan online. Also refer to the sample Skills Focus answers to aid students with their annotations.
Discuss. After students have read the text, use the sample responses to the Skills Focus questions at the bottom of the lesson plan online to discuss the reading and the process of identifying and analyzing tone.	**Extend** **Pair and Share.** In small, heterogeneous groups or pairs, ask students to share and discuss their annotations with a focus on the tone presented in the selection.

Core Path	Access Path
Make sure that students have acquired and accurately use academic-specific words and phrases related to the skill and demonstrate a command of formal English appropriate to the discussion. To help facilitate discussions, refer to Collaborative Discussions in the Speaking & Listening Handbook.	You can provide students with these questions to guide their discussion: 1. Mrs. Dalloway uses the word "fresh" twice to describe the morning. How does this repetition help establish the tone of the text? Cite specific textual evidence to support your statements. (First, Mrs. Dalloway thinks, "what a morning—fresh as if issued to children on a beach." Then, she adds, "How fresh, how calm, stiller than this of course, the air was in the early morning ..." This repetition suggests that Mrs. Dalloway's lightness might be contrived or forced. This is further developed by the description that she felt "that something awful was about to happen.") 2. Which adjectives does Scrope Purvis use to describe Mrs. Dalloway? How do they contribute to her characterization and the tone of the text? Cite specific textual evidence to support your answer. (Purvis describes Mrs. Dalloway as "blue-green, light vivacious," "over fifty," and "very white." These contradictory adjectives suggest that there might be more to Mrs. Dalloway—and the text—that can be seen at first glance.)
	Extend **Tech Infusion** **Highlight.** Remind students that Virginia Woolf uses a stream-of-consciousness style of writing in *Mrs. Dalloway*. Remind students that this means writing thoughts as they come and not always stopping to include punctuation or other clues that let readers know when she is switching to another character's point of view. Paste the second and third paragraphs of *Mrs. Dalloway* into a Google Doc and have students mark the places where Woolf switches points of view. Then, have students edit the text so that it clearly indicates which thoughts belong to which character. Students should be careful to use quotation marks and other punctuation marks correctly as they edit.

3. WRITE

Core Path	Access Path
Prewrite and Plan. Read the prompt as a class and ask students to brainstorm about tone and characterization in the excerpt from *Mrs. Dalloway.* Remind your students to look at the excerpt and their annotations to find textual evidence to support their ideas.	**Beginner & Intermediate** **Plan and Organize.** Have students complete the prewriting activity on the Access 1 and 2 handouts and then explain their ideas to a partner before they write. Explain to students that they need to choose details, examples, or quotes from the text that support their ideas and then explain how those details support their statements. For example, students could include "What a lark! What a plunge!" as evidence of Mrs. Dalloway's cheerful mood at the start of the day. **Approaching** **Plan and Organize.** Have students complete the prewriting activity on the Access 4 handout to organize their thoughts before they write.
Discuss. Project these peer review instructions onto the board and review them with your class, so they know what they are looking for when they begin to provide their classmates with feedback: • How has this essay helped you understand how Virginia Woolf uses tone to develop characters in the novel? • How well did the writer explain how Woolf uses tone to convey different points of view? • What sort of evidence did the writer use from the text to support his or her writing? • How well does the writer explain how that evidence supports his or her ideas? • Does the writer write using standard grammar and punctuation? Are there any weak spots? • What specific suggestions can you make to help the writer improve the response? • What thing(s) does this paper do especially well?	

Core Path	Access Path
After you've looked at the peer review instructions, review the rubric with students before they begin writing. Allow time for students briefly to pose and discuss any questions they may have about the peer review instructions and the rubric. Tell students how many peer reviews they will need to complete once they submit their writing.	
Write. Ask students to complete the writing assignment using textual evidence to support their answers. Once they have completed their writing, they should click "Submit."	
	Extend **Critique.** Assign each student a writing sample to evaluate. Have students identify the elements of writing that are strong as well as those that are weak or in need of improvement. Remind students to consider the writer's ideas and text evidence, not just grammar and mechanics. After students have had an opportunity to evaluate student samples independently, pair students and have them discuss what they marked and why. For the weak spots, have partners brainstorm how to make improvements.
Review. Once students complete their writing assignment, they should submit substantive feedback to two peers.	

FIRST READ:
"The Star-Spangled Banner"

OVERVIEW

Francis Scott Key's song "The Star-Spangled Banner" was written after he witnessed a battle during the War of 1812. More than 100 years later, the song was declared our national anthem. The First Read gives students the opportunity to experience the text with a limited context.

OBJECTIVES

1. Perform an initial reading of a text and demonstrate comprehension by responding to short analysis and inference questions with textual evidence.
2. Practice defining vocabulary words using context.
3. Participate effectively in a range of conversations and collaborations to express ideas and build upon the ideas of others.
4. Practice acquiring and using academic vocabulary correctly.

ELA Common Core Standards:
Reading: Literature - RL.11-12.1, RL.11-12.4, RL.11-12.10
Writing - W.11-12.7
Speaking & Listening - SL.11-12.1.A, SL.11-12.1.B, SL.11-12.1.C, SL.11-12.1.D, SL.11-12.2
Language - L.11-12.4.A, L.11-12.6

RESOURCES

Access 1 handout (Beginner)
Access 2 handout (Intermediate)
Access 3 handout (Advanced)
Access 4 handout (Approaching)

ACCESS COMPLEX TEXT

While most Americans can recite the first verse of "The Star-Spangled Banner," the song's three additional verses are less well known. The entire song leads listeners into a journey symbolizing the United States rising from the depths of war. In the first verse, the speaker asks if the flag is still waving, in the second the speaker catches sight of the flag, the third verse celebrates the United States' victory in battle, and the fourth provides wishes for the country's future. To help students understand the song, use the following ideas to provide scaffolded instruction for a first reading of the more complex features of this text:

- **Genre** - The selection is a song, which contains poetic elements—including rhyme, meter, and figurative language—that might challenge some readers.
- **Prior Knowledge** - Students may be unfamiliar with the War of 1812, which was the second war between the United States and Great Britain. It came less than three decades after the United States gained its independence from Britain during their first war, the American Revolution. In fact, the War of 1812 was often dubbed "The Second War of Independence" even though the war had little impact on either country.
- **Specific Vocabulary** - Key often uses archaic terms, such as "foe" and "doth," as well as figurative language, such as "Their blood has washed out their foul footsteps' pollution." Students may need help understanding the vocabulary and interpreting the imagery.

1. INTRODUCTION

Core Path	Access Path
Read. Individually or as a class, read the introduction for "The Star-Spangled Banner." The introduction provides context for the song.	**English Learners All Levels & Approaching** **Read and Listen.** Ask students to read and listen to the introduction for "The Star-Spangled Banner." Have them refer to the "Introduction Glossary" on their Access 1, 2, 3, and 4 handouts for definitions of key vocabulary terms. If there are unfamiliar words that are not included in their glossary, encourage students to check a dictionary or online reference tool, such as http://dictionary.reference.com.

Core Path	Access Path
Build Background. In pairs or small groups, ask students to research different aspects of the War of 1812. Assign each group a topic to investigate: • Causes of the war • Who fought against the United States • The burning of the capital • The battle at Fort McHenry • Results of the war	**English Learners All Levels & Approaching** **Match.** Pair students with more proficient readers and have them research the War of 1812. Have pairs complete the matching activity on the Access 1, 2, 3, and 4 handouts to guide their research. The correct answers for this activity can be found at the end of the lesson plan online.
	Extend **Discuss the Introduction.** After reading the introduction, use the information provided to facilitate a prereading discussion to get students thinking about the events and themes in "The Star-Spangled Banner." 1. Consider the original title, "The Defence of Fort McHenry." Does that title change your impression of the song? 2. Does it surprise you that a song about the War of 1812 became the national anthem in 1931? Why or why not? 3. What do you expect from a song about a war?

2. READ

Core Path	Access Path
Make Predictions about Vocabulary. There are six bold vocabulary words in the text. As students read the text, ask them to make predictions about what they think each bold vocabulary word means based on the context clues in the sentence. Have students use the annotation tool to make their predictions.	**Note:** This exercise, which extends vocabulary instruction, should be completed when the class shifts from whole-group instruction to individual work during the "Read and Annotate" exercise.

Core Path	Access Path
It might be helpful to model this for students before they begin reading. Either using the board or projecting the actual text, focus in on the sentence that uses the word "reposes": • On the shore, dimly seen through the mists of the deep, Where the foe's haughty host in dread silence reposes, What is that which the breeze, o'er the towering steep, As it fitfully blows, half conceals, half discloses? Model for the class how to use the overall structure and meaning of the sentence and the sentences around it, the word's position, and other clues to define the unfamiliar vocabulary word. In this case, point out these context clues: 1. The sentence that contains "reposes" is long and complex. Let's break it down. The first two lines are setting the scene for the main part of the sentence. The last two lines reveal that the speaker sees something that "fitfully blows" up on top of the fort. 2. So what else does the speaker see? He's looking to the shore, which he can barely make out through the mists, for signs of the flag. The shore is "Where the foe's haughty host in dread silence reposes." 3. We know at this point that the battle is over. We don't know who won, but the foe's host, or army, "reposes" in "dread silence." Dread silence sounds like a description of how a dead body might act. Dead bodies would be lying on the ground after a battle. "Reposes" must mean "lies."	**Beginner, Intermediate & Approaching Pair Practice.** 1. Pair students with more proficient readers. 2. Give them an additional sentence that contains a new vocabulary word. 3. Ask the students to complete a Think Aloud using the teacher-led Make Predictions about Vocabulary activity as a model, while the proficient student actively listens. 4. The student should use the context clues in the sentence to try to determine the meaning of the new vocabulary word. 5. After the student has completed the Think Aloud and made a prediction about the word's meaning, allow time for the proficient reader to add his/her own thoughts and clarify any points of confusion. 6. Once they've completed this Think Aloud, encourage them to use a dictionary to confirm the definition of the new vocabulary word. Have them refer to the "Text Glossary" on their Access 1, 2, and 4 handouts for definitions of key vocabulary terms in the text. Encourage them to add any additional vocabulary words or idioms they find in the text and look up definitions for those words and idioms online or in a dictionary.

Core Path	Access Path
Model Reading Comprehension Strategy. Before students begin reading, model the reading comprehension strategy of visualizing by using this think aloud that talks students through the first paragraph of text. First, explain to your students that visualizing is: *forming a mental picture of something as you read and using new details from the text to add to or change the mental images you have created* Model for students how visualizing will help them better comprehend the selection and help drive their discussions. • The first stanza is very visual. The first line tells us that the setting is the "dawn's early light." I can picture what a fort looks like in the early morning light. • Then the stanza describes the events of the night before. I can picture a flag waving "gallantly" above the fort as bombs burst in the air near it. The scene almost reminds me of the Fourth of July. • Those bombs are described as giving "proof through the night" that the flag was still waving. This line clarifies my mental image. It's so dark that the flag cannot be seen, except when a bomb bursts with a flash of light. • As I read on, I will continue to examine visual details to create a picture in my mind of what is happening.	**Note:** This exercise, which extends instruction around reading comprehension strategies, should be completed when the class shifts from whole-group instruction to individual work during the "Read and Annotate" exercise. **Beginner, Intermediate & Approaching** **Apply Reading Comprehension Strategy.** 1. Have Beginning and Intermediate students listen to the audio version of "The Star-Spangled Banner." As they listen to the audio recording, ask them to follow along in the text and highlight words that appeal to their senses of sight, touch, hearing, taste, and smell. 2. Once students have listened to the audio version and underlined sensory words, have them draw or sketch a picture of what they see in their minds as they visualize the song. Encourage them to include as much detail as possible in the time allowed. 3. Then pair Beginning and Intermediate students with more proficient readers and ask them to describe what they drew and why. Why did they include particular images and/or colors? 4. Allow pairs time to discuss the pictures. Were there any details from the text that were not included in the picture? If so, encourage them to add details to the drawing based on their conversations.

Core Path	Access Path
Read and Annotate. Have students independently read and annotate the song. Ask students to use the annotation tool as they read to: 1. use context clues to analyze and determine the meaning of the bolded vocabulary terms 2. ask questions about passages of the text that may be unclear or unresolved 3. identify key information, events, images, and connections between them 4. note unfamiliar vocabulary	**Beginner** **Coach the Reading.** While other students read, annotate, and discuss the text independently, work with Beginning students, listening to the audio of the text and pausing periodically or when any student has a question. Coach students in articulating their questions for the group and in highlighting and annotating the text. Have students use the Annotation Guide on the Access 1 handout to support them as they highlight and annotate the text. For further support, ask questions about the text such as: • What emotions and reactions do you think Key had as he watched the British attack the US fort? • What feelings do you think Key intended to provoke in readers? • What makes "The Star-Spangled Banner" a better song title than "Defence of Fort McHenry"? **Intermediate** **Listen to the Audio.** Have these students listen to the audio of the text and use the Text Glossary on the Access 2 handout to help them with words or idioms that may be unfamiliar. If students need help with annotating the text, have them use the Annotation Guide on the Access 2 handout. After working with the Beginning students, you may wish to check this group's progress and provide support as needed. **Advanced** **Pair with Proficient Peers.** Have Advanced students work with English-proficient peers to read, annotate, and discuss the text. Have students use the Annotation Guide in the Access 3 handout to support them as they highlight and annotate the text. Encourage them to listen to the audio of the text if needed.

Core Path	Access Path
	Approaching **Use the Annotation Guide.** Have students use the Annotation Guide on the Access 4 handout to support them as they highlight and annotate the text.
Discuss. In small groups or pairs, have students discuss the questions and inferences they made while reading. To help facilitate discussions, refer to Collaborative Discussions in the Speaking & Listening Handbook. 1. What does the speaker of the song think of the enemy? What kinds of words and phrases does he use to describe them? How do these descriptions serve his purpose? (The speaker doesn't think highly of the enemy. He describes them with words such as "haughty" and "foul." These descriptions support the purpose of inspiring pride due to the victory.) 2. Every stanza ends with the same line. What does this line mean? Why might Key have wanted to emphasize this sentiment? (Every stanza ends with "O'er the land of the free and the home of the brave!" This line compliments the country and inspires pride in the reader. The poet likely emphasized this line to express admiration for the country.) 3. What are some vivid examples of figurative language in the song? ("And the rocket's red glare, the bombs bursting in air"; "As it fitfully blows, half conceals, half discloses?") How does visualizing help you understand the figurative language? (Visualizing each image that appears in the song as I read helps me better understand what the poet is trying to say with figurative language.)	**English Learners All Levels & Approaching** Use the extra time while on- and beyond-grade-level students are discussing their first reads of the text to work individually and in small groups with Approaching readers and English Learners as outlined above. Should those students complete their first reads quickly, integrate them into the on- and beyond-grade-level discussion groups. Otherwise, English Learners and Approaching readers will be given an opportunity to participate in text discussions with their peers later in the lesson. **Beyond** **Tech Infusion** **Summarize.** Pair students and ask them to use a word-processing app like Google Docs to summarize each stanza. Remind students to only include the most important ideas and details in their summaries. Have pairs trade their summaries and discuss the choices they made.

3. THINK

Core Path	Access Path
Answer and Discuss. Have students complete the Think questions and then use the peer review instructions and rubric to complete two peer reviews. Refer to the sample answers at the end of the lesson plan online to discuss responses with your students.	**Beginner & Intermediate** **Sentence Frames.** Have students use the sentence frames on the Access 1 and 2 handouts to support their responses to the Think questions. If necessary, distribute sentence frames to Advanced students as well. **Approaching** **Find the Evidence.** Have students use Find the Evidence on the Access 4 handout to help them identify the evidence needed to answer the questions.
	Extend **Tech Infusion** **Write.** Challenge students to write their own song or poem about the American flag. Students should use Key's song as a model, but they do not need to follow his form or set their writing during the War of 1812. When students have written their songs or poems, post them on a class blog. Alternatively, film students reading their work and post them to a class YouTube channel.

SKILL:

Author's Purpose and Author's Point of View

OVERVIEW

In "The Star-Spangled Banner," Francis Scott Key uses rhetorical devices to inspire patriotism in his listeners. This lesson plan provides follow-up questions and useful enrichments to help teachers guide students toward a usable, repeatable method for analyzing author's purpose and author's point of view.

OBJECTIVES

1. Learn the definition of author's purpose and author's point of view.
2. Practice using concrete strategies for identifying and analyzing author's purpose and author's point of view.
3. Participate effectively in a range of conversations and collaborations to express ideas and build upon the ideas of others.

ELA Common Core Standards:
Reading: Literature - RL.11-12.1, RL.11-12.4, RL.11-12.9
Speaking & Listening - SL.11-12.1.A, SL.11-12.1.C, SL.11-12.2

RESOURCES

Access 1 handout (Beginner)
Access 2 handout (Intermediate)
Access 3 handout (Advanced)
Access 4 handout (Approaching)

1. DEFINE

Core Path	Access Path
Watch. Watch the Concept Definition video on author's purpose and author's point of view with your students. Make sure students understand why it's critical to know an author's purpose or point of view when trying to unlock the meaning of a text. Pause the video at these key moments to discuss the information with your students: 1. 1:00 – Can you think of any other purpose (or purposes) an author might have? How does genre affect purpose? In other words, how might the purpose of a work of fiction differ from that of an informational text? In what cases might it be the same? 2. 1:18 – Are there any other elements of a text that might offer clues into an author's purpose or point of view? What are some additional resources we can use if we're having trouble deciphering the purpose or point of view of a text? 3. 2:03 – Why don't authors of fiction or poetry state their purpose clearly in the same way a politician or an essayist might?	**English Learners All Levels & Approaching** **Fill in the Blanks.** Have students complete the fill-in-the-blanks exercise on the Access 1, 2, 3, and 4 handouts as they watch the video. Answers are located at the end of the lesson plan online.
Read and Discuss. After watching the Concept Definition video, have students read the definition of author's purpose and author's point of view. Either in small groups or as a whole class, use these questions to engage students in a discussion about author's purpose and author's point of view: 1. What makes a song or a poem persuasive? (Rhetorical appeals to the reader's emotions or reason make a song or poem persuasive.) Can you think of any examples? (Answers will vary.) 2. Are emotional pleas different in literature as opposed to informational texts? If so, why? (No. Authors of both literature and informational texts use rhetorical devices such as figurative language to appeal to readers' emotions.)	**Beginner & Approaching** **Complete the Chart.** To prepare students to participate in the discussion, have them complete the chart on the Access 1 and 4 handouts as they read the definition. The correct answers are located at the end of the lesson plan online. **Intermediate & Advanced** **Discuss Prompts.** To help these students participate in the discussion, prompt them with questions that can be answered with a few words, such as: • What is the main purpose of most speeches—to entertain or to persuade? (persuade) • What is the primary purpose of scientific articles—to inform, entertain, or persuade? (inform)

Core Path	Access Path
3. What is the effect on readers of using rhetorical questions? (To engage readers and prompt them to read on to answer the questions)	• Which article have you recently read that had more than one purpose? What were the purposes? (Answers will vary.) **Beyond** **Discuss.** Have students select a text they've read and identify the author's purpose(s) and describe the author's point of view. How did the author's purpose and point of view affect the way the author presented the information? What information did the author include on the topic? What information did the author leave out?
	Extend **Define and Present.** Group students and assign each group a rhetorical feature from the following list: • allusion • simile and metaphor • parallelism • repetition • rhetorical question Have each group find a definition for their feature. Then have them find an example of this figure of speech in a persuasive speech or piece of literature. When students have their definition and example, have each group share with the class.

2. MODEL

Core Path	Access Path
Watch. Ask students to take notes on the SkillsTV video on author's purpose and author's point of view in "The Star-Spangled Banner" as you watch together. Remind students to listen for the way the students use academic vocabulary related to the definition of author's purpose and author's point of view during their discussion. Pause the video at these key moments to discuss the information with your students: 1. 1:10 – According to the students, what purpose do the questions in the first stanza have? Is that the author's purpose for the song as a whole? How do you know? 2. 2:06 – Could there be another purpose for the alliteration other than sounding good, as the group concludes? Support your response with evidence from the text. 3. 2:27 – The students say that Key's "five-star words" dazzle the reader. What connotations do "perilous" and "gallantly" have? In what way are those different from the connotations of "dangerous" and "bravely"?	**Beginner, Intermediate & Approaching** **Analyze the Discussion.** Have students watch the video again and complete the chart on the Access 1, 2, and 4 handouts as they watch the video. Sample answers for this exercise are located at the end of the lesson plan online. **Advanced** **Journals.** Have students note in their journals the strategies the students in the SkillsTV video use to find author's purpose and point of view.
Read and Annotate. Have students independently read the Model section. As they read, ask students to use the annotation tool to: • highlight key points • ask questions • identify places where the Model applies the strategies laid out in the Identification and Application section • comment on the effect the author's purpose and point of view has on the text's meaning	**Note:** During this portion of the lesson, instruction shifts from whole-group to individual work. Use this time to work one-on-one or in small groups with Beginning, Intermediate, Advanced, and Approaching students.

Core Path	Access Path
	Beginner & Intermediate **Coach the Reading.** Work with these students (either individually or in small groups) to fill out the guided reading questions on the Access 1 and 2 handouts. Have Beginning students refer to the glossary on the Access 1 handout to help them determine the meaning of difficult words (note: provide the Access 1 handout glossary to Intermediate students if necessary). Let students know they'll use these answers to help participate in the discussion about the Model. Sample answers for this exercise are located at the end of the lesson plan online. **Advanced** **Identify Evidence.** Ask Advanced students to complete the identifying evidence exercise on the Access 3 handout. Let students know that they'll use these answers to help participate in the discussion about the Model. Sample answers for this exercise are located at the end of the lesson plan online. **Approaching** **Guided Reading.** Have students complete the guided reading questions on the Access 4 handout as they read. Let them know that they'll use these answers to help participate in the discussion about the Model. Sample answers for this exercise are located at the end of the lesson plan online.
Discuss. After students read the Model text, use these questions to facilitate a whole-group discussion that helps students understand how to determine and analyze the purpose and point of view of the passage: 1. According to the Model, how does Key use the opening lines to set the scene for the song? (The questions feature visual figurative language to set the scene.) What role do the questions play? (The use of questions adds suspense and encourages the reader to continue to read to find out what happened to the flag.)	

Core Path	Access Path
2. What is alliteration? (repetition of consonant sounds at the beginning of a word) How does Key use alliteration? (Alliteration links words and phrases together, as in "broad stripes and bright stars." It also provides a lyrical quality.) 3. What is the difference between connotation and denotation? (Denotation is a word's dictionary definition. Connotation is the feelings associated with that word.) How does Key use words with strong connotations? (to contrast the danger of the battle with the strength of the flag) 4. What rhetorical device does Key use to stress the importance of key lines? (repetition) Why does this device work? (Repeating lines shows the reader that the author thinks that the repeated line is important and worth remembering.)	
	Extend **Imagine.** What if Francis Scott Key were British rather than American? How would the song be different? Have students rewrite at least the first stanza of the song from the British perspective, with the purpose of either motivating the British forces after a loss or mourning the lost army. When students have finished their rewrites, have them share with a partner and discuss what they changed and why.

3. YOUR TURN

Core Path	Access Path
Assess and Explain. Have students answer the comprehension questions to test for understanding. Share the explanations for Parts A and B (located online) with your students.	

Core Path	Access Path
	Extend **Identify and Discuss.** Have students reread the stanza in the Your Turn question and identify all the rhetorical devices Key uses. Students may wish to use colored highlighters or other annotation tools to clearly note each device. Then, with a partner, have students discuss the effect of each device. • Does each rhetorical device have the same effect? • Which devices are most effective? • Are there any weak lines?

CLOSE READ:
"The Star-Spangled Banner"

OVERVIEW

"The Star-Spangled Banner" by Francis Scott Key has been the national anthem of the United States since 1931. It was written after a key naval battle during the War of 1812. The Close Read gives students the opportunity to analyze Key's rhetoric and purpose.

OBJECTIVES

1. Complete a close reading of a song.
2. Practice and apply concrete strategies for analyzing rhetoric in "The Star-Spangled Banner."
3. Participate effectively in a range of conversations and collaborations to express ideas and build upon the ideas of others.
4. Prewrite, plan, and produce clear and coherent writing in response to a prompt.

ELA Common Core Standards:

Reading: Literature - RL.11-12.1, RL.11-12.2, RL.11-12.4, RL.11-12.9
Writing - W.11-2.2.A, W.11-12.2.B, W.11-12.4, W.11-12.5, W.11-12.6, W.11-12.9.A, W.11-12.10
Speaking & Listening - SL.11-12.1.A, SL.11-12.1.B, SL.11-12.1.C, SL.11-12.1.D, SL.11-12.6
Language - L.11-12.4.A, L.11-12.4.C, L.11-12.4.D

RESOURCES

"The Star-Spangled Banner" Vocabulary handout
"The Star-Spangled Banner" Graphic Organizer
Access 1 handout (Beginner)
Access 2 handout (Intermediate)
Access 3 handout (Advanced)
Access 4 handout (Approaching)

1. INTRODUCTION

Core Path	Access Path
Define and Compare. Project the vocabulary words and definitions onto the board or provide students with handouts so they can copy the vocabulary into their notebooks. Suggest that students consult general and specialized reference materials, both print and digital, to compare the precise meaning of a specific word with their initial vocabulary predictions from the First Read. Review words that students defined incorrectly to understand why they were unable to use context clues to develop usable definitions.	**Beginner & Intermediate** **Complete the Chart.** Have students complete the chart on the Access 1 and 2 handouts by writing the correct word for each of the definitions. **Advanced & Beyond** **Write in Journals.** Have students write a journal entry using all of their vocabulary words. Remind them to write sentences that communicate the meaning of the words they are using. **Approaching** **Graphic Organizer.** To support students in comparing their predictions with the correct meanings, have them complete the graphic organizer on the Access 4 handout to record the vocabulary words, their initial analysis, and the definitions. Then have them write sentences using the words.
Review. Have students complete the fill-in-the-blanks vocabulary worksheet attached to the lesson plan online. Answers for the worksheet are listed at the end of the lesson plan online.	
	Extend **Search.** Have students use dictionaries, thesauruses, or mobile devices to find a synonym and antonym for each vocabulary word. Students should record the word with at least one synonym and antonym in their notes. Student can work individually or collaboratively on this assignment.

2. READ

Core Path	Access Path
Model Close Reading. Project the text onto the board and model a close reading of the first stanza using the annotation strategies mentioned below. While modeling annotation strategies, make notes that tie the text to the focus skill and demonstrate what students are looking for as they read. Some guidance for you as you annotate for your students: • The first stanza is the part of the national anthem we hear before every sporting event and in official occasions. The lyrics are very familiar, but a close look reveals some interesting rhetorical devices. • The first thing I notice when reading the song is its use of punctuation. The second line ends with a question mark, which clarifies that the speaker is asking if the flag is still visible. He doesn't know. • The speaker goes on to say how dangerous, or "perilous," the battle was, but how brave the flag was (by "gallantly streaming"). The battle sounds dramatic, with "bombs bursting in air." According to the speaker, the flag motivated them to keep fighting. • At the end of the stanza, we still don't know what happened to the flag. The final couplet repeats, in different words, the opening question: Does the flag still wave? We'll have to keep reading to find out.	
Read and Annotate. Read the Skills Focus questions as a class, so your students know what they should pay close attention to as they read. Then have students read and annotate the excerpt. Ask students to use the annotation tool as they read to: 1. respond to the Skills Focus section 2. identify the song's rhyme scheme and note the effect of the internal rhyme in some lines	**Note:** While on-grade-level students are reading and annotating, work one-on-one or in small groups with Beginning, Intermediate, Advanced, and Approaching students to support them as they read and annotate the text.

Core Path	Access Path
3. make connections between the song's description of enemies of the United States and Key's purpose in writing the song 4. identify two or three examples of alliteration and repetition in the song 5. analyze how the last two lines of each stanza differ slightly and determine what purpose these differences might serve 6. note unfamiliar vocabulary 7. capture their reaction to the ideas and examples in the text As they reread the text, remind students to use the comprehension strategy of visualizing that they learned in the First Read.	**Beginner & Intermediate** **Summarize and Analyze the Text.** Work with these students to complete the sentence frames on the Access 1 and 2 handouts (note: the sentence frames for Intermediate students on the Access 2 handout contain fewer scaffolds). They will then use the completed sentence frames to help them analyze and annotate the text by completing the Skills Focus questions. Refer to the sample Skills Focus answers to help them complete the sentence frames and annotate the text. **Advanced** **Work in Pairs.** Pair these students with more proficient English speakers to work together on analyzing and annotating the text to complete the Skills Focus questions. If these students need more support, have them use the sentence frames on the Access 3 handout as they work with their more proficient peers. **Approaching** **Summarize the Text.** Have these students discuss and complete the text summary on the Access 4 handout and use their summary to help them analyze and annotate the text by completing the Skills Focus questions. Correct answers for the summary are at the end of the lesson plan online. Also refer to the sample Skills Focus answers to aid students with their annotations.

Core Path	Access Path
Discuss. After students have read the text, use the sample responses to the Skills Focus questions at the bottom of the lesson plan online to discuss the reading and the process of analyzing author's purpose and point of view in the text. Make sure that students have acquired and accurately use academic-specific words and phrases related to the skill and demonstrate a command of formal English appropriate to the discussion. To help facilitate discussions, refer to Collaborative Discussions in the Speaking & Listening Handbook.	**Extend** **Pair and Share.** In small, heterogeneous groups or pairs, ask students to share and discuss their annotations with a focus on the rhetoric presented in the selection. You can provide students with these questions to guide their discussion: 1. Reread the second stanza. How does the speaker's tone change throughout the stanza? Cite specific textual evidence to support your statements. (The tone at the beginning is uncertain: "What is that which the breeze, o'er the towering steep, / As it fitfully blows, half conceals, half discloses?" Then the speaker confirms that he sees the flag, and the tone becomes excited and proud: "'Tis the star-spangled banner! Oh long may it wave.") 2. What words and phrases does the author use in the fourth stanza to describe the United States? ("loved home," "Blest with victory and peace," "heav'n rescued land") 3. How do these phrases support the author's purpose in writing the song? (Key's purpose was to inspire patriotism in readers or listeners. High praise for the United States instills pride.)
	Extend **Tech Infusion** **Create.** Ask students to create a collage using images and words taken from magazines that they believe reflect the theme of patriotism. Alternatively, they can use an online tool, such as Glogster (http://edu.glogster.com) or Google Drawing, to create a virtual collage with a mix of text and media. Invite students to present their collages for the class explaining why they selected particular words and images.

Core Path	Access Path
	Extend **Research.** Have students read about national anthems around the world. Students should discover when national anthems were popularized, what kinds of songs countries tend to choose, and when national anthems are used. Tell students to keep this information in mind as they read "The Star-Spangled Banner" and consider if the anthem fits with world or historical trends.

3. WRITE

Core Path	Access Path
Prewrite and Plan. Read the prompt as a class and ask students to brainstorm about author's purpose and author's point of view in "The Star-Spangled Banner." Remind your students to look at the song and their annotations to find textual evidence to support their ideas.	**Beginner & Intermediate** **Plan and Organize.** Have students complete the prewriting activity on the Access 1 and 2 handouts and then explain their ideas to a partner before they write. Explain to students that they need to choose rhetorical devices such as internal rhyme, repetition, alliteration, and figurative language that support their ideas about the theme. For example, students could include the line, "Where the foe's haughty host in dread silence reposes," which includes alliteration (haughty, host). The device emphasizes that the foe, or enemy, once boasted of winning but has since been silenced by defeat. It helps build the theme that the United States was proudly victorious. **Approaching** **Plan and Organize.** Have students complete the prewriting activity on the Access 4 handout to organize their thoughts before they write.
	Extend **Organize.** Encourage students to complete a graphic organizer (see Resources at the end of the lesson plan online) to organize their ideas before they type their responses.

Core Path	Access Path
Discuss. Project these instructions for the peer review onto the board and review them with your class, so they know what they are looking for when they begin to provide their classmates with feedback: • How has this essay helped you understand how Francis Scott Key uses rhetorical devices in the song? • Did the writer explain the use of rhetorical devices, such as alliteration, repetition, and figurative language? Does that explanation make sense? • What theme did the writer identify? How clear was the writer's explanation of how the rhetorical devices support the theme? • What sort of evidence did the writer use from the text to support his or her writing? • How well does the writer explain how that evidence supports his or her ideas? • Does the writer write using standard grammar and punctuation? Are there any weak spots? • What specific suggestions can you make to help the writer improve the response? • What thing(s) does this paper do especially well? After you've looked at the peer review instructions, review the rubric with students before they begin writing. Allow time for students briefly to pose and discuss any questions they may have about the peer review instructions and the rubric. Tell students how many peer reviews they will need to complete once they submit their writing.	
Write. Ask students to complete the writing assignment using textual evidence to support their answers. Once they have completed their writing, they should click "Submit."	

Core Path	Access Path
	Extend **Critique.** Project a writing sample on the board and use colored highlighters or pens to underline each idea in the text. Have students note where the ideas change and evaluate whether or not the writer used an appropriate transition. If not, discuss how they might use a transition to make the shift clearer. After students have had an opportunity to discuss student samples, work as a class to generate strategies students can use as they complete their peer reviews to ensure they are substantive.
Review. Once students complete their writing assignment, they should submit substantive feedback to two peers.	

BLAST:
What So Proudly We Hailed

OVERVIEW

To continue their study of "The Star-Spangled Banner," students will learn about the history of the song and why some people want to change the national anthem. Research links explore both sides of the argument and disprove myths that both sides use in their arguments.

OBJECTIVES

1. Explore background information about the history of "The Star-Spangled Banner" and how it became the US national anthem.
2. Research using hyperlinks to a range of information about "The Star-Spangled Banner," including articles, a video, and different perspectives.

ELA Common Core Standards:
Reading: Informational Text - RI.11-12.1
Writing - W.11-12.1.A, W.11-12.1.B, W.11-12.5, W.11-12.6
Speaking & Listening - SL.11-12.1.A, SL.11-12.1.C, SL.11-12.1.D

RESOURCES

Access 1 handout (Beginner)
Access 2 handout (Intermediate)
Access 4 handout (Approaching)

TITLE/DRIVING QUESTION

Core Path	Access Path
Discuss. As a class, read aloud the title and driving question for this Blast. Ask students what their opinion of the national anthem is. Do they find the song inspiring? Do they think there's a song that better represents the United States? Taking into account ideas generated by their classmates, should the United States change its national anthem? Remind students that they'll be returning to this question for their formal entries after they've written a draft and read and discussed the Background.	**English Learners All Levels** **Discuss a Visual.** Have students view a photograph of the flag that inspired "The Star-Spangled Banner" on display at the Smithsonian's National Museum of American History, such as the ones at http://tinyurl.com/qzu556n and http://tinyurl.com/pnn3hsq. Discuss how the pictures represent a symbol of American history, prompting students with questions such as: • What words or phrases would you use to describe the flag? Does it look like it is in good condition? Why or why not? • Why do you think the flag was so big? • What is the significance of this flag? Why do you think the flag is on display at the National Museum of American History? • What emotions do you feel when looking at the flag?
Draft. In their notebooks or on scrap paper, have students draft their initial responses to the driving question. This will provide them with a baseline response that they will be altering as they gain more information about the topic in the Background and Research Links sections of the assignment.	**Beginner & Intermediate** **Draft with Sentence Frame.** When drafting their initial response to the driving question, have students refer to this Blast sentence frame on their Access 1 and 2 handouts: • The United States should/should not change its national anthem because ________________. Point out these two key features of the sentence frame: 1. The introductory clause "The United States should / should not change its national anthem" borrows language directly from the Blast driving question and requires students to choose either "should" or "should not" to state their opinion. 2. Ask students to make special note of the word "because," which requires them to give a reason or reasons to support their opinions.

BACKGROUND

Core Path	Access Path
Read. Have students read the Blast background to provide context for the driving question.	**Beginner & Intermediate** **Read with Support.** Have students read the Blast background to provide context for the driving question. When they encounter unfamiliar words or phrases, have students refer to the glossary on their Access 1 and 2 handouts. If there are unfamiliar words that are not included in their glossary, encourage students to check a dictionary or online reference tool, such as http://dictionary.reference.com. **Approaching** **Read and Summarize.** Have students read the Blast background to provide context for the driving question. As they read, ask students to complete the fill-in-the-blanks summary of the background provided on their Access 4 handout. When they encounter unfamiliar words or phrases, have students refer to the glossary on their Access 4 handout.
Discuss. Pair students and have them discuss the following questions: 1. Can you remember any high-profile mistakes made by national anthem singers? (e.g., Christina Aguilera at the Super Bowl) Why do you think people make a big deal out of these mistakes? (e.g., most people know the lyrics by heart; it's disrespectful) 2. Based on your reading of the lyrics, why might "The Star-Spangled Banner" have been popular when it was first written? (The lyrics inspire readers by describing a hopeful moment during a battle. A country at war needs such inspiration.)	**Beginner** **Discuss.** Pair Beginning with Advanced (or Beyond) students and have them use the dialogue starter on their Access 1 handout to discuss the topic. Advise them to return to the dialogue and switch roles if they get stuck. **Intermediate** **Discuss.** Pair Intermediate with Advanced (or Beyond) students and have them use the dialogue starter on their Access 2 handout to discuss the topic. Advise them to return to the dialogue and switch roles if they get stuck. If their conversation is progressing smoothly, encourage them to continue the discussion beyond the dialogue starter sheet. They can expand their conversations to discuss other reasons for and against keeping "The Star-Spangled Banner" as our national anthem.

Core Path	Access Path
3. How did "The Star-Spangled Banner" become the national anthem? Describe the time line. (The song was a popular patriotic song. It was first used by the armed forces in the 1890s and was made the official anthem of the armed forces in 1917. In 1931 it was named the national anthem.) 4. What are some criticisms of "The Star-Spangled Banner"? (It is too militaristic; it is too hard to sing; it celebrates a war that no one cares about anymore.) What do you think of these criticisms? (Answers will vary.)	
Brainstorm. Remind students about the driving question for this Blast: Should the United States change its national anthem? In their notebooks, ask students to make two columns, one for reasons in favor of "The Star-Spangled Banner" remaining the national anthem and one for reasons against. Start with the Background and have them fill in reasons that the Blast suggests people might like the song. After they've finished that, have them begin developing a list of reasons why they or other people might be opposed to the song. Here's a short example of how this might look:	

Reasons For	Reasons Against
Tradition makes the song meaningful.	We shouldn't sing a song celebrating a battle before every sporting event.

RESEARCH LINKS

Core Path	Access Path
Examine and Explore. Use these questions to guide students' exploration of the research links: 1. As a class, listen to the 1814 version of "The Star-Spangled Banner." How is this version different from what you are used to? (It's a lot faster. It uses a harpsichord instead of a full orchestra. There is a backup chorus that repeats some of the lines.) Does listening to this version change your opinion of the song? Should singers return to this version? (Answers will vary.) 2. Ask students to look at "Five Myths about 'The Star-Spangled Banner.'" What does the author have to say to people who think the anthem celebrates war? (While the song is about a battle, it is "more of a hymn of thanks." The author explains that the lyrics are a long question and that Key opposed the war.) Why does the author mention the song's role during the Civil War? (The author points out that the song was embraced after the battle of Fort Sumter. The author thinks this history makes the song the best choice for an anthem.) 3. Have students listen to a few of the famous renditions of "The Star-Spangled Banner" included in "Unconventional Anthems." As a class, discuss what works and what doesn't in each version. How does the singer make you feel? Do you think that was his or her intention? Is the ability of singers to make the song their own positive or negative for the anthem? (Answers will vary.)	
	Extend **Research, Discuss and Present.** 1. Assign each group one link to explore in depth. 2. Ask them to discuss the information: a. What are the key points made in this resource? b. What inferences did you make as you read?

Core Path	Access Path
	c. What did you learn from reading this research? d. How did this help you to better understand the topic? e. What questions does your group have after exploring this link? 3. Allow students time to informally present what they learned.
	Extend **Tech Infusion** **Listen.** After students explore the links, have them find and listen to national anthems from other countries (and English translations of the lyrics, if available). In their small groups, have students discuss what they found in listening to other anthems. In what ways were the songs similar to or different from "The Star-Spangled Banner"? Do they appreciate our anthem more, or do they think another anthem is better? Why?

QUIKPOLL

Core Path	Access Path
Participate. Answer the poll question. Have students use information from the background and research links to explain their answers.	

NUMBER CRUNCH

Core Path	Access Path
Predict, Discuss, and Click. Before students click on the number, break them into pairs and have them make predictions about what they think the number is related to. After they've clicked the number, ask students if they are surprised by the revealed information.	

CREATE YOUR BLAST

Core Path	Access Path
Blast. Ask students to write their Blast response in 140 characters or less.	**Beginner** **Blast with Support.** Have students refer to the sentence frame on their Access 1 handout that they used to create their original Blast draft. Ask them to use this frame to write and enter their final Blast. **Intermediate** **Blast with Support.** Have students attempt to draft their Blast without the sentence frame on their Access 2 handout. If students struggle to compose their Blast draft without the sentence frame, remind them to reference it for support. **Beyond** **Write a Claim.** Ask students to use their answer to the poll question to write a strong claim that could be used as the foundation for a piece of argumentative writing. Once students have written their claims, ask them to read the claims to a small group of their peers. This activity will provide them practice writing claims, as well as expose them to claims written by their peers.
Review. After students have completed their own Blasts, ask them to review the Blasts of their peers and provide feedback.	

Core Path	Access Path
	Extend **Discuss.** As a whole class or in groups, identify a few strong Blasts and discuss what made those responses so powerful. As a group, analyze and discuss what characteristics make a Blast interesting or effective.
	Extend **Revise.** Resend a second version of this Blast assignment to your students and have them submit revised versions of their original Blasts. Do the same responses make the Top 10? How have the answers improved from the first submissions?

BLAST:
Reaching the Masses

OVERVIEW

Before reading two radio speeches by Winston Churchill and Franklin Delano Roosevelt, students will learn about the radio and how technology and media affect politics. Research links explore other aspects of mass media, including articles about radio, television, and new media.

OBJECTIVES

1. Explore background information about the history of radio, television, and other mass media in the 20th century.
2. Research using hyperlinks to a range of information about mass media and politics.

ELA Common Core Standards:
Reading: Informational Text - RI.11-12.1
Writing - W.11-12.1.A, W.11-12.3.A, W.11-12.5, W.11-12.6
Speaking & Listening - SL.11-12.1.A, SL.11-12.1.C, SL.11-12.1.D

RESOURCES

Access 1 handout (Beginner)
Access 2 handout (Intermediate)
Access 4 handout (Approaching)

TITLE/DRIVING QUESTION

Core Path	Access Path
Discuss. As a class, read aloud the title and driving question for this Blast. Ask students what they already know about media coverage of politicians. Have they ever listened to a political speech on the radio or watched one on TV? How do the media treat politicians? Taking into account ideas generated by their classmates, do they have a sense of how mass media affects politics? Remind students that they'll be returning to this question for their formal entries after they've written a draft and read and discussed the Background.	**English Learners All Levels** **Discuss a Visual.** Have students view a photograph of people listening to FDR's "fireside chats," such as the ones at http://tinyurl.com/qykzom2. Discuss how the pictures represent an exchange of information between a sitting president and the American people, prompting students with questions such as: • What are the people doing in the photographs? How can you tell that they are paying close attention? • How many different generations do you see? What does that tell you about the audience of FDR's radio addresses? • What kinds of information do you think FDR shared with the nation this way? • What are the benefits of giving a radio address versus sending a letter or publishing text in a newspaper?
Draft. In their notebooks or on scrap paper, have students draft their initial responses to the driving question. This will provide them with a baseline response that they will be altering as they gain more information about the topic in the Background and Research Links sections of the assignment.	**Beginner & Intermediate** **Draft with Sentence Frame.** When drafting their initial response to the driving question, have students refer to this Blast sentence frame on their Access 1 and 2 handouts: • Politicians have used media effectively to ________________ because. ________________________. Point out these two key features of the sentence frame: 1. Point out that the sentence frame has two blanks the students need to fill. The introductory clause "Politicians have used media effectively to" borrows language directly from the Blast driving question and requires students to write a verb or verb phrase that states what politicians have done effectively.

Core Path	Access Path
	2. The second blank, prompted with the word "because," requires students to offer a reason or reasons to support their opinions.

BACKGROUND

Core Path	Access Path
Read. Have students read the Blast background to provide context for the driving question.	**Beginner & Intermediate** **Read with Support.** Have students read the Blast background to provide context for the driving question. When they encounter unfamiliar words or phrases, have students refer to the glossary on their Access 1 and 2 handouts. If there are unfamiliar words that are not included in their glossary, encourage students to check a dictionary or online reference tool, such as http://dictionary.reference.com. **Approaching** **Read and Summarize.** Have students read the Blast background to provide context for the driving question. As they read, ask students to complete the fill-in-the-blanks summary of the background provided on their Access 4 handout. When they encounter unfamiliar words or phrases, have students refer to the glossary on their Access 4 handout.
Discuss. Pair students and have them discuss the following questions: 1. What is the role of radio in your life? Do you think it will get more or less important to you over time? (e.g., Radio is not important to me. I listen to and discover new music online. Maybe I'd listen to the radio if I had a car.)	**Beginner** **Discuss.** Pair Beginning with Advanced (or Beyond) students and have them use the dialogue starter on their Access 1 handout to discuss the topic. Advise them to return to the dialogue and switch roles if they get stuck.

Core Path	Access Path
2. How was early radio different from today's radio? (Radio was controlled by hobbyists, not big stations.) How is this history similar to other technologies? (Like computers or tablets, some dedicated early adopters need to use a technology first before the public gets on board.) 3. Why did Roosevelt's "fireside chats" become so influential? (Roosevelt gave only 30 radio chats during his 12 years in office, but his personal and casual tone helped people accept his ideas. In addition, most Americans had a radio and listened to it regularly.) 4. How did the introduction of television change politics? (People credit John F. Kennedy's presence on television during the first debate for his close win over Richard Nixon.) What's the role of televised debates today? How is it similar to 1960? (Televised debates get a lot of attention. Media today would comment on a sick-looking candidate, too.)	**Intermediate** **Discuss.** Pair Intermediate with Advanced (or Beyond) students and have them use the dialogue starter on their Access 2 handout to discuss the topic. Advise them to return to the dialogue and switch roles if they get stuck. If their conversation is progressing smoothly, encourage them to continue the discussion beyond the dialogue starter sheet. They can expand their conversations to discuss other ways politicians have used the media to communicate.
Imagine. Ask students to imagine that an alien lands in your town and asks questions about the American political system. The alien has been picking up cable news signals on its ship and wants them explained. Have students write a short description of the role of the media in politics today. Students may include cable news, comedy shows, the Internet, or any other media they consume. If necessary, remind students that this is a creative writing assignment and, although they should be free to stretch their imaginations, they shouldn't use this as an opportunity to be mean-spirited or derogatory. Some sample answers might include: 1. Cable TV includes both serious news channels and comedy shows that make fun of politicians but can reveal some truths about the political process.	

Core Path	Access Path
2. Newspapers and their websites are still the best source for unbiased explanations of elections and politics. 3. The Internet can be a great source of information, but only if you know which sites are trustworthy.	

RESEARCH LINKS

Core Path	Access Path
Examine and Explore. Use these questions to guide students' exploration of the research links: 1. Have students read "A History of Political Radio." How was radio used by politicians in the 1920s? (Radio was used to broadcast conventions and speeches.) What surprised you about the information regarding early political radio? (e.g., no national networks, how expensive it was, selling recordings of speeches) 2. Ask students to look at "How Did the Advent of Television Impact Politics?" How is a candidate's television time "mediated," according to the article? (The producers and people who put together news programs pick and choose what goes on the air.) What difference might that mediation have on voters? (Voters might think they're getting the whole story, but what they're seeing is often edited.) What impacts does the article say television has had on voters? (The focus of news is on soundbites or polls, but it can also shift public opinion, as when Walter Cronkite spoke out against the Vietnam War.) 3. Have students explore "A History of Political Radio" and "How Did the Advent of Television Impact Politics?" Given your understanding of these two pieces, do you think mass media has been good or bad for politics? Debate this in small groups or as a class.	

Core Path	Access Path
	Extend **Research, Discuss and Present.** 1. Assign each group one link to explore in depth. 2. Ask them to discuss the information: a. What are the key points made in this resource? b. What inferences did you make as you read? c. What did you learn from reading this research? d. How did this help you to better understand the topic? e. What questions does your group have after exploring this link? 3. Allow students time to informally present what they learned.
	Extend **Tech Infusion** **Share.** As students explore the links, allow them to create an interactive poster about mass media and politics, using an online poster and collage maker, such as Glogster (http://edu.glogster.com). Students can combine text, music, photos, and video that effectively showcase their story. Consider having students focus on the most recent election. They can share their posters with the class.

QUIKPOLL

Core Path	Access Path
Participate. Answer the poll question. Have students use information from the background and research links to explain their answers.	

NUMBER CRUNCH

Core Path	Access Path
Predict, Discuss, and Click. Before students click on the number, break them into pairs and have them make predictions about what they think the number is related to. After they've clicked the number, ask students if they are surprised by the revealed information.	

CREATE YOUR BLAST

Core Path	Access Path
Blast. Ask students to write their Blast response in 140 characters or less.	**Beginner** **Blast with Support.** Have students refer to the sentence frame on their Access 1 handout that they used to create their original Blast draft. Ask them to use this frame to write and enter their final Blast. **Intermediate** **Blast with Support.** Have students attempt to draft their Blast without the sentence frame on their Access 2 handout. If students struggle to compose their Blast draft without the sentence frame, remind them to reference it for support. **Beyond** **Write a Claim.** Ask students to use their answer to the poll question to write a strong claim that could be used as the foundation for a piece of argumentative writing. Once students have written their claims, ask them to read the claims to a small group of their peers. This activity will provide them practice writing claims, as well as expose them to claims written by their peers.
Review. After students have completed their own Blasts, ask them to review the Blasts of their peers and provide feedback.	

Core Path	Access Path
	Extend **Discuss.** As a whole class or in groups, identify a few strong Blasts and discuss what made those responses so powerful. As a group, analyze and discuss what characteristics make a Blast interesting or effective.
	Extend **Revise.** Resend a second version of this Blast assignment to your students and have them submit revised versions of their original Blasts. Do the same responses make the Top 10? How have the answers improved from the first submissions?

FIRST READ:
"Be Ye Men of Valour"

OVERVIEW

On May 19, 1940, shortly after becoming the prime minister of England, Winston Churchill gave the speech "Be Ye Men of Valour" to inspire the British people during World War II. The First Read gives students the opportunity to experience the text with limited context.

OBJECTIVES

1. Perform an initial reading of a text and demonstrate comprehension by responding to short analysis and inference questions with textual evidence.
2. Practice defining vocabulary words using context.
3. Participate effectively in a range of conversations and collaborations to express ideas and build upon the ideas of others.
4. Practice acquiring and using academic vocabulary correctly.

ELA Common Core Standards:
Reading: Informational Text - RI.11-12.1, RI.11-12.2, RI.11-12.4, RI.11-12.10
Speaking & Listening - SL.11-12.1.A, SL.11-12.1.B, SL.11-12.1.C, SL.11-12.1.D
Language - L.11-12.1, L.11-12.4.A, L.11-12.4.B, L.11-12.4.D, L.11-12.4.6

RESOURCES

Grammar handout: Verb Phrases
Access 1 handout (Beginner)
Access 2 handout (Intermediate)
Access 3 handout (Advanced)
Access 4 handout (Approaching)

ACCESS COMPLEX TEXT

With his speech "Be Ye Men of Valour," Winston Churchill sought to encourage the British during World War II. His rhetoric reflects the strength and courage of a leader, but it may also make the speech difficult to understand for some readers. To help students understand Churchill's rhetoric and the main ideas of this powerful speech, use the following ideas to provide scaffolded instruction for a first reading of the more complex features of this text:

- **Connection of Ideas** - At times, Churchill describes the French as a nation that needs British assistance. At other times, he refers to the French as Britain's partner in the war effort. This complex wartime relationship between the British and the French may be a bit confusing for some readers.
- **Sentence Structure** - Churchill's long sentences and complicated syntax may be difficult for some readers. Students may benefit from breaking sentences with semicolons into two sentences to better understand Churchill's ideas.
- **Specific Vocabulary** - Students may struggle to understand some war-related terminology, such as "front" and "infantry," and British vernacular, such as "lorries."
- **Prior Knowledge** - Some readers may be unfamiliar with background knowledge related to World War I necessary to understand Churchill's speech. For example, references to the Maginot Line, Flanders, and the Western Front are mentioned without explanation. Assist students with research to understand these references as needed.

1. INTRODUCTION

Core Path	Access Path
Read. Individually or as a class, read the Introduction for "Be Ye Men of Valour." The introduction provides context for the speech.	**English Learners All Levels & Approaching** **Read and Listen.** Ask students to read and listen to the introduction for "Be Ye Men of Valour." Have them refer to the "Introduction Glossary" on their Access 1, 2, 3, and 4 handouts for definitions of key vocabulary terms. If there are unfamiliar words that are not included in their glossary, encourage students to check a dictionary or online reference tool, such as http://dictionary.reference.com.

Core Path	Access Path
Access Prior Knowledge. Find out what your students already know about World War II. As a class or in small groups, generate a list (on the board or on paper) of the information and previous knowledge your students have about World War II, especially Britain's role and sacrifices. After compiling a list, ask students to share where their previous knowledge came from—a movie, class, documentary, book, family member? Discuss.	**English Learners All Levels & Approaching** **Build Background.** Create groups of mixed-level students and have them discuss what they already know about World War II, including its participants, its causes, and its outcomes. Have them record their ideas in their journals. As students discuss, encourage them to scan a brief overview of the war, such as the one at http://tinyurl.com/kmqjfn5, to verify the facts and details they recorded and add to them if necessary.
	Extend **Discuss the Introduction.** After reading the introduction, use the information provided to facilitate a prereading discussion to get students thinking about the historical context of the speech. Ask students: 1. What can you infer about the kind of threat Hitler posed at this point in the war? 2. Why might Churchill feel the need to emotionally prepare the British people? 3. During this time of war, would the call-to-arms "Be ye men of valour" apply to soldiers or to all British people? Why?

2. READ

Core Path	Access Path
Make Predictions about Vocabulary. There are five bold vocabulary words in the text. As students read the text, ask them to make predictions about what they think each bold vocabulary word means based on the context clues in the sentence. Have students use the annotation tool to make their predictions.	**Note:** This exercise, which extends vocabulary instruction, should be completed when the class shifts from whole-group instruction to individual work during the "Read and Annotate" exercise.

Core Path	Access Path
It might be helpful to model this for students before they begin reading. Either using the board or projecting the actual text, focus in on the sentence that uses the word "indomitable": • I have received from the Chiefs of the French Republic, and in particular from its indomitable Prime Minister, the most sacred pledges that whatever happens they will fight to the end, be it bitter or be it glorious. Model for the class how to use these context clues to guess the meaning of the word: 1. First, I find the word in the sentence and see that it appears in the phrase "its indomitable Prime Minister." I know that is a person and that "indomitable" is describing him somehow, which means the word is an adjective. 2. Next, I read the rest of the sentence to see what other words or phrases Churchill uses in relation to Prime Minister Reynaud. Churchill says that Reynaud has sent "the most sacred pledges that whatever happens they will fight to the end." 3. I think about what a pledge like this would mean. To promise to keep fighting no matter what makes me think of an unstoppable force. This helps me infer that "indomitable" means "unstoppable" or "not capable of being defeated." 4. I'll check my guess in a dictionary to make sure I was correct.	**Beginner, Intermediate & Approaching Pair Practice.** 1. Pair students with more proficient readers. 2. Give them an additional sentence that contains a new vocabulary word. 3. Ask the students to complete a Think Aloud using the teacher-led Make Predictions about Vocabulary activity as a model, while the proficient student actively listens. 4. The student should use the context clues in the sentence to try to determine the meaning of the new vocabulary word. 5. After the student has completed the Think Aloud and made a prediction about the word's meaning, allow time for the proficient reader to add his/her own thoughts and clarify any points of confusion. 6. Once they've completed this Think Aloud, encourage them to use a dictionary to confirm the definition of the new vocabulary word. Have them refer to the "Text Glossary" on their Access 1, 2, and 4 handouts for definitions of key vocabulary terms in the text. Encourage them to add any additional vocabulary words or idioms they find in the text and look up definitions for those words and idioms online or in a dictionary.

Core Path	Access Path
In addition, point out to students that word part analysis can help them reinforce their understanding of word meanings. For example, tell students that "domitare" is Latin for the verb "to tame." Then ask students to identify the prefix and the suffix in the word and to explain how those affixes change the word's meaning and part of speech. (The prefix "in-" means "not" and reverses the meaning of the word. The suffix "-able" means "capable of" and turns the word into an adjective. Therefore, adding those affixes changes the word's part of speech to an adjective and the meaning to "not capable of being tamed.") Have students think of other words that have the "in-" prefix and the "-able" suffix (such as "inadvisable," "inalterable," and "incomprehensible") and explain the definitions of those words. Finally, have students apply word part analysis to the vocabulary word "imperious" and have them explain how word parts in "imperiously" and "imperiousness" can alter the word's part of speech and meaning.	
Model Reading Comprehension Strategy. Before students begin reading, model the reading comprehension strategy of summarizing by using this Think Aloud that talks students through the second paragraph of text. First explain to your students that summarizing is a process of selecting, organizing, and synthesizing the most important elements in a text. Explain to students how summarizing will help them better comprehend the selection and help drive their discussions. • After I read the text, I reread it with the goal of condensing what it says into a few sentences. Often the main idea is stated at the beginning of the text, so I reread the first paragraph.	**Note:** This exercise, which extends instruction around reading comprehension strategies, should be completed when the class shifts from whole-group instruction to individual work during the "Read and Annotate" exercise. **Beginner, Intermediate & Approaching Apply Reading Comprehension Strategy.** 1. In small groups, have students read the first paragraph of "Be Ye Men of Valour." 2. Ask groups to summarize the paragraph using their own words. Encourage students to talk out the details and events that Churchill discusses in this paragraph. Ask students to record their summaries in the Summarizing Chart on the Access 1, 2, and 4 handouts.

Core Path	Access Path
• In the first two sentences, Churchill says, "I speak to you for the first time as Prime Minister in a solemn hour for the life of our country, of our empire, of our allies, and, above all, of the cause of freedom. A tremendous battle is raging in France and Flanders." Based on this, I can make notes for my summary that the speech is about the state of the country at the beginning of World War II. • Churchill begins the second paragraph by saying, "We must not allow ourselves to be intimidated by the presence of these armored vehicles in unexpected places behind our lines." Based on this, I know that Churchill is trying to inspire bravery in the face of a serious threat. I don't need to insert this quotation in my summary, but I should make a note about Churchill's purpose.	3. Have groups continue to read the speech, tracing Churchill's main ideas. Ask groups to record their summaries of each paragraph or paragraphs as divided by the Summarizing Chart. Allow time for groups to continue the reading comprehension strategy of summarizing until they complete the Summarizing Chart. Check groups' understanding of the strategy by circling around and asking questions.
Read and Annotate. Have students independently read and annotate the excerpt. Ask students to use the annotation tool as they read to: 1. use context clues to analyze and determine the meaning of the bolded vocabulary terms 2. ask questions about passages of the text that may be unclear or unresolved 3. identify key information, events, individuals, and connections between them 4. note unfamiliar vocabulary	**Beginner** **Coach the Reading.** While other students read, annotate, and discuss the text independently, work with Beginning students, listening to the audio of the text and pausing periodically or when any student has a question. Coach students in articulating their questions for the group and in highlighting and annotating the text. Have students use the Annotation Guide on the Access 1 handout to support them as they highlight and annotate the text. For further support, ask questions about the text such as: • Is there anything about the speech that you don't understand? • Recall that this was Churchill's first radio address as prime minister. Why do you think he delivered this speech as his first direct communication with the British people? • How do you think the British people reacted to the speech? Why?

Core Path	Access Path
	Intermediate **Listen to the Audio.** Have these students listen to the audio of the text and use the Text Glossary on the Access 2 handout to help them with words or idioms that may be unfamiliar. If students need help with annotating the text, have them use the Annotation Guide on the Access 2 handout. After working with the Beginning students, you may wish to check this group's progress and provide support as needed. **Advanced** **Pair with Proficient Peers.** Have Advanced students work with English-proficient peers to read, annotate, and discuss the text. Have students use the Annotation Guide in the Access 3 handout to support them as they highlight and annotate the text. Encourage them to listen to the audio of the text if needed. **Approaching** **Use the Annotation Guide.** Have students use the Annotation Guide on the Access 4 handout to support them as they highlight and annotate the text.
Discuss. In small groups or pairs, have students discuss the questions and inferences they made while reading. To help facilitate discussions, refer to Collaborative Discussions in the Speaking & Listening Handbook. 1. What threat do the German armies pose? (They are advancing on France, which is a British ally.) Why does Churchill feel it is best to use bombers to fight back? (Destroying the German air force restricts their mobility, and British bombers can hurt German industry.)	**English Learners All Levels & Approaching** Use the extra time while on- and beyond-grade-level students are discussing their first reads of the text to work individually and in small groups with Approaching readers and English Learners as outlined above. Should those students complete their first reads quickly, integrate them into the on- and beyond-grade-level discussion groups. Otherwise, English Learners and Approaching readers will be given an opportunity to participate in text discussions with their peers later in the lesson.

Core Path	Access Path
2. What are Churchill's goals? (to beat the Germans and reunite Europe; to inspire the British to be courageous) Why is winning the war so important? (Churchill wants to save the world from Hitler, who represents "the foulest and most soul-destroying tyranny.") 3. What are three main ideas of this speech? (German forces are invading France; the Royal Air Force should continue to bomb the Germans; the British need to remain strong and brave during the war.) How would summarizing help you identify Churchill's main ideas? (Churchill's speech contains a lot of information, so summarizing can help identify the most important main ideas and the support for those ideas.)	**Beyond** **Tech Infusion** **Blast and Discuss.** Pair students and ask them to imagine how Churchill's message would be different if he delivered it today via social media. Create a Blast and ask students to "blast out" their own versions of Churchill's speech in statements of 140 characters or less. Encourage them to submit more than one "Blast" if necessary to cover all of Churchill's main ideas. After they've completed their Blasts, have students read them and choose a few that they think best embody the speech's tone, content, and style.
G **Grammar, Usage, and Mechanics.** Distribute the StudySync grammar handout on verb phrases. Review with students what verb phrases and auxiliary, or helping, verbs are, as explained in the handout. Then have students complete the practice exercises. (Answers for the practice exercises appear at the end of the lesson plan online.) Finally, encourage students to apply what they have learned by analyzing "Be Ye Men of Valour." Ask students: 1. What three verb phrases, including auxiliary verbs, does Churchill use in the first paragraph of "Be Ye Men of Valour"? ("is raging," "have broken," and "are ravaging.") 2. What effect do these verb phrases have on the opening of the speech? Consider the meaning suggested by the auxiliary verbs, and give one example from the text to support your ideas. (The auxiliary verbs help Churchill establish a feeling of immediacy. When he says, "A tremendous battle is raging" and "armored vehicles are ravaging," it emphasizes that these events are happening now, so people need to act now.)	**Beginner & Intermediate** **Work with the Teacher.** Remind students that a verb phrase consists of a main verb and all of its auxiliary, or helping, verbs. Write the following sentences on the board: • *The movie is scaring us!* • *The aliens have swallowed hundreds of people.* • *They will destroy more!* For each sentence, ask: *What is the verb phrase?* ("is scaring," "have swallowed," will destroy") *Which word is the main verb?* ("scaring," "swallowed," "destroy") *Which word is the auxiliary verb?* ("is," "has," "will") *What effect do these verb phrases have on you?* (Answers will vary but may include that they make the sentences more frightening by telling what is happening, has happened, and is about to occur.) Pair Beginning and Intermediate students and ask them to come up with their own examples of sentences with verb phrases. Then have them find two more examples of verb phrases in the first paragraph of the speech.

Core Path	Access Path
3. Contrast Churchill's statement at the end of paragraph 3 ("And this spirit must not only animate the High Command, but must inspire every fighting man.") with his call-to-arms at the end of the speech ("Arm yourselves, and be ye men of valour, and be in readiness for the conflict"). Does his choice not to include auxiliary verbs in the second example make his call-to-arms more or less effective? Why? (Answers will vary.)	**Advanced & Beyond** **Extend the Search.** Challenge these students to work in pairs or small groups to find other examples of verb phrases in the text, and to note how they contribute to the impact of the speech. **Approaching** **Analyze Additional Examples.** If students need more support identifying verb phrases, call their attention to the first three sentences in paragraph 4. Ask: *What three verb phrases, including auxiliary verbs, does Churchill use in these sentences? What effect does using these verb phrases have on listeners? Do these verb forms help Churchill make his points? Why or why not?* Encourage students to recognize that this structure helps Churchill emphasize what the British are currently doing to defeat the enemy and move toward victory. Then have students complete the verb phrase handout.
	Extend **Tech Infusion** **Research and Discuss.** Ask students to research Winston Churchill. They should attempt to find out information regarding his biography, his writing and speeches, and his legacy. Create a Lino board (en.linoit.com), and have students work collaboratively to research and post their notes. Then discuss with students whether Churchill was a "man of valour." Remind students to support their opinions with textual evidence.

3. THINK

Core Path	Access Path
Answer and Discuss. Have students complete the Think questions and then use the peer review instructions and rubric to complete two peer reviews. Refer to the sample answers at the end of the lesson plan online to discuss responses with your students.	**Beginner & Intermediate** **Sentence Frames.** Have students use the sentence frames on the Access 1 and 2 handouts to support their responses to the Think questions. If necessary, distribute sentence frames to Advanced students as well. **Approaching** **Find the Evidence.** Have students use Find the Evidence on the Access 4 handout to help them identify the evidence needed to answer the questions.
	Extend **Write a Journal Entry.** Ask students to imagine they lived in England during World War II and that they heard Churchill deliver this speech on the radio. Then have them write a journal entry that addresses the thoughts and feelings they would have at that tense time. Would Churchill's speech have inspired feelings of fear, confidence, patriotism, or something else? Why? Remind students to use precise words and phrases to communicate their reflections.

SKILL:
Author's Purpose and Author's Point of View

OVERVIEW

Winston Churchill's speech "Be Ye Men of Valour" was broadcast live over the radio to a nationwide audience. For such a speech to be effective, the author must provide clues so that the audience can determine his or her purpose and point of view. This lesson plan provides follow-up questions and useful enrichments to help teachers guide students toward a usable, repeatable method for uncovering an author's purpose and point of view.

OBJECTIVES

1. Learn the definitions of author's purpose and author's point of view.
2. Practice using concrete strategies for determining author's purpose and author's point of view.
3. Participate effectively in a range of conversations and collaborations to express ideas and build upon the ideas of others.

ELA Common Core Standards:
Reading: Informational Text - RI.11-12.1, RI.11-12.5, RI.11-12.6
Speaking & Listening - SL.11-12.1.A, SL.11-12.1.C, SL.11-12.2

RESOURCES

Access 1 handout (Beginner)
Access 2 handout (Intermediate)
Access 3 handout (Advanced)
Access 4 handout (Approaching)

1. DEFINE

Core Path	Access Path
Watch. Watch the Concept Definition video on author's purpose and point of view with your students. Make sure students understand why it's critical to know an author's purpose or point of view when trying to unlock the meaning of a text. Pause the video at these key moments to discuss the information with your students: 1. 1:00 – Can you think of any other purpose (or purposes) an author might have? How does genre affect purpose; in other words, how might the purpose of a fiction text differ from that of an informational text? How might it stay the same? 2. 1:18 – Are there any other elements of a text that might offer clues into an author's purpose or point of view? What are some additional resources we can use if we're having trouble deciphering the purpose or point of view? 3. 2:03 – Why don't authors of fiction or poetry state their purpose clearly in the same way a politician or an essayist might?	**English Learners All Levels & Approaching** **Match.** Have students complete the matching exercise on the Access 1, 2, 3, and 4 handouts as they watch the video. Answers are located at the end of the lesson plan online.
Read and Discuss. After watching the Concept Definition video, have students read the definition of author's purpose and author's point of view. Either in small groups or as a whole class, use these questions to engage students in a discussion about author's purpose and author's point of view: 1. How might a text written with a purpose to persuade be different from one that's intended to inform? How might a text that was written to entertain be different? (A text written to persuade might contain more pleas to logic and emotion than one intended to inform. A text written to entertain might be more light-hearted and humorous, whereas an informative text is likely, though not required, to be more serious and formal.)	**Beginner & Approaching** **Fill in the Blanks.** To prepare students to participate in the discussion, have them complete the fill-in-the-blanks activity on the Access 1 and 4 handouts as they read the definition. The correct answers are located at the end of the lesson plan online. **Intermediate & Advanced** **Discuss Prompts.** To help these students participate in the discussion, prompt them with questions that can be answered with a few words, such as: • What are three different purposes authors may have for writing? (to inform, persuade, or entertain) Might an author have more than one purpose? (Yes, writers often write for a combination of purposes.)

Core Path	Access Path
2. Can an informational text, such as a speech, have more than one point of view? Why or why not? (Yes. An author of an informational text might include multiple points of view, although in a persuasive text the author usually has a clear viewpoint and presents alternate viewpoints only in order to refute them.) 3. What is the relationship between an author's purpose and his or her point of view? How might the author's point of view reveal his or her purpose? (An author's point of view, expressed through the text's writing style and content, often reveals the author's purpose.)	• How can you identify the author's purpose? (by reading closely and paying attention to the information an author presents) • What is an author's point of view? (the author's perspective on the subject) **Beyond** **Discuss.** Have students select an article, speech, or nonfiction book they've read and describe its purpose and point of view. Compile a list of examples. Have students discuss how the purpose and point of view of each work affect what the reader learns about the subject and how the reader feels about it. What clues in the text helped students to figure out the author's purpose? Have students explain their responses.
	Extend **Tech Infusion** **Discuss.** Form small groups and have students use the Internet to find the printed text or recording of another famous speech. If students struggle to choose a speech on their own, you might suggest Abraham Lincoln's Gettysburg Address, Sojourner Truth's "Ain't I a Woman?" or John F. Kennedy's inaugural address. Have students read or listen to the speech and look for clues that reveal the author's purpose and point of view. Then have students discuss the clues they found and how they used textual evidence to determine the author's purpose and point of view.

2. MODEL

Core Path	Access Path
Read and Annotate. Have students independently read the Model section. As they read, ask students to use the annotation tool to: • highlight key points • ask questions • identify places where the Model applies the strategies laid out in the Identification and Application section	**Note:** During this portion of the lesson, instruction shifts from whole-group to individual work. Use this time to work one-on-one or in small groups with Beginning, Intermediate, Advanced, and Approaching students. **Beginner & Intermediate** **Coach the Reading.** Work with these students (either individually or in small groups) to fill out the guided reading questions on the Access 1 and 2 handouts. Have Beginning students refer to the glossary on the Access 1 handout to help them determine the meaning of difficult words (note: provide the Access 1 handout glossary to Intermediate students if necessary). Let students know they'll use these answers to help participate in the discussion about the Model. Sample answers for this exercise are located at the end of the lesson plan online. **Advanced** **Identify Evidence.** Ask Advanced students to complete the identifying evidence exercise on the Access 3 handout. Let students know that they'll use these answers to help participate in the discussion about the Model. Sample answers for this exercise are located at the end of the lesson plan online. **Approaching** **Guided Reading.** Have students complete the guided reading questions on the Access 4 handout as they read. Let them know that they'll use these answers to help participate in the discussion about the Model. Sample answers for this exercise are located at the end of the lesson plan online.

Core Path	Access Path
Discuss. After students read the Model text, use these questions to facilitate a whole-group discussion that helps students understand how to determine Churchill's purpose and point of view: 1. For what two purposes does the Model determine the text was written? (to inform and persuade) Why might Churchill have chosen to combine these purposes? (The background information Churchill gives on the state of the war makes his arguments more persuasive because it explains why the British should fight.) 2. How does Churchill make his purpose and point of view clear? (by stating them in the introductory paragraph of his speech) How does revealing his point of view help Churchill achieve his purposes for giving the speech? (By telling his audience about the "magnificent efforts of the Royal Air Force," he stirs their patriotism and inspires them to support the war efforts.) 3. How does the structure of the beginning of the speech help Churchill advance his purpose and point of view? (The introduction prepares listeners for the information Churchill gives in the body paragraphs of the speech. First he tells his audience that the British need to fight; then he explains how and why.)	
	Extend **Brainstorm.** Pair students and have them work together to brainstorm ideas for a speech that presents an opposing point of view to Churchill's. First have students determine the points of view Churchill advances in "Be Ye Men of Valour" and how he communicates them to his audience. Then have them discuss and take notes about how they could counter his points of view in a speech of their own. Last, pairs should work together to compose the opening paragraph of a rebuttal speech. Remind students that their purpose and points of view should be clearly stated.

3. YOUR TURN

Core Path	Access Path
Assess and Explain. Have students answer the comprehension questions to test for understanding. Share the explanations for Parts A and B (located online) with your students.	
	Extend **Evaluate.** Have students reread "Be Ye Men of Valour" and highlight the sentence they think best reveals the author's point of view. Have a few volunteers share which sentence they picked and why. Then, ask if the other students agree or disagree and give reasons why or why not.

CLOSE READ:
"Be Ye Men of Valour"

OVERVIEW

In his speech "Be Ye Men of Valour," Winston Churchill stepped into his role as prime minister as he informed the British people about the current state of World War II in Europe and inspired them to fight against their common enemy. The Close Read gives students the opportunity to identify and analyze the author's purpose and point of view.

OBJECTIVES

1. Complete a close reading of a passage of literature.
2. Practice and apply concrete strategies for determining author's purpose and author's point of view in "Be Ye Men of Valour."
3. Participate effectively in a range of conversations and collaborations to express ideas and build upon the ideas of others.
4. Prewrite, plan, and produce clear and coherent writing in response to a prompt.

ELA Common Core Standards:
Reading: Informational Text - RI.11-12.1, RI.11-12.4, RI.11-12.5, RI.11-12.6, RI.11-12.10
Writing - W.11-12.2.A, W.11-12.2.B, W.11-12.4, W.11-12.5, W.11-12.6, W.11-12.9.B, W.11-12.10
Speaking & Listening - SL.11-12.1.A, SL.11-12.1.B, SL.11-12.1.C, SL.11-12.1.D, SL.11-12.6
Language - L.11-12.4.A, L.11-12.4.C, L.11-12.4.D

RESOURCES

"Be Ye Men of Valour" Vocabulary Review
Access 1 handout (Beginner)
Access 2 handout (Intermediate)
Access 3 handout (Advanced)
Access 4 handout (Approaching)

1. INTRODUCTION

Core Path	Access Path
Define and Compare. Project the vocabulary words and definitions onto the board or provide students with handouts so they can copy the vocabulary into their notebooks. Suggest that students consult general and specialized reference materials, both print and digital, to compare the precise meaning of a specific word with their initial vocabulary predictions from the First Read. Review words that students defined incorrectly to understand why they were unable to use context clues to develop usable definitions.	**Beginner & Intermediate** **Complete the Chart.** Have students complete the chart on the Access 1 and 2 handouts by writing the correct word for each of the definitions. **Advanced & Beyond** **Write in Journals.** Have students write a journal entry using all of their vocabulary words. Remind them to write sentences that communicate the meaning of the words they are using. **Approaching** **Graphic Organizer.** To support students in comparing their predictions with the correct meanings, have them complete the graphic organizer on the Access 4 handout to record the vocabulary words, their initial analysis, and the definitions. Then have them write sentences using the words.
Review. Have students complete the fill-in-the-blanks vocabulary worksheet attached to the lesson plan online. Answers for the worksheet are listed at the end of the lesson plan online.	
	Extend **Charades.** Break students into small groups and assign each group a vocabulary word. Give them a few minutes to plan how they would silently act out the word. Then have a volunteer or volunteers from each group act out clues so the rest of the class can guess the word.

Core Path	Access Path
	Extend **Analyze.** Remind students that there are differences between British English and American English in both spelling and usage. For example, you might point out the *u* in the British spelling of "colour," give them examples of British words such as "flat" (apartment) and "lift" (elevator), or remind them that British English tends to be more formal than American English. Then have students work in pairs to scan the text and look for examples of language that seems particularly British and discuss how these ideas might be expressed differently in American English.

2. READ

Core Path	Access Path
Model Close Reading. Project the text onto the board and model a close reading of the first few paragraphs using the annotation strategies mentioned on the next page. While modeling annotation strategies, make notes that tie the text to the focus skill and demonstrate what students are looking for as they read. Here is some guidance for you as you annotate for your students: • As the Skills lesson that precedes this text makes clear, an author's purpose is his or her reason for writing and an author's point of view is his or her perspective on the topic. • Churchill begins his speech by saying, "I speak to you for the first time as Prime Minister in a solemn hour for the life of our country, of our empire, of our allies, and, above all, of the cause of freedom." Based on this, I can infer that he is speaking to the nation about the war from the perspective as their leader.	

Core Path	Access Path
• In the next sentences, Churchill provides information to explain the current threat the Nazis pose in France. In the first sentence, Churchill lists the empire, their allies, and freedom along with England, so this helps me understand that the prime minister is concerned with the threat Hitler poses on the entire world, not just his country. • The beginning of the second paragraph confirms Churchill's point of view that Britain and their allies should remain strong during this time. He says, "We must not allow ourselves to be intimidated by the presence of these armored vehicles in unexpected places behind our lines." This helps me confirm that Churchill has two purposes in this speech. First, he will inform his audience about why Hitler and the Germans are a significant threat. Then, he will persuade his audience to support him in the fight against the Germans.	
Read and Annotate. Read the Skills Focus questions as a class, so your students know what they should pay close attention to as they read. Then have students read and annotate the excerpt. Ask students to use the annotation tool as they read to: 1. respond to the Skills Focus section 2. identify the use of factual information and note how it is used in the speech to advance Churchill's purpose 3. analyze the use of rhetoric, or persuasive speech, and its relationship to point of view 4. identify the style and tone of the speech and analyze how each relates to purpose and point of view 5. determine the effectiveness of the speech's conclusion	**Note:** While on-grade-level students are reading and annotating, work one-on-one or in small groups with Beginning, Intermediate, Advanced, and Approaching students to support them as they read and annotate the text. **Beginner & Intermediate** **Summarize and Analyze the Text.** Work with these students to complete the sentence frames on the Access 1 and 2 handouts (note: the sentence frames for Intermediate students on the Access 2 handout contain fewer scaffolds). They will then use the completed sentence frames to help them analyze and annotate the text by completing the Skills Focus questions. Refer to the sample Skills Focus answers to help them complete the sentence frames and annotate the text.

Core Path	Access Path
6. note unfamiliar vocabulary 7. capture their reaction to the ideas and examples in the text As they reread the text, remind students to use the comprehension strategy of summarizing that they learned in the First Read.	**Advanced** **Work in Pairs.** Pair these students with more proficient English speakers to work together on analyzing and annotating the text to complete the Skills Focus questions. If these students need more support, have them use the sentence frames on the Access 3 handout as they work with their more proficient peers. **Approaching** **Summarize the Text.** Have these students discuss and complete the text summary on the Access 4 handout and use their summary to help them analyze and annotate the text by completing the Skills Focus questions. Correct answers for the summary are at the end of the lesson plan online. Also refer to the sample Skills Focus answers to aid students with their annotations.
Discuss After students have read the text, use the sample responses to the Skills Focus questions at the bottom of the lesson plan online to discuss the reading and the process of determining the author's purpose and author's point of view. Make sure that students have acquired and accurately use academic-specific words and phrases related to the skill and demonstrate a command of formal English appropriate to the discussion. To help facilitate discussions, refer to Collaborative Discussions in the Speaking & Listening Handbook.	**Extend** **Pair and Share.** In small, heterogeneous groups or pairs, ask students to share and discuss their annotations with a focus on the purpose and point of view presented in the selection.

Core Path	Access Path
	You can provide students with these questions to guide their discussion: 1. Churchill uses first-person singular and plural pronouns throughout his speech. Why is this choice appropriate for the speech, and how might it help him connect with his audience? Cite specific textual evidence to support your statements. (First-person point of view is appropriate for the speech because Churchill is speaking to his people as their leader: "I speak to you for the first time as Prime Minister." The first-person plural pronoun "we" reminds the audience that Churchill is not only their leader, but also their countryman. He says, "We must not allow ourselves to be intimidated," which suggests that he is a part of the same group to whom he is giving this advice. Using first person creates a more intimate connection with the speaker and makes readers feel that Churchill is speaking directly to and about them.) 2. What does Churchill say would be "foolish"? What is the purpose of this part of the speech? Cite specific textual evidence to support your answer. (Churchill says it would be foolish "to disguise the gravity of the hour" and "to lose heart and courage or to suppose that well-trained, well-equipped armies numbering three or four millions of men can be overcome in the space of a few weeks, or even months ..." The purpose of these statements is to inspire the British to remain strong throughout what Churchill believes will be a long, hard war.)

Core Path	Access Path
	3. How are Britain’s strengths and limitations reflected in Churchill’s speech? (Churchill acknowledges that the Royal Air Force has struggled in the past (“the relative balance of the British and German Air Forces is now considerably more favorable to us than at the beginning of the battle”), but he also shows that they have used their limited forces to the best of their ability: “our heavy bombers are striking nightly at the tap-root of German mechanized power, and have already inflicted serious damage upon the oil refineries on which the Nazi effort to dominate the world directly depends.”)
	Extend **Tech Infusion** **Connect.** 1. Ask students to define “valour” in their own words and give an example from history or their own experience that demonstrates their definition. 2. Have students post their definition and example on a Lino board (en.linoit.com) or in a Google Doc. 3. Discuss the definitions and examples as a class. Then apply the discussion to Churchill’s speech. How does Churchill want the British to show their valour? Are his expectations similar to or different from the examples of “valour” the students gave? Why?

3. WRITE

Core Path	Access Path
Prewrite and Plan. Read the prompt as a class and ask students to brainstorm about Winston Churchill's purpose and point of view in "Be Ye Men of Valour." Students can brainstorm together either as a class or in small groups to begin planning their responses. Remind your students to look at the excerpt and their annotations to find textual evidence to support their ideas.	**Beginner & Intermediate** **Plan and Organize.** Have students complete the prewriting activity on the Access 1 and 2 handouts and then explain their ideas to a partner before they write. Explain to students that they need to choose details, examples, or quotes from the text that support their ideas and then explain how those details support their statements. For example, students could include the line, "We must expect that as soon as stability is reached on the Western Front, the bulk of that hideous apparatus of aggression which gashed Holland into ruin and slavery in a few days will be turned upon us," which contributes to Churchill's effort to convince the British people of the great threat against Britain and the need to support the war. **Approaching** **Plan and Organize.** Have students complete the prewriting activity on the Access 4 handout to organize their thoughts before they write.
Discuss. Project these instructions for the peer review onto the board and review them with your class, so they know what they are looking for when they begin to provide their classmates with feedback: • How has this essay helped you understand Churchill's point of view? • Does the writer identify Churchill's purpose or purposes for giving the speech? • Does the writer explain how Churchill used his point of view to advance his purpose(s) for speaking? Does that explanation make sense? • How well does the writer explain how the style or content of the speech helped Churchill's audience understand his purpose(s) and point of view?	

Core Path	Access Path
• What sort of evidence does the writer use from the text to support his or her writing? • How well does the writer explain how that evidence supports his or her arguments? • Does the writer write using standard grammar and punctuation? Are there any weak spots? • What specific suggestions can you make to help the writer improve the response? • What thing(s) does this paper do especially well? After you've looked at the peer review instructions, review the rubric with students before they begin writing. Allow time for students briefly to pose and discuss any questions they may have about the peer review instructions and the rubric. Tell students how many peer reviews they will need to complete once they submit their writing.	
Write. Ask students to complete the writing assignment using textual evidence to support their answers. Once they have completed their writing, they should click "Submit."	
	Extend **Ask Questions.** Before students conduct their peer reviews, have them come up with a list of specific questions or issues they'd like help with. If possible, have students use Google Docs or another word-processing program to highlight the areas or sentences they'd like their peer to focus on, and have partners respond with comments as they peer review.
Review. Once students complete their writing assignment, they should submit substantive feedback to two peers.	

FIRST READ:
"D-Day Prayer"

OVERVIEW

The speech "D-Day Prayer," by President Franklin Delano Roosevelt, was broadcast on June 6, 1944, the date in World War II that Allied forces invaded German-occupied France. Roosevelt sought to rally the public's support behind the invasion. The First Read gives students the opportunity to experience the text with limited context.

OBJECTIVES

1. Perform an initial reading of a text and demonstrate comprehension by responding to short analysis and inference questions with textual evidence.
2. Practice defining vocabulary words using context.
3. Participate effectively in a range of conversations and collaborations to express ideas and build upon the ideas of others.
4. Practice acquiring and using academic vocabulary correctly.

ELA Common Core Standards:
Reading: Informational Text - RI.11-12.1, RI.11-12.4, RI.11-12.10
Speaking & Listening - SL.11-12.1.A, SL.11-12.1.B, SL.11-12.1.C, SL.11-12.1.D, SL.11-12.2
Language - L.11-12.4.A, L.11-12.4.D, L.11-12.6

RESOURCES

Access 1 handout (Beginner)
Access 2 handout (Intermediate)
Access 3 handout (Advanced)
Access 4 handout (Approaching)

ACCESS COMPLEX TEXT

In the "D-Day Prayer," Franklin Roosevelt asks the American people to lend support to US troops fighting in Europe in World War II. He requests that his listeners pray for the soldiers and dedicate themselves to providing other forms of assistance to the war effort. To help students understand the nation's urgent situation, use the following ideas to provide scaffolded instruction for a first reading of the more complex features of this text:

- **Genre** - The text is a prayer that was read during a radio broadcast. US soldiers were involved in a huge and dangerous attack during World War II, and President Roosevelt wanted to provide them with encouragement. The use of a religious form of text to support a military action may be challenging to some students. Remind students that "thee" and "thy" are archaic pronouns used formally in prayer to refer to God.
- **Sentence Structure** - Roosevelt uses lists and other types of parallel structures to emphasize his key points. Encourage students to trace these structures through the prayer and think about why they are effective to use in an oral address.
- **Prior Knowledge** - The context of the Allies' invasion of France in June 1944 may not be familiar to some students. It may be helpful to provide a brief overview of the events that led to this moment in the war.

1. INTRODUCTION

Core Path	Access Path
Read. Individually or as a class, read the introduction for "D-Day Prayer." The introduction provides context for the speech.	**English Learners All Levels & Approaching** **Read and Listen.** Ask students to read and listen to the introduction for "D-Day Prayer." Have them refer to the "Introduction Glossary" on their Access 1, 2, 3, and 4 handouts for definitions of key vocabulary terms. If there are unfamiliar words that are not included in their glossary, encourage students to check a dictionary or online reference tool, such as http://dictionary.reference.com.

Core Path	Access Path
Access Prior Knowledge. Find out what your students already know about D-Day. 1. First, divide your students up into small groups. 2. Ask each group to generate a list of information about D-Day and ask students to share where their previous knowledge came from. 3. Then discuss ways in which the media (movies, books, video games) impact the way we think about war. You may point out that movies such as *Saving Private Ryan*, though bloody, may not show the full challenges of war. Discuss how information about war should be shared with the public.	**Beginner & Approaching** **Access Prior Knowledge.** Have students create a concept map to show what they know about D-Day. Then, as a class, discuss how the media influences our views on war. For example, ask students how movies and TV series sometimes glorify war, such as through the portrayal of heroism, camaraderie, and so on. Discuss which method of informing the public about war is most effective or most accurate (newspapers, TV news, Internet, radio broadcasts, and so forth). If students have limited previous knowledge of D-Day, direct them to the following websites: http://tinyurl.com/nbd9x22, http://tinyurl.com/owp4p8r, and http://tinyurl.com/yrp3ag. **Intermediate & Advanced** **Access Prior Knowledge.** Have students discuss what they already know about D-Day. If they have limited prior knowledge, provide them with the websites for Beginning and Approaching students above. Then, divide students into groups and ask them to discuss things that the media might not portray about wars, whether in the news (actual war) or in fictional accounts (films, novels, and television shows). Call on groups to discuss the importance of reliable public information during wartime. Prompt students with questions such as: • What information about war is often shared or portrayed in the media? What information is rarely or never presented in the media? Why do you think this is? • What method of media would you choose to communicate with the public today if you were the president delivering a wartime speech? Why?

Core Path	Access Path
Analyze Text Features in a Public Document. Explain to students that a public document is a document issued by a government department that is available to the public. Written transcripts of presidential speeches, for example, are considered public documents. Tell students that they can better navigate and comprehend the information available in public documents if they analyze the use of text features (such as graphics, headers, and captions) in the documents. Have students view the scan of Franklin D. Roosevelt's script of the "D-Day Prayer" from the website of the Franklin D. Roosevelt Presidential Library and Museum (http://www.fdrlibrary.marist.edu/_resources/images/msf/msfb0149). Then have students answer these questions about text features as a previewing activity: 1. What do you learn about the document from the header? (The speech was actually a prayer read by the president over the radio. He was at the White House when he read the prayer on June 6, 1944.) 2. Why do you think an introduction was handwritten at the top? (Possible response: That introduction was not part of the originally prepared speech but added by the president to make reference to his speech from the previous night to connect that speech with the prayer.) 3. What can you learn from the use of colons at the beginning of the speech? (The beginning of the speech has three colons. The first colon appears after "My Fellow Americans," indicating that the president is addressing all Americans. The second colon appears after "join me in prayer," and it makes clear that what follows is a prayer. And the third colon appears after "Almighty God" because the prayer is addressed to God.)	

Core Path	Access Path
	Extend **Analyze and Discuss a Quotation.** "I hate war as only a soldier who has lived it can, only as one who has seen its brutality, its stupidity." (General Dwight Eisenhower, architect of the D-Day invasion) Lead students in a discussion of this quote. 1. What do you think Eisenhower's point is? 2. From the quote, what can you infer about Eisenhower's experience during war? 3. In what cases, if any, are wars justified? Can people who have never been in a war understand it?

2. READ

Core Path	Access Path
Make Predictions about Vocabulary. There are five bold vocabulary words in the text. As students read the text, ask them to make predictions about what they think each bold vocabulary word means based on the context clues in the sentence. Have students use the annotation tool to make their predictions. It might be helpful to model this for students before they begin reading. Either using the board or projecting the actual text, focus in on the sentence that uses the word "deter": • Let not the impacts of temporary events, of temporal matters of but fleeting moment—let not these deter us in our unconquerable purpose.	**Note:** This exercise, which extends vocabulary instruction, should be completed when the class shifts from whole-group instruction to individual work during the "Read and Annotate" exercise. **Beginner, Intermediate & Approaching Pair Practice.** 1. Pair students with more proficient readers. 2. Give them an additional sentence that contains a new vocabulary word. 3. Ask the students to complete a Think Aloud using the teacher-led Make Predictions about Vocabulary activity as a model, while the proficient student actively listens.

Core Path	Access Path
Model for the class how to use these context clues to guess the meanings of the words: 1. Look at the structure of the sentence. What part of speech is *deter*? (verb) The subject that goes with the verb *deter* is "these" and the antecedents of this pronoun are "temporary events" and "temporal matters." "Temporal matters" means "minor matters" or "unimportant things." 2. The sentence mentions "our unconquerable purpose" and says that Americans should not let temporary events "deter" them from it. An "unconquerable purpose" sounds like something that the president wants to be a goal for the people. 3. President Roosevelt wants Americans not to be "deterred" from achieving an important goal. The context indicates that *deter* likely means "to stop" or "to prevent."	4. The student should use the context clues in the sentence to try to determine the meaning of the new vocabulary word. 5. After the student has completed the Think Aloud and made a prediction about the word's meaning, allow time for the proficient reader to add his/her own thoughts and clarify any points of confusion. 6. Once they've completed this Think Aloud, encourage them to use a dictionary to confirm the definition of the new vocabulary word. Have them refer to the "Text Glossary" on their Access 1, 2, and 4 handouts for definitions of key vocabulary terms in the text. Encourage them to add any additional vocabulary words or idioms they find in the text and look up definitions for those words and idioms online or in a dictionary.
Model Reading Comprehension Strategy. Before students begin reading, model the reading comprehension strategy of asking and answering questions by using this Think Aloud that talks students through the first paragraph of text. First explain to your students that: *strong readers ask themselves questions before, during, and after reading—not just about surface meaning, but also about big ideas and themes—to check and enhance their understanding* Explain to students how asking and answering questions will help them better comprehend the selection and help drive their discussions. • At the start of the prayer, Franklin Roosevelt mentions the fall of Rome. I ask myself, "How is this connected to D-Day?" • Later in that same sentence, he calls the D-Day invasion a "greater operation."	**Note:** This exercise, which extends instruction around reading comprehension strategies, should be completed when the class shifts from whole-group instruction to individual work during the "Read and Annotate" exercise. **Beginner, Intermediate & Approaching Asking & Answering Questions.** 1. To practice asking and answering questions, have students listen to the audio version of "D-Day Prayer." As they listen to the audio recording, ask them to add a question mark next to portions of the text where they have a question. Pause the audio after the second paragraph. Have them write down a question they have about the text in the chart in their Access 1, 2, and 4 handouts. If students struggle to come up with one, prompt them by asking: *To whom is Roosevelt speaking? About whom is he speaking?*

Core Path	Access Path
• I can use my prior knowledge to try to figure out a logical answer to this question. The fall of Rome was the end of the Roman Empire. Roosevelt must be comparing Rome to a contemporary empire. I know that the Allies were invading German territory (German-occupied France) on D-Day. The empire Roosevelt is referring to must be the Third Reich, what Adolf Hitler called the area controlled by Germany. • As I read, I will continue to ask myself questions about the text.	2. Resume the audio, pausing periodically to allow students to write new questions as well as take notes on their Access handouts to answer their previous questions. Offer guidance to help them notice answers, such as: *Roosevelt is talking about the US troops and the other Allied forces: Britain, France, the Soviet Union, and the other countries that fought against Germany.* 3. As needed, allow additional time after listening for students to answer the questions they've written. Once all their questions have been answered, pair students with more proficient readers and ask them to discuss the strategies they used. Ask: *What led you to ask certain questions? What details answered your questions?* Encourage groups to share their findings with the class.
Read and Annotate. Have students independently read and annotate the speech. Ask students to use the annotation tool as they read to: 1. use context clues to analyze and determine the meaning of the bolded vocabulary terms 2. ask questions about passages of the text that may be unclear or unresolved 3. identify key details, events, individuals, and connections between them 4. note unfamiliar vocabulary	**Beginner** **Coach the Reading.** While other students read, annotate, and discuss the text independently, work with Beginning students, listening to the audio of the text and pausing periodically or when any student has a question. Coach students in articulating their questions for the group and in highlighting and annotating the text. Have students use the Annotation Guide on the Access 1 handout to support them as they highlight and annotate the text. For further support, ask questions about the text, such as: • Is there anything about the text or the situation that you don't understand? • What challenges do the soldiers face, according to Roosevelt? • What kind of support does Roosevelt think the soldiers need?

Core Path	Access Path
	Intermediate **Listen to the Audio.** Have these students listen to the audio of the text and use the Text Glossary on the Access 2 handout to help them with words or idioms that may be unfamiliar. If students need help with annotating the text, have them use the Annotation Guide on the Access 2 handout. After working with the Beginning students, you may wish to check this group's progress and provide support as needed. **Advanced** **Pair with Proficient Peers.** Have Advanced students work with English-proficient peers to read, annotate, and discuss the text. Have students use the Annotation Guide in the Access 3 handout to support them as they highlight and annotate the text. Encourage them to listen to the audio of the text if needed. **Approaching** **Use the Annotation Guide.** Have students use the Annotation Guide on the Access 4 handout to support them as they highlight and annotate the text.
Discuss. In small groups or pairs, have students discuss the questions and inferences they made while reading. To help facilitate discussions, refer to Collaborative Discussions in the Speaking & Listening Handbook. 1. Why does President Roosevelt ask his audience to join him in prayer? (to lend support to the Allied soldiers during the D-Day invasion) Later in the speech, why does he call for a "continuance of prayer"? (Even if the invasion is successful, the road to final victory will be long and difficult.)	**English Learners All Levels & Approaching** Use the extra time while on- and beyond-grade-level students are discussing their first reads of the text to work individually and in small groups with Approaching readers and English Learners as outlined above. Should those students complete their first reads quickly, integrate them into the on- and beyond-grade-level discussion groups. Otherwise, English Learners and Approaching readers will be given an opportunity to participate in text discussions with their peers later in the lesson.

Core Path	Access Path
2. Why does Roosevelt speak of a "struggle to preserve our Republic"? (If the D-Day invasion fails, the United States might lose the war.) 3. How does Roosevelt refer to German troops near the end of the speech? ("the unholy forces of our enemy") Why might he have used such negative language? (to reassure the American people that the struggle will be worth the cost)	**Beyond** **Tech Infusion** **Research.** Have students search the Internet to find one or two ways that civilians in the United States or other countries supported the war efforts "on the home front" during World War II. Have students share what they found with a partner or in groups.

3. THINK

Core Path	Access Path
Answer and Discuss. Have students complete the Think questions and then use the peer review instructions and rubric to complete two peer reviews. Refer to the sample answers at the end of the lesson plan online to discuss responses with your students.	**Beginner & Intermediate** **Sentence Frames.** Have students use the sentence frames on the Access 1 and 2 handouts to support their responses to the Think questions. If necessary, distribute sentence frames to Advanced students as well. **Approaching** **Find the Evidence.** Have students use Find the Evidence on the Access 4 handout to help them identify the evidence needed to answer the questions.
	Extend **Debate.** Present students with an issue from the text that can be debated. Allow students to debate the issue as a class or in smaller groups. Prompt: What is the most helpful way for people to show support for their nation's soldiers and other military personnel? Why?

SKILL:
Connotation and Denotation

OVERVIEW

Understanding connotation and denotation is key to understanding the tone of any piece of writing. This lesson plan provides follow-up questions and enrichments to help teachers guide students toward a usable, repeatable method for identifying connotation and denotation in a work of informational text.

OBJECTIVES

1. Learn the definitions of connotation and denotation.
2. Practice using concrete strategies for determining connotation and denotation.
3. Participate effectively in a range of conversations and collaborations to express ideas and build upon the ideas of others.

ELA Common Core Standards:
Reading: Informational Text - RI.11-12.1, RI.11-12.4
Speaking & Listening - SL.11-12.1.A, SL.11-12.1.C, SL.11-12.2

RESOURCES

Access 1 handout (Beginner)
Access 2 handout (Intermediate)
Access 3 handout (Advanced)
Access 4 handout (Approaching)

1. DEFINE

Core Path	Access Path
Watch. Watch the Concept Definition video on connotation and denotation with your students. Make sure your students write down and understand the definitions of both terms, along with relevant examples for each. Pause the video at these key moments to discuss the information with your students: 1. 0:19 – What does a word's "cultural connection" refer to? Can you think of a word (or words) with a connotative meaning derived from a certain cultural connection? How did this particular connotative meaning come to exist? 2. 0:42 – Similar to the "child" example, brainstorm some other words with neutral denotations and place them in a context in which the connotation gives it a completely different meaning. How do words work together to create meaning? 3. 0:56 – Why do you think authors use words with specific connotations? Why don't they just state what they mean directly?	**English Learners All Levels & Approaching** **Match.** Have students complete the matching exercise on the Access 1, 2, 3, and 4 handouts as they watch the video. Answers are located at the end of the lesson plan online.
Read and Discuss. After watching the Concept Definition video, have students read the definition of connotation and denotation. Either in small groups or as a whole class, use these questions to engage students in a discussion about connotation and denotation: 1. Does every word have a connotation in addition to its denotation? Why or why not? (Yes, because every word has ideas associated with it.) 2. Why do connotations have such a strong impact on the tone of a piece of writing? (Connotations affect the tone of a piece of writing because they call to mind all the ideas and associations associated with the words chosen.) 3. How can you learn the connotations of new vocabulary words? (By looking closely at how the words are used in context)	**Beginner & Approaching** **Fill in the Blank.** To prepare students to participate in the discussion, have them complete the fill-in-the-blanks activity on the Access 1 and 4 handouts as they read the definition. The correct answers are located at the end of the lesson plan online. **Intermediate & Advanced** **Discuss Prompts.** To help these students participate in the discussion, prompt them with questions that can be answered with a few words, such as: • What appears in a dictionary: a word's connotation or denotation? (denotation) • Why does "greasy" take on a negative connotation when it describes food? (because greasy food is unhealthy) • Can you think of another neutral word that becomes positive or negative when used in specific context? (Answers will vary.)

Core Path	Access Path
4. Do you think it is necessary to learn the denotation of a word before its connotation, or can they be learned simultaneously? Why? (Answers will vary. Possible answer: People often learn a word's denotation and connotation simultaneously, using context to determine both the literal meaning and its connotation.)	**Beyond** **Discuss.** Have students select words from the text and discuss their connotations. Compile a list of examples, such as "pride," "darkness," and "conquest." Have students discuss whether each word has a specific connotation in the text and whether the word could have either a positive and negative connotation, depending on the context in which it is used.
	Extend **Pair and Share.** Ask partners to review the bolded vocabulary words from the First Read lesson and identify the connotations of each word. Then have them meet with another pair to compare their list of connotations and discuss similarities and differences.

2. MODEL

Core Path	Access Path
Read and Annotate. Have students independently read the Model section. As they read, ask students to use the annotation tool to: • highlight key points • ask questions • identify places where the Model applies the strategies laid out in the Identification and Application section	**Note:** During this portion of the lesson, instruction shifts from whole-group to individual work. Use this time to work one-on-one or in small groups with Beginning, Intermediate, Advanced, and Approaching students. **Beginner & Intermediate** **Coach the Reading.** Work with these students (either individually or in small groups) to fill out the guided reading questions on the Access 1 and 2 handouts. Have Beginning students refer to the glossary on the Access 1 handout to help them determine the meaning of difficult words (note: provide the Access 1 handout glossary to Intermediate students if necessary). Let students know they'll use these answers to help participate in the discussion about the Model. Sample answers for this exercise are located at the end of the lesson plan online.

Core Path	Access Path
	Advanced **Identify Evidence.** Ask Advanced students to complete the identifying evidence exercise on the Access 3 handout. Let students know that they'll use these answers to help participate in the discussion about the Model. Sample answers for this exercise are located at the end of the lesson plan online. **Approaching** **Guided Reading.** Have students complete the guided reading questions on the Access 4 handout as they read. Let them know that they'll use these answers to help participate in the discussion about the Model. Sample answers for this exercise are located at the end of the lesson plan online.
Discuss. After students read the Model text, use these questions to facilitate a whole-group discussion that helps students understand how to identify and analyze connotation and denotation in the passage: 1. The connotations in the passage are related to the purpose of Franklin Roosevelt's prayer. According to the Model, what is this purpose? (to strengthen the American public's commitment to the Allies' military campaign) 2. Why might Roosevelt use a word such as "righteousness" to characterize the Allies' cause? (to inspire patriotism by associating it with moral purpose) 3. Choose one of the words highlighted in the Model and replace it with a synonym. What effect does this have on the meaning of the sentence? (Sample answer: Using "correctness" instead of "righteousness" might make the prayer seem less persuasive to listeners.) 4. The Model mentions that Roosevelt is seeking to bolster the faith of the American people. What emotional associations does he seek to create in the second passage? (a feeling of family with the word "sons" and a feeling of struggle with a religious overtone with the word "crusade")	

Core Path	Access Path
5. Why do you think Roosevelt chooses to mix words that have positive connotations with words that have negative connotations? (He uses positive connotations for the Allies and negative connotations for their enemy, and for war itself, in order to stir American support for the war.)	
	Extend **Tech Infusion** **Evaluate Genres.** Challenge students to brainstorm genres of writing most likely to contain words with connotations that have strong emotional associations. When students have a list of possibilities, have them locate an example online. Ask volunteers to share what they found with the class.
	Extend **Write.** Have small groups write a paragraph describing a celebrity, using words with positive connotations. Then have groups rewrite the paragraph, using words with negative connotations but keeping the general content the same. Ask groups to read aloud both paragraphs. Discuss how word choice changed the overall tone of the paragraph.

3. YOUR TURN

Core Path	Access Path
Assess and Explain. Have students answer the comprehension questions to test for understanding. Share the explanations for Parts A and B (located online) with your students.	

Core Path	Access Path
	Extend **Write.** Have students write a Your Turn question for a section of the prayer that is not included in the lesson. They should choose an emotional association related to a word's connotation and have the reader identify a word that has that particular connotation. Then have students trade questions with a partner and answer each other's questions.

SKILL:
Compare and Contrast

OVERVIEW

Comparing and contrasting two foundational documents can lead a reader to a deeper understanding of a historical period. This lesson plan provides follow-up questions and enrichments to help teachers guide students toward a usable, repeatable method for comparing and contrasting two speeches.

OBJECTIVES

1. Learn the definition of compare and contrast.
2. Practice using concrete strategies for comparing and contrasting.
3. Participate effectively in a range of conversations and collaborations to express ideas and build upon the ideas of others.

ELA Common Core Standards:
Reading: Informational Text - RI.11-12.1, RI.11-12.8
Speaking & Listening - SL.11-12.1.A, SL.11-12.1.C, SL.11-12.2

RESOURCES

Access 1 handout (Beginner)
Access 2 handout (Intermediate)
Access 3 handout (Advanced)
Access 4 handout (Approaching)

1. DEFINE

Core Path	Access Path
Watch. Watch the Concept Definition video on compare and contrast with your students. Make sure your students understand the difference between comparing and contrasting and how it can help unlock meaning in a given text. Pause the video at these key moments to discuss the information with your students: 1. 1:02 – Which reveals more about two things: comparing or contrasting them? Why? 2. 1:22 – What are some strategies we can use to compare and contrast different kinds of media? What strategies can help get beyond surface media differences? 3. 1:47 – What are character motivations? How can comparing two characters help a reader understand motivations?	**English Learners All Levels & Approaching** **Fill in the Blanks.** Have students complete the fill-in-the-blanks exercise on the Access 1, 2, 3, and 4 handouts as they watch the video. Answers are located at the end of the lesson plan online.
Read and Discuss. After watching the Concept Definition video, have students read the definition of compare and contrast. Either in small groups or as a whole class, use these questions to engage students in a discussion about compare and contrast: 1. Are there any situations in which two informational texts have only differences and no similarities? Why or why not? (Possible answer: This is unlikely. Informational texts usually have some similarities, whether in text structure, content, or author's point of view or purpose.) 2. What are some ways other than content in which two informational texts can be similar? (Possible answers: text structure, author's point of view or purpose, use of rhetoric) 3. How can comparing and contrasting two informational texts help you understand them better than just analyzing them individually? (Comparing and contrasting texts helps you better analyze and understand the content of each text.)	**Beginner & Approaching** **Match.** To prepare students to participate in the discussion, have them complete the matching exercise on the Access 1 and 4 handouts as they read the definition. The correct answers are located at the end of the lesson plan online. **Intermediate & Advanced** **Discuss Prompts.** To help these students participate in the discussion, prompt them with questions that can be answered with a few words, such as: • What do we discover when we compare things? (how they are the same) • What do we discover when we contrast things? (how they are different) • What is something you compare and contrast regularly? (Answers will vary.)

Core Path	Access Path
	Beyond **Discuss.** Have students imagine that they are either US or British citizens during World War II. Have students compare and contrast how citizens of the two nations must have felt and acted during the time period in which the two speeches were given. How were their situations the same? How were they different?
	Extend **Apply.** Ask students to apply information in the Define section to comparison shopping. Students may choose any type of store: supermarket, clothing store, website, and so on. Brainstorm a list of strategies that would help them choose between two items.

2. MODEL

Core Path	Access Path
Read and Annotate. Have students independently read the Model section. As they read, ask students to use the annotation tool to: • highlight key points • ask questions • identify places where the Model applies the strategies laid out in the Identification and Application section	**Note:** During this portion of the lesson, instruction shifts from whole-group to individual work. Use this time to work one-on-one or in small groups with Beginning, Intermediate, Advanced, and Approaching students. **Beginner & Intermediate** **Coach the Reading.** Work with these students (either individually or in small groups) to fill out the guided reading questions on the Access 1 and 2 handouts. Have Beginning students refer to the glossary on the Access 1 handout to help them determine the meaning of difficult words (note: provide the Access 1 handout glossary to Intermediate students if necessary). Let students know they'll use these answers to help participate in the discussion about the Model. Sample answers for this exercise are located at the end of the lesson plan online.

Core Path	Access Path
	Advanced **Identify Evidence.** Ask Advanced students to complete the identifying evidence exercise on the Access 3 handout. Let students know that they'll use these answers to help participate in the discussion about the Model. Sample answers for this exercise are located at the end of the lesson plan online. **Approaching** **Guided Reading.** Have students complete the guided reading questions on the Access 4 handout as they read. Let them know that they'll use these answers to help participate in the discussion about the Model. Sample answers for this exercise are located at the end of the lesson plan online.
Discuss. After students read the Model text, use these questions to facilitate a whole-group discussion that helps students understand how to compare and contrast foundational texts: 1. What does the Model identify as the first key similarity between the two texts? (They are both radio speeches read by leaders of countries to encourage their people during World War II.) 2. How does the speakers' use of pronouns develop tone in both speeches? (The first-person plural pronouns give the speeches an informal tone and put the leaders on the same level as their audience.) 3. What are the core values that Roosevelt and Churchill say will be maintained by victory in the war, according to the Model? (Roosevelt mentions freedom; Churchill mentions truth and justice.) How are these values similar? How are they different? (Answers will vary.) 4. Why is the situation faced by Britain at the time of Churchill's speech more serious than the situation faced by the United States at the time of Roosevelt's speech? (Great Britain faces the threat of invasion by the enemy, whereas the United States does not.)	

Core Path	Access Path
	Extend **Tech Infusion** **Research.** Have small groups do online research to compare and contrast the lives of Franklin Delano Roosevelt and Winston Churchill. Have groups identify three points of similarity and three points of difference. As they work, have each group add their similarities and differences to a class list in a Google Doc or a Padlet wall (http://padlet.com/). Challenge students to make sure no facts are repeated.
	Extend **Write.** Have students imagine they are an average citizen in the United States or Great Britain during World War II. Ask them to write a two-paragraph response to either Roosevelt's speech or Churchill's speech, indicating which sections they find most inspiring and why.

3. YOUR TURN

Core Path	Access Path
Assess and Explain. Have students answer the comprehension questions to test for understanding. Share the explanations for Parts A and B (located online) with your students.	
	Extend **Tech Infusion** **Compile.** Have partners locate two editorials or other opinion pieces on opposite sides of a major political issue. Ask them to write two questions for the editorials, using the same format as that of the Your Turn section. When they are done, have them meet with another pair of students to answer each other's questions.

CLOSE READ:
"D-Day Prayer"

OVERVIEW

On June 6, 1944, President Franklin Delano Roosevelt gave his "D-Day Prayer" to rally the public's support behind the invasion and to comfort people at home. The Close Read gives students the opportunity to analyze Roosevelt's word choice and compare this speech to Winston Churchill's "Be Ye Men of Valour."

OBJECTIVES

1. Complete a close reading of an informational speech.
2. Practice and apply concrete strategies for determining connotation and denotation.
3. Participate effectively in a range of conversations and collaborations to express ideas and build upon the ideas of others.
4. Prewrite, plan, and produce clear and coherent writing in response to a prompt.

ELA Common Core Standards:
Reading: Informational Text - RI.11-12.1, RI.11-12.4, RI.11-12.8, RI.11-12.10
Writing - W.11-12.2.A, W.11-12.2.B, W.11-12.4, W.11-12.5, W.11-12.6, W.11-12.9.B, W.11-12.10
Speaking & Listening - SL.11-12.1.A, SL.11-12.1.B, SL.11-12.1.C, SL.11-12.1.D, SL.11-12.6
Language - L.11-12.4.A, L.11-12.4.C, L.11-12.4.D

RESOURCES

"D-Day Prayer" Vocabulary review
"D-Day Prayer" Venn diagram
Access 1 handout (Beginner)
Access 2 handout (Intermediate)
Access 3 handout (Advanced)
Access 4 handout (Approaching)

1. INTRODUCTION

Core Path	Access Path
Define and Compare. Project the vocabulary words and definitions onto the board or provide students with handouts so they can copy the vocabulary into their notebooks. Suggest that students consult general and specialized reference materials, both print and digital, to compare the precise meaning of a specific word with their initial vocabulary predictions from the First Read. Review words that students defined incorrectly to understand why they were unable to use context clues to develop usable definitions.	**Beginner & Intermediate** **Complete the Chart.** Have students complete the chart on the Access 1 and 2 handouts by writing the correct word for each of the definitions. **Advanced & Beyond** **Write in Journals.** Have students write a journal entry using all of their vocabulary words. Remind them to write sentences that communicate the meaning of the words they are using. **Approaching** **Graphic Organizer.** To support students in comparing their predictions with the correct meanings, have them complete the graphic organizer on the Access 4 handout to record the vocabulary words, their initial analysis, and the definitions. Then have them write sentences using the words.
Review. Have students complete the fill-in-the-blanks vocabulary worksheet attached to the lesson plan online. Answers for the worksheet are listed at the end of the lesson plan online.	
	Extend **Tech Infusion** **Create.** Ask small groups to each create a short video that shows the meaning of the five vocabulary words. Upload the videos to a class YouTube channel for the rest of the class to view.

Core Path	Access Path
	Extend **Make Flashcards.** Ask students to use index cards to create flashcards with a vocabulary word on one side and the definition on the other. On the side of the cards that have definitions, encourage them to add drawings or other memory clues that will help them memorize the definition.

2. READ

Core Path	Access Path
Model Close Reading. Project the text onto the board and model a close reading of the first four paragraphs using the annotation strategies mentioned on the next page. While modeling annotation strategies, make notes that tie the text to the focus skill and demonstrate what students are looking for as they read. Some guidance for you as you annotate for your students: • President Franklin Roosevelt uses words with strong positive connotations when referring to the US soldiers involved in the D-Day invasion. He knows that these soldiers carry the heavy burden of making an Allied victory much more likely if they succeed in this battle. • Look at the word "endeavor" in the third paragraph. Roosevelt could have used a simpler word such as "job" or "task," but he wanted to emphasize the importance of the D-Day invasion. The denotation of "endeavor" is "determined effort," but the connotation of the word involves a major, important effort. Roosevelt used "endeavor" to describe the D-Day invasion because it was much more than a job or a task.	

Core Path	Access Path
• There are many other words in the text whose connotations are more powerful than their denotations. Roosevelt's choice of "stoutness" rather than "courage" and the choice of "steadfastness" rather than "loyalty," both in paragraph four, are two examples. Both "stoutness" and "steadfastness" have stronger connotations than their possible alternatives because the connotations imply a lasting condition. • The use of words with strong connotations allows Roosevelt to express complex feelings in few words.	
Read and Annotate. Read the Skills Focus questions as a class, so your students know what they should pay close attention to as they read. Then have students read and annotate the excerpt. Ask students to use the annotation tool as they read to: 1. respond to the Skills Focus section 2. ask questions to identify President Roosevelt's purpose in giving the speech 3. analyze how the speech's style supports its purpose 4. determine the connotations of key words in the seventh paragraph 5. analyze Roosevelt's use of the word "faith" and explain how its denotation and connotation relate to key ideas in the speech 6. identify and analyze uses of parallelism in the speech 7. note unfamiliar vocabulary 8. capture their reaction to the ideas and examples in the text As students reread the text, remind them to use the comprehension strategy of asking and answering questions that they learned in the First Read.	**Note:** While on-grade-level students are reading and annotating, work one-on-one or in small groups with Beginning, Intermediate, Advanced, and Approaching students to support them as they read and annotate the text. **Beginner & Intermediate** **Summarize and Analyze the Text.** Work with these students to complete the sentence frames on the Access 1 and 2 handouts (note: the sentence frames for Intermediate students on the Access 2 handout contain fewer scaffolds). They will then use the completed sentence frames to help them analyze and annotate the text by completing the Skills Focus questions. Refer to the sample Skills Focus answers to help them complete the sentence frames and annotate the text. **Advanced** **Work in Pairs.** Pair these students with more proficient English speakers to work together on analyzing and annotating the text to complete the Skills Focus questions. If these students need more support, have them use the sentence frames on the Access 3 handout as they work with their more proficient peers.

Core Path	Access Path
	Approaching **Summarize the Text.** Have these students discuss and complete the text summary on the Access 4 handout and use their summary to help them analyze and annotate the text by completing the Skills Focus questions. Correct answers for the summary are at the end of the lesson plan online. Also refer to the sample Skills Focus answers to aid students with their annotations.
Discuss. After students have read the text, use the sample responses to the Skills Focus questions at the bottom of the lesson plan online to discuss the reading and the process of analyzing the author's word choice and rhetorical features. Make sure that students have acquired and accurately use academic-specific words and phrases related to the skill and demonstrate a command of formal English appropriate to the discussion. To help facilitate discussions, refer to Collaborative Discussions in the Speaking & Listening Handbook.	**Extend** **Pair and Share.** In small, heterogeneous groups or pairs, ask students to share and discuss their annotations with a focus on the connotations of the words in the selection. You can provide students with these questions to guide their discussion: 1. How does President Roosevelt want his listeners to feel as they listen to his prayer? Why? Support your answer with textual evidence. (He wants them to feel encouraged and concerned. He is trying to make them understand how urgent the current military situation is for the United States and why Americans need to be thinking of the soldiers in Europe.) 2. Why does Roosevelt say, "They fight not for the lust of conquest. They fight to end conquest"? Cite specific textual evidence to support your answer. (US troops are not fighting because they want to take over other countries; they are fighting against an enemy that wants to take over other countries, including the United States. Later in the prayer Roosevelt says, "Help us to conquer the apostles of greed and racial arrogancies. Lead us to the saving of our country." This makes the Americans seem good while the enemy appears evil.) 3. What are some words in the final paragraph that have positive connotations intended to show that the cause of the US military effort is a good one? ("peace," "freedom," "just," "honest")

Core Path	Access Path
	Extend **Tech Infusion** **Listen.** As a class, listen to a recording of President Roosevelt's speech (available at http://tinyurl.com/o8mtgtu). After listening, discuss how the text is different when reading or listening. • Which parts of the speech were most moving when listening? • Which parts lost their power in the audio version? • Which version did you prefer and why?

3. WRITE

Core Path	Access Path
Prewrite and Plan. Read the prompt as a class and ask students to brainstorm about the similarities and differences between "D-Day Prayer" and "Be Ye Men of Valour." Remind your students to look at the excerpts and their annotations to find textual evidence to support their ideas.	**Beginner & Intermediate** **Plan and Organize.** Have students complete the prewriting activity on the Access 1 and 2 handouts and then explain their ideas to a partner before they write. Explain to students that they need to choose details, examples, or quotes from the text that support their ideas and then explain how those details support their statements. For example, students could include the line, "Lead them straight and true; give strength to their arms, stoutness to their hearts, steadfastness in their faith." This shows the rhetorical feature of parallelism, which helps Roosevelt clearly state the qualities he hopes the troops will have in battle. **Approaching** **Plan and Organize.** Have students complete the prewriting activity on the Access 4 handout to organize their thoughts before they write.

Core Path	Access Path
Discuss. Project these instructions for the peer review onto the board and review them with your students, so they know what they are looking for when they begin to provide their classmates with feedback: • Read the response to see that the writer has made comparisons between the content of the speeches and the rhetorical features. • How has this essay helped you understand how both Roosevelt and Churchill use content to support their purposes? • Did the writer identify rhetorical features in each speech? Were clear comparisons and contrasts made between the features? • What sort of evidence did the writer use from the texts to support his or her writing? • How well does the writer explain how that evidence supports his or her response? • Be sure to tell the writer what he or she does well and what he or she needs to improve. After you've looked at the peer review instructions, review the rubric with students before they begin writing. Allow time for students briefly to pose and discuss any questions they may have about the peer review instructions and the rubric. Tell students how many peer reviews they will need to complete once they submit their writing.	
Write. Ask students to complete the writing assignment using textual evidence to support their answers. Once they have completed their writing, they should click "Submit."	
	Extend **Organize.** Have students complete the Venn diagram attached to the lesson plan online to organize their ideas for the writing prompt. Remind your students to include textual evidence to support their ideas.

Core Path	Access Path
	Extend **Evaluate.** Project a writing sample on the board and have students identify the textual evidence used in the sample. For each piece of evidence, ask students if the writer effectively connects the evidence to his or her thesis or analysis. If not, discuss strategies for clarifying the relationships between evidence and analysis.
Review. Once students complete their writing assignment, they should submit substantive feedback to two peers. Students should use their peers' feedback to improve their writing.	

BLAST:
That's Entertainment!

OVERVIEW

To conclude the unit, students will learn about how world events affected the literary movements of romanticism, realism, and modernism. Research links explore how contemporary entertainment, including books, movies, and TV shows, are influenced by current events.

OBJECTIVES

1. Explore background information about how world events affected romantic, realist, and modernist authors.
2. Research using hyperlinks to a range of information about how current events are reflected in books, movies, and TV shows today.

ELA Common Core Standards:
Reading: Informational Text - RI.11-12.1
Writing - W.11-12.1.A, W.11-12.1.B, W.11-12.5, W.11-12.6
Speaking & Listening - SL.11-12.1.A, SL.11-12.1.C, SL.11-12.1.D

RESOURCES

Access 1 handout (Beginner)
Access 2 handout (Intermediate)
Access 4 handout (Approaching)

TITLE/DRIVING QUESTION

Core Path	Access Path
Discuss. As a class, read aloud the title and driving question for this Blast. Ask students what they think about current events and entertainment. Do they like watching movies or TV shows that directly reflect current events? Why or why not? Taking into account ideas generated by their classmates, do they have a sense of how entertainment reflects current events? Remind students that they'll be returning to this question and responding after they've read the Background and some of the Research Links.	**English Learners All Levels** **Discuss a Visual.** Have students view an image of Pablo Picasso's *Guernica*, such as the one at http://tinyurl.com/o23e8pe. Give the students a brief overview of the painting, including that it was created in 1937 in response to the Spanish Civil War. Then discuss how the picture represents an important achievement from a modernist painter, prompting students with questions such as: • What is happening in this painting? • What emotion is revealed in the painting? How does the artist evoke that emotion in viewers? • Some key ideas in modernism were disillusionment and experimental techniques. How does this painting reflect those ideas? • How does Picasso use abstract images to convey anti-war sentiment?
Draft. In their notebooks or on scrap paper, have students draft their initial responses to the driving question. This will provide them with a baseline response that they will be altering as they gain more information about the topic in the Background and Research Links sections of the assignment.	**Beginner & Intermediate** **Draft with Sentence Frame.** When drafting their initial response to the driving question, have students refer to this Blast sentence frame on their Access 1 and 2 handouts: • Entertainment and pop culture reflect current events by ____________________________. Point out these two key features of the sentence frame: 1. The introductory clause "Entertainment and pop culture reflect current events" borrows language directly from the Blast driving question to provide a response. 2. Ask students to make special note of the preposition "by," which invites them to list a way or ways entertainment and pop culture reflect current events.

BACKGROUND

Core Path	Access Path
Read. Have students read the Blast background to provide context for the driving question.	**Beginner & Intermediate** **Read with Support.** Have students read the Blast background to provide context for the driving question. When they encounter unfamiliar words or phrases, have students refer to the glossary on their Access 1 and 2 handouts. If there are unfamiliar words that are not included in their glossary, encourage students to check a dictionary or online reference tool, such as http://dictionary.reference.com. **Approaching** **Read and Summarize.** Have students read the Blast background to provide context for the driving question. As they read, ask students to complete the fill-in-the-blanks summary of the background provided on their Access 4 handout. When they encounter unfamiliar words or phrases, have students refer to the glossary on their Access 4 handout.
Discuss. Pair students and have them discuss the following questions: 1. How would the French Revolution and the Industrial Revolution change many people's lives? (The French Revolution [temporarily] turned a monarchy into a democracy. The Industrial Revolution led to new jobs, manufactured goods, and a move toward cities.) What effects might these changes have had on literature of the time? (Answers will vary.) 2. What was the focus of realist art? (everyday people, especially issues of class) How does the excerpt from *O Pioneers!* show this focus? (It shows a common man who grew up on a farm.)	**Beginner** **Discuss.** Pair Beginning with Advanced (or Beyond) students and have them use the dialogue starter on their Access 1 handout to discuss the topic. Advise them to return to the dialogue and switch roles if they get stuck. **Intermediate** **Discuss.** Pair Intermediate with Advanced (or Beyond) students and have them use the dialogue starter on their Access 2 handout to discuss the topic. Advise them to return to the dialogue and switch roles if they get stuck. If their conversation is progressing smoothly, encourage them to continue the discussion beyond the dialogue starter sheet. They can expand their conversations to discuss other ways current events affect the way we view the world.

Core Path	Access Path
3. Why was World War I so deadly? (new technologies, such as machine guns and poison gas) How did the war affect artists and writers? (They became disillusioned.) 4. Is it easy to see the connections between current events and literature or art? Why or why not? (Answers will vary.)	
Brainstorm. Remind students about the driving question for this Blast: How do entertainment and pop culture reflect current or recent events? In their notebooks, ask students to make two columns, one for current events and one for art inspired by current events. Have students start by listing some important events of the past ten years. Then have students list books, movies, TV shows, or other art based on those events. Here's a short of example of how this might look:	

Events	Art
Iraq War	*The Hurt Locker*
Rise of smartphones	*Jobs* *Selfie* *Her* *Men, Women & Children*
Social media	*The Social Network* *Catfish*

RESEARCH LINKS

Core Path	Access Path
Examine and Explore. Use these questions to guide students' exploration of the research links: 1. Ask students to read "Why Zombies Rule." What key reason does the author give for the popularity of zombies? (They are a blank slate.) What cultural fears can zombies represent to viewers? (global consumerism, repetitive work life, overconsumption of resources, pandemics) Do you enjoy zombie movies or TV shows? Why or why not? What do they represent to you? 2. Ask students to read "Why Russians are Always Bad Guys." According to the article, why are Russians more likely to be bad guys in movies? (Traditionally, Russia has been a geopolitical threat to the United States, especially during the Cold War.) What other nationalities or ethnicities are more likely to be villains, now or in the past? (Germans, Japanese, Chinese, Arabs) Do you notice the ethnicity of movie villains? Why might it be a problem for movies to portray villains as always coming from the same parts of the world? (Answers will vary.)	
	Extend **Research, Discuss, and Present.** 1. Assign each group one link to explore in depth. 2. Ask them to discuss the information: a. What are the key points made in this resource? b. What inferences did you make as you read? c. What did you learn from reading this research? d. How did this help you to better understand the topic? e. What questions does your group have after exploring this link? 3. Allow students time to informally present what they learned.

Core Path	Access Path
	Extend **Tech Infusion** **Share.** As students explore the links, allow them to crowdsource their findings using a backchannel tool, such as TodaysMeet (https://todaysmeet.com) or Padlet (https://padlet.com). Students can post the research they find individually or in groups to share with the class.

QUIKPOLL

Core Path	Access Path
Participate. Answer the poll question. Have students use information from the background and research links to explain their answers.	

NUMBER CRUNCH

Core Path	Access Path
Predict, Discuss, and Click. Before students click on the number, break them into pairs and have them make predictions about what they think the number is related to. After they've clicked the number, ask students if they are surprised by the revealed information.	

CREATE YOUR BLAST

Core Path	Access Path
Blast. Ask students to write their Blast response in 140 characters or less.	**Beginner** **Blast with Support.** Have students refer to the sentence frame on their Access 1 handout that they used to create their original Blast draft. Ask them to use this frame to write and enter their final Blast. **Intermediate** **Blast with Support.** Have students attempt to draft their Blast without the sentence frame on their Access 2 handout. If students struggle to compose their Blast draft without the sentence frame, remind them to reference it for support. **Beyond** **Write a Claim.** Ask students to use their answer to the poll question to write a strong claim that could be used as the foundation for a piece of argumentative writing. Once students have written their claims, ask them to read the claims to a small group of their peers. This activity will provide them practice writing claims, as well as expose them to claims written by their peers.
Review. After students have completed their own Blasts, ask them to review the Blasts of their peers and provide feedback.	
	Extend **Discuss.** As a whole class or in groups, identify a few strong Blasts and discuss what made those responses so powerful. As a group, analyze and discuss what characteristics make a Blast interesting or effective.
	Extend **Revise.** Resend a second version of this Blast assignment to your students and have them submit revised versions of their original Blasts. Do the same responses make the Top 10? How have the answers improved from the first submissions?

Extended Writing Project

Emotional Currents

EXTENDED WRITING PROJECT:
Informational/Explanatory Writing

OVERVIEW

For this unit's Extended Writing Project, students will be writing an informative/explanatory text in the form of a research paper. Students will develop their writing in stages, with time for reflection, peer review, and revision. This lesson provides students with a definition of informative/explanatory writing and its major features, including aspects of research papers, as well as with a sample student research paper.

OBJECTIVES

1. Discuss and demonstrate an understanding of informative/explanatory writing in the form of a research paper.
2. Practice and apply concrete strategies for identifying the features of informative/explanatory writing and research paper writing.
3. Participate effectively in a range of conversations and collaborations to express ideas and build upon the ideas of others.
4. Generate information for an informative/explanatory research paper.

ELA Common Core Standards:
Reading: Informational Text - RI.11-12.1
Writing - W.11-12.2.A, W.11-12.2.B, W.11-12.2.C, W.11-12.2.D, W.11-12.2.E, W.11-12.2.F, W.11-12.5, W.11-12.8, W.11-12.10
Speaking & Listening - SL.11-12.1.A, SL.11-12.1.C

RESOURCES

Access 1 handout (Beginner)
Access 2 handout (Intermediate)
Access 3 handout (Advanced)
Access 4 handout (Approaching)

1. INTRODUCTION

Core Path	Access Path
Read and Discuss. Have students read the prompt to the Extended Writing Project on informative research paper writing. You might briefly review the concept of a thesis statement, telling students that they will learn more about crafting thesis statements for research papers in a later lesson. Ask them to look at the various parts of the prompt and respond to the following questions: • What is the prompt asking you to do? • What specific requirements does the prompt lay out? • What does the prompt ask you to specifically consider? • What does the prompt ask you to research? • What kinds of sources might best help you answer the prompt?	**Beginner & Intermediate** **Paraphrase.** Have students follow along with the text as they listen to the audio recording of the prompt. After they've heard the audio recording, have them fill in the blanks on their Access 1 and 2 handouts to create their own paraphrased version of the prompt. When they've completed their prompt paraphrase, have students participate in the whole class discussion of the prompt using the questions provided in the Core Path. A sample paraphrase is located in the answer key at the end of the lesson plan online. **Approaching** **Listen and Discuss.** Have students follow along with the text as they listen to the audio recording of the prompt. Then, have them participate in the whole class discussion of the prompt using the questions provided in the Core Path.
Read and Annotate. Individually or as a class, read the Introduction to Informative/Explanatory Writing, including the writing of informative research papers. The introduction defines informative/explanatory writing and research paper writing and offers nine features of the form. If you are reading the introduction as a class, encourage students to take Cornell notes defining informative research paper writing, identifying the purpose of an informative research paper, and putting the nine features of informative research paper writing into their own words. You might also divide students into small groups and have students in each group collaborate on writing a summary of the purpose and features of the informative/explanatory writing form. Point out that students will learn more about these features and about how to incorporate them into their own writing as they craft an informative research paper in response to the Extended Writing Project prompt.	**Beginner & Intermediate** **Fill in the Blanks.** As they read and listen to the introduction, have Beginning and Intermediate students work together to fill in the blanks on the Access 1 and 2 handouts. They can also refer to the introduction glossary provided on those handouts. Provide assistance and clarification as needed. Sample answers are located at the end of the lesson plan online. **Advanced & Approaching** **Identify Features of Informative/Explanatory Writing.** After reading the introduction, have students list the eight features of an informative research paper on their Access 3 and 4 handouts in their own words.

Core Path	Access Path
	Extend **Brainstorm.** Remind students that all research papers are alike in that they require outside research to prove a thesis. However, research papers do differ based on their subject. Have students make a list of subjects (e.g., biology, world history, linguistics) and brainstorm questions they could use as the basis for a research paper in each discipline. Then, with a partner, have students discuss ways their research questions are similar and different for each subject.

2. READ

Core Path	Access Path
Read and Label. Have students read the Student Model research paper "The Making of *Pride and Prejudice*: The Life and Times of Jane Austen" and use the annotation tool to identify the features of an informative research paper: • an introduction with a clear thesis statement • information from credible research sources with formal citations • relevant facts, supporting details, and quotations used to develop the topic • analysis of the details to explain how they support the thesis • a clear and logical organizational structure • precise language and domain-specific vocabulary • a formal and objective style • a concluding statement that supports the thesis and summarizes the topic • a works cited page	**Beginner** **Coach the Reading.** While other students read, annotate, and discuss the text independently, work with Beginning students as they listen to the audio of the text and use the Model glossary on the Access 1 handout. Coach students in articulating their questions for the group and in highlighting and annotating the text using the Annotation Guide on the Access 1 handout. **Intermediate** **Listen to the Audio.** Have Intermediate students listen to the audio of the text and use the Model glossary on the Access 2 handout to help them with words or idioms that may be unfamiliar. If students need help with annotating the text, have them use the Annotation Guide on the Access 2 handout. After working with the Beginning students, you may wish to check this group's progress and provide support as needed.

Core Path	Access Path
Remind students that one goal of an informative research paper writing is to convey information to the reader using credible sources. Ask students to go through the Student Model and indicate all of the phrases and sentences where the writer is conveying information from documented sources.	**Advanced** **Pair with Proficient Peers.** Have Advanced students work with English-proficient peers to read, annotate, and discuss the text. You can also provide them with the Model glossary from the Access 3 handout if necessary. Have these student pairs use the Annotation Guide in the Access 3 handout to support them as they highlight and annotate the text. Encourage them to listen to the audio of the text if needed. **Approaching** **Use the Annotation Guide.** Have students use the Annotation Guide on the Access 4 handout to support them as they highlight and annotate the text.
	Extend **Reread and Highlight.** Have students reread the prompt and take notes about what it requires. Then have students reread the Student Model research paper "The Making of *Pride and Prejudice*: The Life and Times of Jane Austen" and consider how well it meets the requirements of the prompt. As students reread, have them use one color to highlight areas where the essay answers the prompt well and another color to mark the places where the Model needs more support to meet the requirements of the prompt.
Discuss. In small groups or pairs, have students discuss the observations and annotations they made while reading. Have them examine the "Constructed Response—Informative/Explanatory" grading rubric this Student Model was written to satisfy. Inform students that this is the same rubric that will be used to evaluate their completed Informative/Explanatory Extended Writing Project. They should consider how understanding the Student Model can help them as they begin their own essay in response to the prompt.	**English Learners All Levels & Approaching** Use the extra time while on- and beyond-grade-level students are discussing their first reads of the text to work individually and in small groups with English Learners and Approaching readers as outlined above. Should those students complete their first reads quickly, integrate them into the on- and beyond-grade-level discussion groups. Otherwise English Learners and Approaching readers will be given an opportunity to participate in text discussions with their peers in future extended writing project lessons.

3. THINK

Core Path	Access Path
Answer and Discuss. Have students complete the Think questions. Collect papers or discuss answers as a class. Refer to the sample answers at the end of the lesson plan online.	**Beginner** **Answer Questions with Support.** Review all of the Think questions with students to clarify vocabulary and comprehension. Read question 1 aloud. Then, ask students to look at the first paragraph and identify the main idea (Jane Austen's writing was influenced by her family background and by the literary movement of Realism.) and the sentence where it is located (last sentence in the introduction). Once you've completed this instruction with students, have them complete the remaining Think questions using the sentence frames on their Access 1 handout. **Intermediate** **Support.** Have partners review the Think questions and help one another with any terms or concepts that need to be clarified. Tell them that they may ask you about any vocabulary or concepts they cannot clarify for themselves, and then have them use the sentence frames on their Access 2 handout to assist them in writing the answers to the questions. **Advanced** **Discuss.** Have students read and answer the Think questions independently. Then have them discuss their answers to questions with an English-proficient partner. Have them share the ideas they want to develop into their own essay, the reasons why these ideas are interesting to them, and what sources are available. They can take notes on their discussion and save them for their prewrite. **Approaching** **Rewrite the Think Questions.** Preview the Think questions and ask students to rewrite each question in their own words on the Access 4 handout. Have students use their paraphrased versions of the Think questions to help them respond. Sample answers to the Think questions are located at the end of the lesson plan online.

Core Path	Access Path
	Extend **Freewrite and Discuss.** Ask students the following questions and have them freewrite their responses: • What is the purpose of writing a research paper about a literary figure or text? • What sorts of information do you hope to learn through your research on this topic? • When you research a literary topic, what kinds of information will be more helpful than others? Where should you start looking for information? After students finish writing, discuss their responses as a class.

EXTENDED WRITING PROJECT: Prewrite

OVERVIEW

This lesson asks students to complete a prewriting activity in preparation for writing their informative research papers. Students will come up with a list of research questions and then brainstorm credible sources that should help them answer these questions. A Six-Circles Graphic Organizer will help them make sure they address each part of the research paper prompt as they complete their prewriting activities.

OBJECTIVES

1. Demonstrate understanding of features of informative research paper writing.
2. Analyze the prompt and generate information for an informative research paper.
3. Participate effectively in a range of conversations and collaborations to express ideas and build upon the ideas of others.

ELA Common Core Standards:
Reading: Informational Text - RI.11-12.1
Writing - W.11-12.2.A, W.11-12.2.B, W.11-12.4, W.11-12.5, W.11-12.10
Speaking & Listening - SL.11-12.1.A, SL.11-12.1.B, SL.11-12.1.C, SL.11-12.1.D

RESOURCES

Grade 12, Unit 4 Extended Writing Project: Prewrite lesson
Graphic Organizer: Six-Circles web
Access 1 handout (Beginner)
Access 2 handout (Intermediate)

1. WRITE

Core Path	Access Path

Core Path

Brainstorm. Ask students to complete a Six-Circles Graphic Organizer using research questions that will help them answer the prompt.

1. To the side of the web, ask students to identify an author and text from the unit they would like to research.
2. Next, ask students to write research questions about the author's life in two of the smaller circles. Under the questions, have students list what kinds of sources might help them find the answers to their questions.
3. In the four remaining smaller circles, have students write research questions about the author's time period and the literary movement with which his or her work is associated. Under these questions, ask students to list what kind of source might help them find the answers.
4. Last, ask students to write at least one research question that links the text to the author's life, time period, and/or literary movement. Under this question, have them write a quotation from the chosen text that helps them draw this connection.

Discuss with students the questions they will answer in the prewriting activity to generate ideas for their own writing:

- What life events might affect an author's writing?
- What historical events might inspire a writer?
- What are the characteristics of the literary movement with which the author is associated? How are they seen in the text?
- What kinds of print sources might help you answer your research questions?
- What kinds of digital sources might help you answer your research questions?
- How do you know if a source is credible?

Remind students to consider every part of the prompt as they brainstorm.

Access Path

Beginner & Intermediate
Organize and Support the Prewrite.

1. Pair students with proficient English speakers or put them in small mixed-proficiency groups.
2. Assign each group a different author to examine, and have them complete a prewriting brainstorm chart for that author.
3. Have all groups display their brainstorm charts so that all students can then draw from the complete collection of information for their essays (note: Beginning & Intermediate students can then use the Prewrite sentence frames on the Access 1 and 2 handouts to complete their prewrite for the author they wish to write about).
4. Read aloud the example for Jane Austen provided on the Access 1 and 2 handouts. Pause after each section to clarify any concepts related to the content or writing as necessary. Explain that they will use the completed section on Jane Austen as a model for their own prewrite.
5. Have students choose the author they will research and identify research questions in the brainstorm chart. Provide assistance for their writing as necessary (note: In the Plan Lesson they will use these questions as they write their Essay Road Map).

Advanced
Share and Evaluate. Ask partners to share and evaluate their finished brainstorm charts with an English-proficient partner. Have them discuss their research questions and help one another generate additional questions they might have missed before they move on to do their prewrite.

Core Path	Access Path

Review. Once students complete their writing assignment, they should submit substantive feedback to three peers. Students will use the feedback to develop their writing in different stages of the writing process.
 	
Project these instructions for the peer review onto the board and review them with your class, so they know what they are looking for when they begin to provide their classmates with feedback:
• How well did your peer's research questions address the prompt?
    • How well did the research questions address the author's life?
    • How well did the research questions address the author's time period?
    • How well did the research questions address the literary movement with which the author is associated?
• Can you think of any additional questions that may help your peer conduct research? If so, what suggestions can you make?
• How credible and useful are the possible sources your peer listed? Can you think of any other kinds of sources that might be helpful?	

	Extend **Predict.** Have students work in small groups to predict problems they might face in their research. Have them compile a short list and then brainstorm strategies they might use to solve these problems.

BLAST: Audience, Purpose, and Style

OVERVIEW

Students will learn about achieving the appropriate audience, purpose, and style for their informative research papers. They will examine an example from the Student Model essay and then consider how a formal style and objective tone help writers of informative research papers achieve their purpose for writing.

OBJECTIVES

1. Discuss and demonstrate understanding of audience and purpose when writing an informative/ explanatory text, including a research paper.
2. Practice concrete strategies for identifying audience, purpose, and style in a research paper.
3. Write in order to determine audience, purpose, and style for an informative/explanatory research paper.

ELA Common Core Standards:
Reading: Informational Text - RI.11-12.1
Writing - W.11-12.2.E, W.11-12.4, W.11-12.5, W.11-12.6, W.11-12.10
Speaking & Listening - SL.11-12.1.A, SL.11-12.B, SL.11-12.1.C, SL.11-12.1.D

RESOURCES

Access 1 handout (Beginner)
Access 2 handout (Intermediate)
Access 4 handout (Approaching)

TITLE/DRIVING QUESTION

Core Path	Access Path
Read and Discuss. As a class, read aloud the title and driving question for this Blast: How does using a formal style and objective tone help writers achieve their purpose and reach an audience? Ask students to explain their understanding audience, purpose, and style and how they are related. Next, have them discuss how learning about these aspects of writing might apply to writing an informative research paper. Remind students that they should not immediately enter a reply to this question. They'll be returning to this question after they've read and discussed the Background information.	**English Learners All Levels** **Discuss a Visual.** Have students view a photograph of a formal interview, such as the one between Katie Couric and President Obama at http://tinyurl.com/ndo7qkw. Discuss how their clothing and body language reflects style and tone, prompting students with questions such as: • What is happening in this photo? • Is this a formal or informal situation? How do you know? • How might this interview be different if the interviewer were wearing a T-shirt and jeans? Why would that be inappropriate for a meeting with the president? • Why might using an objective tone be important in an interview? How would it help the interviewer achieve her goals?
Draft. In their notebooks or on scrap paper, have students draft their initial responses to the driving question for this Blast: How does using a formal style and objective tone help writers achieve their purpose and reach an audience? This will provide them with a baseline response that they will be developing as they gain more information about the topic in the Background section of the assignment.	**Beginner & Intermediate** **Draft with Sentence Frame.** When drafting their initial response to the driving question, have students refer to this Blast sentence frame on their Access 1 and 2 handouts: • A formal style and objective tone helps writers by / because ____________________. Point out these two key features of the sentence frame: 1. The introductory clause "A formal style and objective tone helps writers" borrows language directly from the Blast driving question to provide a response. 2. Ask students to make special note of the choice "by / because," which invites them to list a way or reasons why using a formal style and objective tone helps writers achieve their purpose and reach an audience.

BACKGROUND

Core Path	Access Path
Read. Have students read the Blast background to provide context for the driving question: How does using a formal style and objective tone help writers achieve their purpose and reach an audience?	**Beginner & Intermediate** **Read with Support.** Have students read the Blast background to provide context for the driving question. When they encounter unfamiliar words or phrases, have students refer to the glossary on their Access 1 and 2 handouts. If there are unfamiliar words that are not included in their glossary, encourage students to check a dictionary or online reference tool, like http://dictionary.reference.com. **Approaching** **Read and Summarize.** Have students read the Blast background to provide context for the driving question. As they read, ask students to complete the fill-in-the-blanks summary of the background provided on their Access 4 handout. When they encounter unfamiliar words or phrases, have students refer to the glossary on their Access 4 handout.
Discuss. Pair students and have them discuss the following questions: 1. Why does a writer need to think about audience, purpose, and style before he or she begins writing? (e.g., Audience, purpose, and style help writers determine why they are writing and what they need to write in order to achieve that purpose.) 2. What is the purpose of an informative research paper? (to explain or inform) 3. Why do writers of informative research papers need to think about their audience as they write? (They need to consider what their audience already knows, what they need to tell their audience, and any questions their audience may have.)	**Beginner** **Discuss.** Pair Beginning with Advanced (or Beyond) students and have them use the dialogue starter on their Access 1 handout to discuss the topic. Advise them to return to the dialogue and switch roles if they get stuck. **Intermediate** **Discuss.** Pair Intermediate with Advanced (or Beyond) students and have them use the dialogue starter on their Access 2 handout to discuss the topic. Advise them to return to the dialogue and switch roles if they get stuck. If their conversation is progressing smoothly, encourage them to continue the discussion beyond the dialogue starter sheet. They can expand their conversations to discuss other ways style and tone affect writing.

Core Path	Access Path
4. How does a writer go about choosing the appropriate style for writing? (by choosing the style that fits their audience and purpose) Why are a formal style and an objective tone appropriate for an informative research paper? (It helps a writer give information clearly and effectively.)	

Brainstorm. Remind students about the driving question for this Blast: How does using a formal style and objective tone help writers achieve their purpose and reach an audience?

In their notebooks, ask students to make three columns: one marked "Style/Tone," one labeled "Effect on Audience," and one titled "Effective for Informative Research Paper?" Have students start with the Style/Tone column and list different styles and tones that they might use when writing. Then have them fill in the effect such a style or tone might have on their audience. Last, have them write whether or not that style or tone would be effective for an informative research paper and why. Here's a short example of how this might look:

Style/Tone	Effect on Audience	Effective for Informative Research Paper?
figurative or sensory use of language	draws audience's attention by engaging their imagination or senses	Not usually; since sensory language is usually used to entertain, it would inform only if the writer wanted to help create an atmosphere of an author's world, for example.

Core Path	Access Path
<table><tr><td>technical language used</td><td>establishes the authority of the writer</td><td>Yes, using technical language specific to a topic provides information and could show audiences that the writer knows what he or she is talking about.</td></tr></table>	

QUIKPOLL

Core Path	Access Path
Participate. Answer the poll question. Have students discuss their reasons for the answers they gave. Students should refer to evidence from the Background to defend their answers. Remind students to follow the rules for collegial discussions.	

NUMBER CRUNCH

Core Path	Access Path
Predict, Discuss, and Click. Before students click on the number, break them into pairs and have them make predictions about what they think the number is related to. After they've clicked the number, ask students if they are surprised by the revealed information.	

CREATE YOUR BLAST

Core Path	Access Path
Blast. Ask students to write their Blast response in 140 characters or less, answering the driving question: How does using a formal style and objective tone help writers achieve their purpose and reach an audience?	**Beginner** **Blast with Support.** Have students refer back to the sentence frame on their Access 1 handout that they used to create their original Blast draft. Ask them to use this frame to write and enter their final Blast. **Intermediate** **Blast with Support.** Have students attempt to draft their Blast without the sentence frame on their Access 2 handout. If students struggle to compose their Blast draft without the sentence frame, remind them to reference it for support. **Beyond** **Write a Claim.** Ask students to use their answer to the poll question to write a strong claim that could be used as the foundation for a piece of argumentative writing. Once students have written their claims, ask them to read the claims to a small group of their peers. This activity will provide them practice writing claims, as well as expose them to claims written by their peers.
Review. After students have completed their own Blasts, ask them to review the Blasts of their peers and provide feedback.	
	Extend **Discuss.** As a whole class or in groups, identify a few strong Blasts and discuss what made those responses so powerful. As a group, analyze and discuss what characteristics make a Blast interesting or effective.
	Extend **Revise.** Resend a second version of this Blast assignment to your students and have them submit revised versions of their original Blasts. Do the same responses make the Top 10? How have the answers improved from the first submissions?

SKILL: Research and Note-Taking

OVERVIEW

This lesson provides students with an overview of research and note-taking practices. Students will review how the writer of the Student Model informative research paper made source cards and turned note cards into a body paragraph. Then they will practice writing their own source cards and note cards.

OBJECTIVES

1. Demonstrate an understanding of informative/explanatory writing: research and note-taking.
2. Identify and practice concrete strategies for developing research and note-taking skills.
3. Participate effectively in a range of conversations and collaborations to express ideas and build upon the ideas of others.

ELA Common Core Standards:
Reading: Informational Text - RI.11-12.1
Writing - W.11-12.2.B, W.11-12.5, W.11-12.7, W.11-12.8, W.11-12.10
Speaking & Listening - SL.11-12.1.A, SL.11-12.1.B, SL.11-12.1.C, SL.11-12.1.D

RESOURCES

Access 1 handout (Beginner)
Access 2 handout (Intermediate)
Access 3 handout (Advanced)
Access 4 handout (Approaching)

1. DEFINE

Core Path	Access Path
Read and Discuss. 1. Either individually or as a class, read the Define section of the lesson. 2. Ask students to take notes on the most important elements of research and note-taking. 3. Then in small groups or as a class ask students to discuss the purpose of research and note-taking. Give them time to discuss these questions: What is the purpose of conducting research and taking notes when preparing to write an informative research paper? (to find information to support the topic of the paper) What is the most important thing to keep in mind when researching? (Answers will vary but should include any of the following: reliable sources, variety of sources, unbiased research, enough information, or other similar examples.)	**Beginner** **In Your Own Words.** Have students read the definition and then use their Access 1 handouts to pause after each bullet point to rewrite the components of research and note-taking in their own words. Once students have completed this activity, ask them to complete the fill-in-the-blanks activity on the Access 1 handout. **Intermediate** **In Your Own Words.** Have students read the definition of research and note-taking and then use their Access 2 handout to pause after each bullet point to rewrite the components of research and note-taking in their own words. After they've rewritten each of the bullet points in their words, work with students to develop their own definitions of the term. **Advanced** **In Your Own Words.** Have Advanced students read the definition and then discuss what they have learned about research and note-taking with an English-proficient partner or in mixed-proficiency groups. After their conversation, have Advanced students write the definition of research and note-taking on the Access 3 handout. **Approaching** **Restate the Definition.** Have students read the define section and then use their Access 4 handouts to restate the most important points in their own words. Clarify questions to aid students' comprehension as needed. Then have students participate in mixed-level groups with the class to discuss the purpose of research and note-taking in the development of an essay.

Core Path	Access Path
	Beyond **Jigsaw.** If students have extra time, put them in small groups and have each group brainstorm the last time they took notes about something. Remind students that taking notes is not exclusive to school projects. The last time they took notes might have been related to driving directions or planning an activity. Then have students discuss. • Do they think of that activity as taking notes? • If not, why not? How is it different from what they think of as note-taking? • Did the research involve any research or sourcing? If not, why not? Allow each group time to share their findings with the class.
	Extend **Debate.** Put students into small groups and give them a few minutes to debate the following question: • When researching, can you ever have too many notes? Then, as a class, discuss their responses and have them explain why or why not.

2. MODEL

Core Path	Access Path
Read and Discuss. 1. Ask students to look over the source cards and note cards for the Student Model essay "The Making of *Pride and Prejudice*." 2. In small groups, have students review the second paragraph of the Student Model essay and consider how well the writer incorporated his or her notes into the essay. • Does this writer use his or her notes effectively? Why or why not? • Based on the writer's note cards, what would you add, change, or remove to improve this paragraph?	**Beginner, Intermediate & Approaching** **Underline Key Words.** Have students look closely at the Student Model note cards alongside the paragraph from the Student Model paper on the Access 1, 2, and 4 handouts. Then ask them to find and underline words and phrases in the paragraph that are based on the research recorded on the note cards. Explain that they can follow this model when they conduct their own research and compose their own papers. **Advanced** **Identify the Parts.** Have students read the note cards and paragraph from the Student Model essay and answer the questions on the Access 3 handout. Once they've completed the questions, pair Advanced students with more proficient students to allow them to share their answers.
Practice. 1. Ask students to create four source cards and four note cards using sources they plan to use in their informative research papers. As they find sources, they may want to reference the research questions they generated for the Six-Circles Graphic Organizer they completed during the Prewrite lesson. 2. Once students have completed their source and note cards, they will need to provide their peers with constructive feedback. 3. Students should use their peers' feedback as they continue to research their topic.	**Beginner** **Find a Source and Take Notes.** 1. Pair students and have pairs work together to come up with search terms related to their essay topic. Then have pairs help each other evaluate source material for credibility. If necessary, direct students to reliable sources related to their chosen texts or topics. 2. Once students have found a reliable source with relevant information, have them complete the Finish the Sentences activity on the Access 1 handout to record their information and source material. Students can use these frames for all their note cards. 3. After students have answered the questions, ask them to discuss with their partner what information they found and how it relates to their topic. Encourage partners to give each other feedback on the paraphrases.

Core Path	Access Path
	Intermediate **Finish the Sentences.** Have students fill in the sentence frames in the Apply section of the Access 2 handout. Review their answers with them, and after making any clarifications needed, allow them to join Advanced students to discuss and edit their note cards. **Advanced** **Clarify and Edit.** Have students refer to their Prewrite Worksheet and the writing prompt as they come up with ideas for research. Once they have their note cards completes, have them read their notes aloud to another Intermediate or Advanced student to check for language that needs to be clarified and to answer the following questions: • Have you used quotation marks for any exact quotations? • Did you include all of the essential information? • Is the information relevant to the topic? • Did you record complete source information? Allow students time to make edits to their note cards as necessary. **Approaching** **Finish the Sentences** 1. Before they begin their research, encourage students to work with a partner to come up with strong search terms. 2. Once they have search terms, have them complete the sentences on the Access 4 handout to guide their note-taking. Pair students and have them explain why the information they found relates to their topic.

Core Path	Access Path
	Extend **Take Notes.** If students have extra time, have them make a note card for their chosen author's selection from the unit. Ask students to reread the selection and highlight the key words, phrases, or quotations they might use in their own research papers. Then have students record the words, phrases, and quotations they've highlighted and take notes about how they might incorporate them into their papers.
	Extend **Write.** Create four source cards and four note cards that properly record quoted or paraphrased information from four sources. When you are finished, trade with a partner and offer each other feedback. Do the cards contain all of the necessary source information? Do direct quotes appear in quotations? Do the notes make it clear why your peer has included the information? Offer each other suggestions, and remember that they are most helpful when they are constructive.
	Extend **Tech Infusion** **Note-Taking.** Ask students to use a word-processing program, such as Google Docs, or a note-taking application, such as Evernote, to take notes on the four sources they chose to use for the Practice activity. Then divide students into pairs and have them discuss the benefits and drawbacks of online note-taking compared to making note cards.

3. YOUR TURN

Core Path	Access Path
Assess and Explain. Have students answer the comprehension questions to test for understanding. Share the explanations for Parts A and B (located online) with your students.	
	Extend **Pair and Share.** After completing the assessment, put students in pairs and ask them to discuss the Your Turn questions. • Did they struggle with either question? • What strategies did they use to figure out the answers? • Do they have any additional questions about the Your Turn activity?

SKILL:
Thesis Statement

OVERVIEW

As students move toward the planning stage of their Extended Writing Project, they'll need to think about a thesis statement for their informative research papers. This lesson provides students with a definition of thesis statement and its purpose. Students will analyze and critique the thesis statement in the Student Model. Then they will practice writing a thesis statement for their informative research papers.

OBJECTIVES

1. Demonstrate an understanding of informative/explanatory writing: thesis statements.
2. Identify and practice concrete strategies for writing a strong thesis statement.
3. Participate effectively in a range of conversations and collaborations to express ideas and build upon the ideas of others.

ELA Common Core Standards:
Reading: Informational Text - RI.11-12.1
Writing - W.11-12.2.A, W.11-12.5, W.11-12.10
Speaking & Listening - SL.11-12.1.A, SL.11-12.1.C, SL.11-12.1.D

RESOURCES

Access 1 handout (Beginner)
Access 2 handout (Intermediate)
Access 3 handout (Advanced)
Access 4 handout (Approaching)

1. DEFINE

Core Path	Access Path
Read and Discuss. 1. Either individually or as a class, read the Define section of the lesson. 2. Ask students to take notes on the most important elements of a thesis statement. 3. Then in small groups or as a class ask students to discuss the purpose of the thesis statement in an essay. Give them time to discuss this question: What is the purpose of the thesis statement in an informative research paper? (It introduces the topic and previews what the writer is going to explore in the paper based on research.) What makes the thesis statement of an informative research paper different from the thesis statement of an argumentative essay? (Answers will vary but should include the idea that the main difference has to do with the writer's purpose. The thesis statement of an informative research paper focuses on ideas that a writer will explore and explain, whereas a thesis statement for an argumentative essay states something the writer will prove and defend.)	**Beginner** **In Your Own Words.** Have students read the definition and then use their Access 1 handouts to pause after each bullet point to rewrite the components of a thesis statement in their own words. Once students have completed this activity, ask them to complete the fill-in-the-blanks activity on the Access 1 handout. **Intermediate** **In Your Own Words.** Have students read the definition of a thesis statement and then use their Access 2 handout to pause after each bullet point to rewrite the components of a thesis statement in their own words. After they've rewritten each of the bullet points in their words, work with students to develop their own definitions of the term. **Advanced** **In Your Own Words.** Have Advanced students read and then discuss what they have learned about thesis statements with an English-proficient partner or in mixed-proficiency groups. After their conversation, have Advanced students write the definition of thesis statement on the Access 3 handout. **Approaching** **Restate the Definition.** Have students read the Define section and then use their Access 4 handouts to restate the most important points in their own words. Clarify questions to aid students' comprehension as needed. Then have students participate in mixed-level groups with the class to discuss the purpose of a thesis statement in an essay.

Core Path	Access Path
	Beyond **Jigsaw.** If students have extra time, put them in small groups and give each group a body paragraph from an essay. Then challenge them to work together to write a thesis statement in the text they are assigned. • How did you determine what the thesis statement should be? • What challenges did you face in writing a thesis statement for a body paragraph? Allow each group time to share their findings with the class.
	Extend **Freewrite.** Ask students to define thesis statement in their own words and freewrite about why a thesis statement for an informative research paper is similar to and different from one for an argument.

2. MODEL

Core Path	Access Path
Read and Discuss. 1. Ask students to read the Model section of the lesson, including the introduction to the Student Model research paper "The Making of *Pride and Prejudice:* The Life and Times of Jane Austen." Have them highlight the original thesis statement and use the annotation tool to label it. ("A look at Austen's biography and a short overview of literary realism provide helpful context for better understanding this novel.") Also have them highlight and label the revised thesis statement that is suggested in the Model. ("A look at Jane Austen's biography and a short overview of literary realism can give readers insight into characterization in *Pride and Prejudice*.")	**Beginner, Intermediate & Approaching** **Underline Key Words.** Have students look closely at the writing prompt alongside the Student Model thesis statement on the Access 1, 2, and 4 handouts. Students may use the Model Glossary to help them with words or idioms that may be unfamiliar. Then ask them to find and underline words and phrases in the thesis statement of the Student Model that directly respond to the writing prompt, such as "literary realism," which refers to one of the "literary movements" of the prompt. After underlining the phrase, students should write which elements of the prompt their annotation relates back to. Explain that they can use the writing prompt as a guide for formatting their own thesis statement when they write their essay.

Core Path	Access Path
1. Then, as a class, discuss the following questions: • What positive feedback would you give the writer of the Student Model essay for his or her original thesis statement? (It lists three key parts of the prompt: the author, the literary movement, and historical context.) • What constructive criticism would you give the writer? (The thesis statement could be more specific and explain how this information will help readers understand the text.) • Do you agree that the revised thesis statement would help strengthen the introduction of the research paper? Why or why not? Do you have another suggestion? (Answers will vary but should include a sample thesis statement that connects to the information that follows in the Student Model, unless students have suggestions for revisions tied to the new thesis statement.)	**Advanced** **Identify the Parts.** Have students read the Student Model thesis statement and answer the questions on the Access 3 handout. Once they've completed the questions, pair Advanced students with more proficient students to allow them to share their answers.
Practice. 1. Ask students to review the prompt for the Extended Writing Project and the skill definition of "thesis statement" before they draft a thesis statement for their own informative research papers. Remind them to use all of their prewriting notes and research to guide their writing. 2. Remind students that they will be able to use either this thesis statement or a revised version when they write their research papers. 3. Students can complete this draft of their thesis statement on paper, or you can create a write assignment on StudySync, and they can submit their drafts online for anonymous peer review.	**Beginner** **Write Your Thesis.** 1. Prior to having them write their thesis statements, ask students to complete the sentence frames on the Access 1 handout. 2. After students have answered the questions, ask them to discuss with a partner what they plan to write about, clarifying any language as needed before writing their thesis statements. 3. Then students should write their own thesis statements using language from the writing prompt in their thesis. Encourage them to refer back to the writing prompt and to the Prewrite Worksheet they completed. 4. Have them use the fill-in-the-blanks thesis statement in the Access 1 handout to help them write their thesis statement.

Core Path	Access Path
	Intermediate **Finish Sentences.** Have students fill in the sentence frames in the Apply section of the Access 2 handout. Review their answers with them, and after making any clarifications needed, allow them to use their answers to craft their thesis statements. Then allow them to join Advanced students to discuss and edit their thesis statements. If needed, students may use the fill-in-the-blanks thesis statement in the Access 2 handout for additional support. **Advanced** **Clarify and Edit.** Have students refer to their Prewrite Worksheet and the writing prompt as they write their thesis statements. Have them read their statement aloud to another Intermediate or Advanced student to check for language that needs to be clarified and to answer the following questions: • Have you made a clear statement about your central idea? • Where do you let the reader know what to expect in the body of the research paper? • Did you respond fully and completely to the prompt? • Have you used grammar such as pronouns, prepositions, and subject/verb agreement correctly? Allow students time to make edits to their thesis statements as necessary. **Approaching** **Finish the Sentences & Complete the Fill-in-the-Blanks Thesis.** 1. Prior to having them write their thesis statements, ask students to complete the sentence frames on the Access 4 handout.

Core Path	Access Path
	2. Once they have completed the statements with the information they plan to write about, allow them to use the fill-in-the-blanks thesis statement provided on the Access 4 handout to construct a thesis. Remind students to complete the missing parts of the fill-in-the-blanks thesis with information they plan to write about in their own essays. Additionally, you may want to explain that they should complete the first blanks with the title of the text they plan to write about and its author's name. The next blank should identify an element or elements of that author's life or time period that affected that text. Then the final blank should identify how that text reflects the literary movement with which that author or work is associated.
	Extend **Write.** Write a thesis statement for your informative research paper that articulates your central idea in relation to the essay prompt. When you are finished, trade with a partner and offer each other feedback. How clear is the writer's main point or idea? Is it obvious what this paper will focus on? Does it specifically address all aspects of the prompt? Offer each other suggestions, and remember that they are most helpful when they are constructive.
	Extend **Tech Infusion** **Reread and Rewrite.** If students have extra time, have them reread the entire Student Model informative research paper, using the annotation tool to trace the writer's main ideas. Then have them work with a partner to draft a new thesis statement that better reflects how the writer uses information in the paper. Have groups share their revisions with the class and discuss the changes they made.

Core Path	Access Path
	Extend **Tech Infusion.** Ask students to share their revised thesis statements using a shared TodaysMeet back channel. Project the back channel onto the board and discuss the thesis statements as a class. • What do students notice about the thesis statements? Are there commonalities? • Which thesis statements are particularly effective? Why? What elements make them strong?

3. YOUR TURN

Core Path	Access Path
Assess and Explain. Have students answer the comprehension questions to test for understanding. Share the explanations for Parts A and B (located online) with your students.	
	Extend **Pair and Share.** After completing the assessment, put students in pairs and ask them to discuss the Your Turn questions. • Did they struggle with either question? • What strategies did they use to figure out the answers? • Why might Churchill have included his thesis statement as the first sentence of the second paragraph? Does that strategy work for his speech?

SKILL:
Organize Informative Writing

OVERVIEW

As students research and gather evidence for their Extended Writing Project, they'll need to consider the manner in which they will organize information in their informative research papers. This lesson identifies the variety of structures that writers use to organize informative writing. Then students will identify and analyze the text structures used in the Student Model to apply to their own writing.

OBJECTIVES

1. Demonstrate an understanding of informative/explanatory writing: organize informative writing.
2. Identify and practice concrete strategies for organizing informative writing.
3. Participate effectively in a range of conversations and collaborations to express ideas and build upon the ideas of others.

ELA Common Core Standards:
Reading: Informational Text - RI.11-12.1, RI.11-12.5
Writing - W.11-12.2.A, W.11-12.5, W.11-12.7, W.11-12.10
Speaking & Listening - SL.11-12.1.A, SL.11-12.1.B, SL.11-12.1.C, SL.11-12.1.D

RESOURCES

Access 1 handout (Beginner)
Access 2 handout (Intermediate)
Access 3 handout (Advanced)
Access 4 handout (Approaching)

1. DEFINE

Core Path	Access Path
Read and Discuss. 1. Either individually or as a class, read the Define section of the lesson. 2. Ask students to take notes on the basic text structures used to organize informative writing. 3. Then in small groups or as a class ask students to discuss the purpose of organization in an essay. Give them time to discuss these questions: What is the purpose of organizing information in an informative research paper? (to structure the information in a clear and logical manner) How do text structures serve this purpose? (Text structures provide a common template for writing that helps both writers and readers understand the connections between ideas.)	**Beginner** **In Your Own Words.** Have students read the definition and then use their Access 1 handouts to pause after each bullet point to rewrite the definition of organizing informational writing in their own words. Once students have completed this activity, ask them to complete the chart on the Access 1 handout. **Intermediate** **In Your Own Words.** Have students read the definition of organizing informative writing and then use their Access 2 handouts to pause after each bullet point to rewrite the components of organizing informative writing in their own words. After they've rewritten each of the bullet points in their own words, work with students to develop their own definitions of the term. **Advanced** **In Your Own Words.** Have Advanced students read and then discuss what they have learned about organizing informative writing with an English-proficient partner or in mixed-proficiency groups. After their conversation, have Advanced students write the definition of organizing informative writing on the Access 3 handout. **Approaching** **Restate the Definition.** Have students read the Define section and then use their Access 4 handouts to restate the most important points in their own words. Clarify questions to aid students' comprehension as needed. Then have students participate in mixed-level groups with the class to discuss organizing informative writing.

Core Path	Access Path
	Beyond **Jigsaw.** If students have extra time, put them in small groups and assign each group an informational text structure: chronological, sequential, cause and effect, and compare and contrast. Then challenge them to work together to identify as many texts they can that use their structure. Students should think about texts they've read in this unit or other classes, or genres that often use the structure. • Is there one clear structure in each text? If a text mixes structures, is it successful? Why? • How does the structure support the author's purpose? Would another structure have worked equally well, or better? Allow each group time to share their findings with the class.
	Extend **Tech Infusion** **Compare and Contrast.** Draw the following chart on the board. Then ask volunteers to fill out the empty boxes. In the "Description" column, they should describe the characteristics of each structure. In the "Type of Text" box, they should write a type of text (i.e., recipe, biography, literary analysis) that could use each structure. Encourage students to include each type of text under multiple structures, if applicable. Then discuss the advantages and disadvantages of each text structure.

Text Structure	Description	Type of Text
Chronological		
Sequential		
Cause and Effect		
Compare and Contrast		

2. MODEL

Core Path	Access Path
Read and Discuss. 1. First, have students reread the prompt for the Extended Writing Project and then ask them to identify the type of organizational structure they think might work best to answer the prompt. (Answers may vary. Students are likely to choose chronological, sequential, or cause and effect.) 2. Then ask students to read the Model section of the lesson that analyzes the organizational structure of "The Making of *Pride and Prejudice*: The Life and Times of Jane Austen." Have students identify the different text structures the writer uses throughout the paper. 3. Last, in small groups ask students to discuss the following questions: • Overall, does the writer of "The Making of *Pride and Prejudice*: The Life and Times of Jane Austen" blend informational structures effectively? Why or why not? • Where in the paper does the writer organize information most clearly? • How does the writer indicate when information is based on research? • Where could the organization be improved?	**Beginner, Intermediate & Approaching** **Analyze the Model.** Have students read the sentences from "The Making of *Pride and Prejudice*: The Life and Times of Jane Austen" in the chart on their Access 1, 2, and 4 handouts. They may use the Glossary to help them with words or idioms that may be unfamiliar. Then ask them to write a word or phrase from the sentence that signals a specific kind of text structure. Finally have them identify the text structure and explain how that word or phrase signals it. When students have finished the chart, pair students with more proficient peers to discuss how the different text structures work together to support the main ideas of the essay. **Advanced** **Analyze the Model.** Have students read the excerpt from "The Making of *Pride and Prejudice*: The Life and Times of Jane Austen" and answer the questions on the Access 3 handout. Once they've completed the questions, pair Advanced students with more proficient students to allow them to share their answers.
Practice. 1. Ask students to complete a short writing assignment and apply the skills they have learned for organizing informative writing. 2. Before students write an outline for organizing information, review with them both the writing prompt and the definition of organize informative/explanatory writing. Then have students locate their prewriting, thesis statements, and the note cards and source cards they created based on their research.	**Beginner** **Choose an Organizational Structure.** 1. Prior to having students choose an organizational structure, review the structure options from the definition and explain how each could support an informative essay. 2. Then ask students to complete the sentence frames on the Access 1 handout. 3. After students have answered the questions, ask them to discuss with a partner how they plan to organize their writing. Have them give each other feedback or suggest other options if applicable.

Core Path	Access Path
3. Remind students that they will be able to use this initial outline or a revised version when they begin to plan their informative research papers. 4. Students can complete this draft of their outlines on paper, or you can create a write assignment on StudySync, and they can submit their drafts online for anonymous peer review.	**Intermediate & Approaching** **Finish Sentences.** Have students fill in the sentence frames in the Apply section of the Access 2 handout. Review their answers with them, and after making any clarifications needed, allow them to use their answers to choose a structure. Then allow them to join Advanced students to discuss and edit their sentence frames. **Advanced** **Clarify and Edit.** Have students refer to their Prewrite Worksheet and the writing prompt as they fill out their graphic organizer. Have them share their graphic organizer with another Intermediate or Advanced student to check for language that needs to be clarified and to answer the following questions: • Have you made the relationship between your ideas clear? • What does a reader need to know to help them understand your ideas? Allow students time to make edits to their graphic organizers as necessary.
	Extend **Plan.** Encourage students to think about the structure they will use to write their own informative research papers. Pair students with a partner who has chosen the same author and ask them to discuss how to organize evidence effectively. Encourage them to consider how choosing a structure might reveal gaps in their research or analysis.

3. YOUR TURN

Core Path	Access Path
Assess and Explain. Have students answer the comprehension questions to test for understanding. Share the explanations for Parts A and B (located online) with your students.	
	Extend **Pair and Share.** After completing the assessment, put students in pairs and ask them to discuss the Your Turn questions. • Did they struggle with either question? • How could these paragraphs be rewritten to use a different structure? • Would the new structure be more or less effective than the current structure? Why?

SKILL:
Supporting Details

OVERVIEW

This lesson provides students with a definition of supporting details and an explanation of their use in developing a topic thoroughly. Students will analyze and critique the use of supporting details, including precise language, in the Student Model. Then they will fill out their own *Textual Evidence Charts* and practice analysis by making an inference based on supporting details that develop their own informative research papers.

OBJECTIVES

1. Demonstrate an understanding of informative/explanatory writing: supporting details.
2. Identify and practice concrete strategies for including relevant facts, extended definitions, and other concrete supporting details in an informative research paper.
3. Identify and practice concrete strategies for using precise language, domain-specific vocabulary, and techniques to manage the complexity of a research topic.
4. Participate effectively in a range of conversations and collaborations to express ideas and build upon the ideas of others.

ELA Common Core Standards:
Reading: Informational Text - RI.11-12.1
Writing - W.11-12.2.A, W.11-12.2.B, W.11-12.2.D, W.11-12.5, W.11-12.10
Speaking & Listening - SL.11-12.1.A, SL.11-12.1.C, SL.11-12.1.D

RESOURCES

Textual Evidence Chart
Access 1 handout (Beginner)
Access 2 handout (Intermediate)
Access 3 handout (Advanced)
Access 4 handout (Approaching)

1. DEFINE

Core Path	Access Path
Read and Discuss. 1. Either individually or as a class, read the Define section of the lesson. 2. Ask students to take notes on the role of supporting details in an informative piece of writing. 3. Then in small groups or as a class ask students to discuss the purpose of the supporting details in an essay. Give them time to discuss these questions: What are the various kinds of supporting evidence writers include to develop a topic? (Details include the most significant and relevant facts, extended definitions, concrete details, quotations, or other information, such as photographs, paintings, or other media, as appropriate to the audience and topic.) What is the purpose of supporting details in a research paper? (Details help the writer develop his or her thesis statement, support ideas, and demonstrate the level of research the writer has done.) What are some ways to manage a complex topic to make it more accessible to the audience? (Precise language, vocabulary specific to the subject, and techniques such as using metaphors, similes, and analogies can help make a topic clearer to readers.)	**Beginner** **In Your Own Words.** Have students read the definition and then use their Access 1 handouts to pause after each bullet point to rewrite the definition of supporting details in their own words. Once students have completed this activity, ask them to complete the fill-in-the-blanks activity on the Access 1 handout. **Intermediate** **In Your Own Words.** Have students read the definition of supporting details and then use their Access 2 handout to pause after each bullet point to rewrite the definition of supporting details in their own words. After they've rewritten each of the bullet points in their words, work with students to develop their own definitions of the term. **Advanced** **In Your Own Words.** Have Advanced students read the Define section and then discuss what they have learned about supporting details with an English-proficient partner or in mixed-proficiency groups. After their conversation, have Advanced students write the definition of supporting details on the Access 3 handout. **Approaching** **Restate the Definition.** Have students read the Define section and then use their Access 4 handouts to restate the most important points in their own words. Clarify questions to aid students' comprehension as needed. Then have students participate in mixed-level groups with the class to discuss the purpose of supporting details in an essay.

Core Path	Access Path
	Beyond **Brainstorm.** The definition says that students need to carefully evaluate information before using it in an essay. Have Beyond students work in groups to create a checklist that all students in the class can use to evaluate sources for their informational research essays. If available, have students create their checklist in a collaborative app like Google Docs. Allow each group time to share their checklist with the class.
	Extend **Tech Infusion** **Share and Discuss.** Put students into small groups based on the author they have chosen. Ask each group member to share one relevant supporting detail and one irrelevant detail he or she found while conducting research. Then have students discuss how they determined which details were relevant and which were not.

2. MODEL

Core Path	Access Path
Read and Discuss. 1. Ask students to examine the *Textual Evidence Chart* used by the writer of the Student Model "The Making of *Pride and Prejudice*: The Life and Times of Jane Austen." 2. In groups ask them to discuss the supporting details the writer chose and the inference he or she made: • What kinds of supporting details does the writer use? Are these supporting details relevant to the writer's thesis? Why or why not? • Based on these details, is the inference the writer made valid? Why or why not?	**Beginner, Intermediate & Approaching** **Fill in the Blanks.** Have students read the Identification and Application section. Then have them use that information to complete the fill-in-the-blanks activity on the Access 1, 2, and 4 handouts. When they have finished, create mixed-proficiency pairs and have students discuss how the textual evidence in the Identification and Application section and in the Model support the Student Model thesis statement. Beginning and Intermediate students can use the Glossary on their Access 1 and 2 handouts with any difficult vocabulary.

Core Path	Access Path
• What examples of precise language, domain-specific vocabulary, or techniques do you see in the evidence? How do these support the thesis?	**Advanced** **Explain the Evidence.** Have students read the paragraph from the Student Model and complete the chart on the Access 3 handout. Once they've completed the chart, pair Advanced students with more proficient students to allow them to share their answers.
Practice. 1. Ask students to fill out a *Textual Evidence Chart* with some of the quotations and other supporting details they might use to develop their informative research papers. Remind them to keep their thesis statements in mind as they choose the most relevant evidence. 2. Ask students to underline precise language and any domain-specific vocabulary in their evidence. If they don't see any, point out that as they continue doing research, they will want to look for such language to include in their writing. 3. Remind students that they can use the details from the *Textual Evidence Chart* to help them in the planning stage of their research papers. 4. Once students have completed their charts and made an inference using the supporting details they have chosen, they will need to provide their peers with constructive feedback. 5. Students should use their peers' feedback to improve their use of supporting details.	**Beginner** **Identify Supporting Details.** 1. Ask students to complete the sentence frames on the Access 1 handout to help them identify textual evidence for their essays. Encourage them to refer back to the writing prompt and to the Prewrite Worksheet and Organize Informational Writing handout they completed. 2. After students have completed the sentence frames, ask them to discuss their chosen details with a partner. Partners should provide feedback and help each other clarify their ideas. 3. After students have discussed their responses, have them transfer the best supporting details to their Textual Evidence Chart. **Intermediate** **Finish Sentences.** Have students fill in the sentence frames on the Access 2 handout. Review their answers with them, and after making any needed clarifications, allow them to join Advanced students to discuss and edit their supporting details. **Advanced** **Clarify and Edit.** Have students refer to their Prewrite Worksheet, thesis statement, and the writing prompt as they compile a list of supporting details. Have them share their lists with another Intermediate or Advanced student to answer the following questions: • Does every supporting detail relate to the thesis?

Core Path	Access Path
	• Which supporting details are weak? Is there another piece of evidence that might be better? • Are any supporting details irrelevant? Allow students time to make edits to their Textual Evidence Charts as necessary. **Approaching** **Identify Supporting Details.** 1. Ask students to complete the sentence frames on the Access 4 handout to help them start their list of supporting details. 2. Once they have completed the three statements with the information they plan to write about, allow them to use the blank spaces to continue adding supporting details that support their thesis statements before they complete the Textual Evidence chart.
	Extend **Evaluate Supporting Details.** 1. If students have extra time, have them reread the entire Student Model research paper "The Making of *Pride and Prejudice*: The Life and Times of Jane Austen" and evaluate the supporting details the author has used. 2. First, have students highlight relevant supporting details and use the annotation tool to take notes about why these details are helpful. 3. Then, have students read the essay again and look for irrelevant supporting details. Have students highlight these and use the annotation tool to comment on why these details could be cut from the paper.

Core Path	Access Path
	Extend **Write.** Using a Textual Evidence Chart like the one you have just studied, fill in information you've gathered about your chosen author's biography, time period, or literary movement. Then make an inference based on this information that supports your thesis statement. When you are finished, share your chart with a partner and evaluate each other's inferences. Is the inference logically drawn from the evidence presented? Is there any additional information that the writer could include to strengthen the support for the inference or thesis? Offer each other suggestions, and remember that they are most helpful when they are constructive.

3. YOUR TURN

Core Path	Access Path
Assess and Explain. Have students answer the comprehension questions to test for understanding. Share the explanations for Parts A and B (located online) with your students.	
	Extend **Pair and Share.** After completing the assessment, put students in pairs and ask them to discuss the Your Turn questions. • Did they struggle with either question? • What strategies did they use to figure out the answers? • What strategies are most useful when choosing supporting details that best support a thesis?

EXTENDED WRITING PROJECT:
Plan

OVERVIEW

This lesson asks students to plan the draft of their informative research paper by referencing their prewriting, thesis statements, research note cards, source cards, outlines, and their Textual Evidence Charts to help them create a road map for their papers. In this stage of the writing process, students will examine information they've collected in their research and analyze the relevance of the supporting details they have chosen and the organization they have used. Students will use the planning process to determine the direction of their writing and the quality of their research prior to drafting.

OBJECTIVES

1. Discuss and demonstrate understanding of organizing informative/explanatory writing.
2. Plan an informative research paper by ensuring that ideas, concepts, and information are organized logically and support a thesis statement.
3. Participate effectively in a range of conversations and collaborations to express ideas and build upon the ideas of others.

ELA Common Core Standards:
Reading: Informational Text - RI.11-12.1
Writing - W.11-12.2.A, W.11-12.2.B, W.11-12.4, W.11-12.5, W.11-12.6, W.11-12.7, W.11-12.8, W.11-12.9.B, W.11-12.10
Speaking & Listening - SL.11-12.1.A, SL.11-12.1.C

RESOURCES

Grade 12, Unit 4 Extended Writing Project: Plan lesson
Completed *Textual Evidence Chart*
Completed research note cards and source cards
Access 1 handout (Beginner)
Access 2 handout (Intermediate)
Access 4 handout (Approaching)

1. WRITE

Core Path

Discuss. Ask students to review their thesis statements, their audience and purpose, the supporting details they have gathered, and the characteristics of the organizational structure they plan to use in their informative research paper. Remind students of the research questions they generated in preparation for completing their prewriting assignment in the Prewrite lesson of the Extended Writing Project. Then ask them to consider the following questions:

- What is the topic of your research paper?
- How much does your audience know about the topic?
- What is your central idea or thesis?
- What are the sources of your information?
- How much research have you completed? Is there enough information to begin planning?
- When organizing the information, does comparing and contrasting ideas or information make sense?
- To develop the topic, is it helpful to recount events and facts in chronological order?
- Are there natural cause-and-effect relationships in your evidence?
- What kinds of supporting details and precise language will help your audience understand the research paper?

Allow time for students to share some of their answers to these questions and to begin planning their writing. Then point out that planning an informative research paper involves identifying as precisely as possible which information from sources, placed in their note cards, should be included in each paragraph of the writing. In planning, writers need to identify the topic of each of their paragraphs and ensure that their topics relate to their thesis statement. They also need to be certain that the information and details in each paragraph are relevant to and support that paragraph's topic.

Access Path

Beginner & Intermediate
Use Sentence Frames. Include Beginning and Intermediate students in the whole class discussion. Then work with small groups to discuss their own writing ideas using the following questions and sentences below:

- The main idea of my essay is ______________________________.
- What author and text will you write about? What literary movement do they relate to?
- Does that text relate to that author's life or time period? How?
- What are some key qualities of the literary movement? How does the text reflect those qualities?
- What details can you use to support your thesis?
- I plan to use a ____________________ organizational structure to write my essay.

Once they've had a chance to discuss their own ideas, ask them to complete the final sentence frame stating which organizational structure they think will work best for their essays.

Core Path	Access Path
Organize. Remind students to refer to their prewriting, thesis statements, research note cards, source cards, outlines, and Textual Evidence Charts to help them create a road map for their papers. As an alternative to plan their informative research papers, they may find that another organizer or an outline is a better fit for the writing structure they have planned. As they create the plan, remind students that other options include modifying the thesis statement, finding additional resources, changing the structure, or finding other supporting details to develop the thesis. Remind students to always keep their audience and purpose in mind.	**Note:** As the on- and beyond-grade level students begin the organization and writing stage of this lesson, support Beginning, Intermediate & Approaching students to ensure they understand what type of information they need to include in their essay road maps. **Beginner & Intermediate** **Preview Essay Road Map.** Give students the Research Paper Road Map on the Access 1 and 2 handouts, and explain what kind of information they will write in each section. Have them review their previously completed assignments to identify and underline information and details they can use in each section of their Research Paper Road Maps. **Approaching** **Use Organizational Supports.** Make sure students have access to all of their previous assignments to draw upon. Then give them the Research Paper Road Map on the Access 4 handout to structure their organization. Go over each of the categories. Explain that as they write they can add additional paragraphs as needed.
Write. Instruct students to refer to their thesis statements, notes, organizer(s), and other prewriting materials to complete the Research Paper Road Map or similar exercise and create a more detailed, in-depth plan for their informative research papers. Point out that, as they organize their ideas for the paper, students may find it necessary to structure their writing using a different strategy than they had originally planned to use. In that case, work with them to suggest various organizational tools they might use to plan and structure their ideas. Finally, have students make note of additional research they might do, as needed.	**Beginner & Intermediate** **Write and Discuss.** Remind students that they can use what they have underlined in the previous assignments, as well as the Research Paper Road Map on the Access 1 and 2 handouts, to plan their writing. Have partners or small groups discuss questions about the content of their completed Essay Road Maps such as: • What is your thesis? My thesis is ______________________. • What is the subject of this paragraph? The subject of this paragraph is ____________________________. • What details in the paragraph help strengthen your thesis? The details that strengthen my thesis are ____________________________.

Core Path	Access Path
	Have them make any changes necessary before submitting their writing for further peer review. **Advanced** **Clarify Organization.** Have students share their completed Research Paper Road Map with another Advanced or English-proficient partner. Have them work together to answer the following questions about their writing and make changes if necessary: • Is this organized in a way that makes sense? • Do the details in each section or paragraph strengthen my thesis? • Are there any other details I want to include? **Approaching** **Complete a Research Paper Road Map.** Provide students with the following questions to help them complete and review their Research Paper Road Map on the Access 4 handout: • Does my thesis statement address all of the points in the writing prompt? Do I need to add anything that is missing? • Do all of the details in this paragraph support my thesis? • Are there additional details I want to add to the paragraph to strengthen my ideas? • Would it make sense to put my paragraphs in a different order?
Review. Once students complete their writing assignments, they should submit substantive feedback to three peers. Students will use the feedback to develop their writing in different stages of the writing process. Project these instructions for the peer review onto the board and review them with your class so they know what they are looking for when they begin to provide their classmates with feedback.	

Core Path	Access Path
Review your peer's road map assignment and provide feedback. Consider the following questions as you review their road map: • How well does the road map activity address the actual writing prompt? • How can the thesis statement be improved? What should the writer add or edit to make it stronger? • What suggestions do you have for improving the paragraph topics? How can they better support the thesis statement? • What kinds of supporting details (such as facts, definitions, and quotations) and precise language has the writer included? Is there enough research in evidence? • How strong are the supporting details? How can the relevance of the supporting details be improved? Provide suggestions for improvement.	
	Extend **Explore Organizational Features.** Explain that although using an appropriate text structure is one way to clarify ideas for readers, other organizational tools are also available to writers. Discuss the use of the following text and visual features, connecting each to its function in organizing and clarifying content: • Titles • Subheads • Photographs and illustrations • Charts and tables • Diagrams and maps Form pairs or small groups and assign each a specific text or visual feature. Have groups explore how they might incorporate that feature into an informative research paper before sharing their ideas with the entire class.

SKILL:
Introductions and Conclusions

OVERVIEW

This lesson provides students with a definition of introductions and conclusions and an explanation of each section's purpose in an informative research paper. Students will analyze and critique the introduction and conclusion in the Student Model. Then they will practice writing an introduction and a conclusion for their informative research papers.

OBJECTIVES

1. Demonstrate an understanding of informative/explanatory writing: introductions and conclusions.
2. Identify and practice concrete strategies for writing a strong introduction and conclusion.
3. Participate effectively in a range of conversations and collaborations to express ideas and build upon the ideas of others.

ELA Common Core Standards:
Reading: Informational Text - RI.11-12.1
Writing - W.11-12.2.A, W.11-12.2.F, W.11-12.4, W.11-12.5, W.11-12.10
Speaking & Listening - SL.11-12.1.A, SL.11-12.1.C, SL.11-12.1.D

RESOURCES

Access 1 handout (Beginner)
Access 2 handout (Intermediate)
Access 3 handout (Advanced)
Access 4 handout (Approaching)

1. DEFINE

Core Path	Access Path
Discuss. 1. Either individually or as a class, read the Define section of the lesson. 2. Ask students to take notes on the most important elements of the introduction and the conclusion. 3. Then in small groups or as a class ask students to discuss the purpose of the introduction and the conclusion in an essay. Give them time to discuss these questions: • What is the purpose of the introduction? (to introduce the topic, to present and explain the thesis statement, to engage readers) • What is the purpose of the conclusion? (to sum up the information presented, to restate the thesis, to give the reader a sense of closure) • How are the two related? (The conclusion should restate the thesis from the introduction and sum up all of the ideas presented in the introduction. Neither should contain information that isn't in the rest of the essay.)	**Beginner** **In Your Own Words.** Have students read the definitions and then use their Access 1 handouts to pause after each bullet point to rewrite the components of an introduction and conclusion in their own words. Once students have completed this activity, ask them to complete the fill-in-the-blanks activity on the Access 1 handout. **Intermediate** **In Your Own Words.** Have students read the definitions of introductions and conclusions and then use their Access 2 handouts to pause after each bullet point to rewrite the definition of introductions and conclusions in their own words. After they've rewritten each of the bullet points in their words, work with students to develop their own definitions of the terms. **Advanced** **In Your Own Words.** Have Advanced students read the Define section and then discuss what they have learned about introductions and conclusions with an English-proficient partner or in mixed-proficiency groups. After their conversation, have Advanced students write the definition of introductions and conclusions on the Access 3 handout. **Approaching** **Restate the Definition.** Have students read the Define section and then use their Access 4 handouts to restate the most important points in their own words. Clarify questions to aid students' comprehension as needed. Then have students participate in mixed-level groups with the class to discuss the purpose of an introduction and conclusion in an essay.

Core Path	Access Path
	Beyond **Brainstorm.** If students have extra time, put them in small groups and have them brainstorm hooks and closing statements for a research paper about an assigned topic, such as an overview of endangered species or the history of baseball. Have groups try to come up with as many examples as they can. Then have students post their ideas to a collaborative tool such as a Google Doc or Tricider (http://www.tricider.com/). As a class, have students vote on which hooks would get them to keep reading and which closing statements would give them a sense of closure.
	Extend **Tech Infusion** **Annotate.** Organize the class into groups. Have each group locate an online magazine article that includes an introduction that identifies the topic, states or hints at a thesis, and includes a hook. Then have students read the conclusion of the same article. Have students use Diigo (www.diigo.com) or another online annotation tool to highlight and annotate the features of the introduction and the conclusion. Finally, have groups share their annotations with the class and discuss the effectiveness of the introductions and conclusions.

2. MODEL

Core Path	Access Path
Read and Discuss. 1. Ask students to read the introductory and concluding paragraphs of the Student Model research paper, "The Making of *Pride and Prejudice*: The Life and Times of Jane Austen." Then have students read the Model text.	**Beginner, Intermediate & Approaching** **Identify the Parts.** Have students reread the Student Model introduction and conclusion on the Access 1, 2, and 4 handouts. They may use the Glossary to help them with words or idioms that may be unfamiliar. Then ask them to find and underline words and phrases that provide clues to what the essay's hook, central or main idea, and possible structure are. Then have students answer the questions. When they have finished, have students share their annotations and answers with a partner and discuss.

Core Path	Access Path
2. In groups, ask students to answer the following questions about the Model text: • According to the Model, which elements of a strong introduction does the Student Model essay contain? • Does the conclusion of "The Making of *Pride and Prejudice*: The Life and Times of Jane Austen" effectively wrap up the essay? Why or why not? • What would your group add, change, or edit to improve the introduction or conclusion?	**Advanced** **Identify the Parts.** Have students read the Student Model introduction and conclusion and answer the questions on the Access 3 handout. Once they've completed the questions, pair Advanced students with more proficient students to allow them to share their answers.
	Extend **Critique.** Project a conclusion onto the board and ask the class to identify its different parts (e.g., reinforcement of thesis and other main points, call to action or other final thoughts). Ask them which elements of the writing they think are particularly strong, as well as those that are weak or in need of improvement. Alternatively, you can put students in small groups and give them photocopies to collaboratively evaluate. After students have had a chance to evaluate the sample, work as a class to generate strategies students can use when they complete their peer reviews to ensure that the critiques are substantive.
Practice. 1. Ask students to review the essay prompt for the Extended Writing Project and to write an introduction and conclusion for their paper. Remind them to use their prewriting notes and road maps to guide their writing. They will want to reference the main points they generated during the prewriting and planning stages in their introduction and sum up their evidence in their conclusion.	**Beginner** **Write Your Introduction and Conclusion.** 1. Prior to having them write their introductions and conclusions, ask students to complete the introduction and conclusion map on the Access 1 handout. 2. After students have completed the map, ask them to discuss with a partner what they plan to write about, clarifying any language as needed before writing their introductions. Make sure partners discuss tone and how to establish it.

Core Path

2. Once students have completed their rough draft paragraphs either on a piece of paper in class or online (note: you will need to create a write assignment if they are going to submit their introductions and conclusions online), they will need to provide their peers with constructive feedback either on paper or online.
3. Students should use their peers' feedback to improve their introductions and conclusions.

Access Path

3. Then students should write their own introductions and conclusions. Encourage them to refer back to the writing prompt and to the Plan Worksheet they completed.

Intermediate
Write an Introduction and Conclusion. Have students fill in the introduction and conclusion map in the Access 2 handout. Review their answers with them, and after making any clarifications needed, allow them to use their answers to craft their introductions and conclusions. Then allow them to join Advanced students to discuss and edit their introductions and conclusions.

Advanced
Clarify and Edit. Have students refer to their Plan Worksheet and the writing prompt as they write their introductions and conclusions. Have them read their paragraph aloud to another Intermediate or Advanced student to check for language that needs to be clarified and to answer the following questions:

- Did you engage the reader with an interesting hook?
- Have you made a clear statement about your central idea? Did you restate that central idea in the conclusion?
- Where do you let the reader know what to expect in the body of the essay?
- Does the conclusion follow logically from the rest of the ideas in the essay?
- Did you provide your reader with a sense of closure?

Allow students time to make edits to their introductions and conclusions as necessary.

Core Path	Access Path
	Approaching **Write an Introduction and Conclusion.** 1. Prior to having them write their introductions and conclusions, ask students to complete the introduction and conclusion map on the Access 4 handout. 2. Once they have completed the map, allow them to use it to write an introduction and conclusion. Remind students to add transitions to link the sentences from the map together into a coherent paragraph.
	Extend **Write.** Write an introduction for your informative research paper that includes a hook, the topic, and the thesis statement. Then write a conclusion that sums up your essay's key points and restates the thesis statement. When you are finished, trade with a partner and offer each other feedback. How strong is the language of your partner's thesis statement? How clear is the topic? Were you hooked? Did the conclusion effectively restate the thesis statement and sum up the writer's ideas? Offer each other suggestions, and remember that they are most helpful when they are constructive.
	Extend **Pair and Share.** Ask students to share their revised introductions with a new partner. 1. Have partners write a list, based on the introduction, of what they expect to be in the research paper. 2. Then have them read the conclusion and add to their list if necessary. 3. Finally, have students share their lists with their partner. Are there items on the list that aren't in their paper? Does the list miss any key points of the paper? Students should use this information to revise their introductions or body paragraphs later in the writing project.

3. YOUR TURN

Core Path	Access Path
Assess and Explain. Have students answer the comprehension questions to test for understanding. Share the explanations for Parts A and B (located online) with your students.	
	Extend **Write.** Have students work in pairs or groups to write two Your Turn questions about the features of the introduction of the Student Model research paper. The questions should focus on the thesis, topic, or hook in the text's introduction. Students should include multiple-choice answers to their questions and identify the answers. Have groups share their questions with another group. Give the groups time to answer the questions. Then lead a class discussion about what students learned from completing the questions.

SKILL:

Body Paragraphs and Transitions

OVERVIEW

This lesson provides students with a definition of body paragraphs and transitions and their role in an informative research paper. Students will analyze and critique the composition of body paragraphs in the Student Model, including the way the writer uses transitions and how they affect cohesion and clarity. Then students will practice writing a body paragraph for their own Extended Writing Projects.

OBJECTIVES

1. Demonstrate an understanding of informative research paper writing: body paragraphs and transitions.
2. Practice and apply concrete strategies for writing strong body paragraphs and clear transitions.
3. Participate effectively in a range of conversations and collaborations to express ideas and build upon the ideas of others.

ELA Common Core Standards:
Reading: Informational Text - RI.11-12.1
Writing - W.11-12.2.A, W.11-12.2.B, W.11-12.2.C, W.11-12.4, W.11-12.5, W.11-12.7, W.11-12.9.B, W.11-12.10
Speaking & Listening - SL.11-12.1.A, SL.11-12.1.C, SL.11-12.1.D

RESOURCES

Access 1 handout (Beginner)
Access 2 handout (Intermediate)
Access 3 handout (Advanced)
Access 4 handout (Approaching)

1. DEFINE

Core Path	Access Path
Read and Discuss. 1. Either individually or as a class, read the Define section of the lesson. 2. Ask students to take notes on the most important elements of body paragraphs and transitions. 3. Then in small groups or as a class ask students to discuss the purpose of each element in an essay. Give them time to discuss these questions: What is the purpose of body paragraphs in an essay? (Body paragraphs make up the majority of an essay. The writer uses body paragraphs to present evidence and analysis in support of the thesis statement.) What is the purpose of transitions? (Transitions are essential to help the reader follow the flow of ideas in an essay.)	**Beginner** **In Your Own Words.** Have students read the definition and then use their Access 1 handouts to write the meaning of the listed terms in their own words. Once students have completed this activity, ask them to complete the Structure a Body Paragraph activity on the Access 1 handout. **Intermediate** **In Your Own Words.** Have students read the definitions of body paragraphs and transitions. Work with students as they use their Access 2 handout to write the meanings of the listed terms in their own words. **Advanced** **In Your Own Words.** Have Advanced students read and then discuss what they have learned about body paragraphs and transitions with an English-proficient partner or in mixed-proficiency groups. After their conversation, have Advanced students write the definition of each term on the Access 3 handout. **Approaching** **Restate the Definition.** Have students read the Define section and then use their Access 4 handouts to rewrite the definitions of each listed term in their own words. Clarify questions to aid students' comprehension as needed. Then have students participate in mixed-level groups with the class to discuss the purpose of a body paragraph or transitions in an essay.

Core Path	Access Path
	Beyond **Jigsaw.** If students have extra time, put them in small groups and give each group a stack of six index cards with sentences from a body paragraph written on them. Do not include any transitions on the cards. Challenge students to organize the cards in the correct order. Then bring groups together and discuss the results. Did everyone sort the cards the same way? If not, why? Would transitions have made the connections more clear?
	Extend **Tech Infusion** **Brainstorm.** Pair or group students and have them brainstorm a list of transition words and phrases that might be useful in a research paper. Have groups collect their words and phrases in a Google Doc or a Padlet wall (http://padlet.com/). Tell students they can use this list as they draft to aid their writing.

2. MODEL

Core Path	Access Path
Read and Discuss. 1. Ask students to read the Model text. For each paragraph from "The Making of *Pride and Prejudice*: The Life and Times of Jane Austen" have students use the annotation tool to note the purpose of each sentence in the paragraph. 2. In groups ask them to review the writing prompt, the research paper's thesis statement, and the body paragraphs in the Student Model: • Do all of the body paragraphs add worthwhile information that supports the thesis statement? If not, what changes would you make? Is more or different research needed? • What would your group add, change, or edit to improve the paper's transitions?	**Beginner, Intermediate & Approaching** **Underline Transitions.** Have students read the paragraph from "The Making of *Pride and Prejudice*: The Life and Times of Jane Austen" on the Access 1, 2, and 4 handouts. They may use the Glossary to help them with words or idioms that may be unfamiliar. Then ask them to find and underline transition words and phrases in the text. Make sure students understand these phrases. Explain that they can use these words and others like them in their own body paragraphs to connect ideas.

Core Path	Access Path
	Advanced **Identify the Parts.** Have students read the Student Model paragraph and answer the questions on the Access 3 handout. Once they've completed the questions, pair Advanced students with more proficient students to allow them to share their answers.
	Extend **Practice.** Pair or group students and have them return to the Student Model research paper "The Making of *Pride and Prejudice*: The Life and Times of Jane Austen" Ask students to highlight every transition in the essay. For each instance, have students note the purpose of that transition. As they go, students should also note places where a transition could be added to clarify the writer's ideas.
Practice. 1. Tell students they will complete a short writing assignment and apply the skills they have learned for writing a body paragraph and using effective transitions. 2. Before students write their body paragraphs, review with them the informative research paper prompt for the Extended Writing Project. Next, have students review their topics, texts, research, and thesis statements. Remind them to use their prewriting notes and road maps to guide their writing. 3. Remind students that they should include one main idea and any supporting evidence, as well as correct citations in their sample paragraphs. Students should also be sure to use transitions where needed to make their paragraphs cohesive.	**Beginner** **Write a Body Paragraph.** 1. Prior to having them write their body paragraphs, ask students to complete the fill-in-the-blanks body paragraph map on the Access 1 handout. Make sure students use complete sentences. Encourage them to refer back to the writing prompt and to the Plan Worksheet they completed. 2. After students have completed the map, ask them to discuss with a partner what they plan to write about, clarifying any language as needed before writing their complete paragraphs. 3. Then students should write their own body paragraphs using language from their map. At this point, have students add clear transitions between sentences.

Core Path	Access Path
4. Remind students that they will be able to use either this body paragraph or a revised version when they write their informative research papers. 5. Students can complete this draft of their body paragraphs on paper, or you can create a write assignment on StudySync, and they can submit their drafts online for anonymous peer review.	**Intermediate** **Complete a Map.** Have students fill in the body paragraph map in the Apply section of the Access 2 handout. Review their answers with them, and after making any clarifications needed, allow them to use their answers to craft their full paragraphs. Remind students to add clear transitions between sentences. Then allow them to join Advanced students to discuss and edit their body paragraphs. **Advanced** **Clarify and Edit.** Have students refer to their Plan Worksheet and the writing prompt as they write their body paragraphs. Have them read their statement aloud to another Intermediate or Advanced student to check for language that needs to be clarified and to answer the following questions: • Does your paragraph focus on one clear idea? • What evidence did you include? Did you explain how the evidence supports the central idea? • Did you include a concluding sentence? • Did you include clear transitions? • Have you used grammar such as pronouns, prepositions, and subject-verb agreement correctly? Allow students time to make edits to their thesis statements as necessary. **Approaching** **Complete the Body Paragraph Map.** 1. Prior to having them write their body paragraphs, ask students to complete the fill-in-the-blanks body paragraph map on the Access 4 handout. If needed, review each element of body paragraphs with students before they begin writing. 2. Once they have completed the statements with the information they plan to write about, allow them to write their body paragraphs. Remind students to use transition words and phrases when they write their full paragraphs.

Core Path	Access Path
	Extend **Revisit.** Pair or group students and have them revisit the excerpt from "The Making of *Pride and Prejudice:* The Life and Times of Jane Austen." Have them reread the excerpt and look for evidence that would better support the thesis statement of the Student Model research paper. When students have a sentence or sentences in mind, they should write a one- or two-sentence explanation connecting the evidence to the thesis statement. Allow groups to share their findings with the class.

3. YOUR TURN

Core Path	Access Path
Assess and Explain. Have students answer the comprehension questions to test for understanding. Share the explanations for Parts A and B (located online) with your students.	
	Extend **Pair and Share.** After completing the assessment, have students write their own concluding sentence for the paragraph. Then have students share their sentence with a partner and discuss which sentence does the best job concluding the paragraph and transitioning to the next.

EXTENDED WRITING PROJECT:
Draft

OVERVIEW

This lesson asks students to write a draft of their informative research papers. To do so, they will use relevant facts and details collected from the texts in this unit as well as outside research. Students are instructed to use their prewriting, thesis statements, source cards, note cards, and the road maps they created in the Plan lesson to help them assemble and structure information. As students draft, they should focus on the clarity of their thesis statement, the logic and flow of their organizational structure, the relevance of their textual evidence, the appropriateness of their transitions, and the effectiveness of their conclusion. Before they submit their drafts, students should check to be sure they have fully addressed the writing prompt.

OBJECTIVES

1. Review notes, outlines, or other organizers before writing an informative/explanatory text.
2. Draft an informative research paper in response to a prompt.
3. Participate effectively in a range of conversations and collaborations to express ideas and build upon the ideas of others.

ELA Common Core Standards:
Reading: Informational Text - RI.11-12.1
Writing - W.11-12.2.A, W.11-12.2.B, W.11-12.2.C, W.11-12.2.D, W.11-12.2.E, W.11-12.2.F, W.11-12.4, W.11-12.5, W.11-12.6, W.11-12.7, W.11-12.9.B, W.11-12.10
Speaking & Listening - SL.11-12.1.A, SL.11-12.1.D
Language - L.11-12.1.B, L.11-12.6

RESOURCES

Grade 12, Unit 4 Extended Writing Project: Draft lesson
Access 1 handout (Beginner)
Access 2 handout (Intermediate)
Access 3 handout (Advanced)
Access 4 handout (Approaching)
Grammar handout: Usage

1. WRITE

Core Path	Access Path
Discuss. Before students begin to write, review with the class the writing prompt/directions for their informative research papers. Have a volunteer read them aloud. Ask whether students have any questions either about the prompt or the directions. Respond to their questions, and explain the importance of addressing the prompt fully and completely. Then read aloud the peer review instructions that students will use to comment on one another's work. Students will use the feedback to develop their writing in different stages of the writing process. Point out that understanding the peer review instructions can help students focus their writing on important features of informative/explanatory texts. Remind students to use academic vocabulary correctly when participating in a discussion. The peer review instructions ask students to consider the following questions: • Has the writer included a clear thesis statement in an engaging introduction? • Does the writer effectively support all historical background with information from reliable sources? Are the sources cited? • How well does the writer include concrete details, quotations, and other information to support the thesis? Are there any irrelevant details? • Does the writer clearly link the author's biography and literary movement to the text from the unit? Are there any weak connections? • How has the essay helped you understand the author or the literary movement described? What questions do you still have about the topic?	**English Learners All Levels & Approaching** **Review Writing Draft Checklist.** Read aloud the Informative/Explanatory Writing Draft Checklist on the Access 1, 2, 3, and 4 handouts with students. Encourage students to circle unfamiliar words and underline anything that is confusing or unclear. Then take a few minutes to clarify unknown vocabulary, answer questions, and provide examples for any items that students do not understand. Explain that they will need to include each of these items in their writing. For each checklist item, point out an example in the Student Model and read it aloud. **Beyond** **Critique.** If students have extra time, give small groups photocopies of an informative/explanatory writing sample to collaboratively evaluate. Have them identify the elements of writing that are strong as well as those that are weak or in need of improvement. Then ask them to generate strategies students can use when they complete their peer reviews to ensure their critiques are substantive. Have them make a list of their strategies to share with the class.

Core Path	Access Path
• Does the writer maintain a formal style and objective tone? • What specific suggestions can you make to help the writer improve the essay? Remind students that a peer reviewer's comments are most useful when they are clear, constructive, and presented with a positive attitude. Make sure students understand your expectations for all aspects of the assignment before beginning their work.	
Organize. Remind students to review their topics, text choices, and thesis statements, as well as consider audience and purpose as they begin to draft. Next, have them refer to any outlines, lists, road maps, source cards, note cards, and other organizers, including the Six-Circles Web they completed in the Prewrite lesson and their Textual Evidence Chart from the Plan lesson, before they begin writing. Students may also wish to reread relevant portions of the texts that they have selected for inclusion in their informative research paper. They should review the practice drafts they wrote for an introduction, body paragraph, and conclusion as well. At this time, they may also want to look up the definitions of any unfamiliar vocabulary from their reading, and use all or portions of these as they write a complete draft.	**Beginner & Intermediate** **Add Transition Words to Essay Road Map.** Before students write their draft, have them talk through their completed Essay Road Map from the Plan lesson. Have them read each paragraph or section aloud and help them identify places where they can use transition words such as *furthermore*, *therefore*, *in addition*, and *in order* to connect ideas. Have them write the transition words on their Essay Road Map, and then reread each section aloud with the transition words in place.
G **Grammar, Usage, and Mechanics.** Distribute the grammar handout on usage and discuss the instruction provided on the handout with students. Have students respond individually to the questions on the handout and then discuss their responses as a class. Answers to the questions appear at the end of the lesson plan online. Before students submit their drafts, have them reread their essays to make sure that they don't contain usage errors. Encourage students to consult a reference material, such as *Garner's Modern American Usage*, if they have any questions.	**Beginner** **Support Grammar Comprehension.** 1. Read the grammar handout aloud with students, pausing to clarify concepts as needed. Model an example of usage rules 1, 2, 4, and 5 for students by writing sentences on the board. First follow the rule, and then revise the sentence to break it. For example, model the first rule by writing, "The team is late for the game." Then explain that since the noun *team* refers to more than one person, it is also acceptable to say, "The team are late for the game."

Core Path	Access Path
	2. Work directly with small groups to complete the practice items by reading each sentence aloud and having students identify the nonstandard usage and the rule it breaks. Then help them to explain why a writer might choose to break that rule in a sentence. 3. Read students' drafts with them to help them check for nonstandard usage in their own writing. **Intermediate** **Support Grammar Comprehension.** Have Intermediate students join with Beginning students for the instruction portion of the lesson. Then allow them to work with an Advanced or English-proficient partner to complete the practice items and check their drafts for nonstandard usage. Remind these students that such "errors" are not necessarily wrong if they are made sparingly to achieve a certain effect. **Advanced** **Check for Nonstandard Usage.** Have Advanced students complete the practice items individually, and check and discuss their answers with an English-proficient partner. Then have them check their drafts for nonstandard usage. Remind these students that such "errors" are not necessarily wrong if they are made sparingly to achieve a certain effect. **Approaching** **Partner Work.** Check in with Approaching students before they complete the grammar exercise. Ask them to explain what they understand about each grammar rule, and offer clarification as necessary. Allow them to complete the practice items with a partner. When they are done, have them check and discuss their answers. Have them continue working with their partner to check their drafts for nonstandard usage. Remind these students that such "errors" are not necessarily wrong if they are made sparingly to achieve a certain effect.

Core Path	Access Path
Write. Ask students to complete the writing assignment using textual evidence, such as relevant facts, details, and quotations, from their selection and outside research to support their thesis statement. Once they have completed their writing, they should click "Submit."	**Beginner** **Write with Support.** Preview the Informative/Explanatory Draft Checklist on the Access 1 handout with students before they write. Then have students use their Essay Road Map to complete their draft with teacher support as needed. Prior to having them write each paragraph, ask students to state orally what they want to say in each paragraph. They can do this in small groups with support from the teacher or in pairs with an on-level partner who can provide quality feedback. Talking through their writing before they put pen to paper will help them clarify their language and use of transition words before they write. **Intermediate & Advanced** **Use Transition Words.** Have students use the Informative/Explanatory Writing Draft Checklist on the Access 2 and 3 handouts as they write. Remind them to focus on using transition words to smoothly connect ideas, sentences, and paragraphs. They may refer to the words listed in the student lesson on Body Paragraphs and Transitions. **Approaching** **Use Essay Road Map to Write a Draft.** Remind students to consult all the prewriting documents they have created—structure graphic organizer, thesis statement, and Essay Road Map—to help them craft their essay. It may be particularly useful for Approaching students to use their Essay Road Map to structure their writing. Explain that they can follow the order of the outline they created, but in their draft they will need to add details and develop their writing. Have them use the Informative/Explanatory Writing Draft Checklist on the Access 4 handout to make sure they include a strong introduction with a hook and thesis statement, smooth transitions, precise language, and a conclusion that restates the thesis and wraps up the essay in an interesting way.

Core Path	Access Path
Review. Once students complete their writing assignment, they should submit substantive feedback to two peers. Students should use their peers' feedback to improve their writing.	**Beginner** **Review the Checklist.** Help students to go through the Informative/Explanatory Draft Checklist item-by-item on the Access 1 handout to check their writing. Provide support to help them make changes as needed. **Intermediate & Advanced** **Use the Checklist.** Have mixed-proficiency partners read their completed drafts aloud to one another and use the Informative/Explanatory Draft Checklist on the Access 2 and 3 handouts to check their writing. Remind them to check that they used transition words appropriately and make suggestions for how transitions could be improved or clarified.

SKILL:
Sources and Citations

OVERVIEW

This lesson provides students with definitions of both sources and citations and an explanation of their purposes. Students will recognize the need for multiple sources to demonstrate an understanding of a subject under investigation, as well as analyze and critique the citations in the Student Model. Then they will practice formatting the citations for their research writing project.

OBJECTIVES

1. Demonstrate an understanding of informative/explanatory texts: sources and citations.
2. Identify and practice concrete strategies for using multiple sources and correctly formatting citations for an informative research paper.
3. Participate effectively in a range of conversations and collaborations to express ideas and build upon the ideas of others.

ELA Common Core Standards:
Reading: Informational Text - RI.11-12.1
Writing - W.11-12.5, W.11-12.7, W.11-12.8, W.11-12.10
Speaking & Listening - SL.11-12.1.A, SL.11-12.1.C, SL.11-12.1.D

RESOURCES

Access 1 handout (Beginner)
Access 2 handout (Intermediate)
Access 3 handout (Advanced)
Access 4 handout (Approaching)

1. DEFINE

Core Path	Access Path
Read and Discuss. 1. Either individually or as a class, read the Define section of the lesson. 2. Ask students to take notes on the most important elements of sources and citations. 3. Then in small groups or as a class, ask students to discuss the purpose of citations in an essay. Give them time to discuss these questions: Writers of research papers must consult multiple sources. How does this research help a writer demonstrate understanding of a subject under investigation? (Possible response: Writers need to find sources that offer different perspectives and a variety of information. This means consulting, either in print or online, sources such as books, magazines, academic papers, or scientific articles by various authors.) What is the purpose of citations in an informative research paper? (Citations tell readers exactly where the writer located his or her information. The reader knows the information came from a credible source, and that the information is not plagiarized.) What is plagiarism? (Plagiarism is the act of claiming someone's words or ideas as your own, in writing.) Why do you think writers plagiarize? How might they be convinced not to? (Possible response: Writers may not bother to cite sources because they want to avoid the work involved, or even because they forget. Possibly, though, writers want to claim original thinking as their own in order to appear smart. To deter writers from doing this, readers should expect citations and demand to see the sources of all factual details when reading arguments and informational texts. Also, readers, including teachers and classmates, need to praise writers for thorough research used either to prove a point or to provide correct information.)	**Beginner** **In Your Own Words.** Have students read the definition and then use their Access 1 handouts to pause after each bullet point to rewrite the important points about sources and citations in their own words. Once students have completed this activity, ask them to complete the chart on the Access 1 handout. **Intermediate** **In Your Own Words.** Have students read the definitions of sources and citations and then use their Access 2 handouts to pause after each bullet point to rewrite the important points about sources and citations in their own words. After they've rewritten each of the bullet points in their own words, work with students to develop their own definitions of the terms. **Advanced** **In Your Own Words.** Have Advanced students read the Define section and then discuss what they have learned about sources and citations with an English-proficient partner or in mixed-proficiency groups. After their conversation, have Advanced students write the definitions of sources and citations on the Access 3 handout. **Approaching** **Restate the Definition.** Have students read the Define section and then use their Access 4 handouts to restate the most important points in their own words. Clarify questions to aid students' comprehension as needed. Then have students participate in mixed-level groups with the class to discuss the purpose of sources and citations in an essay.

Core Path	Access Path
	Beyond **Discuss.** If students have extra time, put them in small groups and have students discuss how using information from reliable sources impacts their own writing. How does using sources help them make their own ideas more credible? What function do citations serve (besides avoiding plagiarism), and why are they important to include? Would a paper be just a strong without sources and citations? Why or why not? Allow time for groups to share their conclusions with the class.
	Extend **Tech Infusion** **Connect.** Pair or group students and have them briefly research the question of anonymous sources in journalism. As a class, host a short debate about the issue. Should all sources in journalism be named? Why or why not?

2. MODEL

Core Path	Access Path
Read and Discuss. 1. Ask students to read the Model text and the explanation of the citations in the Student Model research paper. 2. In groups ask them to discuss the citations in the Student Model: • What kinds of sources has the writer consulted to do the research? Why are multiple and varied resources a good idea when doing research? • Is all the information that needs to be credited cited? Why or why not? • Are there additional citations that need to be added? If not, why?	**Beginner, Intermediate & Approaching** **Identify Citations.** Have students read the Model text and then look at the excerpt from "The Making of *Pride and Prejudice*: The Life and Times of Jane Austen" listed on the Access 1, 2, and 4 handouts. They may use the Glossary to help them with words or idioms that may be unfamiliar. Ask them to make an inference about the writer's sources based on the citations listed. Make sure students understand each component of a citation. Explain that they can use these rules when they add citations to their own essays.

Core Path	Access Path
	Advanced **Write a Citation.** Have students read the sentence and citation from the Student Model and answer the questions on the Access 3 handout. Once they've completed the questions, pair Advanced students with more proficient students to allow them to share their answers.
	Extend **Practice.** Compile a list of the types of sources students likely used for their research essays, such as books, online articles, and articles from scholarly journals. Pair students and give each pair a list of bibliographic information for several sources. Do not format the information in MLA style. Challenge pairs to create the Works Cited entry and list all the ways the source could be cited in running text. When pairs finish, have them trade with another pair and check each other's work. Some sample sources: Book - *Becoming Jane Austen* by Jon Spence. Published by Bloomsbury Academic in London in 2007 Web article - "Jane Austen" in *Encyclopaedia Britannica* online. Written by Brian C. Southam. Last updated 9-23-2013 Journal article (online) - "The Closeness of Sisters: Imagining Cassandra and Jane" by Juliette Wells. Published in *Persuasions*, the publication of the Jane Austen Society of North America in volume 30 number 1 (Winter 2009)
Practice. 1. Ask students to review their research paper drafts in order to create a Works Cited section and to add in-text citations to their research papers. Remind them to use their source and note cards from the Research and Note-Taking lesson. Students should consult multiple sources in order to demonstrate an understanding of the subject.	**Beginner** **Write a Citation.** 1. Prior to having them write their citations, have students fill in all the information about their sources on the Access 1 handout. You may wish to give students multiple copies so they can have one list for each source.

Core Path	Access Path
2. Point out to students that if they have information for which they cannot find a source, they will have to review their research and locate it in order to create the appropriate citation. 3. Remind students that they will be able to include both the Works Cited section and the in-text citations as they write the revisions of their informative research papers. 4. Students can complete this draft of their Works Cited sections and in-text citations on paper, or you can create a write assignment on StudySync, and they can submit their drafts online for anonymous peer review.	2. After students have filled in all the information for each source, have them add a citation to a sentence from their essay and write the works cited entry for that source, using the blanks at the bottom of the Access 1 handout. 3. Then have students share their sentence and works cited entry with a partner. Have partners check the format of each and provide feedback if necessary. **Intermediate** **Write a Citation.** Have students fill in the source information on the Access 2 handout. You may wish to give students multiple copies so they can have one list for each source. Review their source information with them, and after making any clarifications needed, allow them to use their answers to write a citation and works cited entry in the space below. Then allow them to join Advanced students to discuss and edit their citations. **Advanced** **Clarify and Edit.** Have students refer to their drafts and their notes as they write their citations. Have them read their citations aloud to another Intermediate or Advanced student to check for language that needs to be clarified and to answer the following questions: • Does this sentence include information that came from a source and needs to be cited? • Have you included the correct source information? • Is the Works Cited entry complete and correctly formatted? Allow students time to make edits to their citations as necessary.

Core Path	Access Path
	Approaching **Write a Citation.** Prior to having them write their citations, ask students to gather their source information on the Access 4 handout. Once they have completed the source information, allow them to use the blanks provided on the Access 4 handout to add a citation to a sentence and write a Works Cited entry for that source. Remind students to use the first blank for a sentence from their essay, and then fill in the parentheses with the in-text citation. Additionally, you may want to explain that the second line of the Works Cited entry is indented to remind them to do the same in their complete list.
	Extend **Write.** Write citations for quoted information in your research paper. When you are finished, trade with a partner and offer feedback. Are all citations done according to MLA style? Is there any information that seems like it came from an outside source that wasn't cited? How varied were the types of sources cited? Offer each other suggestions, and remember that they are most helpful when they are constructive.
	Extend **Explore.** For more information about formatting sources and citations, direct students to an online MLA style guide, such as the one from the Purdue University Online Writing Lab: https://owl.english.purdue.edu/owl/resource/747/01/. Tell students to bookmark this site and use it as they add citations to their research papers.

3. YOUR TURN

Core Path	Access Path
Assess and Explain. Have students answer the comprehension questions to test for understanding. Share the explanations for Parts A and B (located online) with your students.	
	Extend **Pair and Share.** After completing the assessment, put students in pairs and ask them to discuss the Your Turn questions. • In what situation is it correct to only include a page number in a citation? • What strategies did they use to figure out the answers? • Do they have any additional questions about the Your Turn activity?

EXTENDED WRITING PROJECT:
Revise

OVERVIEW

This lesson asks students to revise the drafts of their informative research papers. Students are first asked to include any peer suggestions they previously received on their draft, provided they think the suggestions help improve the paper. Then they are asked to focus on revisions to maintain a formal style suited to their audience and purpose. They are also asked to carefully review their content, citations, and format and to check that they have fully supported their thesis statement with solid textual evidence.

OBJECTIVES

1. Identify elements of a writing style appropriate to an informative/explanatory text or research paper.
2. Revise an informative research paper to improve content and organization, to maintain a formal style and objective tone, and to add citations and a list of sources.
3. Participate effectively in a range of conversations and collaborations to express ideas and build upon the ideas of others.

ELA Common Core Standards:
Reading: Informational Text - RI.11-12.1
Writing - W.11-12.2.A, W.11-12.2.B, W.11-12.2.C, W.11-12.2.D, W.11-12.2.E, W.11-12.2.F, W.11-12.4, W.11-12.5, W.11-12.6, W.11-12.7, W.11-12.8, W.11-12.9.B, W.11-12.10
Speaking & Listening - SL.11-12.1.A
Language - L.11-12.2.A

RESOURCES

Grade 12, Unit 4 Extended Writing Project: Revise lesson
Grammar handout: Hyphenation Conventions
Access 1 handout (Beginner)
Access 2 handout (Intermediate)
Access 3 handout (Advanced)
Access 4 handout (Approaching)

1. WRITE

Core Path

Discuss. Before students begin to revise, review with the class the writing prompt/directions for their informative research papers. Ask whether students have any questions either about the prompt or the revision process. Respond to their questions, and explain the importance of thoughtful, focused revisions. Then read aloud the peer review instructions that students will use to comment on one another's work. Students will use the feedback to develop their writing in different stages of the writing process. Point out that understanding the peer review instructions can help students focus their writing on important features of informative/explanatory texts. The peer review instructions ask students to consider the following questions:

- What elements of a formal style has the writer included? Is the tone objective?
- Do you see any of the writer's personal opinions expressed in the paper?
- Are there any weak spots that could be strengthened with a quotation or more evidence from the writer's research?
- Which general words could be replaced with more precise language?
- Is there any vocabulary or are there any concepts that need further explanation?
- Check that there is a Works Cited list. Is the list formatted correctly?
- Do the in-text citations match the Works Cited list? Are any citations missing or improperly formatted?
- How has the research paper helped you understand the subject's life, the text, and a literary movement?
- What specific suggestions can you make to help the writer improve the paper?

Access Path

Beginner, Intermediate & Approaching
Review the Revision Checklist.
Read aloud the Informative/Explanatory Writing Revision Checklist with students. As the teacher reads each item on the checklist, students should read along on their Access 1, 2, and 4 handouts. Encourage students to circle unfamiliar words and underline anything that is confusing or unclear. Then take a few minutes to clarify unknown vocabulary, answer questions, and provide examples for any items that students do not understand. Explain to students that they will need to check their own writing for each of these items.

Advanced
Read and Discuss. Pair Advanced students with an on-level partner and ask them to review the Informative/Explanatory Writing Revision Checklist. Allow time for them to discuss each item to ensure the students understand what they are being asked to do.

Beyond
Create Action Items.

1. Give small groups a writing sample and ask them to identify and underline the elements of informative/explanatory writing.
2. Have students generate strategies they can use to ensure that their peer reviews are focused and substantive.
3. Ask them to create a list of action items for their revision to focus their efforts. Have them organize these items into a checklist.
4. Create a shared Google doc that all students in the class can add to, edit, and use to revise their work.

Core Path	Access Path
Remind students that a peer reviewer's comments are most useful when they are clear, constructive, and presented with a positive attitude. Students should also understand that even though the peer reviewer may make several recommendations for revisions, it's important that students use their own judgment to ensure the changes will improve the research paper. Make sure students understand your expectations for all aspects of the assignment before beginning their revisions.	
Grammar, Usage, and Mechanics. Distribute the grammar handout on hyphenation conventions and discuss the instruction provided on the handout with students. Have students respond individually to the questions on the handout and then discuss their responses as a class. Answers to the questions appear at the end of the lesson plan online. Finally, encourage students to apply what they have learned by making sure that their own writing observes hyphenation conventions.	**Beginner** **Support Grammar/Usage Comprehension.** 1. Read the grammar handout aloud with students, pausing to clarify concepts as needed. Demonstrate the proper use of hyphens to join compound words by using a sample sentence for each rule. Then have students work together to write more examples in small groups. 2. Work directly with small groups to complete the practice items by reading the sentences aloud and having students identify the hyphens and the rules they follow. 3. Read students' drafts with them to help them identify where hyphenated compound words could be included to clarify the writing. **Intermediate** **Support Grammar/Usage Comprehension.** Have Intermediate students join with Beginning students for the instruction portion of the lesson. Then allow them to work with an Advanced or English-proficient partner to complete the practice items and check their drafts for correct usage of hyphenated compound words. **Advanced** **Check for Correct Usage.** Have Advanced students complete the practice items individually, and check and discuss their answers with an English-proficient partner. Then have them check their draft for correct usage of hyphenated compound words.

Core Path	Access Path
	Approaching **Partner Work.** Check in with Approaching students before they complete the grammar handout. Ask them to explain what they understand about hyphens and hyphenated compound words. Allow them to complete the practice items with a partner. When they are done, have them check and discuss their answers. Have them continue working with their partner to check their drafts for correct usage of hyphenated compound words.
Highlight. Each student should start this activity with a copy of his or her draft either printed on paper or open in a word-processing program. Students will conduct three rereads of their own paper, each with a different focus. 1. First, have students read through their draft to be sure they have included previous peer suggestions, as appropriate. 2. Next, ask students to look for aspects of informal style. Students should be on the lookout for slang, personal pronouns and opinions, incorrectly used pronouns (especially reflexive or intensive pronouns), imprecise words, and a casual tone. Advise students to highlight in blue any instances of informal style and note corrections in the margins. 3. Finally, instruct students to read through a third time. This time, students should look for opportunities to broaden audience appeal while maintaining a formal style (e.g., improving supporting details or using more vivid language). Challenge students to find at least two places where they could create interest for their target audience and to highlight these places in yellow.	**English Learners All Levels & Approaching** **Mixed-Level Partner Editing.** Have all students form mixed-level pairs in which partners vary one level up or down from one another. Then have them work together on their drafts to identify and highlight areas they need to improve when they edit their drafts.

Core Path	Access Path
Write. Ask students to complete the revision using textual evidence from the text or their research to support any additional ideas they present. They should also include in-text citations and a Works Cited section at the close of their papers. Once they have completed their writing, they should click "Submit."	**English Learners All Levels** **Use Checklist.** Have all English Learners use the Informative/Explanatory Writing Revision Checklist to help guide their revisions. Provide additional differentiated support as indicated below. **Beginner** **Focus on Hyphens.** Focus on properly using hyphens to join compound words. Walk students through the activity on the Access 1 handout. Then have them join in the discussion of compound modifiers with Intermediate students (below). Afterward, help them to check their writing for correct hyphen usage and to find and eliminate hyphens they have used incorrectly. **Intermediate** **Focus on Hyphens.** Have Intermediate students participate in the hyphens activity on the Access 2 handout. Then display the following two sentences: *Austen, however, proved to be self-sufficient.* *This seven-volume work focused on the history of a marriage and was full of scandalous behavior and interesting characters (27).* Explain that the use of compound modifiers can help create precision in writing. Help students to identify the underlined word *self-sufficient* in the first sentence. Explain that this modifier comes after the proper noun *Austen* but it still uses a hyphen because it includes the word *self.* Help students to identify the underlined word *seven-volume* in the second sentence. Explain that this compound word is used as a modifier as part of the phrase "*seven-volume work*" as a way to give readers more information. It contains a hyphen because it appears before the noun it modifies. Discuss how the rules for hyphenating compound modifiers can change based on the location of the word within the sentence. Then have partners review their own writing for correct use of compound modifiers with teacher assistance as needed.

Core Path	Access Path
	Advanced **Use Precise Language.** 1. Ask students to work with an English-proficient partner to identify and underline places in their essay where language could be made more clear or vivid. 2. Then have them use the two-column chart on the Access 3 handout to list words students underlined in their essay that need revision. Brainstorm a list of new words to replace these words. 3. Give students time to discuss which words are strongest (related to the topic, showing clear and vivid description) and choose the best to include in their essay. **Approaching** **Practice Editing.** 1. Approaching students should practice identifying instances of personal opinion, incorrectly hyphenated compound words, words that could be replaced with more vivid or exact language, and places where they need to include additional textual evidence using the exercise on the Access 4 handout. 2. After they edit the example paragraph, allow them to work with an on-level partner to read through their own drafts. They should focus on identifying and underlining instances of personal opinion, incorrectly hyphenated compound words, words that could be replaced with more vivid or exact language, and places where they need to include additional textual evidence in their own writing. 3. Then have them make their revisions independently. Have them check their revised essay against the Informative/Explanatory Revision Checklist before they submit their revision.

Core Path	Access Path
Review. After completing their writing assignment, students should submit substantive feedback to two peers.	**Beginner** **Review with Teacher Support.** In a small group, help students to go through the Informative/Explanatory Writing Revision Checklist on the Access 1 handout item-by-item to review one another's writing. Provide individual support to help them make changes as needed. **Intermediate & Advanced** **Use Checklist.** Have mixed-proficiency partners read their completed drafts aloud to one another and use the Informative/Explanatory Writing Revision Checklist on the Access 2 and 3 handouts to check that their writing includes all of the required revisions. With teacher guidance as necessary, encourage them to suggest ways their partner could make any needed changes. **Approaching** **Use Checklist.** Have partners use the Informative/Explanatory Writing Revision Checklist on the Access 4 handout to make sure their completed revisions include all of the necessary elements.

EXTENDED WRITING PROJECT: Edit/Proofread/Publish

OVERVIEW

This lesson asks students to edit, proofread, and publish the edited and corrected version of their informative research paper revisions. Students are instructed to edit for final improvements in information, style, and organization, and to proofread for the correct use of grammar, spelling, and punctuation. Finally, students are encouraged to explore ways of publishing their work.

OBJECTIVES

1. Identify editing, proofreading, and publishing skills.
2. Edit and proofread an informative research paper to finalize information, style, and organization, and to eliminate errors in grammar, punctuation, and spelling.
3. Use technology to produce and publish writing.
4. Participate effectively in a range of conversations and collaborations to express ideas and build upon the ideas of others.

ELA Common Core Standards:
Writing - W.11-12.2.A, W.11-12.2.B, W.11-12.2.C, W.11-12.2.D, W.11-12.2.E, W.11-12.2.F, W.11-12.4, W.11-12.5, W.11-12.6, W.11-12.7, W.11-12.8, W.11-12.9.B, W.11-12.10
Speaking & Listening - SL.11-12.1.A, SL.11-12.1.B, SL.11-12.1.C, SL.11-12.1.D, SL.11-12.6
Language - L.11-12.2.A, L.11-12.2.B, L.11-12.3.A, L.11-12.6

RESOURCES

Grade 12, Unit 4 Extended Writing Project: Edit/Proofread/Publish lesson
Grammar handout: Spelling
Access 1 handout (Beginner)
Access 2 handout (Intermediate)
Access 3 handout (Advanced)
Access 4 handout (Approaching)

1. WRITE

Core Path	Access Path
Test. Have students submit their paper to PaperRater (www.paperrater.com). This site checks for grammar and spelling errors. Students can also select from the dropdown menus to have the engine provide feedback for style, word choice, and citations. Invite students to do a round of edits on their own before submitting a section of their text to the website to check their own work. Make sure students understand that the application by itself might make suggestions that do not improve the paper. Students will need to exercise judgment as they review suggestions for changes. In particular, have them edit and proofread for the following: • use of transitional words and phrases • varied syntax and sentence length • correct use of hyphens • errors in spelling	**English Learners All Levels** **Use Technology to Check Clarity.** Have students conduct a check for the clarity of their writing using Hemingway (www.hemingwayapp.com). This app is designed to make the writing clear and concise. It will suggest eliminating embellishments and revising syntax for readability. Emphasize, however, that the app's suggestions may not be consistent with what the writer wishes to say. There is no substitute for the writer's own judgment.
Discuss. Before students begin to edit and proofread, review with the class the writing prompt/directions. Have a volunteer read them aloud. Ask whether students have any questions either about the prompt or the process of editing and proofreading. Respond to their questions, and then review criteria that can help students make final adjustments and corrections in their texts. Remind students that: • The text should reflect skill in research paper writing, including features such as a clear thesis statement, effective organization of information, relevant supporting details, precise language, varied transitions, appropriate syntax, and a concluding paragraph. • The text should support the thesis statement with textual evidence and include accurate citations of sources. The sources should be listed in a Works Cited section at the close of the paper.	**Beginner** **Use Writing Support.** Walk Beginning students through the Proofreading Checklist on the Access 1 handout item-by-item. Help them to identify and underline the sections of their essay they will need to edit. **Intermediate and Advanced** **Use Checklist.** Have Intermediate and Advanced students preview the Proofreading Checklist on the Access 2 and Access 3 handouts before they begin their final editing process. Make sure they understand everything on the checklist. As needed, help individual students identify the items on the checklist that they need to pay special attention to as they edit their essay.

Core Path	Access Path
• The text should have a formal style, including the use of third-person pronouns, and reflect an objective tone, removing any personal opinions. • Any hyphens should be used correctly. • The text should be free from other errors in grammar, punctuation, and spelling. Before or after students make final adjustments to their essays, brainstorm publishing ideas with them. Students have already been using technology to create, revise, and submit their work on StudySync, as well as to collaborate with their peers. Now, students will want to share information with one another about additional appropriate online publication opportunities, as well as about possible print outlets for their work. Ask students to collaborate on creating a list of these opportunities and outlets for their own use to help them when they are ready to publish. Once students have submitted the final versions of their informative research papers, you might also suggest that they adapt their writing to an oral report format and deliver their essay as a presentation to the class. Remind them to use formal rather than informal language in their presentations. To help students prepare and deliver their presentations, refer them to the Presentation Skills in the Speaking & Listening Handbook.	**Approaching** **Support Proofreading.** Walk students through each item on the Proofreading Checklist on the Access 4 handout. Encourage students to circle unfamiliar words and underline anything that is confusing or unclear. Then take a few minutes to clarify unknown vocabulary, answer questions, and provide examples for any items that students do not understand. If you have identified individual students' challenges, circle those items on the checklist that they need to pay special attention to and provide individual support, or pair them with an on- or above-level student to make their final edits.
Grammar, Usage, and Mechanics. Distribute the grammar handout on spelling and discuss the instruction provided on the handout with students. Have students respond individually to the questions on the handout and then discuss their responses as a class. Answers to the questions appear at the end of the lesson plan online. Finally, ask students to reread their essays to make sure that they have followed all spelling rules, especially those regarding "ie" and "ei." Encourage students to use a dictionary when they are unsure of a word's spelling.	**Beginner & Intermediate** **Focus on Spelling.** Have students join in as you review the spelling rules with the class. Then in small groups have them complete the exercises on the Access 1 and 2 handouts by identifying the misspelled words. Encourage them to read each word aloud several times, listening for the vowel sounds and noting any exceptions as listed on the grammar handout. Circulate among the groups, helping them as needed. When their work is complete, check their answers. Review any incorrect answers by reviewing the spelling rules as needed.

Core Path	Access Path
	Advanced **Work with a Partner.** After the instruction, have Advanced students complete the exercise with an English-proficient partner. Encourage them to read each example word aloud together, listening for the vowel sounds and noting any exceptions as listed on the grammar handout. **Approaching** **Support Understanding.** Read aloud the instruction portion of the handout with students, focusing on vowel sounds and exceptions in each of the examples. Remind students that these examples are exceptions to the general rule. Ask students: *In general, does an "i" come before or after an "e"?* (before) Then ask: *What is an exception to this rule?* (when they both follow "c" or when they make the sound of a long "a") Then have them complete the exercise and check their answers with an on-level partner.
Write. Ask students to complete the writing assignment. Suggest, if there's time, that they set their informative research papers aside for a few minutes, and that they then proofread it one more time. Once they have completed their writing, they should click "Submit."	**Beginner & Intermediate** **Check Spelling and Proofread.** Before students begin proofreading, remind them of the spelling activity they just completed. Have them read through their essay with a partner and circle any word with an "ie" or "ei" that they may have spelled incorrectly. Then have them read the circled words aloud and try to use what they have learned to correct the spelling themselves before confirming it using a dictionary or spell-checker. They can continue proofreading their essay with a teacher or partner using the Proofreading Checklist on the Access 1 and 2 handouts.

Core Path	Access Path
	Intermediate & Advanced **Read Aloud to Proofread.** Explain to students that reading their work aloud is a great way to check for errors they might have otherwise missed. After students have completed their proofreading using the Proofreading Checklist, have them read their essay aloud to an English-proficient partner. Tell them that if they stumble in their reading it may indicate a place where they need to adjust punctuation or sentence structure. Have their partner listen for correct use of grammar and suggest corrections if needed. **Approaching** **Support Writing.** Have students check their final draft against the checklist on their Access 4 handout to make sure they made all of the edits needed. Ask them if they have questions or if they found any part of the assignment challenging. If so, provide clarification and assistance so that they can make their final edits and proofread before submitting their work.

Research

Emotional Currents

TYPE

Research

TITLE

Grade 12 Unit 4: Emotional Currents

TIME

185 minutes (research and presentations)

OBJECTIVES

1. Complete topic-specific group research project connected to the unit theme and driving question.
2. Practice and apply research strategies to produce a presentation with multimedia features.
3. Practice, apply, and reinforce the following Grades 11-12 ELA Common Core Standards for reading literature and informational texts, writing explanatory pieces, conducting research projects, and speaking and listening:
   - Reading: Informational Text - RI.11-12.7
   - Writing - W.11-12.7, W.11-12.8, W.11-12.9.B, W.11-12.10
   - Speaking & Listening - SL.11-12.1, SL.11-12.1.C, SL.11-12.2, SL.11-12.3, SL.11-12.4, SL.11-12.5, SL.11-12.6

RESOURCES

Library, online resources, links to topics

OVERVIEW

In order to better understand how the literary movements of the past two centuries still affect us today, students will research the movements and their influence on contemporary literature and pop culture. If introduced in the first half of the unit, this research project can serve as a resource for the Extended Writing Project students will produce at the unit's close.

As students work to complete their research projects, remind them of the skills they have practiced and applied during the unit. They should incorporate this knowledge into their work as they discuss, plan, research, and create the project, and as they deliver their presentations.

Suggested topics for small-group research and presentations include:

- Choose either romanticism, realism, or modernism and research the visual art of that movement. Who were the key artists of the movement, and what are some key works of art? How did visual arts change at that time?
- Why are Jane Austen's novels still popular today? What is it about her books that lend themselves well to film and television adaptations?
- Using "The Star-Spangled Banner" as a starting point, think about the role of patriotic songs and art today. Are they still relevant? Was there a time in the past when patriotic art was more popular? Why?
- How are the supernatural and gothic elements of romanticism reflected in popular culture today? Find examples of supernatural or gothic pop culture and explain the similarities and differences between modern examples and classic romantic literature.
- What is the role of female authors in contemporary literature? Are female authors well represented among best-selling or highest paid authors today? Is that a change from the past?
- Is reality TV an extension of realism, or is it its own phenomenon? Why do people like reading about or watching "real" people?

Links to some of these topics and more can be found on the Big Idea Blast and other Blasts throughout the unit.

REVIEW AND DISCUSS (10 MINUTES)

1. **Revisit the Big Idea Blast and Unit Preview** *(SL.11-12.1-2)*. As a group, reread the Big Idea Blast and watch the Unit Preview again. Use the following questions to guide a discussion prior to research:
    a. What is the most interesting or surprising literary movement in this unit? Which texts stand out in your mind as possibly influential?
    b. What elements of the literary movements can you see reflected in twenty-first century literature? television? movies?
    c. What historical period from the unit are you most interested to learn more about?

CONDUCTING THE RESEARCH (80 MINUTES)

2. **Break Students Into Small Groups. Assign Each Group a Topic, or Let Groups Self-Select. (40 minutes)**
    a. **Make a Research Plan** *(W.11-12.7)*. Instruct students to formulate research questions for their topic. After students prepare questions, collaborate with them on the best places to search for information, the most useful keywords to use in their search, and the types of resources available to them during the research process. Remind students that their research should focus on how the literary movements of the past two centuries still affect us today.
    b. **Gather Resources** *(W.11-12.8)*. Instruct students to gather a selection of the following: print and digital text resources, video, audio recordings, graphics, and photos. Remind students to evaluate the validity of a source before using information from that source.
    c. **Review and Discuss** *(SL.11-12.1-2 and RI.11-12.7)*. Advise groups to assign each member a research task. Tasks should be completed and presented to the group by each member individually.

3. **Assemble the Research in Each Group (40 minutes)**
    a. **Share** *(SL.11-12.1-2)*. Instruct students in each group to share what they have learned about their individual research and why this information is important.
    b. **Focus** *(W.11-12.8)*. Ask students to review the information they have gathered and to select the information that is most relevant. Encourage students to revise their research questions, as needed. Each group should then create a bibliography of their resources.
    c. **Write Explanations of Facts** *(W.11-12.8)*. Instruct group members to write brief explanations of any facts they uncovered during their research. These facts can be included in the group presentation. Have students be sure to cite the sources of all information.
    d. **Plan a Short Presentation** *(SL.11-12.1.3 and SL.11-12.4)*. Ask groups to plan a short presentation of the information they compiled. Students should follow the format below:
        i. **Title:** *(W.11-12.7)* The title should provide information about the topic.
        ii. **Introduction:** *(W.11-12.7)* The introduction should include a general description of the topic and research questions.
        iii. **List of Top Facts:** *(W.11-12.9.B)* The list should include five to ten key facts about the subject.
        iv. **Multimedia Element:** *(SL.11-12.5)* Remind each group to include a visual resource (video, graphic, photo) or a recording in their presentation.
        v. **Conclusion:** Explain how this topic is relevant today.

PRESENT THE RESEARCH (35 MINUTES)

4. **Group Multimedia Presentations (5-7 minutes per group)**
    a. **Present** *(SL.11-12.5-6)*. Each group should take turns presenting their findings to the class. Remind students that a good presentation involves speaking clearly. This includes using appropriate grammar, an effective volume, a proper tone, and meaningful gestures to keep the audience's attention and to emphasize key points. To introduce quoted material or specific facts, remind students that they can say "According to" and follow this with the source of the information.
    b. **Summarize** *(SL.11-12.4)*. Ask each group to briefly summarize their presentation.
    c. **Questions** *(SL.11-12.1.C)*. If time allows, students in the audience should ask relevant questions.

EXTENSION: RESPOND TO AND POST THE PRESENTATIONS (10 MINUTES)

5. **Write** *(W.11-12.10)*. Have students write about what they have learned from the presentations by:
    a. listing three things they know now that they didn't know before
    b. writing a paragraph explaining how the presentations informed their understanding of how the literary movements of the past two centuries affect us today

POST THE RESEARCH (10 MINUTES)

Create an area in the room for students to review the research of other groups. Alternatively, have groups post their research to a blog or website to keep as a portfolio of their work.

Full-text Study

Pride and Prejudice

Pride and Prejudice

Jane Austen

INTRODUCTION

In this classic novel, Jane Austen explores love, marriage, and social mores in Georgian England at the end of the 18th century. Revolution was in the air—first in the American colonies, then in France—and the Enlightenment in Europe betokened a new respect for reason and individuality, as opposed to the feudal trappings of traditional authority. Against this background, the story of the Bennet daughters—Jane, Elizabeth, and Lydia—and their suitors illustrates the dilemma of the middle class in Great Britain, dependent on the fortunes of the upper class to keep from slipping down to the dreaded and desperate underclass. More impressive, in a plot of proposal, refusal, deception, and revelation, Austen, not yet 25, changed the novel from a yarn of high adventure to the drama of the domestic and everyday.

Jane Austen, the daughter of a rector at a country parish, began writing as a teenager, completing her first draft of *Pride and Prejudice* in her early twenties. Although her novel *Sense and Sensibility* was published first, both that novel and *Pride and Prejudice*, as well as her works *Mansfield Park* and *Emma*, achieved great popularity and acclaim during Austen's life. (Her final two novels, *Persuasion* and *Northanger Abbey*, were published after her death.) Despite the success of Austen's books, she herself remained anonymous, which likely prevented the outrage, criticism, and censure that she might have encountered as a female writer, perhaps especially as one so willing to provide pointed commentary about members of various genders and social classes.

As students read *Pride and Prejudice*, they might consider how different characters in the book view the purpose of marriage, and what those characters prioritize as they seek out matches for themselves or their family members. Students can also compare the novel's conversation of marriage to their own more contemporary experience of the institution, considering what has and has not changed since Austen's time.

USING THIS READING GUIDE

This reading guide presents lessons to support the teaching of *Pride and Prejudice*. Organized by sections of grouped chapters, the lessons preview key vocabulary words and include close reading questions tied to the Common Core State Standards. The lessons identify a key passage in each section that will help you guide students through an exploration of the essential conflicts, themes, and questions in *Pride and Prejudice*. This passage will also serve as the jumping-off point from which students will engage in their own StudySyncTV–style group discussion.

Each section of the reading guide also includes a list of comparative texts—provided in the *Pride and Prejudice* Full-text Unit in the StudySync Library—that go along with that section. For each comparative text, the reading guide includes important contextual notes and ideas for relating the text to *Pride and Prejudice*. The reading guide concludes with two writing prompts that allow students to revisit *Pride and Prejudice* both creatively and summatively, with reference to the comparative texts.

PRIDE AND PREJUDICE

TEXT SECTIONS

CHAPTERS 1-9: Two Social Worlds, One Village

The wealthy bachelor John Bingley moves to Longbourn, where he and his wealthy bachelor friend Fitzwilliam Darcy meet the Bennet family. Although Bingley becomes enamored with the eldest Bennet daughter, Jane, the social divisions between the young men and the Bennets do not favor Jane's prospects, especially after Jane falls ill and she and her sister Elizabeth are forced to stay at Bingley's estate, Netherfield.

CHAPTERS 10-22: A Chance for Security

In addition to Darcy and Bingley, the reader is introduced to several more eligible bachelors, including a regiment of bivouacked soldiers and the Reverend Mr. Collins, who is due to inherit the Bennets' property. After the ball at Netherfield, Mr. Collins proposes to Elizabeth, but she refuses, much to her mother's chagrin.

CHAPTERS 23-34: Too Much Pride, Too Much Prejudice

Bingley's sisters scheme to keep Bingley in London for the winter, away from Jane, and close to Darcy's sister, whom they and Darcy believe to be a more appropriate partner. Elizabeth spends some time with Charlotte Collins (Lucas) at Rosings Park, where she sees quite a bit of Mr. Darcy. Although an attraction seems to be growing between them, his misgivings about her family status and her bad opinion of him, based on what she's heard, continue to keep them apart.

CHAPTERS 35-45: Reconsideration, But Too Late?

A letter from Darcy, a visit to his estate at Pemberley, and an awkward encounter with a soldier, Mr. Wickham, all cause Elizabeth to feel that she has been wrong in her judgments about Darcy. Although Elizabeth tries to prevent this, Mr. Bennet lets Lydia stay in Brighton, where Wickham's regiment is now stationed.

CHAPTERS 46-52: The Trouble with Wickham

Lydia Bennet runs away with Mr. Wickham, but he is persuaded to marry her once his debts are paid off and he is given an income on which the couple can live. Elizabeth later learns that Mr. Darcy is responsible for finding Wickham and brokering his marriage to Lydia.

CHAPTERS 53-61: Resolution, Happiness, Marriage

Bingley and Darcy return to Netherfield, and with Darcy's blessing this time, Bingley quickly proposes to Jane. When Lady Catherine attempts to interfere with the marriage of Darcy and Elizabeth, the estranged couple becomes aware of each other's true feelings.

CHAPTERS 1-9: Two Social Worlds, One Village

KEY PASSAGE | Chapter 1, Paragraphs 1–16

It is a truth universally acknowledged, that a single man in possession of a good fortune, must be in want of a wife.

However little known the feelings or views of such a man may be on his first entering a neighbourhood, this truth is so well fixed in the minds of the surrounding families, that he is considered the rightful property of some one or other of their daughters.

"My dear Mr. Bennet," said his lady to him one day, "have you heard that Netherfield Park is let at last?"

Mr. Bennet replied that he had not.

"But it is," returned she; "for Mrs. Long has just been here, and she told me all about it."

Mr. Bennet made no answer.

"Do you not want to know who has taken it?" cried his wife impatiently.

"You want to tell me, and I have no objection to hearing it."

This was invitation enough.

"Why, my dear, you must know, Mrs. Long says that Netherfield is taken by a young man of large fortune from the north of England; that he came down on Monday in a chaise and four to see the place, and was so much delighted with it, that he agreed with Mr. Morris immediately; that he is to take possession before Michaelmas, and some of his servants are to be in the house by the end of next week."

"What is his name?"

"Bingley."

"Is he married or single?"

"Oh! Single, my dear, to be sure! A single man of large fortune; four or five thousand a year. What a fine thing for our girls!"

"How so? How can it affect them?"

"My dear Mr. Bennet," replied his wife, "how can you be so tiresome! You must know that I am thinking of his marrying one of them."

WHY IT'S KEY

Central Concept: As the introduction to the novel's themes and concerns, this passage raises the question of social class in Austen's England, and shows how the institution of marriage played a central role in defining and preserving social class. While contemporary society might be more inclined to view marriage as an institution driven by personal choice and individual emotion, this passage makes clear the degree to which property and prosperity are at stake for Austen's single female characters, their families, and the bachelors they encounter. Although comic in nature, this passage shows how the middle-class Bennet family must use their daughters' marriages to preserve their own social status; a rich bachelor moving to the neighborhood is a "fine thing for our girls." Although Mrs. Bennet is particularly eager to use her daughters' beauty in the service of the family's financial security, the passage indicates that this approach to marriage was a vital concern for many middle-class families, especially those without sons. Mrs. Bennet's valuation of Mr. Bingley shows the importance of status, as she comments not on his character but on his income and the style in which he travels to visit Netherfield Park.

Character: This passage introduces the reader to several characteristics of the Bennet family that will play significant roles later in the novel. Mrs. Bennet's crass pursuit of wealthy husbands for her daughters marks the Bennets as socially precarious, as if she presumes too much in thinking anyone of her status would be deserving of a more noble marriage. Her inability to pick up on social cues, such as her husband's sarcastic response to her machinations, will also harm the family's prospects in the future. Similarly, Mr. Bennet's lack of seriousness about the fates of his daughters will have grave consequences for the family later on. Mrs. Bennet is a typical Austen character in that she serves not only as a source of comedy but also provides commentary on the social mores and situations that determine the lives of the novel's heroines.

Point of View: This passage establishes the third-person narrator that characterizes much of Jane Austen's fiction, and it is a hallmark of her literary style. In addition to telling her story, Austen provides biting insight into the social expectations of the time, such as the novel's opening line, "It is a truth universally acknowledged, that a single man in possession of a good fortune, must be in want of a wife.... this truth is so well fixed in the minds of the surrounding families, that he is considered the rightful property of some one or other of their daughters." Austen suggests here that for wealthy men, the choice of a wife must be made with status in mind, a truth that will later trouble both Mr. Darcy and Mr. Bingley when they fall in love with women who are below them socially. Notably, Austen doesn't limit her criticisms to the upper class; she is equally harsh on upwardly mobile middle-class families such as the Bennets, who similarly reduce potential marriage partners to assets or, as she says here, "property." Although the characters in this novel are constrained by their social environment, Austen's narrative also provides insight into how they emerge as individuals within it; the principle characters are neither entirely villainous nor victims of their circumstances.

YOUR STUDYSYNC® TV

Discussion Prompt: In this passage, it appears clear that Mrs. Bennet wants her daughters to marry men of fortune. Why might Austen be mocking such ambitions? Is it ever appropriate to marry for wealth? Why or why not? Are the Bennet sisters more in need of wealthy husbands than women today, and if so, why?

Standards: RL.11-12.1, RL.11-12.4; SL.11-12.1.A, SL.11-12.1.C, SL.11-12.1.D

VOCABULARY

caprice
ca•price *noun*
A quick or unexpected shift in attitude, comportment, or plan
He was prone to caprices while on vacation, which made him an unpredictable travel partner.

complacency
com•pla•cen•cy *noun*
The state of being overly pleased with one's situation, often from a reluctance to question or challenge oneself
After his team won three shutout games, the soccer coach set up a friendly match with a more skilled team, to make sure his players would not drift into complacency.

solicitude
so•lic•i•tude *noun*
Concern for the well-being or situation of others
She was known for her solicitude toward her neighbors, always quick to offer a pot of hot soup if one had a cold.

substantial
sub•stan•tial *adjective*
Of significant size or value
The family received substantial assistance when their house was hit by the tornado, allowing them to completely rebuild.

witticism
wit•ti•cism *noun*
A clever, humorous comment
Although he worked as a standup comedian, his everyday conversation contained almost no witticisms.

CLOSE READ

QUESTION 1: How do the Bennet sisters finally meet Bingley, and why does it happen in this manner?

Sample Answer: They meet Bingley at a ball, since he had not been able to accept their family's dinner invitation, and there are strict rules for social contact between single men and women (Chapter 3).

Standards: RL.11-12.1

QUESTION 2: What first impressions do the Bennet family form about Bingley and Darcy? Use language from the text to support your answers.

Sample Answer: They are quite impressed with Bingley, as Jane finds him to be "sensible, good-humoured, lively; and I never saw such happy manners" (Chapter 4). Because

Darcy refused to dance with Elizabeth, however, they think he is a snob: "so high and so conceited that there was no enduring him" (Chapter 3).

Standards: RL.11-12.1

QUESTION 3: How do Elizabeth Bennet and her friend Charlotte Lucas differ in their views on how well one should know a potential spouse before marriage?

Sample Answer: Elizabeth believes that one must make a careful study of a person's character, but Charlotte thinks that the happiness of two people can't ever be predicted or certain, and one might as well marry quickly (Chapter 6).

Standards: RL.11-12.1

QUESTION 4: When Mr. Bennet dies, who will inherit his money and property, and why?

Sample Answer: Mr. Bennet's property is entailed, which means it will go to a male relative, since none of his daughters are allowed to inherit it (Chapter 7).

Standards: RL.11-12.1

QUESTION 5: How do Darcy and various members of the Bingley family respond when Elizabeth travels by foot to Netherfield to be with her sick sister Jane? Use language from the novel to support your answer.

Sample Answer: Bingley thinks that this proves how much she loves her sister: "it shows an affection for her sister that is very pleasing." The Bingley sisters think it isn't very ladylike: "Her hair, so untidy, so blowsy!" Darcy doesn't think it is proper, but he does find her more beautiful from making the effort; her eyes "were brightened by the exercise" (Chapter 8).

Standards: RL.11-12.1

COMPARATIVE TEXTS

Text: *Jane Austen: A Life* by Claire Tomalin

Compare to: Chapters 1-7 of *Pride and Prejudice*

Connection: The wealthy nobles were under attack for being wealthy. Many in the laboring class were spurning society's rules, even disdaining marriage. Amid this era of change, Jane Austen grew up in Hampshire, England, born in 1775, the daughter of a clergyman and one of eight children, including a sister named Cassandra, who was her closest confidante. Jane grew up an avid reader of the novels of the day, and her early talent for writing was manifest in shrewd parodies. Her aborted romance with a would-be suitor, Tom Lefroy, directly precedes her work on what would become *Pride and Prejudice*, as told in Claire Tomalin's biography. Students might consider how the novel's social world both resembles and differs from Austen's life as described in the biography.

Text: *How to Get a Rich Man* by Donna Spangler

Compare to: Chapter 9 of *Pride and Prejudice*

Connection: In *How to Get a Rich Man*, author Donna Spangler shares her tips on why and how to snag Mr. Moneybags. Who among Jane Austen's characters in *Pride and Prejudice* would agree with Spangler's "Princess Formula" for happiness and fulfillment? Who would take exception and why? Students will explore how the rules of the courtship game have or haven't changed since Jane Austen's day.

CHAPTERS 10-22: A Chance for Security

KEY PASSAGE | Chapter 19, Paragraphs 13–17

"I am not now to learn," replied Mr. Collins, with a formal wave of the hand, "that it is usual with young ladies to reject the addresses of the man whom they secretly mean to accept, when he first applies for their favour; and that sometimes the refusal is repeated a second, or even a third time. I am therefore by no means discouraged by what you have just said, and shall hope to lead you to the altar ere long."

"Upon my word, sir," cried Elizabeth, "your hope is a rather extraordinary one after my declaration. I do assure you that I am not one of those young ladies (if such young ladies there are) who are so daring as to risk their happiness on the chance of being asked a second time. I am perfectly serious in my refusal. You could not make me happy, and I am convinced that I am the last woman in the world who could make you so. Nay, were your friend Lady Catherine to know me, I am persuaded she would find me in every respect ill qualified for the situation."

"Were it certain that Lady Catherine would think so," said Mr. Collins very gravely—"but I cannot imagine that her ladyship would at all disapprove of you. And you may be certain when I have the honour of seeing her again, I shall speak in the very highest terms of your modesty, economy, and other amiable qualification."

"Indeed, Mr. Collins, all praise of me will be unnecessary. You must give me leave to judge for myself, and pay me the compliment of believing what I say. I wish you very happy and very rich, and by refusing your hand, do all in my power to prevent your being otherwise. In making me the offer, you must have satisfied the delicacy of your feelings with regard to my family, and may take possession of Longbourn estate whenever it falls, without any self-reproach. This matter may be considered, therefore, as finally settled." And rising as she thus spoke, she would have quitted the room, had Mr. Collins not thus addressed her:

> *"When I do myself the honour of speaking to you next on the subject, I shall hope to receive a more favourable answer than you have now given me; though I am far from accusing you of cruelty at present, because I know it to be the established custom of your sex to reject a man on the first application, and perhaps you have even now said as much to encourage my suit as would be consistent with the true delicacy of the female character."*

WHY IT'S KEY

Character: This passage shows Elizabeth Bennet's independent nature. In refusing Mr. Collins because she doesn't think their union will be a mutually satisfying or happy one, she goes against the social expectations of her time. Although she has no long-term financial security, she chooses not to marry Mr. Collins, even though their marriage would ensure that her family's property stays in the family. One can also see how Elizabeth's actions defy the expectations for female behavior in the middle and upper classes. She forgoes the "delicacy" that Mr. Collins assumes would be in her nature as a woman by refusing him. Although Mr. Collins's suit is quite comic in this passage, Austen clearly satirizes the unwillingness to see women as individuals willing to express themselves in a direct manner. His continued refusal to ascribe value to Elizabeth's words provides a great contrast to the more rebellious nature of her decision-making in this passage. The belief that women have a duty of self-sacrifice, as Elizabeth would be doing if she married Mr. Collins to preserve her family's wealth, is clearly not one to which she subscribes.

Central Concept: This passage develops the concept that in Austen's world, marriage was an institution that preserved social status and reinforced divisions between the classes. This is true in this passage in the most practical sense: because middle- and upper-class women had no legal ability to work, the Bennet sisters depend on their husbands for long-term financial security. In more subtle ways, marriage is also an institution that protects the more privileged classes from others, an institution that preserves their privilege. Collins's noble patron, Lady Catherine, would approve of the match between Collins and Elizabeth because of their relatively equal middle-class status. (Later in the novel, she will not approve of a union between Elizabeth and Darcy, because of Elizabeth's inferiority.) The obsession with maintaining one's social status, for both the middle- and upper-class characters in the novel, comes in part from the broad social backdrop against which Austen's novel is set: in the final decades of the 18th century, social revolutions in France and growing working-class unrest in England have made previously inviolable institutions such as nobility and social status seem more precarious.

Author's Craft: In this passage, one can see how much Austen uses social convention and manners to narrate this novel. The formal exchange between Elizabeth and Mr. Collins can seem absurd to modern readers, as Elizabeth must use conventions of polite social interaction, such as compliments, to demand that Mr. Collins accept her answer: "pay me the compliment of believing what I say." Austen's ability to reenact the manners of her time, but also to comically question them, is a key feature of her narrative style. Although Elizabeth is hardly the kind of woman that Mr. Collins assumes her to be, the reader might consider the "delicacy" of this exchange. This passage and the novel as a whole are filled with delicate conventions—the visits, the balls, the dances. It is worth keeping in mind that such institutions of courtship are important because in Austen's world, marriage is not about the search for love, but instead is an area of life through which social status is protected or maintained, and knowing how to behave in the proper manner was part of this process.

YOUR STUDYSYNC® TV

Discussion Prompt: Do you agree with Elizabeth's decision to refuse Mr. Collins, and the manner in which she makes her refusal? What are the dangers of such a decision, and given those dangers, what might motivate or justify her to act as she did?

Standards: RL.11-12.1, RL.11-12.4; SL.11-12.1.A, SL.11-12.1.C, SL.11-12.1.D

VOCABULARY

iniquitous
in•i•qui•tous *adjective*
Unjust or wrong on an ethical level
The country still used an iniquitous legal system, which favored those with more money regardless of their innocence or guilt.

antagonist
an•ta•go•nist *noun*
A person with whom one is hostile or in confrontation; an enemy
The mayor was known for being fair and even-handed, even dining out with his political antagonists.

veracity
ver•a•ci•ty *noun*
The quality of being truthful, factual, legitimate
Although she usually trusted her children, when they told her they had no homework for the entire week, she doubted their veracity.

implicit
im•plic•it *adjective*
Understood to be true, from indirect evidence; implied
When the gardener called the choice of flowers "a bit unusual," her implicit criticism of the client's garden was unmistakable.

disapprobation
dis•ap•pro•ba•tion *noun*
Severe moral or ideological disapproval
Although some in her community at first expressed disapprobation, the senator staunchly defended the legality of same-sex marriage.

CLOSE READ

QUESTION 1: Why does Mr. Collins want to come visit the Bennet family at Longbourn, their estate, even though his father and Mr. Bennet have a bad history?

Sample Answer: Mr. Collins feels guilty that he will inherit the Bennet property and the daughters will have nothing. He seems to want to get to know the daughters and to find some way to make amends for the situation (Chapter 13).

Standards: RL.11-12.1

QUESTION 2: How does Mr. Collins feel one should act toward people who have higher social status than oneself? Use language from the novel to support your answer.

Sample Answer: Mr. Collins feels that people should appreciate any gesture of friendliness or overture from someone of higher status. He thinks that less wealthy people are enriched by the presence of wealthier ones, even if they are only driving by: "she is perfectly amiable, and often condescends to drive by my humble abode in her little phaeton and ponies" (Chapter 14).

Standards: RL.11-12.1

QUESTION 3: What do the Bennet sisters notice about Mr. Wickham when they meet him in Meryton? Use language from the novel to support your answer.

Sample Answer: Mr. Wickham appears to be attractive in many ways: "... he had all the best part of beauty, a fine countenance, a good figure, and very pleasing address." Elizabeth notices that there seems to be some bad blood between him and Mr. Darcy: "Both changed colour, one looked white, the other red. Mr. Wickham, after a few moments, touched his hat—a salutation which Mr. Darcy just deigned to return" (Chapter 15).

Standards: RL.11-12.1

QUESTION 4: What does Mr. Wickham claim that Darcy has done to wrong him, and why does Elizabeth believe Wickham's story?

Sample Answer: Wickham says that Darcy did not give Wickham an inheritance that Darcy's father had promised, as reward for Wickham's family's service to the Darcys. Elizabeth has heard Darcy speak about his own tendency to hold a grudge: "I do remember his boasting one day, at Netherfield, of the implacability of his resentments" (Chapter 16).

Standards: RL.11-12.1

QUESTION 5: Why does Elizabeth's friend Charlotte Lucas say yes to Mr. Collins, and how does her approach to marriage differ from Elizabeth's? Use language from the text to support your answer.

Sample Answer: Charlotte Lucas says yes because Mr. Collins can provide a secure life for her. She doesn't believe that love should be the guiding force in decisions about marriage: "I am not romantic, you know; I never was. I ask only a comfortable home" (Chapter 22).

Standards: RL.11-12.1

COMPARATIVE TEXTS

Text: *Bridget Jones's Diary* by Helen Fielding

Compare to: Chapter 18 of *Pride and Prejudice*

Connection: Helen Fielding readily admits to basing her *Bridget Jones* books on *Pride and Prejudice*, even naming one of her characters Mark Darcy, after Elizabeth's suitor. Fielding began writing *Bridget Jones's Diary* in 1995 as a weekly column in a London newspaper, as a satire of the life of the single British working woman in her thirties. The column was instantly popular and led to three Bridget Jones novels, as well as three movies, becoming part of the Jane Austen craze following a hit BBC-TV series of *Pride and Prejudice* in 1995 with Colin Firth as Mr. Darcy. Students can discuss what the two novels share and how they diverge in tone, attitude, language, and characterization.

CHAPTERS 23-34: Too Much Pride, Too Much Prejudice

KEY PASSAGE | Chapter 34, Paragraphs 26–32

"You could not have made the offer of your hand in any possible way that would have tempted me to accept it."

Again his astonishment was obvious; and he looked at her with an expression of mingled incredulity and mortification. She went on:

"From the very beginning—from the first moment, I may almost say—of my acquaintance with you, your manners, impressing me with the fullest belief of your arrogance, your conceit, and your selfish disdain of the feelings of others, were such as to form the groundwork of disapprobation on which succeeding events have built so immovable a dislike; and I had not known you a month before I felt that you were the last man in the world whom I could ever be prevailed on to marry."

"You have said quite enough, madam. I perfectly comprehend your feelings, and have now only to be ashamed of what my own have been. Forgive me for having taken up so much of your time, and accept my best wishes for your health and happiness."

And with these words he hastily left the room, and Elizabeth heard him the next moment open the front door and quit the house.

The tumult of her mind was now painfully great. She knew not how to support herself, and from actual weakness sat down and cried for half-an-hour. Her astonishment, as she reflected on what had passed, was increased by every review of it. That she should receive an offer of marriage from Mr. Darcy! That he should have been in love with her for so many months! So much in love as to wish to marry her in spite of all the objections which had made him prevent his friend's marrying her sister, and which must appear at least with equal force in his own case—was almost incredible! It was gratifying to have inspired unconsciously so strong an affection. But his pride, his abominable pride—his shameless avowal of what he had done with respect

> *to Jane—his unpardonable assurance in acknowledging, though he could not justify it, and the unfeeling manner in which he had mentioned Mr. Wickham, his cruelty towards whom he had not attempted to deny, soon overcame the pity which the consideration of his attachment had for a moment excited.*
>
> *She continued in very agitated reflections till the sound of Lady Catherine's carriage made her feel how unequal she was to encounter Charlotte's observation, and hurried her away to her room.*

WHY IT'S KEY

Central Concept (Pride): While many events and passages of the novel reveal the degree to which marriage in Austen's time was an institution related to social privilege and exclusion, this section of the novel and this passage in particular reveal the deeper flaws that emerge when individuals live inside such a system. Austen's intricate plotting showcases the pitfalls of pride for both Elizabeth and Darcy, as the events whose climax readers have just witnessed are shaped by pride in both their cases. Elizabeth accuses Darcy of "abominable pride," of "your arrogance, your conceit, and your selfish disdain of the feelings of others." In her understanding of events thus far, his actions show a destructive pride in his decision to convince Bingley not to marry Jane, and his shameless honesty about the matter. He also seems proud in his unwillingness to accept or explain the wrongs that Elizabeth believes he has committed against Mr. Wickham. From Darcy's perspective, Elizabeth seems too proud to admit when her family's behavior, especially her mother's bald pursuit of wealthy sons-in-law, might actually give some pause to a reasonable person. He sees his disclosure of his own actions toward Bingley and Jane as honesty, not pride, and believes that if Elizabeth were less defensive about her own family's social situation, she would also understand that.

Central Concept (Prejudice): In addition to the complex troubles of pride as detailed above, this passage shows the degree to which prejudice, or rigid assumptions about the relative worth of others, can interfere with one's pursuit of happiness and stability in life. In this passage, Austen reveals the degree to which all of Elizabeth's judgments about Darcy compound each other, leading her to an inflexible view of his character; each impression forms a "groundwork of disapprobation" that becomes impossible for Elizabeth to dismantle, even when some evidence, such as Mr. Wickham's blatant pursuit of a wealthy widow earlier in this section or Colonel Fitzwilliam's general goodness and regard for Darcy, might suggest the limits of her perceptions. (Darcy's prejudices against Elizabeth on account of her family's behavior and social dignity will likely seem more obvious and problematic to the contemporary reader.) Although both her relative social status and her gender render her more of a victim in this social system than Darcy, the detail with which Austen explores her flaws and the trouble of her character is evidence of Austen's complex social analysis. Austen refuses to write Elizabeth as a helpless object in this social system, and the heroine's flaws and complexity have likely led to the lasting appeal of her character, even centuries after Austen's novel was first published.

Character: This passage shows the independence with which both Elizabeth and Darcy function, even as they are both confined or troubled by the judgments and expectations of the social system in which the novel takes place. Students might consider how differently Elizabeth refuses Darcy, as compared to her earlier refusal of Mr. Collins. Here, she is abrupt and direct, pulling no punches for the sake of Darcy's feelings: "I had not known you a month before I felt that you were the last man in the world whom I could ever be prevailed on to marry." Although Darcy seems a bit surprised by her lack of social graces in refusing him, he admits that he too does not bother with such social graces, and has chosen not to conceal or deceive her as to his misgivings about her social status. By now, the reader can understand how shocking this type of direct and honest communication—especially about matters of love, marriage, and social class—might seem in the world of Austen's novel. (Students might also consider the ways in which it might still be taboo to talk so directly about social class.) Unlike Bingley and Jane, who are both passively accepting of when social expectations and divisions interfere with their affection, Elizabeth and Darcy emerge in this passage as characters more willing to fly in the face of convention.

YOUR STUDYSYNC® TV

Discussion Prompt: In this passage from *Pride and Prejudice*, as in many stories both tragic and comic, the growing love between two main characters is thwarted by other circumstances and forces. What gets in the way of love succeeding between Elizabeth and Darcy? Do the forces that separate the two characters apply and exist in contemporary society? Why or why not?

Standards: RL.11-12.1, RL.11-12.4; SL.11-12.1.A, SL.11-12.1.C, SL.11-12.1.D

VOCABULARY

rapturous
rap•tur•ous *adjective*
Showing or resulting from passion or great happiness
When she saw her friend at the baggage claim, back from his tour of duty in Iraq, she greeted him with a rapturous shout.

commendation
com•men•da•tion *noun*
Recognition for something positive
He had always been a dedicated student, so no one was surprised when he graduated with commendations from his teachers.

duplicity
du•plic•i•ty *noun*
Dishonest behavior; lying
We listened to her story with great skepticism because she had a reputation for duplicity.

avarice
av•a•rice *noun*
Greed or miserly behavior; a desire to gain wealth at the expense of others
Because of his extreme avarice, the landlord raised our rent three times this year,

affability
af•fa•bil•i•ty *noun*
The quality of being kind and easy to get along with
His affability made him a great waiter, coaxing a smile from even the crankiest customers.

impertinent
im•per•ti•nent
Disrespectful or improper; rude
Dan's boss explained that taking a phone call in the middle of the board meeting was impertinent behavior.

CLOSE READ

QUESTION 1: In Chapter 24, what differences of perspective can be seen between Elizabeth and Jane, as they react to the news that Bingley's affection for Miss Darcy may growing?

Sample Answer: Jane seems more likely to think well of people, as she thinks that the Bingley sisters want their brother to marry Miss Darcy because she is a deserving bride, but Elizabeth thinks they are trying to save Bingley from what they see as a dangerous marriage to Jane.

Standards: RL.11-12.1

QUESTION 2: How does Elizabeth explain and react when Mr. Wickham ceases to pay so much attention to her and her sisters? Use language from the novel to support your answer.

Sample Answer: She assumes that Mr. Wickham has chosen to pursue Miss King because of her fortune, and she thinks that such behavior is perfectly reasonable for a man who has no money, since " handsome men must have something to live on, as well as the plain" (Chapter 26).

Standards: RL.11-12.1

QUESTION 3: In Chapter 29, what sorts of criticisms does Lady Catherine make about the Bennet family, when she spends the evening with Elizabeth?

Sample Answer: She seems shocked that the daughters were raised without a governess to give them an education. She thinks it isn't appropriate for the younger daughters to be out in society before the elder ones are married.

Standards: RL.11-12.1

QUESTION 4: In Chapter 33, which of Darcy's private actions does Colonel Fitzwilliam tell to Elizabeth, and why does he confide in her about this information?

Sample Answer: Colonel Fitzwilliam tells Elizabeth that Darcy has prevented Bingley from making an imprudent marriage. He does this because he is trying to give an example of how devoted Darcy is to his friend, and the Colonel doesn't realize that the questionable family from whom Darcy saved Bingley is Elizabeth's family.

Standards: RL.11-12.1

COMPARATIVE TEXTS

Text: *The Fatal Shore* by Robert Hughes

Compare to: Chapter 29 of *Pride and Prejudice*

Connection: *Pride and Prejudice* presents a limited view of late-18th-century England. Austen's genteel world of desperate housewives seeking monied marriages for their sons and daughters tells a very small part of the story. In *A Fatal Shore*, Robert Hughes exposes the desperation of England's very poor who lived in squalor and turned to crime as a useful vehicle for social advancement. Students will consider a novelist's obligation to deal with the most urgent issues of the day and explore the degree to which Jane Austen does or doesn't meet that responsibility. Does Austin sidestep the pressing issues of poverty, social desperation, the criminal underclass, and the tone-deafness of the landed gentry? Or does she address them in different ways—indirectly, through subplots and minor characters? Students might consider Lady Catherine in relationship to this question.

CHAPTERS 35-45: Reconsideration, But Too Late?

KEY PASSAGE | Chapter 35, Paragraphs 11–12

"I must now mention a circumstance which I would wish to forget myself, and which no obligation less than the present should induce me to unfold to any human being. Having said thus much, I feel no doubt of your secrecy. My sister, who is more than ten years my junior, was left to the guardianship of my mother's nephew, Colonel Fitzwilliam, and myself. About a year ago, she was taken from school, and an establishment formed for her in London; and last summer she went with the lady who presided over it, to Ramsgate; and thither also went Mr. Wickham, undoubtedly by design; for there proved to have been a prior acquaintance between him and Mrs. Younge, in whose character we were most unhappily deceived; and by her connivance and aid, he so far recommended himself to Georgiana, whose affectionate heart retained a strong impression of his kindness to her as a child, that she was persuaded to believe herself in love, and to consent to an elopement. She was then but fifteen, which must be her excuse; and after stating her imprudence, I am happy to add, that I owed the knowledge of it to herself. I joined them unexpectedly a day or two before the intended elopement, and then Georgiana, unable to support the idea of grieving and offending a brother whom she almost looked up to as a father, acknowledged the whole to me. You may imagine what I felt and how I acted. Regard for my sister's credit and feelings prevented any public exposure; but I wrote to Mr. Wickham, who left the place immediately, and Mrs. Younge was of course removed from her charge. Mr. Wickham's chief object was unquestionably my sister's fortune, which is thirty thousand pounds; but I cannot help supposing that the hope of revenging himself on me was a strong inducement. His revenge would have been complete indeed.

"This, madam, is a faithful narrative of every event in which we have been concerned together; and if you do not absolutely reject it as false, you will, I hope, acquit me henceforth of cruelty towards Mr. Wickham. I know not in

> *what manner, under what form of falsehood he had imposed on you; but his success is not perhaps to be wondered at. Ignorant as you previously were of everything concerning either, detection could not be in your power, and suspicion certainly not in your inclination."*

WHY IT'S KEY

Plot: This passage highlights a classical moment of reversal and recognition in the novel. After reading Darcy's letter, Elizabeth has no choice but to recognize the falseness of her early perceptions of both him and Mr. Wickham, as well as the prejudices that have kept her from seeing the situation more clearly. From this point on, she will rank the male characters in the novel in a different order, moving toward a higher opinion of Darcy and more skepticism concerning Mr. Wickham, especially as Wickham continues to have relationships with her sisters. Although Austen's novel is quite different in both style and social context from an Aristotelian tragedy, the momentum of her plot does borrow something from that narrative tradition, as seen in this passage. That the story turns on a moment of internal realization and epiphany, as well as action, marks Austen as a forerunner of more modern narrative traditions.

Point of View: This passage also highlights Austen's use of the epistolary form. *Pride and Prejudice* can't be considered an epistolary novel in its entirety; the omniscient third-person narrative used elsewhere is a key aspect of Austen's style and social commentary. That said, the use of letters throughout the novel, especially in key moments of development and revelation, connects Austen to a more personal style of writing that was popular in the late 18th and early 19th centuries. For Austen and her characters, the letter was an essential means of communication. Students might consider the role that written correspondence plays in the lives of these characters. In this novel, there is a great deal at stake in one's manner of speaking and writing about oneself, as judgments about character are often linked to one's manner of expression. Students might consider in what ways this remains true in contemporary society, even as the lengthy letter has fallen out of fashion.

Central Concept: In more explicit ways than the novel's earlier developments, the story of Mr. Wickham and Georgiana Darcy reveals the dangers that sometimes accompany passion for middle- and upper-class women in Austen's world. Because Georgiana is too young to understand the social context and significance of marriage, Wickham is able to manipulate her feelings in the service of his own more mercenary desires; he performs love when it allows him to secure income and fortune. Many of Austen's characters can seem ridiculously cynical to more contemporary and romantic readers, but it is important to understand the context for such caution and the stakes that faced these women if they failed to recognize predatory affections such as Wickham's. (This will become clearer as students read about Lydia's situation in the next section.) Students might also consider how Austen's novel develops the difference between these dramatic types of love and the more considered, slow-moving, and reflective relationship that develops between Elizabeth and Darcy, in part through correspondence such as this letter.

YOUR STUDYSYNC® TV

Discussion Prompt: Why do you think Darcy decides to reveal the truth behind his actions toward Bingley and Wickham in a letter? How does the use of this medium change the impact that this information has on Elizabeth? What role do you think letters play in Austen's world, and why are they so important? Do letters still have a place in more contemporary society, and what is their purpose now?

Standards: RL.11-12.1, RL.11-12.4; SL.11-12.1.A, SL.11-12.1.C, SL.11-12.1.D

VOCABULARY

profligacy
prof•li•ga•cy *noun*
The quality of being foolish or wasteful with money
Her parents believed that profligacy was the greatest evil, so she never bought anything unless it was absolutely necessary.

mercenary
mer•ce•nar•y *adjective*
Willing to ignore moral or ethical considerations in pursuit of financial gain
Many fans condemned the basketball star as mercenary when he left his hometown team to play for their rival at a higher salary.

irksome
irk•some *adjective*
Causing irritation or bother
He found it irksome when his mother entered his bedroom without knocking first.

vexation
vex•a•tion *noun*
When one is concerned or annoyed about a situation
The fact that her daughter never called to say she'd be home late caused the mother a great deal of vexation.

ascertain
as•cer•tain *verb*
To find out something that isn't known with certainty
She knew the recovery process after her friend's car accident would be long and slow, but she kept trying to ascertain how she could help.

CLOSE READ

QUESTION 1: Why does Elizabeth choose to believe Mr. Darcy's version of events, instead of that of her former friend Mr. Wickham? Use evidence from the novel to support your answer.

Sample Answer: Elizabeth realizes that Mr. Wickham's good impression on her came mostly from his manner, and not from any kind acts: "she could see him instantly before her, in every charm of air and address; but she could remember no more substantial good" (Chapter 36). She sees his actions toward Miss King as more predatory: "his attentions to Miss King were now the consequence of views solely and hatefully mercenary" (Chapter 36).

Standards: RL.11-12.1

QUESTION 2: Why does Elizabeth try to convince her father not to let Lydia stay with Colonel Forster's wife in Brighton, where the regiment will be stationed? Use language from the novel to support your answer.

Sample Answer: She is aware how much Lydia's improper behavior has already hurt their family: "my dear father, can you suppose it possible that they will not be censured and despised wherever they are known, and that their sisters will not be often involved in the disgrace?" (Chapter 41).

Standards: RL.11-12.1

QUESTION 3: How have Elizabeth's observations about her parents' marriage influenced her own views on the institution? Use language from the text to support your answer.

Sample Answer: It is important to her to find a partner who suits her character, since she sees how her own badly matched parents have created a harmful environment for her and her sisters: "she had never felt so strongly as now the disadvantages which must attend the children of so unsuitable a marriage" (Chapter 42).

Standards: RL.11-12.1

QUESTION 4: How does Mrs. Reynolds, the servant at Pemberley, influence Elizabeth's opinion of Darcy and Wickham? Use language from the novel to support your answer.

Sample Answer: Mrs. Reynolds confirms Elizabeth's growing sense that Darcy is a man of good character—"he was always the sweetest-tempered, most generous-hearted boy in the world"—and that Wickham's character is more dubious: "he has turned out very wild" (Chapter 43).

Standards: RL.11-12.1

QUESTION 5: What motivates Miss Bingley in her continued efforts to criticize Elizabeth or make her look bad? Use language from the novel to support your answer.

Sample Answer: Miss Bingley is jealous of Darcy's love for Elizabeth, as she herself has feelings for the man: "Miss Bingley was venting her feelings in criticisms on Elizabeth's person, behaviour, and dress" (Chapter 45).

Standards: RL.11-12.1

CHAPTERS 46-52: The Trouble with Wickham

KEY PASSAGE | Chapter 52, Paragraph 18

The contents of this letter threw Elizabeth into a flutter of spirits, in which it was difficult to determine whether pleasure or pain bore the greatest share. The vague and unsettled suspicions which uncertainty had produced of what Mr. Darcy might have been doing to forward her sister's match, which she had feared to encourage as an exertion of goodness too great to be probable, and at the same time dreaded to be just, from the pain of obligation, were proved beyond their greatest extent to be true! He had followed them purposely to town, he had taken on himself all the trouble and mortification attendant on such a research; in which supplication had been necessary to a woman whom he must abominate and despise, and where he was reduced to meet, frequently meet, reason with, persuade, and finally bribe, the man whom he always most wished to avoid, and whose very name it was punishment to him to pronounce. He had done all this for a girl whom he could neither regard nor esteem. Her heart did whisper that he had done it for her. But it was a hope shortly checked by other considerations, and she soon felt that even her vanity was insufficient, when required to depend on his affection for her—for a woman who had already refused him—as able to overcome a sentiment so natural as abhorrence against relationship with Wickham. Brother-in-law of Wickham! Every kind of pride must revolt from the connection. He had, to be sure, done much. She was ashamed to think how much. But he had given a reason for his interference, which asked no extraordinary stretch of belief. It was reasonable that he should feel he had been wrong; he had liberality, and he had the means of exercising it; and though she would not place herself as his principal inducement, she could, perhaps, believe that remaining partiality for her might assist his endeavours in a cause where her peace of mind must be materially concerned. It was painful, exceedingly painful, to know that they were under obligations to a person who could never receive a return. They owed the restoration of Lydia, her character, every thing, to him. Oh! how

> *heartily did she grieve over every ungracious sensation she had ever encouraged, every saucy speech she had ever directed towards him. For herself she was humbled; but she was proud of him. Proud that in a cause of compassion and honour, he had been able to get the better of himself. She read over her aunt's commendation of him again and again. It was hardly enough; but it pleased her. She was even sensible of some pleasure, though mixed with regret, on finding how steadfastly both she and her uncle had been persuaded that affection and confidence subsisted between Mr. Darcy and herself.*

WHY IT'S KEY

Plot: This passage reveals the growing closeness and understanding between Elizabeth and Darcy, even as the circumstances at this moment in the novel still make a possible union between them seem doubtful to Elizabeth. Although she has yet to discuss the matter with him, her interpretations of his motivations in assisting Lydia seem much more accurate than earlier judgments about his character. Both the nuance of her feeling toward him and her own self-awareness have changed since the beginning of the novel: "for herself she was humbled; but she was proud of him." These developments show the degree to which Austen's novel, while using the traditional form of the marriage plot, also argues for a notion of relationship, understanding, and character-driven love that develops independently of the institution of marriage.

Central Concept: This passage in particular, and the entire narrative turn involving Lydia and Wickham, might show the limits of Austen's social criticism when it comes to matters of class. While her novel skewers and satirizes many social customs and institutions with which she takes issue, the character of Wickham seems to reinforce the concept of the "deserving poor," a common way of explaining social inequality. Wickham's trouble results from his bad character and his wasteful and wild behavior, not from any socioeconomic circumstances that might limit his options. In contrast, his father, who is referred to throughout the novel as a good man, received generous economic support from the Darcy family. In this worldview, individuals are responsible for their own poverty, poverty relates to inherent flaws or wickedness, and noble individuals such as Darcy have the power and duty to elevate those who are deserving. (In this passage, Elizabeth rightly guesses that his actions to elevate Wickham Jr. come from his growing belief that she is deserving of his assistance.) Some scholars debate about the degree to which Austen's novels criticize or reinforce such an explanation of poverty, and students might engage in a similar debate.

Author's Craft: Jane Austen has a complicated relationship to the Romantic tradition, as her concern with social institutions and her tendency toward satire often hold a more significant place in readings and understandings of her novels, including *Pride and Prejudice*. In general, the subtlety of her plots and the attention to manners do not seem to match the melodramatic tendencies of some Romantics. That said, passages such as this one show how she relates to the Romantic tradition of which she is indeed a part. The "flutter of spirits" that Elizabeth experiences here seems Romantic. In this passage, the author allows her some "whispers of the heart," and the experience of emotion seen here, both the pleasure and the pain, seem to be the kind of sentiment with which many Romantic authors are concerned.

YOUR STUDYSYNC® TV

Discussion Prompt: In your analysis of this passage, what kinds of obligation exist between the different social classes in the world of the novel? Why does Elizabeth say she is "under obligations to a person who could never receive a return"? What, if anything, obligates Darcy to Wickham in this situation? To whom, if anyone, is Wickham obligated? Do these questions of class and obligation apply to contemporary society? Should they? Why or why not?

Standards: RL.11-12.1, RL.11-12.4; SL.11-12.1.A, SL.11-12.1.C, SL.11-12.1.D

VOCABULARY

palliate
pal•li•ate *verb*
To make an illness or other hardship less severe
Although the absence of her now-grown son made her sad, the company of her friends helped to palliate her loneliness.

acquiescence
ac•qui•es•cence *noun*
A concession or acceptance of something that may not be wanted
Despite her doubts, she gave her acquiescence to helping the girls with the prank because she wanted to be their friend.

expeditious
ex•pe•di•tious *adjective*
Done easily and efficiently
Faced with a long line at her register, the cashier was expeditious in the attention she gave each customer.

vestibule
ves•ti•bule *noun*
The lobby or front hallway of a building
The hostess asked her early guests to wait in the vestibule while she finished dimming the lights.

trifling
tri•fling *adjective*
Insignificant; of no great importance
They had been friends for so long that he was sure his trifling comment about her hair would be quickly forgotten.

cogent
co•gent *adjective*
Reasonable, clear, and persuasive
The boy made a cogent case for riding the bus by himself, so his parents allowed it.

CLOSE READ

QUESTION 1: Why, in Chapter 46, does Elizabeth feel that her sister Lydia is "lost"?

Sample Answer: Given that Lydia has no inheritance, Elizabeth doesn't believe that Wickham has any intention of marrying her, and living with a man unmarried would be a kind of social ruin from which women such as the Bennet sisters could not recover.

Standards: RL.11-12.1

QUESTION 2: Why does Elizabeth feel guilty about the fate that awaits her sister if the worst fears about Wickham's intentions prove to be true? Use language from the novel to support your answer.

Sample Answer: She thinks she could have prevented this, if she had told more people what she'd known about Wickham's character: "neither Jane, to whom I related the whole, nor I, thought it necessary to make our knowledge public" (Chapter 47).

Standards: RL.11-12.1

QUESTION 3: How or why is Wickham finally convinced to marry Lydia Bennet?

Sample Answer: He marries Lydia once his own debts have been settled by someone else, and once he is promised that someone will pay him an annual income as her husband.

Standards: RL.11-12.1

QUESTION 4: On first hearing of Wickham's marriage to Lydia, why does Elizabeth regret telling Darcy about the situation? Use language from the novel to support your answer.

Sample Answer: Since the matter has been resolved in a way that will save her family from great public shame, Elizabeth wishes that Darcy didn't know about it because she fears that his knowledge of this embarrassing situation will decrease his feelings for her: "from such a connection she could not wonder that he would shrink" (Chapter 50).

Standards: RL.11-12.1

CHAPTERS 53-61: Resolution, Happiness, Marriage

KEY PASSAGE | Chapter 59, Paragraphs 35–39

"Lizzy," said her father, "I have given him my consent. He is the kind of man, indeed, to whom I should never dare refuse anything, which he condescended to ask. I now give it to you, if you are resolved on having him. But let me advise you to think better of it. I know your disposition, Lizzy. I know that you could be neither happy nor respectable, unless you truly esteemed your husband; unless you looked up to him as a superior. Your lively talents would place you in the greatest danger in an unequal marriage. You could scarcely escape discredit and misery. My child, let me not have the grief of seeing you unable to respect your partner in life. You know not what you are about."

Elizabeth, still more affected, was earnest and solemn in her reply; and at length, by repeated assurances that Mr. Darcy was really the object of her choice, by explaining the gradual change which her estimation of him had undergone, relating her absolute certainty that his affection was not the work of a day, but had stood the test of many months' suspense, and enumerating with energy all his good qualities, she did conquer her father's incredulity, and reconcile him to the match.

"Well, my dear," said he, when she ceased speaking, "I have no more to say. If this be the case, he deserves you. I could not have parted with you, my Lizzy, to anyone less worthy."

To complete the favourable impression, she then told him what Mr. Darcy had voluntarily done for Lydia. He heard her with astonishment.

"This is an evening of wonders, indeed! And so, Darcy did every thing; made up the match, gave the money, paid the fellow's debts, and got him his commission! So much the better. It will save me a world of trouble and economy. Had it been your uncle's doing, I must and would have paid him; but these violent young lovers carry every thing their own way. I shall offer to pay him to-morrow; he will rant and storm about his love for you, and there will be an end of the matter."

WHY IT'S KEY

Plot: In the final chapters of *Pride and Prejudice*, Austen appears to be using marriage as it has been used in English literature since Shakespeare's time and earlier, as narrative code for a happy ending. Since marriage has long symbolized the restoration of proper order in literature, the end of Austen's novel can therefore be seen as another story that fits in that tradition; despite the biting social commentary throughout the novel, both Jane and Elizabeth do fulfill their tiresome mother's wishes by securing themselves wealthy husbands. That said, this passage shows how Austen's take on the marriage plot, or the relationship between marriage and happy endings, might be a bit more complicated. Mr. Bennet's insightful observations about his daughter seem to articulate Austen's own views on the topic of marriage. For intelligent and independent women, happiness and resolution depend not on the economic security of marriage but on a situation in which one is able to "respect [one's] partner in life," a marriage of equals.

Author's Craft: The delicacy with which Austen makes her social commentary is evident in this passage. These ideas about marriage—that women have a right to consider their own happiness, that marriage should be an equal partnership, that not all marriages have an inherent social value, even when money or security is present—may seem obvious to modern readers, but they were far from obvious in Austen's time. While some might see Mr. Bennet's words as indicative of proto-feminist views on Austen's part, they are also spoken by a male character, and can be understood as an individual case of a father's far more traditional paternal concern for his daughter. They might also be read as a criticism of Elizabeth's mother, as the heroine has already observed the inequalities of intelligence in her own parents' marriage. Students might discuss whether this scene gives the novel a broader concern about the nature of women's lives, or if instead it presents a more catty view of women with limited intelligence. One can also see how Austen lightens her own romantic ending with Mr. Bennet's sarcasm; the artful resolution of the novel's complex plot becomes the laughable "rant and storm about ... love."

Central Concept: Regardless of how one views the sometimes ambiguous qualities of Austen's social critiques, this passage does assert her particular idea that the single most important quality to be considered in advance of a marriage is the "disposition" of the people involved. More so than her financial insecurity, the fact that her affection toward Darcy has increased over time and with greater knowledge of his character is what convinces her father to approve the match. The novel's conclusion presents Lydia's marriage and Elizabeth's marriage as contrasting possibilities for the institution. One represents rash decisions based on financial matters while the other represents more measured decisions based on character. In this passage, and elsewhere in the novel's final chapters, it becomes quite clear for which vision of marriage Austen's novel advocates.

YOUR STUDYSYNC® TV

Discussion Prompt: Why is Mr. Bennet concerned about Elizabeth's marriage to Darcy? What various forces compel him to give permission for the match? Why does tradition indicate that a father needs to give permission for a marriage? Does this tradition persist in contemporary society? Should it? Why or why not?

Standards: RL.11-12.1, RL.11-12.4; SL.11-12.1.A, SL.11-12.1.C, SL.11-12.1.D

VOCABULARY

prodigious
pro•di•gious *adjective*
Significant in amount or extent
The new point guard pleased the team's shooters by making a prodigious number of assists in his first few games.

panegyric
pan•e•gyr•ic *noun*
A speech or piece of writing whose purpose is to give praise
At the campaign fundraiser, the candidate's mother delivered a panegyric about all the positive things that her son had done for the community.

infatuation
in•fat•u•a•tion *noun*
A strong but passing affection for someone; a crush
Before he even knew her name, Joseph had developed an infatuation for the new girl in his homeroom.

frivolous
friv•o•lous *adjective*
Without substantive meaning or worth
He often made frivolous purchases at the grocery store, like the time he bought six different flavors of ice cream.

sagacity
sa•gac•i•ty *noun*
The quality of having strong powers of perception; wisdom
Her years as a counselor had given her the sagacity to hear the student out before giving advice.

CLOSE READ

QUESTION 1: What is the state of Bingley's feelings for Jane after he returns to Netherfield and visits the Bennet house, and how does it seem that Mr. Darcy feels about this?

Sample Answer: After seeing Jane, Bingley seems to be in love with her all over again. Because Darcy comes with Bingley to visit Jane, Darcy no longer seems to be trying to stop their union (Chapter 53).

Standards: RL.11-12.1

QUESTION 2: How and why does the general social perception of the Bennet family change, even though the scandal of Lydia's elopement is still fresh in many minds of their community?

Sample Answer: Although Lydia's elopement seemed to spell disgrace and disaster for the Bennet family, the news of Jane's engagement to the noble and wealthy Bingley means that Jane and her family will soon be elevated above their current social status.

Standards: RL.11-12.1

QUESTION 3: What news causes Lady Catherine to visit the Bennet house, and why is the noble lady so upset about this rumor?

Sample Answer: She's heard that Darcy is going to propose to Elizabeth. Not only does she think that the match is socially unequal, she also believes that Darcy is already engaged, if unofficially, to her daughter.

Standards: RL.11-12.1

QUESTION 4: What impact does Lady Catherine's visit to Longbourn ultimately have on the possibility of a marriage between Darcy and Elizabeth, and why?

Sample Answer: Lady Catherine uses the conversation with Elizabeth as a reason to warn her nephew about the dangers of such a marriage, but this warning only gives Darcy encouragement that Elizabeth may still have feelings for him.

Standards: RL.11-12.1

COMPARATIVE TEXTS

Text: "How to Marry Well" by Mary Wolfe Hungerford

Compare to: Chapter 55 of *Pride and Prejudice*

Connection: As *Pride and Prejudice* draws to a close, all the young people approach marriage with a more somber sensibility. Even Bingley and Jane, whose romance seemed destined to run unimpeded from its very start, come to a deeper realization of just how significant a step marriage can be. This fact has never been lost on Margaret Wolfe Hungerford, who in her article "How to Marry Well" communicated to her readers that marrying a man of means cannot be an end in itself.

Text: *The Science of Love* by Robin Dunbar

Compare to: Chapter 58 of *Pride and Prejudice*

Connection: In *The Science of Love*, British scientist Robin Dunbar explores the essential physiological aspects of love. He makes the point that romantic expressions differ because of cultural norms, but the underlying chemical and physiological aspects are the same. In *Pride and Prejudice*, the social rules governing couplehood tend to be at war with the chemistry.

WRITE TO REVISIT

ARGUMENTATIVE WRITING

Prompt: Richard Price was a Welsh clergyman who was no doubt a thorn in the side of King George III. He was both a firm supporter of the American colonies in their war for independence and a fierce critic of the tyranny of the monarchy. In 1789, Price delivered a sermon "on the Love of Country" that laid out his views championing the American Revolution, the ongoing French Revolution, and Britain's own Glorious Revolution of 1688: all expressions of the power of self-determination and a further weakening of the rule of aristocracy. In 1795, when Jane Austen wrote the first draft of *Pride and Prejudice*, titled *First Impressions*, the French Revolution was in its seventh year, the Age of Enlightenment had established a bias toward individualism, and Romanticism was taking art, music, and literature in a more personal direction. How does Jane Austen fit in? Starting with the ideas in Richard Price's "Discourse" and doing research of your own, write an essay of at least 400 words arguing to what extent *Pride and Prejudice* was (or wasn't) a revolutionary novel of its time, giving reasons supported by facts or textual details.

Standards: RL.11-12.1; RI.11-12.1; W.11-12.1.A, W.11-12.1.B, W.11-12.1.C, W.11-12.1.D, W.11-12.1.E

COMPARATIVE WRITING

Prompt: *Pride and Prejudice* has proven to be very adaptable to the 20th and 21st centuries, lending itself to four films and seven TV miniseries. In April 2012, *Pride and Prejudice* conquered another format in "The Lizzie Bennet Diaries," a Web series consisting of videos and various social media outlets, mainly focused on Lizzie Bennet, a live-at-home grad student inspired by that other Elizabeth Bennet in *Pride and Prejudice*. The series was later "novelized" as *The Secret Diary of Lizzie Bennet*. Students will compare the novelization to its two sources: the original novel and the Web series. In this essay, consider three corners of a triangle: *Pride and Prejudice*; "The Lizzie Bennet Diaries"; and *The Secret Diary of Lizzie Bennet*. How would you characterize the three connections? Some questions to think about: Does Jane Austen's novel depend on the other two in any way? Which does the novelization have more in common with, the Web series or the novel? Likewise, which print version is a more relevant adaptation of "The Lizzie Bennet Diaries"? Finally, do we need all three? Why or why not?

Standards: RL.11-12.1, RL.11-12.3, RL.11-12.5, RL.11-12.6, RL.11-12.7; W.11-12.1.A, W.11-12.1.B, W.11-12.2.A, W.11-12.2.B

[illegible]

Prompt: Richard Price was a Welsh clergyman who was no doubt a thorn in the side of King George III. He was both a firm supporter of the American colonies in their war for independence and a fierce critic of the tyranny of the monarchy. In [illegible] Price delivered a sermon, "On the Love of Country," that laid out his views, championing the American Revolution, the ongoing French Revolution, and Britain's own Glorious Revolution of 1688 as expressions of the power of self-determination and a further [illegible] of the rule of [illegible]. In [illegible], when Jane Austen wrote the first draft of Pride and Prejudice, titled First Impressions, the French Revolution was in its seventh year, the Age of Enlightenment had established a new trend toward individualism, and [illegible]. Starting with the ideas in Richard Price's "Discourse" and doing research of your own, write an essay of at least 500 words arguing to what extent Pride and Prejudice is a revolutionary novel of its time, [illegible] supported by facts or textual details.

Standards: RL.11-12.2, RL.11-12.3, W.11-12.1.A, W.11-12.1.B, W.11-12.1.C, W.11-12.1.D, W.11-12.1.E

[illegible]

Prompt: Pride and Prejudice has proven to be very adaptable to the 20th and 21st centuries, leading to both four films and seven TV miniseries. In April 2012, Pride and Prejudice continued another format in "The Lizzie Bennet Diaries," a Web series consisting of videos and various social media outlets, mainly focused on Lizzie Bennet, a [illegible] student inspired by the [illegible] Elizabeth Bennet in Pride and Prejudice. The series was later novelized, as The Secret Diary of Lizzie Bennet. Students will compare the novelization to its two sources: the original novel and the Web series. In an essay, consider these forms of the story: Pride and Prejudice, "The Lizzie Bennet Diaries," and The Secret Diary of Lizzie Bennet. How would you characterize the three connections? Some questions to think about: Does Jane Austen's novel depend on the other two in any way? Which does the novelization more closely align with: the Web series or the novel? [illegible] which point [illegible] a more relevant adaptation of "The Lizzie Bennet Diaries"? Finally, do we need all three? Why or why not?

Standards: RL.11-12.2, RL.11-12.3, RL.11-12.6, RL.11-12.7, W.11-12.1.A, W.11-12.1.B, W.11-12.2.A, W.11-12.2.B

PHOTO/IMAGE CREDITS:

Cover, ©iStock.com/CostinT, ©iStock.com/alexsl, ©iStock.com/ dorian2013
p. iii, ©iStock.com/wellglad, ©iStock.com/Leonardo Patrizi, ©iStock.com/franckreporter, ©iStock.com/ dorian2013
p. v, Apic/contributor/Getty Images, ©iStock.com/gaiamoments, ©iStock.com/kertlis, ©iStock.com/ABDESIGN, ©iStock.com/technotr, ©iStock.com/poco_bw, ©iStock.com/Leonsbox, ©iStock.com/ alexey_boldin
p. vi, ©iStock.com/skegbydave, ©iStock.com/alexey_boldin, ©iStock.com, ©iStock.com/Massonstock, ©iStock.com/RMAX, ©iStock.comprudkov, fair use, ©iStock.com/szefei, ©iStock.com/ gaiamoments, ©iStock. com/technotr ©iStock.com/Marilyn Nieves, ©iStock.com/welcome-to-carol-world, ©iStock.com/adisa, Yale Joel/Yale Joel/Getty Images, ©iStock.com/StephenSewell, Archive Photos/Archive Photos, ©iStock.com/ DNY59, ©iStock.com/dblight
p. vii, Hero Images/Getty Images
p. ix, Apic/contributor/Getty Images
p. x, ©iStock.com/alexey_boldin, ©iStock.com
p. xii, ©iStock.com/MorelSO, ©iStock.com/bizoo_n, ©iStock.com/dtokar, ©iStock.com/gkuchera
p. xiii, ©iStock.com/gkuchera
p. xv, ©iStock.com/dtokar, ©iStock.com/Bunyos, ©iStock.com/ThomasVogel
p. xvii, ©iStock.com/Kamchatka, ©iStock.com/moevin
p. xviii, ©iStock.com/bizoo_n
p. xix, ©iStock.com/DNY59
p. xxi, ©iStock.com/kemie, ©iStock.com/belchonock, ©iStock.com/melissasanger, ©iStock.com/ErikaMitchell
p. xxiii, ©iStock.com/Toa55, ©iStock.com/sturti, ©iStock.com/IzabelaHabur, Stephen F. Somerstein/Getty Images
p. xxiv, ©iStock.com/TuomasKujansuu
p. xxv, ©iStock.com/Caval, ©iStock.com/kamonlai, ©iStock.com/ImagineGolf
p. xxvi, ©iStock.com/GeorgePeters, ©iStock.com/Aleksander, ©iStock.com/duncan1890, ©iStock.com/ aniszewski, ©iStock.com/ExcellentPhoto, WIN MCNAMEE/Getty Images
p. xxvii, ©iStock.com/PhotoZidaric, ©iStock.com/neoblues, ©iStock.com/DaveAlan, ©iStock.com/ stockstudioX
p. xxvii, ©iStock.com/makosh, ©iStock.com/m-imagephotography, ©iStock.com/sam74100
p. 1, ©iStock.com/naphtalina, ©iStock.com/dorian2013, ©iStock.com/alexey_boldin, ©iStock.com/ skegbydave
p. 2, ©iStock.com/naphtalina

Text Fulfillment Through StudySync

If you are interested in specific titles, please fill out the form below and we will check availability through our partners.

ORDER DETAILS

Date:

TITLE	AUTHOR	Paperback/ Hardcover	Specific Edition *If Applicable*	Quantity

SHIPPING INFORMATION

Contact:
Title:
School/District:
Address Line 1:
Address Line 2:
Zip or Postal Code:
Phone:
Mobile:
Email:

BILLING INFORMATION ☐ *SAME AS SHIPPING*

Contact:
Title:
School/District:
Address Line 1:
Address Line 2:
Zip or Postal Code:
Phone:
Mobile:
Email:

PAYMENT INFORMATION

☐ CREDIT CARD — Name on Card:

Card Number: Expiration Date: Security Code:

☐ PO — Purchase Order Number:

StudySync Text Fulfillment, BookheadEd Learning, LLC
610 Daniel Young Drive | Sonoma, CA 95476